I0095978

**ecpr** PRESS
monographs

Series Editor: Alan Ware
University of Oxford

# paying for democracy:
political finance and state funding for parties

Kevin Casas-Zamora

*The doctoral thesis upon which this book is based was awarded the ECPR's
2004 PhD Prize*

**ecpr** PRESS

© Kevin Casas-Zamora

First published by the ECPR Press in 2005

The ECPR Press is a department of the European Consortium for Political
Research (ECPR), a scholarly association, which supports and encourages the
training, research and cross-national cooperation of political scientists in institutions throughout Europe and beyond. The ECPR's Central Services are located at
the University of Essex, Wivenhoe Park,
Colchester, CO4 3SQ, UK

All rights reserved. No part of this book may be reprinted or reproduced or
utilised in any form or by any electronic, mechanical, or other means, now
known or hereafter invented, including photocopying and recording, or in any
information storage or retrieval system, without permission in
writing from the publishers.

Typeset in Times 10pt by the ECPR Press


British Library Cataloguing in Publication Data
A catalogue record for this book is available from the British Library


ISBN 0-9547966-3-2

**ecpr**PRESS
monographs

The ECPR Monographs series is published by the ECPR Press, the publishing imprint of the European Consortium for Political Research (ECPR).

As an independent, scholarly institution, one of the ECPR's objectives is to facilitate research in political science among European universities. To that end, the ECPR has developed a strong publishing portfolio since the 1970s.

The policy to extend that portfolio by launching its own publishing imprint was discussed by the Executive Committee of the ECPR in 2002, and the decision to proceed was taken in early 2003.

It was decided that the first two series to be published under the imprint should be complementary. The ECPR Classics series facilitates scholarly access to significant works from earlier eras of political science by re-publishing books that have been out of print. It believes this will enable contemporary students and researchers to develop their own work more effectively.

The ECPR Monographs series publishes major new research in all sub-disciplines of political science including revised versions of manuscripts that were originally submitted as PhD theses, as well as manuscripts from established members of the profession

Alan Ware
Editor, ECPR Classics and ECPR Monographs
Worcester College, Oxford University, UK


Editorial Board:
Richard Bellamy, University of Essex
Dionyssis G. Dimitrakopoulos, University of London
Sergio Fabbrini, Universita degli studi di Trento
Andrew Hurrell, University of Oxford
Beate Jahn, University of Sussex
Darina Malova, Comenius University in Bratislava
Alina Mungiu-Pippidi, European University Institute
Carlos Closa Montero, Universidad de Zaragoza
Gerald Schneider, University of Konstanz
Jan Sundberg, University of Helsinki
Yves Surel, Université de Grenoble
Stefaan Walgrave, University of Antwerp

Other titles in this series:

*Citizenship: The History of an Idea*, Paul Magnette
*Representing Women? Female Legislators in West European Parliaments*, Mercedes Mateo Diaz

Titles in the ECPR Classics series:

*System and Process in International Politics*, Morton A. Kaplan
*Political Elites*, Geraint Parry
*Parties and Party Systems: A Framework for Analysis*, Giovanni Sartori

# acknowledgements

This volume is an abridged and updated version of a doctoral dissertation presented at the University of Oxford in early 2003. Thus, the debts of gratitude incurred for this book are wholly inseparable from those, very extensive ones, already mentioned and acknowledged in the thesis. I would like, nonetheless, to recognise again some particularly profound debts and add a few new ones.

This work benefited from exceptionally apt academic advice at Oxford and beyond. For that I have to thank my supervisors, Alan Angell and Laurence Whitehead, as well as Michael Pinto-Duschinsky, Peter Pulzer and Karl-Heinz Nassmacher. Alan Ware is responsible not just for turning my final examination into an uncommonly pleasant rite of passage, but also for encouraging me to submit the original manuscript to the ECPR Press. The publication of this book would have never taken place without his kind help.

The research that supports this monograph was possible with the economic support of the Ronald Falconer Scholarship, the Ford / Macarthur / Hewlett Scholarship Programme for Post-graduate Studies in the Social Sciences, the University of Costa Rica, and the various travel funds of the University of Oxford. For that, Rodolfo Cerdas at CIAPA in Costa Rica, María Antonieta Sáenz at the Law School of the University of Costa Rica, and María Teresa San Román at the Institute of International Education in Mexico deserve a very special thank you.

In Costa Rica and Uruguay, my research was helped in many different ways by a group of remarkably generous people. The list is long and it would be pointless to repeat it here. They all know of my gratitude. A few collective acknowledgements may be more appropriate. I would like to thank, in particular, the personnel of Costa Rica's Legislative Assembly and Supreme Elections Tribunal, as well as the colleagues and friends at the Legislative Palace, CLAEH and the University of the Republic's Institute of Political Science in Uruguay. In both countries, special recognition is due to all my interviewees, who put up with my intrusion in their schedules and my irritating questions with invariable grace and good will.

Last but not least, I must mention two personal debts that defy any attempt to be brief. The first one is to my wife, Simone, who has a unique talent for making my work and my life far better and worthier than they would otherwise be. The second one, and deepest, is to my parents, Antonio and Carmen. For more than fifty years they have supported their children through the travails of life with unfailing love and wisdom. This book is dedicated to them.

# contents

# tables and graphs

# acronyms and abbreviations

| | |
|---|---|
| ACCR | Constitutional Assembly of Costa Rica (Asamblea Constitucional de Costa Rica) |
| AD | *Al Día* (Costa Rica) |
| AGU | General Assembly of Uruguay (Asamblea General del Uruguay) |
| AHD | Honorable Directorate's Archives (Archivo del Honorable Directorio del Partido Nacional – Uruguay) |
| ALCR | Legislative Assembly of Costa Rica (Asamblea Legislativa de Costa Rica) |
| ANDEBU | National Association of Uruguayan Broadcasters (Asociación Nacional de Broadcasters Uruguayos) |
| AP | Progressive Alliance (Alianza Progresista – Uruguay) |
| AU | Asamblea Uruguay |
| BAC | Anglo-Costa Rican Bank (Banco Anglo Costarricense) |
| BCCR | Central Bank of Costa Rica (Banco Central de Costa Rica) |
| BCU | Central Bank of Uruguay (Banco Central del Uruguay) |
| BHU | Mortgage Bank of Uruguay (Banco Hipotecario del Uruguay) |
| BNCR | National Bank of Costa Rica (Banco Nacional de Costa Rica) |
| BRE | *Semanario Brecha* (Uruguay) |
| BROU | Bank of the Republic of Uruguay (Banco de la República Oriental del Uruguay) |
| BUS | *Semanario Búsqueda* (Uruguay) |
| CAP | Popular Alliance Coalition (Coalición Alianza Popular – Costa Rica) |
| CE | Electoral Court (Corte Electoral – Uruguay) |
| CELADU | Centre for the Study of Democracy in Uruguay (Centro para el Estudio de la Democracia en Uruguay) |
| CEPAL or ECLA | United Nation's Economic Commission for Latin America |
| CEst | State Council of Uruguay (Consejo de Estado del Uruguay) |
| CGR | General Comptroller of the Republic (Contraloría General de la República – Costa Rica) |
| ChR or CRU | Chamber of Representatives of Uruguay (Cámara de Representantes del Uruguay) |
| CNA | National Administration Council (Consejo Nacional Administrativo – Uruguay) |
| COE | Council of Europe |
| COM | Uruguayan Communist Party (Partido Comunista Uruguayo) |
| CPU | United People Coalition (Coalición Pueblo Unido – Costa Rica) |
| CRO | *Semanario Crónicas* (Uruguay) |
| CSJ | Supreme Court of Justice of Costa Rica |
| CSNP | Centre for the Study of the National Problems (Centro para el |

|        | Estudio de los Problemas Nacionales – Costa Rica) |
|--------|----------------------------------------------------|
| CSU    | Senate Chamber of Uruguay (Cámara del Senado del Uruguay) |
| CU     | Unity Coalition (Coalición Unidad – Costa Rica) |
| DCR    | *Diario de Costa Rica* |
| DEMOS  | *Semanario Demos* (Uruguay) |
| DS     | Daily Proceedings (Diario de Sesiones) |
| DSF    | Direct State Funding |
| DSV    | Double Simultaneous Voting |
| EC     | Electoral Code (Código Electoral – Costa Rica) |
| ECO    | *El Eco* (Uruguay) |
| ED     | *El Día* (Uruguay) |
| EF     | *Semanario El Financiero* (Costa Rica) |
| EJPR   | European Journal of Political Research |
| ELP    | *El Popular* (Uruguay) |
| ENP    | Effective Number of Parties |
| EO     | *El Observador* (Uruguay) |
| EP     | *El País* (Uruguay) |
| EPR    | Progressive Encounter (Encuentro Progresista – Uruguay) |
| ESTD   | *Este Diario* (Uruguay) |
| EU     | European Union |
| EXC    | *Excelsior* (Costa Rica) |
| EXT    | *Diario Extra* (Costa Rica) |
| FA     | Broad Front (Frente Amplio – Uruguay) |
| FB     | Foro Batllista (Uruguay) |
| FDP    | Free Democratic Party (Germany) |
| FEC    | Federal Election Commission (US) |
| FIDEL  | Left Liberation Front (Frente Izquierda de Liberación – Uruguay) |
| ILO    | International Labour Organisation |
| IMM    | Municipal government of Montevideo (Intendencia Municipal de Montevideo – Uruguay) |
| INE    | National Statistics Institute (Instituto Nacional de Estadística – Uruguay) |
| IPU    | Inter-Parliamentary Union |
| L15    | Lista 15 (Uruguay) |
| L1999  | Lista 1999 (Uruguay) |
| L99000 | Lista 99000 (Uruguay) |
| LG     | *La Gaceta* (Costa Rica) |
| LM     | *La Mañana* (Uruguay) |
| LN     | *La Nación* (Costa Rica) |
| LPL    | *La Prensa Libre* (Costa Rica) |
| LR     | *La República* (Costa Rica) |
| LRU    | *La República* (Uruguay) |
| MH     | Movimiento Herrerista (Uruguay) |
| ML     | Libertarian Movement (Movimiento Libertario – Costa Rica) |

| | |
|---|---|
| MOPT | Ministry of Public Works and Transport (Ministerio de Obras Públicas y Transportes – Costa Rica) |
| MP | Member of Parliament |
| MPP | Popular Participation Movement (Movimiento de Participación Popular – Uruguay) |
| NDP | New Democratic Party (Canada) |
| NE | New Space Party (Partido del Nuevo Espacio – Uruguay) |
| NYT | The New York Times |
| OAS | Organisation of American States |
| OIF | International Organisation of the Francophonie |
| OPI | *Semanario Opinión* (Uruguay) |
| PAC | Citizen Action Party (Partido Acción Ciudadana – Costa Rica) |
| PACs | Political Action Committees |
| PAD | Democratic Action Party (Partido Acción Democrática – Venezuela) |
| PADA | Alajuelense Democratic Action Party (Partido Acción Democratica Alajuelense – Costa Rica) |
| PAL | Limonense Authentic Party (Partido Auténtico Limonense – Costa Rica) |
| PALA | Agrarian Labour Action Party (Partido Acción Laborista Agrícola – Costa Rica) |
| PC | Colorado Party (Partido Colorado – Uruguay) |
| PDC | Christian Democrat Party (Partido Demócrata Cristiano – Costa Rica) |
| PDCU | Christian Democrat Party (Partido Demócrata Cristiano – Uruguay) |
| PFD | Democratic Force Party (Partido Fuerza Democrática - Costa Rica) |
| PFS | Political Finance System |
| PGP | People's Government Party (Partido por el Gobierno del Pueblo – Uruguay) |
| PI | Independent Party (Partido Independiente – Costa Rica) |
| PIN | National Integration Party (Partido Integración Nacional – Costa Rica) |
| PLN | National Liberation Party (Partido Liberación Nacional – Costa Rica) |
| PN | National Party (Partido Nacional – Uruguay) |
| PNI | National Independent Party (Partido Nacional Independiente – Costa Rica) |
| PNIU | Independent National Party (Partido Nacional Independiente – Uruguay) |
| POS | *Revista Posdata* (Uruguay) |
| PR | Proportional Representation |
| PRC | Republican Party (Partido Republicano – Costa Rica) |
| PRCO | Costa Rican Renovation Party (Partido Renovación Costarricense) |
| PRD | Democratic Renovation Party (Partido Renovación Democrática – Costa Rica) |

| | |
|---|---|
| PRDP | Democratic Revolution Party (Partido de la Revolución Democrática – Panamá) |
| PRI | Revolutionary Institutional Party (Partido Revolucionario Institucional – Mexico) |
| PS | Uruguayan Socialist Party (Partido Socialista Uruguayo) |
| PSD | Social Democratic Party (Partido Social Demócrata – Costa Rica) |
| PT | Workers' Party (Partido de los Trabajadores – Costa Rica) |
| PU | National Unification Party (Partido Unificación Nacional – Costa Rica) |
| PUAC | Cartaginesa Agricultural Union Party (Partido Unión Agrícola Cartaginesa – Costa Rica) |
| PUGEN | Generaleña Union Party (Partido Unión Generaleña – Costa Rica) |
| PUN | National Union Party (Partido Unión Nacional – Costa Rica) |
| PUP | Popular Union Party (Partido Union Popular – Costa Rica) |
| PUSC | Social Christian Unity Party (Partido Unidad Social Cristiana – Costa Rica) |
| PV | *Prensa de los Viernes* (Uruguay) |
| PVP | People's Vanguard Party (Partido Vanguardia Popular – Costa Rica) |
| ROU | Oriental Republic of Uruguay (República Oriental del Uruguay) |
| SCCR | Constitutional Court of Costa Rica (Sala Constitucional de Costa Rica) |
| SDP | Social Democratic Party (Germany) |
| SI | Socialist International |
| SPC | Servicios Publicitarios Computarizados (Costa Rica) |
| SU | *Semanario Universidad* (Costa Rica) |
| TI | Transparency International |
| TRES | *Revista Tres* (Uruguay) |
| TSE | Supreme Elections Tribunal (Tribunal Supremo de Elecciones – Costa Rica) |
| UC | Civic Union Party (Partido Unión Cívica – Uruguay) |
| UN | *Ultimas Noticias* (Uruguay) |
| UNDP | United Nations Development Program |
| UP | Popular Union (Unión Popular – Uruguay) |
| UR | Re-adjustable Unit (Unidad Reajustable) |
| VA | Vertiente Artiguista (Uruguay) |

# | introduction

Campaign finance is the great reenactment of the dancing images on the walls of Plato's cave. We political scientists think we see the reality, the dancers themselves, and we think the public watches the heightened, exaggerated, even grotesque images of contemporary campaign finance projected on the distant walls of the cave. (…) In a perverse way, it may even be because the facts and realities of campaign finance are so hard to grasp that the pseudo-fact and codified explanations are so gripping and so convincing.

Frank Sorauf[1]

## COMPARATIVE POLITICAL FINANCE: WHY DOES IT MATTER?

'The relation between money and politics has come to be one of the great problems of democratic government.' Thus James Kerr Pollock opened his pioneering study of political finance practices in Britain, Germany and France, published in 1932. His dictum, as well as his call for public opinion to realise 'that healthy political life is not possible as long as the use of money is unrestrained', ring truer today than in Pollock's time.[2] Successive waves of democratisation, an increased complexity in electoral processes, and the growing awareness of the risks posed by corruption to the viability of democratic institutions have moved the funding of political activity to the centre of public debates all over the world. The issue has become both global and pressing.

The signs of its prominence are unmistakable. In October 2000, a public statement by the anti-corruption organisation Transparency International (TI) singled out questionable political finance practices as a growing threat to democracy. TI's Chairman, Peter Eigen, noted that 'the current wave of corruption scandals we are witnessing across Europe is not about personal enrichment – it's about the purchase of access to policy-makers, and political parties are the prime target in this game'.[3] In a similar vein, the Inter-American Democratic Charter, adopted by the Organisation of American States (OAS) in 2001, pledged that 'special attention will be paid to the problems associated with the high cost of election campaigns and the establishment of a balanced and transparent system for their financing'.[4] Analogous pronouncements have been forthcoming from organisations as diverse as the Inter-Parliamentary Union (IPU), the International Organisation of the Francophonie (OIF), the Council of Europe (COE), and the European Union (EU).[5] The pace and depth of political finance legislation has markedly increased at the national level as well. In March 2002, US lawmakers approved the most comprehensive package of political finance regulation in a generation, claiming that it would 'help untangle the web of money and influence that has made the Congress and the White House so vulnerable to the appearance of corruption'.[6] In the course of the past decade, far-reaching political finance reforms have also been enacted in Canada, Colombia, Costa Rica, Mexico, Panama, France, Germany, Japan and the United Kingdom, to name but a few cases.

While the profusion of regulatory efforts may be new, the anxieties that surround money's role in politics are old and entrenched. Pollock's words and the early passage of comprehensive pieces of regulation in the UK (1883 Corrupt and Illegal Practices [Prevention] Act) and the US (1907 Tillman Act), already betray the notion that as much as money is indispensable for political activity – and precisely *because* it is indispensable – it can endanger democracy in fundamental ways. Three are of particular consequence:

a) The flow and distribution of political funds impinge directly on electoral equality, on the actual possibilities enjoyed by candidates and parties to put their message across to the voters. A lopsided distribution of electoral funds erodes – although not necessarily impedes – the uncertainty of electoral results, a fundamental prerequisite for their legitimacy.

b) Money bestows on individuals and groups an unevenly distributed opportunity to directly participate in elections and/or exert political influence through their contributions to candidates and parties. This is of critical importance for democracy. When political power merely reflects economic power, the principle of 'one man, one vote' loses its significance and democracy ceases to be, in Schattschneider's words, an 'alternative power system, which can be used to counterbalance the economic power'.[7]

c) Fundraising processes offer obvious opportunities for the articulation of *quid pro quos* between private donors and policy makers, or, at a minimum, for the emergence of continuous conflicts of interest for the latter. At best, political fundraising processes can jeopardise the public interest; at worst, they destroy the integrity and autonomy of policy makers and privatise their decisions.

For all its relevance for key democratic values, the funding of political activities remains an under-researched and under-theorised topic. A systematic corpus of knowledge on political finance, able to illuminate the numerous regulatory efforts that continue to emerge all over the world, is still a long way away. Despite a growing industry of national case studies, truly comparative works are scarce.[8] The weak development of comparative political finance as a field of study is hardly mystifying. First and foremost, the field remains crippled by the dearth of reliable data in most countries. Not surprisingly, academic production has generally focused on the legal contours of political finance systems, their changes and the menu of regulatory instruments found in comparative practice. Less attention has been devoted to the rules' impact and implementation problems, and hence to *actual* political finance practices. The field faces the same conundrum identified by Duverger in his seminal study of political parties: how do we uncover the facts in the absence of a general theory to suggest relevant hypotheses? How do we generate a general theory without a pool of reliable information?[9]

Moreover, the field is yet to come to grips with the remarkable heterogeneity of political finance regulations and their complex linkages to their surrounding political and institutional framework, which frequently conditions heavily their features and effects. Somewhat paradoxically, despite the crucial role ascribed to political finance processes in the fate of elections, parties and democratic regimes, the study of political finance has remained largely isolated from the literature on electoral systems, party systems and political regimes, three of the areas that have best shown the promise of a comparative science of politics. The results of this unfortunate dissociation have been, on the one hand, a general overestimation of the effects of political finance rules and, on the other, the appearance of sweeping claims about those effects, which, on close inspection, travel badly across political systems. In many cases these generalisations appear more like the product of normative preconceptions – which the topic clearly invites – than of empirical rigour.

## GAPS IN OUR KNOWLEDGE: POLITICAL FINANCE IN LATIN AMERICA AND DIRECT STATE FUNDING

The gaps in our knowledge of political finance are especially glaring in some geographic areas. Indeed, while political finance issues have been extensively explored in the US – thanks, in large part, to the wealth of information made available by the Federal Electoral Commission (FEC) after 1976 – they have received far less systematic treatment in Western Europe, and next to no academic consideration in the rest of the world. In Latin America, where a turbulent political history has spawned a rich literature on parties, regimes and democratisation processes, the topic is still shrouded in secrecy and on the margins of academic discussion. To this day, only a handful of academic works on political finance exist in Latin America, nearly all of them reflecting the long fascination of the region's social scientists with legal frameworks and normative prescriptions, even when the latter show a poor grounding in reality.[10] The generation of an empirically grounded picture of political finance remains a pending assignment in Latin America.

The weakness of political finance research in Latin America is hardly testimony to the topic's irrelevance for the region. In fact, as democratic elections have expanded in the continent, *all* Latin American democracies have introduced some kind of political finance legislation, often quite extensive. Moreover, political finance practices have become a recurrent threat to the already frail credibility of politicians and governments in the region. The profound political crises unleashed in Colombia and Panama in the mid-1990s by the evidence of the participation of drug cartels in the funding of presidential campaigns stand as reminders of the destabilising effects of political finance corruption on Latin America's frail democratic institutions.[11] Rather than the topic's lack of salience, the dearth of empirical political finance works in Latin America reflects the formidable obstacles faced by researchers in a region historically marred by corrupt, opaque and authoritarian political mores. In a way, the same reasons that render important the systematic inquiry of political finance practices in the region – namely the pervasive lack of transparency, the endemic corruption and, increasingly, the threat posed by drug trafficking to political institutions in some countries – make such a probe very difficult.

What has been said about Latin America also applies to most political finance topics, even crucial ones. Conspicuous amongst the unexplored themes within the field is the effect of Direct State Funding (DSF), i.e., the cash grants allocated by the state to parties and candidates with the aim of supporting their political activities, according to a procedure laid out in the law.[12] The spread of DSF is, arguably, the most important trend in contemporary political finance and one whose consequences have come to dominate academic and political debates in the field, notably in Western Europe. Following its early introduction in Uruguay in 1928, and during the last four decades in particular, DSF has been adopted in nearly fifty countries. No other regulatory instrument – from restrictions on private political contributions to electoral spending ceilings and financial disclosure rules – is so widely diffused around the world. Moreover, no other instrument has been so laden with expectations and criticisms.

The adoption and consolidation of DSF as a political finance regulation device has been marked by acute controversies ranging from its fiscal cost for taxpayers to the legitimacy of exacting resources from the public in order to sustain political parties. More importantly for political science, disputes have also touched upon the *practical* consequences of DSF for democratic systems in three areas: (a) autonomy of political actors and prevention of corruption; (b) political equality and electoral competition; (c) organisation and institutionalisation of political parties.

The standard case in favour of DSF, often articulated by the same politicians that enact it, may be summarised as follows:

a) *DSF strengthens the autonomy of politicians, prevents political-finance-related corruption and enhances financial transparency.* By providing a source of income with no strings attached, subsidies protect parties and elected officials from economic dependence on large private donors and reduce the likelihood of corrupt exchanges between contributors and politicians. By virtue of being public, DSF is an entirely transparent source of political money.

b) *DSF protects political equality of opportunity and electoral competition.* Subsidies prevent the political dominance of groups with vast economic resources to put their message across and mobilise voters. They allow parties and candidates to compete fairly in elections regardless of the socio-economic condition of their supporters, and thus reduce entry barriers to political competition.

c) *DSF provides political actors with adequate resources for essential democratic activities, increasing the institutionalisation and stability of parties.* Traditional sources of funding are unable to sustain an adequate level of democratic activity. DSF helps political actors cover the cost of increasingly sophisticated campaigns and provides parties with steady income. It does so in an optimal way, minimising fundraising costs and dependence on large private contributors.

In recent years, these claims have come under attack. Critics have charged DSF with negative consequences that, in most cases, are the mirror image of the lofty claims put forward by supporters of public subventions. The typical indictment of DSF includes one or more of the following arguments:

a) *DSF does not replace private political donations and has a limited effectiveness against corruption.* Subsidies become an addition rather than a substitute for private contributions. If they replace anything it is 'healthy' money from membership dues and small donations, rather than large private contributions, which require less effort and organisation to collect. The effectiveness of DSF against corruption is, at best, severely limited.

b) *DSF stifles electoral competition and ossifies the party system.* Since incumbents enact DSF, subsidies create a bias in favour of the status quo. They raise entry barriers for newcomers and help to freeze the party system.

c) *DSF provides parties with resources that jeopardise their social embeddedness, internal democracy and autonomy.* By reducing the financial relevance of members, DSF diminishes the parties' incentives to reach out for new recruits, leading to falling rates of party membership. Subsidies also alter the parties' internal distribution of power, curbing the power of the rank-and-file and enhancing that of party bureaucracy. Finally, DSF becomes addictive for parties, leading to their loss of autonomy vis-à-vis the state.

In reviewing a very similar list of arguments in favour and against the introduction of general state subventions for British parties, the Committee on Standards in Public Life concluded that 'many of these arguments have merit and, taken together, they are finely balanced'.[13] In fact, despite the intensity of the debate, its most remarkable trait has been its limited empirical content and, if anything, the suspect scientific merits of the arguments put forward by both sides. Empirical works on the effects of public funding are scarce and even rarer are those that offer a comparative assessment of any kind.[14] The political finance literature lacks even a comprehensive survey of DSF arrangements and a typology of their striking, and generally unnoted, diversity. Discussions on the effects of DSF have usually failed to account for the heterogeneity of subsidy rules and, more importantly, for the mediating impact that other institutional and political factors – from the configuration of the electoral and party systems to the presence of other political finance regulations – may have on subsidy arrangements. Often impelled by normative preconceptions or by a positivistic urge to find covering laws, the discussion has proceeded, in many ways, as if in an institutional and political void. Any sweeping claim about the effects of DSF rests on distinctly shaky foundations.

## OBJECTIVES AND PROPOSITIONS

Whatever their shortcomings, the general assertions made by supporters and critics of DSF are very useful heuristic devices. At a minimum, they constitute a set of working hypotheses deserving systematic and comparative examination. This book will thus offer, first, a comparative appraisal of state funding systems and their effects on parties, party systems and political finance practices. Second, through an in-depth exploration of the effects of DSF in Costa Rica and Uruguay, it will construct a detailed empirical account of political finance practices in two Latin American democracies. The latter task is, in some ways, the more important of the two. Uncovering and systematising *empirical* political finance information is the prerequisite for an informed discussion on the issue in Latin America, as much as for the advancement of comparative political finance research as an academic field. However difficult the probe, probe we must.

Within the framework of both objectives, this book will advance the following propositions:

a) That state funding systems are extraordinarily heterogeneous and their effects contingent on the subsidy's own design and the political and institutional environment in which they are introduced. It will argue that electoral systems, party system formats, regime structures and the parties' historical evolution and organisational culture impinge on the features and effects of state funding schemes, and, ultimately, mould political finance practices as much as the subsidy's own presence.

b) That to the extent that the effects of state funding can be ascertained, they point towards a mixed picture that offers very partial vindication of the claims made by the subsidies' staunchest advocates and critics. Thus, while more often than not subsidies protect electoral equality and competition, they appear to offer a rather modest protection against questionable political finance practices. The case in favour of DSF seems to rests more comfortably on its importance for the value of political equality, than on its relevance for political integrity.

c) That DSF is a far less powerful instrument for shaping parties, party systems and even political finance practices than envisaged by both sides of the debate. By showing that the consequences of political finance rules, and of state funding systems in particular, can be understood or predicted only within a certain institutional and political context, this work will advocate a more restrained view of political finance regulation than that which has come to dominate discussions on the issue in most democracies.

## METHODOLOGICAL UNDERPINNINGS

In placing political finance rules within a broader network of incentives and constraints, and emphasising the contingency of political outcomes, the book expresses a preference for a particular approach to comparative political science. It is infused, on the one hand, with the belief in the pivotal role of institutions in explaining political behaviour. As noted by Thelen and Steinmo, 'by shaping not just actors' strategies (as in rational choice), but their goals as well, and by mediating their relations of cooperation and conflict, institutions structure political situations and leave their own imprint on political outcomes'.[15] On the other hand, the monograph embraces the notion of a political science that is less oriented towards the formulation of covering laws with strong predictive power than towards the explanation and interpretation of political behaviour in specific contexts. This methodological stand implies:

a) *A profound scepticism with respect to universal, one-dimensional, a priori explanations of political behaviour, typically exemplified by rational choice approaches.* This book embraces a more complex view of politics, in which permanent and conjunctural, normative and instrumental, social and individual factors shape political outcomes. In this sense, it advocates for comparative political science a procedure that is more inductive than deductive, aptly described, once again, by Thelen and Steinmo:

> Rather than deducing hypotheses on the basis of global assumptions and prior to the analysis, historical institutionalists generally develop their hypotheses more inductively, in the course of interpreting the empirical material itself... (I)nstitutional analyses focus on illuminating how different variables are linked. None... proposes a simple, single-variable explanation. All demonstrate the relationships and interactions among a variety of variables in a way that reflects the complexity of real political situations.[16]

b) *A pluralistic view of comparative methods.* Clearly, the generation of law-like generalisations requires the stringent methodological conditions eloquently laid out by Przeworski and Teune (1970) and King et al. (1994), to name two canonical texts in the field. These conditions include, first and foremost, a careful selection of cases according to their fit for 'most-similar systems' or 'most-different systems' research designs. However, even the strictest practitioners are keen to recognise that valuable insights about political behaviour may be obtained from comparative research that falls well short of such methodological strictures.[17] A single-minded quest for empirical regularities downplays, and probably misses altogether, the cultural and normative understandings that shape political behaviour in specific contexts, which often provide as good a guide for political practice as the most sophisticated generalisation. As we will see in these pages, the subtle social codes that rule interaction within small business elites, which are essentially un-modellable, are an indispensable element in any explanation of political finance practices in Costa Rica and Uruguay. In many ways, political science is at its best and most useful when solidly grounded on political history, sociology and anthropology, even if that reduces significantly the parsimony and leverage of its conclusions.[18] While *desirable*, covering laws – and the strict methods that may generate them – are not *essential* for the understanding of political behaviour.

Such an approach underpins one of the growing trends in comparative political science, i.e. the use of studies in which a small number of cases are explored in great depth, emphasising the role of context in the production of political outcomes. Generally speaking, such works are geared more towards *descriptive* than *causal* inference, are more reliant on qualitative evidence than on sophisticated quantitative techniques, and more oriented towards the generation of new hypotheses than towards the conclusive validation of old ones.[19] Aware of its merits and limitations, this work partakes of this tendency, embracing it as the best way forward for the development of a discipline of comparative political finance. The bulk of this volume thus comprises a comparative study of state funding systems and political finance practices in Costa Rica and Uruguay.

## THE CASES: WHY COSTA RICA AND URUGUAY?

Amongst Latin American countries, Costa Rica and Uruguay are uniquely suited to this research. They have long been recognised as two of the most stable democracies in the region and indeed in the entire developing world. While Costa Rica has enjoyed a spell of more than fifty years of unbroken democratic rule, a sequence unparalleled in the developing world, democratic institutions, notably elections and political parties, had a precocious development in Uruguay since the mid-nineteenth century, making the country one of the world's oldest polyarchies. Today, both countries boast some of the highest levels of democratic legitimacy, electoral participation, and party system institutionalisation in Latin America.[20]

The solidity of their democratic institutions hardly exhausts the list of similarities between these two countries. They indeed share central features in their political and institutional configuration, from the nature of the political regime – presidential in both cases – to the historically dominant presence of the state in society. More importantly for this work, both countries exhibit a similar long-term approach to political finance, defined by a lengthy tradition of direct state support to parties and a liberal attitude towards private contributions, only recently and ambiguously altered in Costa Rica. In fact, their state funding schemes are the two oldest in the world, preceding – in the Uruguayan case by several decades – the West European systems that have attracted much of the discussion on the topic. Their public funding schemes share important features, including their electoral orientation, and the proportional allocation and generosity of the disbursed funds.[21]

Beyond political and institutional realities, Costa Rica and Uruguay display a striking resemblance in their social structure and socio-economic development.

Table A.1: *Costa Rica and Uruguay, selected socio-economic indicators, c.2000*

| | | Costa Rica | Ranking in Latin America | Uruguay | Ranking in Latin America |
|---|---|---|---|---|---|
| A | Population (millions) | 3.9 | 18th | 3.2 | 19th |
| B | Population in capital city (millions) | 1.2 (1) | --- | 1.4 (2) | --- |
| C | GNP per capita (US$) (3) | 7,980 | 5th | 8,800 | 3rd |
| D | Literacy (% age 15 and above) | 95.5 | 4th | 97.7 | 1st |
| E | Human Development Index (4) | 0.821 | 4th | 0.828 | 2nd |
| F | Income distribution (top quintile/ bottom quintile) (5) | 6.9 | 2nd | 4.5 | 1st |
| G | Poor households (%) | 21.1 | --- | 15.5 (6) | --- |

Notes: (1) 1994, Metropolitan Area of San José. (2) 1991, city of Montevideo. (3) Adjusted for PPP. (4) Index of per capita income and selected health and education indicators, elaborated by the UNDP. (5) 1997. Lower figures are ranked higher. (6) Urban households only.
Sources: See Appendix.

Table A.1 shows that Costa Rica and Uruguay are very small societies, with significant spatial-demographic concentration and a relatively egalitarian socio-economic structure, where some of the worst inequalities and social tensions that characterise Latin America have been considerably tempered.

This long catalogue of shared features does not obscure, however, the existence of many political and historical differences between Costa Rica and Uruguay. The recent authoritarian experience undergone by Uruguay (1973–85) merely points towards more profound and permanent contrasts in the evolution of political actors and cleavages in both countries. Even in purely institutional terms, critical differences remain in the format of the party system and the workings of electoral rules in each case. As we will see below, the long-term use of Double Simultaneous Voting (DSV) – a peculiar system of preferential voting – has long conferred on Uruguayan electoral rules a clearly distinctive identity, not bereft of financial consequences.

Such a complex blend of systemic similarities and differences makes the selection of Costa Rica and Uruguay problematic from the standpoint of a 'most-similar' or 'most-different systems' comparative inquiry. Clearly, this paired comparison does not fall in either category. It is, however, a highly appropriate pairing for a project purporting to show that the historical, political, social and institutional context – which includes both shared and divergent traits – is essential to understand political finance practices. In a way, the politico-institutional context in Costa Rica and Uruguay is similar enough to make the comparison intelligible, but not so similar as to render it pointless. It is, moreover, a fortunate selection for a research that aims to show how contextual peculiarities and relatively minor differences in the subsidy's design may lead rather similar party funding schemes to affect political finance practices in quite distinct ways.

Above and beyond methodological suitability, however, strong practical motives underpin the choice of Costa Rica and Uruguay. As noted above, empirical information on political finance is a most scarce commodity in Latin America. In a topic riddled with secrecy and weak reporting practices, the construction of a pool of empirical data involves a painstaking investigative effort in the course of which a wide range of qualitative and quantitative sources must be probed and cross-checked. Clearly, such an endeavour stands a far better chance of succeeding in very small countries, with solidly established institutions – notably political parties – and age-old traditions of political openness. This is a rare combination of traits in Latin America. Indeed, with the partial exception of Chile, it may be found in Costa Rica and Uruguay alone. Moreover, they are the region's only cases that allow for a long-term examination of the role and effects of state funding systems. Quite simply, if any kind of comparative research on the effects of party subsidies and political finance practices is to be carried out in Latin America, all the roads lead to Costa Rica and Uruguay.

## LIMITS AND CAVEATS

Far from making it easy, such a choice makes this project feasible. Indeed, the feasibility of this research imposes, in many ways, strict limits to it. Four considerations about what this book is *not* and does *not* seek to achieve must be explicitly stated:

a) A first limit should be evident by now: this book will not offer conclusive validation or refutation of any hypothesis regarding the effects of state funding systems. Its theoretical aims are more modest: to offer an empirical critique of the available hypotheses, suggest that a view emphasising the contingency rather than the regularity of political outcomes is a valid standpoint to analyse those effects, and draw attention to phenomena and relations largely neglected in available political finance analyses. In that sense, it aims at attaining *heuristic* rather than *theoretical* value.

b) The reconstruction of political finance practices in Costa Rica and Uruguay deals, indeed, with *general practices* and how they relate to state funding systems and their context. The book does not seek to identify *specific* sources of political funding and *specific* political pay-offs eventually derived from their presence. If at all possible, the identification of conclusive empirical links between contributions and political decisions poses almost insurmountable methodological obstacles. What will be attempted here is an admittedly oblique way of dealing with the consequences of state funding systems on the autonomy and integrity of politicians and parties, i.e., by studying the subsidies' effects on fundraising practices. Such an indirect approach is based on the following premise: if DSF is to protect the integrity of political actors and enhance their autonomy from moneyed interests, then it should at least have a moderating impact on the fundraising practices of parties and candidates and, ultimately, on the financial influence of private donors.

If DSF fails to achieve this, then its relevance as a protector of political integrity must be seriously questioned.

c) The book deals with political finance, i.e., the funding of political activities in general. However, it will privilege the analysis of *campaign* finance issues over *party* finance ones. This implies a limited consideration of the funding of the parties' permanent (i.e. non-electoral) activities as well as of the long-term organisational effects of DSF (for instance on the parties' incentives to attract members, their institutionalisation and autonomy from the state). Though these issues will feature, in some length, in the review of the hypotheses on the effects of state funding, they will be almost completely absent from the book's case studies, due to reasons of space. The reduced focus on party finance is a far less serious shortcoming for this particular comparison than it would otherwise be. With very few exceptions – Uruguay's Broad Front (FA) the most important one – parties in both countries remain largely dormant between electoral tournaments. Their financial turnover, membership levels and permanent activities remain pitifully weak.[22] That parties in Costa Rica and Uruguay are considered amongst the most institutionalised in Latin America is more a commentary on the extraordinary feebleness of party organisations elsewhere in the region than a reflection of their peculiar solidity in both countries. To put it shortly: in Costa Rica and Uruguay political finance is campaign finance.

d) Even in Costa Rica and Uruguay, the study of campaign finance remains beset by the secular weakness of transparency rules and the corresponding scarcity of reliable information, particularly with regard to private sources of funding. Thus, while an effort has been made to provide the analysis of campaign finance practices with a historical perspective, a comprehensive quality, and a reasonable balance between both countries, the book's focus will be on the recent rather than the distant past (i.e. the 1990, 1994 and 1998 elections in Costa Rica, and the 1994 and 1999 elections in Uruguay), on presidential rather than congressional contests, and on Costa Rica more than on Uruguay. The latter emphasis owes more to the acute dearth of political finance information and the topic's long-standing neglect in Uruguay, than to the author's inevitable proclivities.

## THE CHAPTERS THAT FOLLOW

The book is divided into five chapters. Chapter one is a comparative survey of political finance regulations and state funding schemes. The chapter seeks to emphasise the extraordinary diversity of political finance regulations, the complexity of their components, and the frequently contradictory and unexpected consequences of their combination. The chapter also dissects DSF systems, offers a typology of them and engages in an appraisal of their political effects. Making use of sources of primary information (notably Katz and Mair's [1992] comprehensive handbook on party organisations in twelve developed democracies) as well as the scattered evidence collected in the available literature, the chapter scrutinises the empirical fit of the alternative hypotheses about DSF's effects on: (a) the parties' dependence on private donors and the prevention of corruption; (b) political equality, electoral competition and the dynamics of the party system; and (c) the organisation and strength of parties. Basic statistical tools are employed to test possible links between DSF and party system fragmentation, electoral volatility, and membership and bureaucratisation levels in political parties. This survey yields neither a victory for the subsidies' advocates nor one for their critics, but a rather mixed picture where the effects of DSF are contingent on an extraordinary diversity of political and institutional factors, not least the subsidy's own design. In the face of contingency, the chapter calls for more textured, context-sensitive analyses of political finance.

The rest of the volume embarks on such an analysis. Chapter two provides the historical, political and institutional backdrop against which political finance practices must be seen in Costa Rica and Uruguay. The chapter provides the reader with a basic understanding of the evolution and features of the political regime, electoral rules, party system, and political finance and state funding regulations in both countries. It is, in other words, an attempt to *frame* the case studies that will be developed in subsequent chapters. Chapter two pulls together the rich political literature on both countries (particularly on Uruguay) as well as a range of archival sources on the emergence and evolution of political finance arrangements. The chapter relates the latter to each country's broader political milieu and ends by taking stock of the key similarities and differences between the politico-institutional contexts of both cases.

The following two chapters should be considered as a unit and, in many ways, the core of the book. They are an exploration of the role of state funding in shaping campaign finance practices and in moderating exchanges between politicians and private donors in Costa Rica (Chapter three) and Uruguay (Chapter four). Employing a wide array of primary sources, including official documents, newspapers, media monitoring records and more than 100 interviews with active and retired politicians, party officials, electoral authorities and leading businesspersons, these chapters reconstruct the cost of campaigns, the nature of election expenses, the relative financial weight of DSF, and the procedures and codes that govern the parties' fundraising activities in both countries.[23] More than merely offering a description of campaign finance practices, the chapters connect these practices and the role of state funding to the politico-institutional traits laid out in Chapter two. What emerges from this paired account is a picture in which electoral rules and the format of the party system affect decisively fundraising dynamics and the subsidy's own relevance. Moreover, this picture is one in which subtle social and institutional mechanisms prove as important a constraint on exchanges between politicians and private contributors as the availability of public funding. As in the case of Chapter one, these chapters do not provide unalloyed confirmation of the best hopes and worst fears that infuse debates on DSF, but rather a more subdued view of its power to shape political behaviour. These chapters do suggest, nonetheless, that subsidies may be an important instrument for the protection of electoral equality, and that the acute pro-business bias of fundraising processes – even in Latin America's most egalitarian societies – may well turn DSF into a democratic necessity in the region.

Chapter five returns to the issue of the effects of DSF on electoral competition and the dynamics of the party system, already raised in Chapter one. Through a long-term analysis of electoral volatility and party-system fragmentation in Costa Rica and Uruguay, the chapter reinforces what the review made in Chapter one already suggests: very little evidence exists of the ability of DSF to block changes in the party system. If anything, the chapter argues that certain subsidy designs – such as the Uruguayan one – may actually *foster* party-system transformation and the subversion of the status quo rather than protecting it. Ultimately, the configuration of party systems and their evolution respond to deeper historical and institutional phenomena, which political finance rules can hardly counteract. A brief conclusion follows Chapter five, summarising the main lessons drawn from the case studies and suggesting new hypotheses and directions for future comparative work on political finance.

This book seeks to enrich the empirical content of an important discussion for the quality of democracy in Latin America and beyond. But, above all, it is an attempt to place political finance debates in a better informed and more objective perspective. While positive and even necessary, the current media infatuation with political finance issues has propagated a powerful mythology of the topic, populated by greedy contributors, corrupt politicians, bought-and-sold policies, and all-knowing reformers. Populated, that is, by the disfigured shadows that Frank Sorauf's epigraph rightly decries. Luckily for this work, and for political science in general, political finance realities are far more interesting and complex than their cardboard version suggests. The truth is that political money rarely determines political outcomes, and that regulation instruments seldom achieve more than a fleeting and moderate success in curbing its influence. Even the author would be happy to admit that, fortunately, the subject of this volume is less urgent than often appears.

## NOTES

Sorauf (1994), pp. 1359, 1367.
1   Pollock (1932), p. 328.
2   Transparency International (2000).
3   OAS, Inter-American Democratic Charter (Article 5), 11/9/2001.
4   International Parliamentary Union [IPU], Resolution adopted without a vote by the 94th
5   Inter-Parliamentary Conference (paragraph 5.c), 13/10/1995; International Organisation of the Francophonie [OIF], Declaration of Bamako (paragraph 5.b.11), 3/11/2000; COE, Parliamentary Assembly, Recommendation 1516, 22/5/2001; EU, Treaty of Nice (Declaration 11), 26/2/2001; Commission of the European Communities, Proposal for a Council Regulation on the Statute and Financing of European Political Parties, 13/2/2001.

Senator R. Feingold in *The Washington Post*, 19/3/2002.

6  Schattschneider (1975 [1960]), p. 119.

7  For a comprehensive bibliography of political finance works and a good survey of the com-
8  parative efforts see Nassmacher (2001a) and (2001b).

Duverger (1988 [1951]), p. 9.

9  Del Castillo and Zovatto (1998) is, by far, the most comprehensive collection of studies on
10  Latin American political finance.

On the case of Colombia: Posada-Carbó (n.d.). On the case of Panama: *The Economist*,
11  25/5/1996 and 29/6/1996. Illegal fundraising practices also played a role in the downfall of
former Brazilian President Fernando Collor de Melo in 1992.

On the difference between direct, indirect and specific state funding see Chapter one, pp. 28–9.
12  For the rest of this volume, the expressions 'state funding', 'state financing', 'state subsidy',
'public funding', 'public financing', 'public subsidy' and 'public subvention' will be used inter-
changeably and be taken to mean Direct State Funding, unless otherwise stated.

Committee on Standards in Public Life (1998), p. 92.

13  Although most political finance works deal with DSF in one way or another, the only vol-
14  umes published in English or Spanish specifically devoted to its study are, to the best of my
knowledge: Leonard (1975), Committee on Financial Aid to Political Parties (1976), Centro
de Estudios para la Justicia Social con Libertad (CEJUL) (1989), Wiberg (1991a), Alexander
et al. (1992) and Corrado (1993).

Thelen and Steinmo (1992), p. 9.

15  Thelen and Steinmo (1992), pp. 12–13.

16  King et al. (1994), pp. 211–12.

17  See Almond and Genco (1977); MacIntyre (1978); Skocpol and Somers (1980); Thelen and
18  Steinmo (1992); Whitehead (1996) and (2002).

Mair (1996), pp.328–31.

19  Costa Rica and Uruguay have routinely topped the rankings of support of and satisfaction
20  with democracy in Latin America. See, for instance, Latinobarómetro (2002). See also
International IDEA (1997), Figure 12, and Mainwaring and Scully (1995), Table 1.6.

The mean level of subsidisation over the past fifty years is very similar in both countries:
21  US$7.7 per voter and election cycle in Costa Rica, US$6.9 per voter in Uruguay (US$ of
1995).

A few facts should clarify the point. Between March 1994 and July 1997, i.e. between the
22  1994 election and the onset of the next presidential campaign, *total* expenditures at the headquarters of Costa Rica's National Liberation Party (PLN) – the most institutionalised in the
country – amounted to US$20,500 per month on average (PLN [1994–8]). In January 1996,
two years before the 1998 election, its main contender, the Social Christian Unity Party
(PUSC), had only seven full-time employees on its payroll. The figure climbed to 633 in
January 1998, only to plummet, once again, to seven in January 2000, halfway through the
electoral cycle (CCSS [various years]). Top directing posts in both parties – such as
President of the Political Directorate, Secretary General and Treasurer – carry no salary,
despite being, in some cases, full-time occupations. The situation is not essentially different
in Uruguay. Monthly expenses at the headquarters of the long ruling Colorado Party (PC)
have been estimated at US$10,000. One of its largest internal sectors, Lista 15, does not have

affiliates or offices outside the campaign season. Even the central office of the left-wing Broad Front (FA) – far and away the most expensive political operation in the country between campaigns – has a routine turnover of less than US$1 million per year. This pales when compared with the almost US$10 million spent by the party in the course of the 1999–2000 election cycle. In both countries, parties are, for all intents and purposes, electoral machines.

Indeed, the book's case studies – particularly their reconstruction of campaign finance prac-
23 tices – rely heavily, although far from exclusively, on information provided by the following interviews: A) In Costa Rica: Altmann [28/9/1999]; Alvarez [7/12/1999]; Araya [4/12/1999]; Araya-Fernández [27/1/2000]; Arias [30/8/1999]; Berhorst [21/10/1999]; Burgués, [11/11/1999]; Calderón-Fournier [16/9/1999]; Carazo [29/9/1999]; Cerdas [20/9/1999]; Chacón [7/9/1999]; Chacón-González [21/12/1999]; Chávez [22/10/1999]; Chinchilla [9/9/1999]; Constenla [20/9/1999]; Coto [6/9/1999]; De la Cruz [13/9/1999]; Dent [22/12/1999]; Fachler [22/9/1999]; Feoli [20/9/1999]; Figueres [3/11/1999]; Fishman [1/12/1999]; Flórez-Estrada [28/1/2000]; Fonseca [24/11/1999]; González [17/9/1999]; Guardia [20/10/1999]; Guevara [24/9/1999]; Gutiérrez-Sáenz [1/11/1999]; Laclé [7/9/1999]; León-Páez [1/12/1999]; Méndez [15/11/1999]; Montero [21/12/1999]; Muñoz [21/10/1999]; Pacheco [20/1/2000]; Pacheco-Salazar [23/11/1999]; Palma [15/10/1999], Ruíz [10/12/1999]; Schyfter [9/12/1999]; Sobrado [8/9/1999]; Spaett [22/10/1999]; Tovar [1/11/1999]; Trejos [25/10/1999]; Urcuyo [23/11/1999]; Vargas [28/10/1999]; Vargas-Aguilar [6/12/1999]; Vargas-Artavia [4/10/1999]; Vargas-Benavides [23/9/1999]; Villalobos [25/11/1999]; Villegas [17/9/1999]; Weisleder [23/9/1999]; Yankelewitz [20/10/1999]. B) In Uruguay: Abdala [25/4/2000]; Achard [17/5/2000]; Advertising executive [10/5/2000]; Aguirre [9/6/2000]; Ahumada [16/6/2000]; Alonzo [9/5/2000]; Andreoli [13/6/2000]; Arbilla [3/7/2000]; Astori [1/6/2000]; Baráibar [17/4/2000]; Barandiarán [25/4/2000]; Barbé [20/3/2000]; Batlle [2/6/2000]; Bayardi [4/5/2000]; Benecke [4/7/2000]; Businessperson No. 1 [15/5/2000]; Businessperson No. 2 [2/6/2000]; Businessperson No. 3 [24/5/2000]; Businessperson No. 4 [5/7/2000]; Carlevaro [14–16/6/2000]; Castro [18/5/2000]; Cataldi [5/6/2000]; Da Silva [29/6/2000]; De Cuadro [13/6/2000]; FA media advisor [27/4/2000]; Flores-Silva [14/4/2000]; Gandini [12/4/2000]; Giuria [25/4/2000]; Heber [26/5/2000]; Lacalle [4/7/2000]; Lamorte [31/5/2000]; Lassús [14/6/2000]; Lorenzo [3/4/2000]; Macedo [9/6/2000]; Martin [6/6/2000]; F.Michelini [11/5/2000]; R.Michelini [10/5/2000]; Mieres [20/3/2000]; Millán [26/5/2000]; Nunes [10/4/2000]; Penino [20/6/2000]; Radiccioni [23/5/2000]; Ramírez [28/6/2000]; Rodríguez-Camusso [28/4/2000]; Rosas [21/6/2000]; Sanguinetti [12/4/2000]; Urruty [23/2/2000]; Vaillant [28/4/2000]; Valdez [10/4/2000]; Visillac [23/5/2000]; Xavier [1/6/2000]. For reasons of space, as well as to facilitate the reading, I have decided, with few exceptions (particularly cases of direct quotation), not to attribute points made in the text to particular interviews. Other sources have been largely kept in the endnotes. Attribution details may be found in Casas-Zamora (2002) or obtained from the author at kevin_casas@yahoo.com.

# chapter one | political finance systems and direct state funding: a comparative survey

## INTRODUCTION

The regulation of the role of money in politics has become a central part of political agendas across the world. All democracies are routinely faced with the consequences of political fundraising for pivotal democratic values such as equality, fairness, transparency and integrity. Not surprisingly, in the last three decades – which have seen a dramatic expansion of democratic regimes – regulatory efforts have proliferated. Today, virtually every democracy exerts *some* legal control over the flow of money to and from election campaigns and other party activities. More than any other option, the introduction of Direct State Funding (DSF) for parties and candidates has been at the centre of these regulatory efforts. In many ways, the story of contemporary political finance regulation is the story of the emergence and expansion of DSF.

This chapter offers a basic survey of state funding schemes and their consequences. It is, primarily, an attempt to test the empirical fit of the hypotheses advanced by advocates and critics of DSF regarding its effects on the financial dependence of political actors on private sources of income, on the dynamics of the party system, and on the organisation and social embeddedness of parties. This empirical exercise will be preceded, however, by an attempt to map out the diversity of subsidy arrangements that can be found in contemporary democracies and, more broadly, the heterogeneity of political finance regulatory frameworks, of which DSF schemes are but a part. The chapter shows that DSF is a remarkably versatile instrument, whose mutations are underpinned by several and frequently opposed logics. Furthermore, it demonstrates that DSF co-exists with a plethora of regulations over other aspects of political finance, often at cross-purposes with state funding schemes, which endow every regulatory framework with a distinct character and peculiar (and often unintended) consequences.

This chapter starts with a survey of political finance regulations in a sample of more than forty (mostly) North American, Latin American and West European democracies, seeking to frame state funding and its effects in a broader institutional context. More importantly, it aims to dispel the notions that there are easy, obvious and standard regulatory solutions to the vexing dilemmas of money in politics, and that the effects of particular regulation instruments – including DSF – can be accurately predicted in isolation from their institutional surroundings.

### POLITICAL FINANCE SYSTEMS: A GLANCE AT THE OPTIONS

In a classic work, Alexander Heard noted that the financial costs of nominating and electing public officials are as inevitable for democratic politics as a certain level of demagogy in public debate.[1] A political finance system (PFS) is the set of rules that deals with the indispensable flow of money into the political system and from it. It provides the framework within which parties and candidates can legally act to obtain money for their activities and spend it, and within which citizens and organisations – private and public – fund those activities. It also defines the legal instruments that oversee and enforce the operation of that framework.

PFS are complex institutional arrangements that combine a variety of regulatory instruments. For the sake of simplicity, and according to their function, these instruments may be classified in three groups:
• Regulations of the sources of income of candidates and parties,
• Regulations of political expenditure;
• Regulations of financial transparency for the activities of candidates and parties.

As will soon become evident, each of these categories hosts a striking variety of policy options. Furthermore, each is affected by normative dilemmas and practical shortcomings. When it comes to political finance regulation the options are many but the choices are seldom easy.

### Controlling political finance income

This set of rules includes all the instruments that regulate the flow of money into the political system, either by restricting/banning the use of certain sources of political funds (negative regulations) or by providing/stimulating specific types of funding (positive regulations). As shown in Graph 1.1 the sources of political funding are numerous and diverse, covering the whole spectrum from the highly legitimate, such as party membership fees, to the outright corrupt, such as 'kickbacks', 'toll-gating' and 'macing'.[2]

Amongst legitimate sources of funding, private political donations are subject to the most extensive controls. Table 1.1 shows that most democracies restrict the use of at least some kinds of private donations, albeit with widely different levels of intensity. While some countries (e.g. Greece) merely impose a cap on contribution amounts, more than half of the countries in the sample ban the use of some sources altogether. Ceilings on individual contributions range from US$350 per election in Israel to more than US$250,000 per year in Japan. Bans most commonly affect foreign donations – forbidden in more than twenty countries – and specific kinds of business contributions, typically those from state-owned firms or

Graph 1.1: *Sources of political funding*

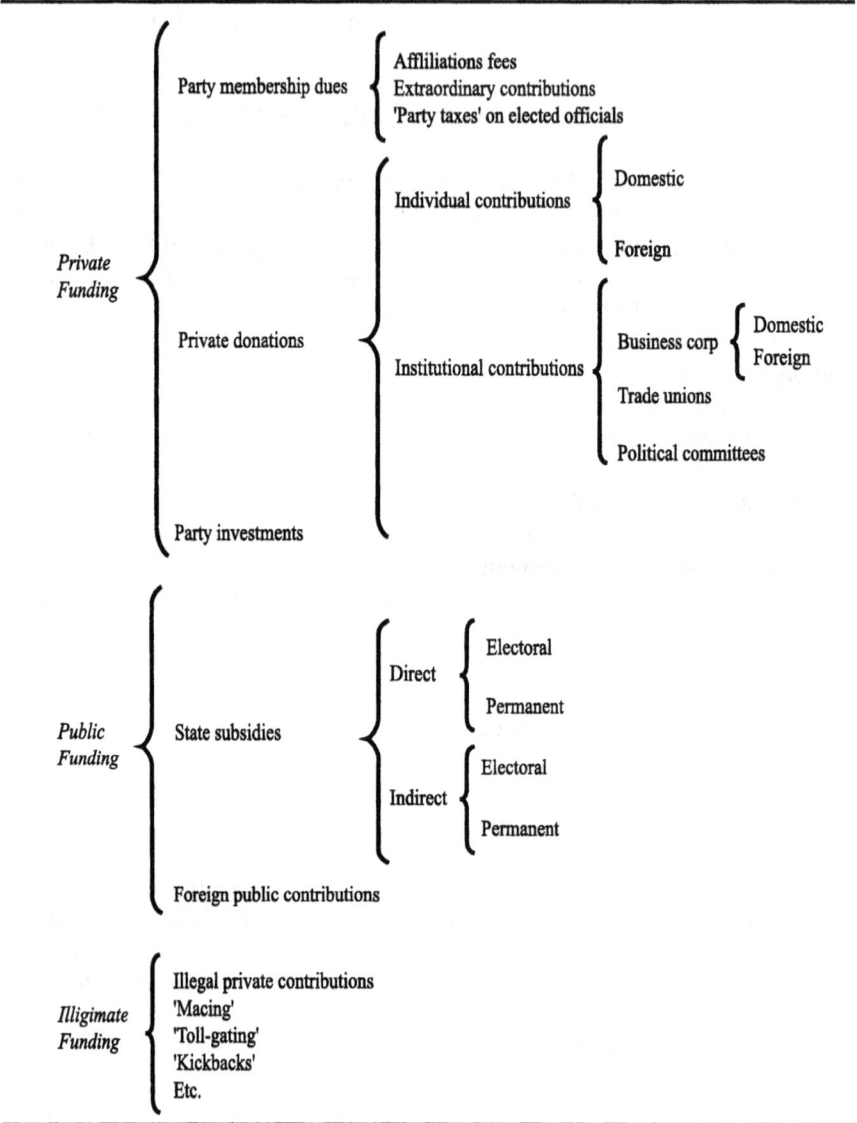

---

*Private Funding*
- Party membership dues
  - Afflilations fees
  - Extraordinary contributions
  - 'Party taxes' on elected officials
- Private donations
  - Individual contributions
    - Domestic
    - Foreign
  - Institutional contributions
    - Business corp
      - Domestic
      - Foreign
    - Trade unions
    - Political committees
- Party investments

*Public Funding*
- State subsidies
  - Direct
    - Electoral
    - Permanent
  - Indirect
    - Electoral
    - Permanent
- Foreign public contributions

*Illigimate Funding*
- Illegal private contributions
- 'Macing'
- 'Toll-gating'
- 'Kickbacks'
- Etc.

---

firms which benefit from state contracts or licences.

Restrictions on private sources of funding are meant to thwart the purchase of political influence by large and/or controversial donors. In the words of the US Supreme Court, they are a legitimate means to limit 'the danger of actual *quid pro quo* arrangements... (and) the impact of the appearance of corruption'.[3] Particularly severe restrictions tend thus to follow major corruption scandals, as seen in the US – where limits were introduced in the wake of Watergate in 1974,

Table 1.1: *Comparative political finance income regulation*[4]

| Country | Contribution limits (1) | | | | State funding (2) | | |
|---|---|---|---|---|---|---|---|
| | | | | | Direct subsidies | | Indirect subsidies/ |
| | Individuals | Corporations | Trade Unions | Foreign | Permanent | Electoral | specific grants |
| Argentina | Yes | Forbidden | Forbidden | Forbidden | Yes | Yes | Yes |
| Australia | No | No | No | No | Yes | Yes | Yes |
| Austria | No | No | No | No | Yes | Yes | Yes |
| Belgium | Yes | Forbidden | Yes | Yes | Yes (4) | No | Yes |
| Bolivia | No | No (3) | Forbidden | Forbidden | No | Yes | Yes |
| Brazil | Yes | Yes (3) | Forbidden | Forbidden | Yes | No | Yes |
| Canada | Yes | Yes | Yes | Forbidden | Yes | Yes | Yes |
| Chile | No | No | No | Forbidden | No | Yes | Yes |
| Colombia | No | No | No | No | Yes | Yes | Yes |
| Costa Rica | Yes | Yes | Yes | Forbidden | No | Yes | Yes |
| Denmark | No | No | No | No | No | Yes | Yes |
| Dominican Rep. | No | No | No | Forbidden | Yes | Yes | Yes |
| Ecuador | No | Yes (3) | Yes | Forbidden | Yes | Yes | Yes |
| El Salvador | No | No | No | No | No | Yes | No |
| Finland | No | No | No | No | Yes | No | Yes |
| France | Yes | Forbidden | Forbidden | Forbidden | Yes | Yes | Yes |
| Germany | No | No | No | Yes (8) | Yes | No | Yes |
| Greece | Yes | Yes | Yes | Yes | Yes | No | Yes |
| Guatemala | No | No | No | No | Yes | No | Yes |
| Honduras | No | No (3) | No | Forbidden | No | Yes | Yes |
| India | No | Yes | No | Forbidden(5) | No | No | Yes |
| Ireland | Yes | Yes | Yes | Forbidden | Yes | No | Yes |
| Israel | Yes | Forbidden | Forbidden | Forbidden | Yes | Yes | Yes |
| Italy | Yes (6) | Yes (3) | Yes | Yes | Yes | Yes | Yes |
| Japan | Yes | Yes (3) (7) | Yes (7) | Forbidden | Yes | No | Yes |
| Luxembourg | No | No | No | No | No | No | Yes |
| Mexico | Yes | Forbidden | Yes | Forbidden | Yes | Yes | Yes |
| Netherlands | No | No | No | No | Yes | No | Yes |
| New Zealand | No | No | No | No | No | No | Yes |
| Nicaragua | No | No | No | No | No | Yes | Yes |
| Norway | No | No | No | No | Yes | No | Yes |
| Panama | No | No | No | No | Yes | Yes | Yes |
| Paraguay | Yes | Yes (3) | Forbidden | Forbidden | Yes | Yes | Yes |
| Peru | Yes | Yes (3) | Yes | Forbidden | Yes | No | Yes |
| Portugal | Yes | Yes (3) | Yes | Forbidden | Yes | Yes | Yes |
| South Korea | Yes | Yes | Forbidden | Forbidden | Yes | Yes | No |
| Spain | Yes | Yes (3) | Yes | Forbidden | Yes | Yes | Yes |
| Sweden | No | No | No | No | Yes | No | Yes |
| Switzerland | No | No | No | No | No | No | Yes |
| Taiwan | Yes | Yes | Yes | Forbidden | No | Yes | Yes |
| Turkey | Yes | Yes | Forbidden | Forbidden | Yes | No | Yes |
| UK | No | No | No | No | No | No | Yes |
| Uruguay | No | No | No | No | No | Yes | Yes |
| USA | Yes | Forbidden | Forbidden | Forbidden | No | Yes | Yes |

Notes to Table 1.1
(1) 'Yes' means the presence of limits, 'No' their absence, and 'Forbidden' the complete banning of the source. (2) 'Yes' means the presence of subsidies, 'No' their absence. (3) Specific kinds of business donations are forbidden. (4) An annual grant is paid to the non-profit institution designated by the parties. (5) No party, association or political group is allowed to accept any foreign contribution without the permission of the central government. (6) No limit exists for contributions to the parties' routine expenses. (7) Donations to individual politicians are banned. (8) Except for contributions from EU nationals.
Sources: See Appendix.

---

– France (1988–1990), Belgium (1989) and Brazil (1995), to name but a few cases. Whether these constraints live up to the goals that inspire them is, however, an uncertain matter. As is the case with other restrictive regulatory measures, contribution limits pose major implementation problems, demanding the presence of an extensive system of reporting and auditing of political money, a difficult requirement even for developed democracies.[5] Moreover, contribution limits, particularly of the extensive kind, frequently lead to perverse outcomes. Thus, draconian measures to ban private contributions altogether, such as those employed in France before 1988 and India during 1969–85, fostered singularly opaque fundraising practices.[6] Even less extreme policies, such as the set of limits enacted in 1974 in the US, gradually toughened by their lack of indexation, drove political actors towards less transparent funding sources, while becoming an important obstacle to funding viable electoral challenges to incumbents.[7] It is no surprise that many democracies, notably West European ones, have shied away from comprehensive contribution controls, opting to curb the financial influence of donors through other means, such as extensive public subsidy systems, short election campaigns and severe restrictions on electoral publicity.

PFS can also *actively* shape the inflow of political money, by providing parties and candidates with public money, goods or services. As Table 1.1 attests, the use of direct, indirect and specific public subsidies is the single most common feature of contemporary PFS: *all* the countries in the sample display some kind of public support for political activities. However, as the third section of this chapter will make clear, such a statement disguises the heterogeneity of subsidy schemes, a miscellaneous group of funding instruments united only by the feature of being funded with taxpayer money.

## Controlling political finance expenditure

The second group of instruments regulates the electoral expenditures of candidates and parties, either through general spending limits or itemised ceilings, typically restricting advertising outlays during campaigns.

General spending ceilings are relatively rare amongst democracies. This is a reflection of their significant normative and practical drawbacks. Ostensibly aimed at restraining the cost of politics and obstructing the translation of econom-

Table 1.2: *Comparative political finance expenditure regulation*

| Country | Spending ceilings for parties or presidential candidates (national level) | | Spending ceilings for parties or parliamentary candidates (constituency level) | |
|---|---|---|---|---|
| | General | Advertising (1) | General | Advertising (1) |
| Argentina | Yes | No | Yes | No |
| Australia | No | No | No | No |
| Austria | No | No | No | No |
| Belgium | Yes | Yes (2) | Yes | Yes (2) |
| Bolivia | No | No | No | No |
| Brazil | No | No | No | No |
| Canada | Yes | Yes | Yes | No |
| Chile | Yes | Yes (2) | Yes | Yes |
| Colombia | Yes | Yes | Yes | Yes |
| Costa Rica | No | No | No | No |
| Denmark | No | Yes (2) | No | Yes (2) |
| Dominican Rep. | No | No | No | No |
| Ecuador | Yes | No | Yes | No |
| El Salvador | No | No | No | No |
| Finland | No | No | No | No |
| France | Yes | Yes (2) | Yes | Yes (2) |
| Germany | No | No | No | No |
| Greece | Yes | Yes (2) | No | Yes (2) |
| Guatemala | No | No | No | No |
| Honduras | No | No | No | No |
| India | No | Yes (2) | Yes | Yes (2) |
| Ireland | Yes | Yes (2) | Yes | Yes (2) |
| Israel | Yes | Yes (2) | National constituency only | |
| Italy | Yes | No | Yes | No |
| Japan | No | Yes | No | Yes |
| Luxembourg | No | No | No | No |
| Mexico | Yes | No | Yes | No |
| Netherlands | No | No | National constituency only | |
| New Zealand | Yes | Yes (2) | Yes | Yes (2) |
| Nicaragua | No | No | No | No |
| Norway | No | Yes (2) | No | Yes (2) |
| Panama | No | No | No | No |
| Paraguay | No | Yes | No | No |
| Peru | No | Yes | No | No |
| Portugal | Yes | No | Yes | No |
| South Korea | Yes | Yes (3) | Yes | Yes (3) |
| Spain | Yes | Yes (4) | No | Yes (2) |
| Sweden | No | Yes (5) | No | Yes (5) |
| Switzerland | No | Yes (2) | No | Yes (2) |
| Taiwan | No | Yes (3) | Yes | Yes (3) |
| Turkey | No | Yes (2) | No | Yes (2) |
| UK | Yes | Yes (2) | Yes | Yes (2) |
| Uruguay | No | No | No | No |
| USA | Yes (6) | No | No | No |

22 | paying for democracy

Notes to Table 1.2

(1) 'Yes' means an explicit policy of restricting publicity outlays or part of them, such as TV advertising. Clearly, the enactment of general limits for electoral expenditure implies, by definition, a limit to advertising spending. In this table, such 'implicit' limits on publicity outlays have been classified as 'No.' (2) Paid political advertising is not allowed on TV. Parties are allocated time on state-owned and/or private broadcasters. (3) There is no political broadcasting, either free or paid. (4) Similar to (2), but there is also a cap on advertising expenses in general. (5) Similar to (2) with regards to national broadcasting, but parties are allowed to buy advertising in local and regional stations. (6) Spending limits operate only for presidential candidates that have accepted public funding. In that case, the spending ceiling equals the subsidy.

Sources: See Appendix

ic power into electoral advantage, spending limits impose a tax on freedom of expression[8] and, occasionally, on the same electoral fairness that they purport to protect. In the absence of countervailing mechanisms, spending caps can reinforce the electoral position of incumbent candidates and parties. Abundant international evidence, notably from US congressional elections, suggests that large electoral disbursements are frequently essential to counteract the inherent advantages of incumbency (e.g. superior name recognition, access to patronage, etc.). In the context of democratic politics, money can often be suppressing; yet, under specific circumstances, it can also be liberating.

The empirical record of general spending limits is mixed at best. Even the most successful examples, such as Britain and Canada, where caps have been rigorously enforced and generally praised, attest to the vexing practical questions implied by their implementation. In Britain, the relevance of constituency-based ceilings was gradually eroded by the secular growth of the parties' national expenditures, only recently harnessed by legislation.[9] In Canada, meanwhile, the regulation of third-party expenditures – i.e., disbursements made by non-party groups aiming to affect electoral results – has proved intractable in spite of the visible role often played by such outlays.[10] In most other instances, inadequacies in the definition of electoral expenses, unrealistically low ceilings, poor enforcement mechanisms, and strong incentives towards electoral spending derived from other institutional features, have undermined decisively the efficacy of expenditure caps. Thus, while ceilings were for a long time too high to be useful in Spain, in other countries, such as Australia, Colombia, India, Israel, Japan, Russia, South Korea, the Ukraine and the US (1925–1974), political actors have consistently ignored them.[11]

Trying to avert some of these consequences, other PFS focus their restrictions on singularly visible and expensive items, such as election advertising. As shown in Table 1.2, most West European democracies ban paid political advertising on television, while providing parties with advertising slots in state-owned broadcasters. Though generally regarded as an efficient way to cut down the costs of electoral activity and reduce the economic pressure on parties, the general applicability of the West European model is dubious. It requires the presence of powerful state-owned broadcasting systems – an oddity among non-West European democracies – and, probably, the existence of strongly party-based political systems to prevent the atomisation of advertising. More importantly, the effects of this model in protecting political equality are ambiguous. As with general spending ceilings, strict advertising limits may become an unfair protection of incumbent parties and a significant obstacle for political newcomers, particularly if incumbents continue to enjoy unlimited access to official information outlets.

### Securing political finance transparency

The third set of political finance rules includes all the norms that compel parties, candidates and other political actors to report to the public authorities the origin of the economic resources used in their activities and/or the uses given to those resources.

As Table 1.3 shows, these rules exhibit considerable variation between countries. Generally speaking they involve financial reports from political parties rather than candidates, reports on routine as well as electoral activities, disclosure of both income and expenditure, and auditing of the information by a competent authority

Transparency rules are meant to shed light on the sources of support of parties and candidates as well as on the latter's compliance with political finance legislation. While unveiling such information may have an intrinsic value for democracy, transparency rules also have a decisive instrumental relevance for the success of particular political finance reforms, such as contribution and expenditure limits. In many ways, the efficacy of the latter is entirely contingent on the presence of a solid system of political finance disclosure.

While they remain the cornerstone of political finance regulation in many countries –most notably the US – disclosure rules are not exempt from acute normative and practical dilemmas. On the one hand, they imply the public knowledge of critical information about the internal life of political organisations and a degree of state control over them. On the other, these norms reflect the notion that the collective benefits of disclosing the sources of financial support of political actors outweigh the donors' right to privacy. Both notions have been consistently rejected in many democracies, even some strongly consolidated ones (e.g. Sweden and Switzerland). These issues are of particular concern in democracies haunted by a recent authoritarian past, where fear of government harassment is still fresh in the minds of many political actors.[12] Moreover, a copious comparative experience suggests that a demanding set of requisites must be met if political finance disclosure is to be enforced. It includes thorough auditing of financial reports, independence and resourcefulness in the authority that receives and audits the reports, and strong sanctions attached to non-compliance. The presence of such requisites is by no means guaranteed. The post-1974 experience in Italy offers a particularly poignant reminder of the futility of a complex system of reporting if the auditing of the information is left in the hands of the same politicians that submit the reports.

Table 1.3: *Comparative political finance transparency rules (reporting and auditing)*

| Country | Interval | | Reporting subject | | Report's object | | Controlling authority | Report's audit | Agency doctrine (1) |
|---|---|---|---|---|---|---|---|---|---|
| | Annual | Campaign | Campaign | Others | Income | Others | | | |
| Argentina | X | X | | | X | X | Federal judge | No | |
| Australia | X | | X | | X | X | Electoral Commission | Yes | X |
| Austria | X | | X | | X | X | Prime Minister's Office | Yes (2) | |
| Belgium | X | | | X (3) | X | X | Parliamentary Control Committee | Yes | |
| Bolivia (2) | | X | X | | | X | National Electoral Court | Yes | |
| Brazil | X | X | X | | X | X | Electoral tribunals | Yes | |
| Canada | X (5) | X | X | | X | X | Chief Electoral Officer | Yes | X |
| Chile | X | | | | X | X | Chief Electoral Officer | Yes | |
| Colombia | X | X | X | X (4) | X | X | National Electoral Council | Yes | |
| Costa Rica | X (5) | X | | | X | X | Supreme Elections Tribunal/National Comptroller | Yes (2) | |
| Denmark | X | | | | X | X | Electoral authorities | Yes | |
| Dominican Republic | X | X | | | X | X | Central Electoral Junta | No | |
| Ecuador (2) | | X | | | X | X | Supreme Electoral Tribunal | No | |
| El Salvador | | | | | | | No reporting | | |
| Finland | X | X | X | | X | X | Ministry of Justice | Yes | |
| France | X | X | X | | X | X | National Commission for Political Funding/Constitutional Council (6) | Yes | X |
| Germany | X | | X | | X | X | Speaker of Congress/Nat. Accounts Tribunal | Yes | |
| Greece | X | X | X | | X | X | Parliament Speaker/Minister of Interior | Yes | |
| Guatemala(2) | Undefined | | | | | X | Supreme Electoral Tribunal | Yes | |
| Honduras (2) | | X | | | X | X | National Elections Tribunal | No | |
| India | | X | X | | X | X | Election Commission | Yes | |
| Ireland | X | X | | | X | X | Election Commissioner | Yes | |
| Israel | | X | | | X | X | Chair of Parliament /State Comptroller | No | |
| Italy | X | X | X | | X | X | Speaker of Chamber of Deputies/State Auditor/Regional Electoral Authority (7) | Yes | X |

Table 1.3: (Cont)

| Country | Interval | | Reporting subject | | | Report's object | Controlling authority | Report's audit | Agency doctrine (1) |
|---|---|---|---|---|---|---|---|---|---|
| | Annual | Campaign | Party | Candidate | Others | | | | |
| Japan | X | | X | X | X (8) | X | Minister of Home Affairs/Local Electoral Commission | No | |
| Luxembourg | | | | | | | No reporting | | |
| Mexico | X | X | X | | X (9) | X | Federal Electoral Institute | Yes | |
| Netherlands | X | X | X | | | X | Ministry of Home Affairs | Yes | |
| New Zealand | X | X | X | | | X | Electoral Commission | Yes | |
| Nicaragua (2) | | X | X | | | X | National Comptroller | Yes | |
| Norway | X | X | X | | | X | Ministry of Labour | Yes | |
| Panama (2) | X | X | X | | | X | Electoral Tribunal | Yes | |
| Paraguay | X | X | X | X | | X | Supreme Tribunal of Electoral Justice | Yes | |
| Peru | X | X | X | | | X | National Elections Jury | Yes | |
| Portugal | X | X | X | | | X | Constitutional Tribunal/National Election Commission (10) | Yes | |
| South Korea | X | X | X | X | X (11) | X | Central Election Management Committee | Yes | |
| Spain | X | X | X | | | X | Accounts Tribunal | Yes | |
| Sweden | | | | | | | No reporting | | |
| Switzerland | | | | | | | No reporting | | |
| Taiwan | | X | X | X | | X | Election Commission | Yes | |
| Turkey | X (5) | X | X | | | X | Constitutional Court/Attorney General | Yes | |
| U.K. | X (5) | X | X | | | X | Electoral Commission | Yes | X |
| Uruguay | | X | X | | | X | No reporting | | |
| USA | X (12) | X (12) | X | X | X (13) | X | Federal Election Commission | Yes | |

Notes to Table 1.3

(1) The election agent is an innovation introduced in Britain in 1883, aimed at centralising the control of and responsibility for the financial activities of candidates. Candidates must appoint a financial manager for their campaign. All electoral contributions and expenditures must be channelled through the electoral agent, who is legally responsible for the campaign's compliance with political finance laws (Blackburn [1995], pp.270–271). (2) Legal reporting and auditing requirements cover only state-provided funds. (3) Party foundations and institutes. (4) Social movements, ad-hoc organisations formed in support of candidates, and independent candidates must also report their campaign accounts. (5) Quarterly reports required. (6) Presidential candidates report to the Constitutional Council. (7) Parties' routine operations are reported to the Chamber's Speaker. Their campaign income and expenses is reported to the State Auditor. Candidates declare their expenses to the regional electoral authority. (8) *Habatsu* or financial organisations formed to support individual candidates. (9) Political groupings: associations created to support the development of democracy and civic life, which may participate in elections allied to a party. (10) Routine operations reported to Constitutional Tribunal. Campaign operations reported to National Election Commission. (11) Sponsors' Associations: conveyor organisations formed to channel funds from individuals and corporations to specific politicians and parties. (12) Most political committees must file semi-annual reports during non-election years and quarterly reports during election years. Principal campaign committees of presidential candidates must submit monthly and quarterly reports. All committees must submit pre-electoral reports fifteen days before the election and post-electoral reports within one month of the election. (13) Political committees: any committee, club, association, or other group of persons that receives political contributions or makes expenditures in excess of US$1000 during a year.
Sources: See Appendix.

## A basic typology of PFS

This cursory review of the basic instruments of political finance regulation hints at three crucial points. First, there are no obvious regulatory solutions to the challenges raised by the use of money in politics. The rhetorical excesses that populate discussions on political finance reform in most countries are simply misguided: political finance regulation implies hard practical and normative choices, whose success is by no means guaranteed. Second, no matter how prominent, state funding systems are, more often than not, merely one part of a complex regulatory ensemble. Extricating the effects of DSF from those of the latter as a whole is difficult in the best of cases. Third, the frameworks chosen by modern democracies to deal with political finance are extraordinarily diverse. For the time being, the complex question of why different political systems travel along different regulatory paths will be sidelined. It suffices to point out that those choices are as much determined by normative predisposition (e.g. extensive state funding has been more generally preferred in Western Europe than in the US), as by institutional incentives (e.g. broadcasting regulations are widespread in Western Europe but not elsewhere; permanent party subsidies are more common in parliamentary regimes), and conjunctural pressures (e.g. major corruption scandals tend to lead to the adoption of contribution limits). Whichever motives may underpin regulatory choices, the diversity of PFS is the point to emphasise. As shown in Table 1.4, even a limited typology of contemporary PFS reveals at least ten existing combinations of the basic policy instruments, while many more are possible. In fact,

Table 1.4: *A typology of comparative political finance systems*

| Category ⟶ | A<br>Limited regulation of expenditure + Limited transparency rules | B<br>Limited regulation of expenditure + Extensive transparency rules | C<br>Extensive regulation of expenditure + Limited transparency rules | D<br>Extensive regulation of expenditure + Extensive transparency rules |
|---|---|---|---|---|
| 1. Limited regulation of contributions + Limited subsidisation | El Salvador<br>Luxembourg<br>Switzerland | | | India<br>New Zealand<br>United Kingdom |
| 2. Limited regulation of contributions + Extensive subsidisation | Austria<br>Bolivia<br>Netherlands<br>Nicaragua<br>Norway<br>Dominican Rep.<br>Guatemala<br>Panama<br>Honduras<br>Sweden<br>Uruguay | Australia<br>Denmark<br>Finland<br>Germany | Ecuador | Chile<br>Colombia<br>Greece<br>Italy |
| 3. Extensive regulation of contributions + Limited subsidisation | | USA | | |
| 4. Extensive regulation of contributions + Extensive subsidisation | | Brazil<br>Costa Rica<br>Japan<br>Paraguay<br>Peru<br>Turkey | Argentina<br>Ireland | Belgium<br>Canada<br>France<br>Israel<br>Mexico<br>Portugal<br>South Korea<br>Spain<br>Taiwan |

Sources and method: See Appendix

such a typology cannot but yield an impressionistic picture that greatly underestimates the actual diversity of PFS, since neither the countless nuances allowed by each instrument, nor their varied levels of implementation or their surrounding institutional framework are included.

Such heterogeneity is mirrored, and enhanced, at the level of subsidy arrangements. Indeed, in the next section we will see how the attempt to ascribe, in general, beneficial or harmful effects to the 'institution' of DSF largely fails due to the extreme diversity of subsidy arrangements, their various underlying rationales and the influence of numerous institutional variables to which subsidies are inextricably linked.

## DIRECT STATE FUNDING: ARGUMENTS, OPTIONS, EVIDENCE

No matter how widespread, DSF schemes are heterogeneous and controversial instruments. Our analysis of direct subsidy systems must thus start by clarifying basic definitional issues and reminding the reader of the empirical content of debates on DSF.

### Definition and claims

What does DSF mean? How is DSF to be distinguished from other forms of subvention? In principle, DSF comprises cash grants disbursed to parties and/or candidates according to a public procedure laid down in the law. As such, they exclude any law-enacted subvention delivered in kind to political actors – such as access to state-owned broadcasters, public buildings or publicly printed material – and, equally, the loss of state revenue derived from tax incentives for private political contributors, parties or candidates, or from the enjoyment of public service franchises by political actors. Throughout this analysis these instruments will be grouped under the concept of *indirect subsidies*. The definition also excludes *extra-legal subsidies*, such as the secret funnelling of state funds to some political actors, and the legitimate or illegitimate use of state goods, services and powers by incumbents.

More problematic is the classification of yet another group of public subventions: cash grants earmarked for party-related or party-controlled organisations, such as parliamentary caucuses, ancillary groups (women's and youth, mainly), newspapers and research institutes. While, in principle, these *specific grants* may be considered as no more than particular examples of direct subvention, it seems advisable to group them in a separate category. Specific grants are frequently outside the control of the parties' central or local organs and, in fact, are frequently disbursed to entities with a separate legal existence from the party (e.g. a newspaper or a research foundation). Moreover, in the case of parliamentary subsidies the extent to which public funds help to sustain the activities of parties rather than the workings of parliament is unclear.

Hence, this book will employ a restricted concept of DSF, covering only in-cash electoral subsidies for parties and candidates as well as generic grants disbursed to the parties' core organs. In most cases, direct subventions thus defined comprise the majority of public resources allocated by law to sustain political activities.[13] Other forms of subvention will be treated as separate categories and remain on the margins of the present analysis. Although this solution is not universally shared,[14] it leaves within the concept of DSF only those cash subventions that primarily, directly and unequivocally benefit candidates and parties.

Table 1.5: *Arguments in favour of and against Direct State Funding*

| Area of debate | In favour | Against |
|---|---|---|
| Autonomy of political actors and prevention of corruption | DSF strengthens the autonomy of politicians, prevents political finance-related corruption and enhances financial transparency | DSF does not replace private donations and has a limited effectiveness against corruption |
| Political equality and electoral competition | DSF protects political equality of opportunity and electoral competitiveness | DSF stifles electoral competitiveness and freezes the party system |
| Organisation and strength of political parties | DSF provides political actors with adequate resources for essential democratic activities, increasing the institutionalisation and stability of parties | DSF provides parties with resources that jeopardise their social embeddedness, internal democracy and autonomy |

Moreover, it denotes a certain fidelity to debates on state funding and its effects. So far the thrust of the discussion and criticism of DSF has been focused on electoral and generic party subventions, reflecting an implicit consensus that their enactment is *different* from the implementation of specific party grants or indirect subsidies, and in many ways a more fundamental political change than the latter.[15]

As noted above, beyond heated normative disputes, advocates and critics of DSF have offered contrasting assessments of its practical consequences for democracy. The core arguments of both sides of the debate are summarised in Table 1.5.

As noted in the introductory chapter, these arguments, particularly the more sophisticated set of causal connections suggested by the subsidies' critics, provide researchers with a valuable set of hypotheses and, indeed, constitute the backbone of the empirical assessment of the following pages. Such an assessment must start, however, by addressing a basic issue: is there *an* institution of state funding whose effects may be readily defended or criticised? Let us see.

## The regulation of DSF

Every system of direct political subvention must explicitly define four central issues:
• Which political actors will receive the subsidy?
• How often will the grants be paid?
• What eligibility and allocation rules will be followed? and,
• Who is to define the amount of the subvention and how?

These questions provide the axis along which direct subsidy arrangements may be classified, and a typology of them constructed. Table 1.6 summarises the basic features of state funding rules, with emphasis on DSF, in forty-four democracies.

Table 1.6: *Comparative Direct State Funding and other state subventions*

| Country | Year of enactment of DSF | Recipients | | | Interval | | Threshold of eligibility | Allocation | | |
|---|---|---|---|---|---|---|---|---|---|---|
| | | Party | Candidates (Pres./Parliament) | Other | Annual | Election | | Per vote | Per seat | Other (inc. flat grants) |
| Argentina | n.a | X | | | X | X | No | X | | X |
| Australia | 1984 | X | X | | | X | 4% of vote | X | | |
| Austria | 1975 | X | | | X | X | Various | X | | X |
| Belgium | 1989 | | | X | X | | 1 MP | X | | X |
| Bolivia | 1997 | X | | | | X | 1 MP | X | | |
| Brazil | n.a. | X | | | X | | 1 MP | X | | X |
| Canada | 1974 | X | X | | X | X | Various | X | | X |
| Chile | 2003 | X | X | | | X | No | X | | |
| Colombia | 1994 | X | | X | X | X | Various | X | X | X |
| Costa Rica | 1956 | X | | | | X | 4% of vote or 1 MP | X | | |
| Denmark | 1986 | X | | | | X | Various | X | | |
| Dominican Rep. | 1997 | X | | | X | X | No | X | | X |
| Ecuador | 1978 | X | X | | X | X | 5% of vote | X | | X |
| El Salvador | 1988 | X | | | | X | No | X | | X |
| Finland | 1968 | X | | | X | | 1 MP | | X | |
| France | 1988 | X | X | | X | X | Various | X | X | X |
| Germany | 1959 | X | X | | X | | 0.5% of vote | X | | X |
| Greece | 1984 | X | | | X | | 3% of vote | X | | X |
| Guatemala | 1985 | X | | | X | | 4% of vote | X | | |
| Honduras | 1981 | X | | | | X | No | X | | X |
| India | | | | | | | No DSF | X | | |
| Ireland | 1997 | | | | X | | 2% of vote | X | X | |
| Israel | 1969 | X | | | X | X | 1 MP | | | X |
| Italy | 1974 | X | X | | X | X | Various | X | | |
| Japan | 1994 | X | | | X | | 5 MP or 2% of vote | X | | |
| Luxembourg | | | | | | | No DSF | | | |
| Mexico | 1986 | X | | | X | X | 1 MP | X | X | X |
| Netherlands | 1999 | X | | | X | | 1 MP | | | X |
| New Zealand | | | | | | | No DSF | | | |
| Nicaragua | 1984 | | | | | X | 4% of vote | X | | |
| Norway | 1970 | X | | | X | | 2.5% of vote | X | | |
| Panama | 1997 | X | X | | X | X | Various | X | X | X |
| Paraguay | 1990 | | | | X | X | No | X | | |
| Peru | 2003 | | | | X | | 1 MP | | | X |
| Portugal | 1977 | X | | | X | X | Various | X | X | X |
| South Korea | 1981 | X | | | X | X | 2% of vote | | X | X |
| Spain | 1977 | X | | | X | X | 1 MP | X | X | |
| Sweden | 1965 | X | | | X | | 4% of vote of 1 MP + 2.5% v. | | | |
| | | X | | | | | | | | |
| Switzerland | | | | | | | No DSF | | | |
| Taiwan | 1989 | | X | | | X | 75% of votes required to elect 1 MP | X | X | |
| Turkey | n.a | X | | | X | | 7% of vote | X | | |
| UK | | | | | | | No DSF | | | |
| Uruguay | 1928 | X | X | | | X | No | X | | |
| USA | 1974 | | X | | | X | Various | | | X |

Table 1.6: *(Cont)*

| Country | Defined by law | Variable budget allocation | Other | Parliamentary subsidies | Free broadcasting | Tax benefits for donors | Press/research subsidy | Other |
|---|---|---|---|---|---|---|---|---|
| Argentina |  | X |  | X | X |  |  | X |
| Australia | X |  |  |  | X |  |  |  |
| Austria |  | X |  | X | X |  | X |  |
| Belgium | X |  |  | X | X |  |  |  |
| Bolivia | X |  |  |  | X |  |  |  |
| Brazil |  | X |  |  | X |  |  |  |
| Canada | X |  |  |  | X | X |  |  |
| Chile | X |  |  |  | X |  | X | X |
| Colombia | X |  |  |  | X |  |  | X |
| Costa Rica | X |  |  | X |  |  |  | X |
| Denmark | X |  |  | X | X |  | X |  |
| Dominican Rep. | X |  |  |  |  |  |  |  |
| Ecuador | X |  |  |  |  | X |  | X |
| El Salvador | X |  |  |  |  |  |  |  |
| Finland |  | X |  | X | X |  | X | X |
| France | X | X |  | X | X | X |  |  |
| Germany | X |  |  | X | X | X | X |  |
| Greece | X |  |  |  | X |  |  |  |
| Guatemala | X |  |  |  | X | X |  | X |
| Honduras | X |  |  |  | X |  |  | X |
| India |  |  |  |  | X |  |  |  |
| Ireland | X |  |  | X | X |  |  |  |
| Israel |  |  | X |  | X |  |  | X |
| Italy | X |  |  |  | X |  | X | X |
| Japan | X |  |  |  | X | X | X | X |
| Luxembourg |  |  |  | X |  |  |  | X |
| Mexico |  |  | X |  | X | X | X | X |
| Netherlands | X |  |  | X | X | X | X |  |
| New Zealand |  |  |  | X | X |  |  |  |
| Nicaragua | X |  |  |  |  | X |  |  |
| Norway |  | X |  | X |  |  | X | X |
| Panama | X |  |  | X | X |  |  | X |
| Paraguay | X |  |  |  | X |  |  | X |
| Peru | X |  |  |  | X |  |  | X |
| Portugal | X |  |  | X |  | X |  | X |
| South Korea | X |  |  |  |  |  |  |  |
| Spain |  | X |  | X | X |  |  | X |
| Sweden | X |  |  | X | X |  | X | X |
| Switzerland |  |  |  | X | X |  |  | X |
| Taiwan | X |  |  |  | X |  |  | X |
| Turkey | X |  |  |  | X |  |  | X |
| UK |  |  |  | X | X |  |  | X |
| Uruguay |  | X |  | X | X |  |  | X |
| USA | X |  | X |  |  |  |  | X |

Sources: See Appendix

*Subsidy recipients*
As Table 1.6 shows, parties are the main recipients of DSF in the vast majority of countries. Among the cases examined, only Belgium, Taiwan and the US have chosen not to subsidise the parties' central office. The Belgian case is dubious, however, while in the US a few states have enacted public funding for parties even if the federal government has not.[16] Indeed, the US is not alone in supporting sub-national party organs. Party branches at the state/regional level also receive public funding, in some cases extensively, in Australia, Canada, Denmark, Germany, Norway, Spain, Austria and Sweden. In the latter two, in particular, sub-national entities provide the lion's share of DSF.[17]

Direct support of individual candidates, either presidential or parliamentary, is less common. Presidential nominees may directly receive public funding only in Ecuador, France, Uruguay and the US. In the US, the scheme covers even candidates to the parties' presidential nomination, the only case anywhere where intra-party campaigns are directly subsidised.

*Interval and timing*
The important divide here is between *permanent* and *electoral* subsidies. Both categories differ in the frequency of the subvention, their recipients and the object of the funding. Thus, in contrast with electoral subsidies, permanent subventions are normally annual, payable only to parties and directed towards a wide array of activities beyond campaigning, noticeably the building up and day-to-day running of party organisations. While some systems have enacted only one type of subven-

Table 1.7: *Distribution of DSF according to interval and region*

| Type of subsidy → / ↓ Region | Only electoral subsidies | Only permanent party subsidies | Electoral and premanent subsidies |
|---|---|---|---|
| Western Europe | Denmark | Belgium Netherlands Finland Norway Germany Portugal Greece Sweden Ireland | Austria France Italy Portugal Spain |
| Latin America | Bolivia Honduras Chile Nicaragua Costa Rica Uruguay El Salvador | Brazil Guatemala Peru | Argentina Mexico Colombia Panama Dom. Rep. Venezuela Ecuador Paraguay |
| North America | USA | | Canada |
| Others | Australia Taiwan | Japan Turkey | Israel South Korea |

Sources: See Appendix

tion, others combine both permanent and electoral subsidies. As we see in Table 1.7, the distribution of these three options exhibits an interesting pattern.

While virtually all West European democracies provide parties with permanent funding, in Latin and North America electoral financing is the more widespread of the two. Such clustering reflects a different understanding of the nature and functions of parties. In the US, for example, subsidy rules reflect the notion that parties primarily exist to wage electoral battles and are, in any case, less important than individual candidates.[18] The strong electoral orientation of party organisations is also a pervasive phenomenon in Latin America, even amongst the most institutionalised party systems. West European systems, on the other hand, assume a more comprehensive idea of the role of parties, as permanent organisations upon which responsible government rests and which ought to be subsidised accordingly. These different perceptions are not alien to the overlapping institutional divide between presidential regimes in North and Latin America and parliamentary regimes in Western Europe.[19]

The timing of the disbursement of electoral grants is also consequential. In some countries (e.g. Australia, Costa Rica) the state subvention operates as a post-electoral reimbursement of expenditures, while other systems (e.g. Dominican Republic, US) have enacted rules that guarantee entitled parties or candidates full access to the subsidy before the election. In a few countries (e.g. Spain, Uruguay) both principles are mixed, combining in different measures a post-election reimbursement with a pre-electoral advance. These advances normally function as guaranteed loans against future subsidies, allocated according to the parties' previous electoral history. The availability of subsidies before the election or, alternatively, their configuration as a post-electoral reimbursement can influence the financial barriers experienced by newcomers and the dependence of political actors on non-public income sources. As we will see below, this issue has proved very divisive in Costa Rica.

*Eligibility and allocation rules*
Virtually all countries with DSF have enacted a threshold of eligibility for the subsidy. This barrier is intended to discourage the proliferation of candidates and parties, particularly of the frivolous or rent-seeking kind. The eligibility barrier is frequently defined by the achievement of parliamentary representation in the previous election (e.g. Bolivia, Finland), but it may also consist of an absolute number of votes (e.g. Denmark, Portugal), a given percentage of the vote (e.g. Germany, Nicaragua) or a combination of representation and votes (e.g. Costa Rica, Sweden). Other countries have implemented multiple thresholds for different subsidies (e.g. Austria, Colombia). The complete absence of threshold is less common and normally restricted to specific kinds of public funding (e.g. El Salvador, Uruguay).

Once the threshold has been applied, allocation rules operate. Almost every country included in Table 1.6 allocates the bulk of DSF according to the share of vote or representation obtained by each eligible recipient in the previous election (e.g. Belgium, Greece [per vote]; Finland, Sweden [per seat]). The use of vote or seat-based allocation rules is not, however, universal or unqualified. Out of normative choice or political expediency reformers frequently enact rules that qualify election-based subsidy distributions and make the system move towards absolute equality. This is done normally by disbursing part of the subsidy in flat grants for all recipients (e.g. Israel, Mexico).

Other systems display even more radical departures from the vote- or seat-based allocation procedure. The Canadian and French systems isolate the allocation of electoral subsidies from electoral results, by establishing a flat rate of reimbursement for parliamentary candidates (50 per cent of the spending limit in both cases), as well as presidential candidates (only in France: one-third of the spending ceiling) and parties (only in Canada: 22.5 per cent of the ceiling). Other obvious examples are the matching grant schemes implemented in Germany and the US, which allocate a significant share of public funds according to the parties' (in Germany) or presidential candidates' (in the US) ability to attract small private contributions.

*Amount definition procedures*

In every country, the definition of the subsidy's initial amount rests in the hands of legislators. The initial legislation may follow, however, one of several paths, including one that gives politicians a blank authorisation to define the subsidy's amount on an ad-hoc basis through the budget or a special law (e.g. Austria, Uruguay). This *unconstrained* system leaves the subsidy open to short-term manipulation and rapid increase.

*Constrained* amount definition systems do not eliminate these dangers, but at least lay down clear rules for the calculation of DSF. In some countries the electoral law may define in detail the amount of subsidy to be paid for each seat or vote (e.g. Honduras, Italy). Alternatively, legislators may choose to fix the total sum of the subvention or the spending limits that will, in turn, define the amount of public funds available (e.g. electoral subsidies in Canada, France). Though the manipulation of legislated subsidy rates, spending ceilings or total subventions is within the reach of politicians, the latter's future intervention is frequently minimised by indexing the figures fixed by law (e.g. Australia, Paraguay). The prevention of political tampering of DSF amounts is taken one step further in Israel and Mexico, where the subsidy is entirely defined by a non-political organ. In Israel's case this reform (of 1994) follows a long history of legislated increases of the public subvention per seat in order to shore up party finances.[20]

The US system of political subvention deserves a further reflection. As opposed to all the previous examples, DSF in the US is not based on a forced exaction on taxpayers. Instead, taxpayers voluntarily direct US$3 of their annual liability to the Presidential Election Campaign Fund. This means that, in principle, the latter grows insofar as taxpayers are willing to contribute to the scheme.[21]

*A standard system of DSF?*

This brief overview suggests that, as with PFS, there is a remarkable diversity in subsidy arrangements. Table 1.8 summarises and combines the basic policy

Table 1.8: *A typology of Direct State Funding systems*

| Eligibility/allocation + Amount definition procedure → Recipients + Interval ↓ | A Egalitarian eligibility/allocation + Unconstrained amount definition procedure | B Non-egalitarian eligibility/allocation + Unconstrained amount definition procedure | C Egalitarian eligibility/allocation + Constrained amount definition procedure | D Non-egalitarian eligibility/allocation + Constrained amount definition procedure |
|---|---|---|---|---|
| 1. Party-oriented + permanent | | Brazil Finland Norway | Peru | Belgium Greece Guatemala Ireland Japan Netherlands Sweden Turkey |
| 2. Party-oriented + electoral | | | Denmark El Salvador Honduras | Bolivia Costa Rica Nicaragua Taiwan |
| 3. Party-oriented + permanent/electoral | Argentina Austria | Spain | Dominican Rep. Mexico Portugal South Korea | Israel Paraguay |
| 4. Candidate-oriented + electoral | | | USA | |
| 5. Party/candidate-oriented + permanent | | | Germany | |
| 6. Party/candidate-oriented + electoral | Uruguay | | Chile | Australia |
| 7. Party/candidate-oriented + permanent/electoral | France | | Canada Colombia Ecuador Panama | Italy |

Sources and method: See Appendix

options derived from the previous overview.

The dispersion of the cases is striking. Even after reducing the four sets of subsidy regulations to their barest options we can still find cases in seventeen boxes out of the possible twenty-eight, with significant clustering occurring only in box 1D. Besides the already observed correlation between West European cases and permanent subsidies, on the one hand, and North/Latin American cases and electoral subsidies, on the other, no obvious rationale emerges from this picture as to why political systems combine DSF regulations the way they do.

In short, there is no standard subsidy system, but a myriad of them, pointing in different directions, shaped by various institutional environments and historical conjunctures, and, in turn, creating different incentives and constraints for different political actors. As noted by Bradley A. Smith, 'to say that one favors government financing of campaigns is a bit like saying that one enjoys sports. Are we talking football? Kayaking? Downhill skiing? Ballroom dancing? Chess? The options are endless'.[22] Any defence or criticism of DSF for other than ideological motives should probably start by specifying *which* subsidy system is being advocated or criticised. Even the subsidies' most common feature – the exaction that they imply for taxpayers – is neither universal nor inevitable, as the example of the US Presidential Election Campaign Fund shows.

## DSF: an appraisal of its political effects

Now that we know the definitions, arguments and rules, it is time to examine what the facts have to say about the consequences of DSF on the three areas of debate summarised in Table 1.5.

*Autonomy of political actors, dependence on private donors and prevention of political finance corruption*
Does DSF protect the autonomy of parties and elected officials vis-à-vis their financial backers and thereby reduce the likelihood of *quid-pro-quos* between both? As noted in the introductory chapter, the measurement of causal effects on this front poses daunting methodological obstacles, not least derived from the inherent imprecision of the notion of 'autonomy'. Focusing the analysis on the extent to which DSF helps to moderate the financial influence of large private contributions offers a more operational approach for research. Even this oblique route gives, however, limited ground for hope in the quest for law-like generalisations. As we will see throughout this book, countries differ widely in the numerous factors that shape the *demand* for resources by political actors, which are hardly affected by the mere presence of DSF. These factors include the presence or absence of spending limits, the existence of publicly owned media, the length of campaigns, the relative importance of the parties' permanent and electoral functions, the institutional incentives for intra-partisan competition, the size of the floating electorate, to name a few. Perhaps more crucially, democracies exhibit large differences in the supply of public funds (see Table 1.9).

Given such ostensible differences it is unsurprising that evidence of the impact of DSF in curbing the financial influence of large private donors is inconclusive. A few examples should suffice to illustrate the point.

In Israel and the US, the porosity of electoral spending ceilings and a fluid electoral market structured around loose-knit catch-all parties, have favoured a rapid increase in electoral expenditure and, therefore, in the need to attract the large private donations that DSF was meant to prevent. Since 1976, US presiden-

Table 1.9: *DSF per year and registered voter in twenty-five democracies (1990s)*

| Country | US$ | Years (1) |
| --- | --- | --- |
| Israel | 11.2 | 1996–8 |
| France | 6.5 | 1995–6 |
| Mexico | 3.3 | 1997–9 |
| Austria | 2.8 (2) | 1998 |
| Japan | 2.8 | 1995–9 |
| Sweden | 2.6 (2) | 1999 |
| Germany | 2.0 | 1995–8 |
| Australia | 1.9 | 1996–8 |
| Panama | 1.8 | 1999–2004 |
| Uruguay | 1.7 | 1999–2004 |
| Spain | 1.6 | 1998–2000 |
| Costa Rica | 1.4 | 2002–6 |
| Italy | 1.4 | 1999–2001 |
| Nicaragua | 1.2 | 2001–6 |
| Ireland | 1.1 | 1997–8 |
| Portugal | 1.0 | 1995–6 |
| Bolivia | 0.6 | 1997–2002 |
| El Salvador | 0.5 | 1999–2004 |
| Netherlands | 0.4 | 1999 |
| Honduras | 0.2 | 2001–2005 |
| USA | 0.2 | 1992–6 |
| Canada | 0.2 | 1993–7 |
| Denmark | 0.2 | 1988–90 |
| Ecuador | 0.2 | 1995–7 |
| Guatemala | 0.02 | 1999–2003 |

Notes: (1) Includes one electoral year for all countries, except Austria, Sweden and The Netherlands. In the latter two, parties do not receive additional direct subsidies on electoral years. (2) Excludes direct subsidies paid by sub-national entities, which are greater than national subsidies. Sources: See Appendix.

tial candidates have benefited from a 100 per cent public subsidy in return for an equivalent spending ceiling. By controlling the cost of presidential elections and eliminating the role of private donors, this policy, a crucial element of the sweeping electoral reforms enacted in the wake of Watergate, largely fulfilled the expectations of reformers in the 1976 and 1980 election cycles. After 1984, however, the growth of unregulated 'soft money'[23] consistently undermined the existing contribution and spending limits and, therefore, the replacement effect of DSF. 'Soft money' skyrocketed from US$45 million in 1988 to US$495 million in the 2000 election, well above the federal subsidy for presidential candidates. During the 1999–2000 election cycle, forty-four corporate donors contributed more than US$1,000,000 to both parties in 'soft-money'.[24] Similarly, the introduction of DSF in Israel in 1969 initially helped to reduce the alarming costs of politics and the role of private donations. Subventions were tied to limits on the parties' fundraising and electoral spending. In the course of the following two decades, which saw the emergence of a competitive party system, all sanctions attached to spending limits were eliminated while campaign expenditure soared from US$17.6 million in 1981 to US$41.6 million in 1988. In the words of Mendilow, 'money to cover such expenditure came from loans guaranteed by anticipated subsidies as well as from large donations from corporations and wealthy individuals, which public party funding had intended to eliminate.'[25]

A different set of political features has also given an additive quality to DSF in Latin American countries. There, the absence of spending ceilings, the scarcity of fee-paying party members, the feebleness of trade unions, and the weakness of political organisations founded in the wake of democratic transitions confer on business a central role in campaign funding. Kinzo reports that 93 per cent of the private donations that funded F. H. Cardoso's 1994 presidential bid in Brazil came from private firms, particularly those in the civil construction and banking sectors, a phenomenon repeated throughout the country's gubernatorial elections.[26] The presence of DSF has failed to dent business dominance of campaign finance not only in Brazil, but also in Argentina, Colombia, Ecuador, Guatemala and, as we will see below, Costa Rica and Uruguay.[27]

As opposed to the previous examples, the enactment of DSF in Canada seems to have ostensibly reduced the financial role of pressure groups and, particularly, corporate donors. However, causality in this case is uncertain, for DSF was enacted as part of a complex policy package that included tax incentives for small contributions and tightly enforced spending ceilings. Tax incentives, in particular, have been successful in greatly enlarging the pool of individual donors and reducing the heavy reliance of the traditional parties on business contributors.[28] As most analysts have noted, this has been a remarkable change in a country where, before 1974, traditional parties were almost exclusively funded by fewer than 500 large corporations.[29]

The experience of most, albeit not all, West European countries appears to be even clearer: the available information shows that the role of private political donations has generally gone down as extensive subsidy systems become widespread. As in the Canadian case, other institutional factors have played a prominent role in this process. Short electoral campaigns, widespread public ownership of broadcasting stations, the banning of TV and radio political advertising outside the slots allocated by the state and, in general, a less election-centred understanding of parties, have helped to ease rising electoral costs and thus the urgency to raise large sums in private donations. Quoting data from Germany, Sweden, Austria and Italy for the 1974–1989 period, when DSF was already in place, Nassmacher reports that the importance of private donations for the headquarters of bourgeois parties declined during the 1980s.[30] Moreover, in Germany large private donations to all parties virtually halved in number and amount after the enactment of the 1994 reform to the party funding law, which significantly shifted the structure of incentives from large to small contributions.[31] The Canadian and West European experiences with DSF – even allowing for the unreliability of the latter[32] – thus tend to show that public subsidies can indeed help significantly to reduce the weight of large interested donations to the parties' coffers. Yet, this outcome seems to be contingent on the presence of a complex set of institutional features, rather than merely on the availability or generosity of DSF.

More importantly, even such an outcome fails to guarantee the eradication of questionable fundraising practices. Ostensible *quid-pro-quos* between parties and corporations persist in countries with comprehensive political subsidy schemes, such as Israel, France, Spain, Italy, Austria and Germany.[33] To be sure, the extent of these corrupt practices varies as widely as the social and political structures where DSF has been implanted, ranging from highly visible but largely atypical cases in Germany to the systematic political finance pathologies uncovered by the Italian judges in the 1990s. Indeed, Italy, where DSF coexisted with the perverse incentives for patronage created by preferential voting, fragmented parties and one-party rule, offers a singularly powerful reminder that curbing political finance corruption requires considerably more than the mere enactment of generous party subsidies.

If the direct effects of subsidies in fending off political finance corruption appear to be limited, in some countries their indirect consequences may be far-reaching and lasting. The enactment of DSF frequently stimulates the adoption of comprehensive rules to deal with illegal political finance practices. As shown by the experience of countries as diverse as the US, Canada, Israel, Denmark, Germany and Bolivia, tougher transparency rules are often the price paid by political actors in return for the use of taxpayers' money.[34] For Mendilow, the enhanced awareness of party funding corruption and of the importance of tougher rules to deal with it is an important achievement derived from the enactment of DSF in Israel.[35]

The consequences of DSF for the prevention of questionable exchanges between parties and donors are thus uncertain, blurred by numerous intervening factors, and not particularly suitable to law-like generalisations. Yet, all things considered, the unsystematic evidence available leans more closely towards the claims of critics of DSF: subsidies are not necessarily an antidote to financial dependence on private sources of funding and, even less, to unsavoury fundraising practices. As we shall see below, the evidence yielded by the Costa Rican and Uruguayan cases lends further support to this conclusion.

*Political equality, electoral competition and the dynamics of the party system*
Does DSF protect or harm electoral competitiveness? Three issues need to be distinguished here: the effects of DSF in keeping political newcomers at bay, in constraining the electoral opportunities of minor parties and, finally, in redressing political inequalities derived from the distribution of wealth in society. The first two, in particular, are central to the critics' contentions that direct subventions contribute to ossifying the party system.

**Eligibility barriers and political newcomers.** At first glance, the review of subsidy eligibility rules suggests one conclusion: because of the widespread use of thresholds and rare funding of new political actors, DSF raises electoral barriers for newcomers. However, this generalisation does not take the discussion very far. DSF has on not a few occasions lowered electoral barriers and fostered the multiplication of political actors. The matching-grants system for primary elections in the US is a case in point. These funds are available for first-time presidential contestants, and, according to most observers, have been instrumental in helping lesser-known aspirants, notably Jimmy Carter in 1976, who would have otherwise been financially overrun.[36] Similarly, the immediate availability of annual grants for new party groups in Israel's Knesset has clearly lessened the costs of establishing a new political group and, ultimately, the costs of political dissent.[37] Pizarro-Leongómez reports how the egalitarian features of the subsidy system in Colombia, in particular the opening up of the system to loose ad-hoc political groups, has generated a veritable explosion of political actors trying to capture rents, a phenomenon also observed in Nicaragua by Fiallos.[38]

Secondly, even when DSF is loaded against political newcomers, it has proved very difficult to establish the importance of this disadvantage. Newcomers may be kept at bay in those systems that impose taxing requisites to achieve representation, by either using majority election rules, representation thresholds or the small size of multi-member electoral districts. In those cases, the effects of subsidies are nearly impossible to extricate from those of the electoral system. Conversely, when the institutional incentives favour the multiplication of political actors, it is dubious that any amount of subsidies will suffice to debar newcomers. Newcomers certainly have not been excluded in Israel, where twenty-six new parties achieved parliamentary representation between 1969 (when DSF was enacted) and 1996, or Italy, where twenty-five new parties gained seats after the introduction of direct subventions in 1974, nine of them in the 1994 'earthquake' election alone.[39] Research on Finland and Canada has demonstrated that even in countries where DSF was set in motion as part of an explicit effort to limit the proliferation of parties, new groups have doggedly continued to break into the political system, in some cases with far-reaching effects.[40] The emergence of the Reform Party and the Bloc Quebecois in the 1993 election in Canada provides a vivid example of this.

**Allocation rules, minor parties and electoral competition.** The effects of DSF on minor parties within the system are more interesting and somewhat counterintuitive. Though in most countries electoral results remain the central subsidy allocation instrument, many countries have introduced corrections to purely proportional rules. In those cases, small parties receive, almost by definition, a larger proportion of DSF than their share of votes would warrant. While it is true that in very few countries are minor and large parties placed on an absolutely equal financial footing, it would be mistaken to assume that DSF allocation rules are systematically biased against minor parties (see Table 1.10).

Albeit this is not a comprehensive sample of subsidy systems, the consistency with which minor parties are over-subsidised is remarkable. In some cases, notably the four countries at the top of the table, where flat grants of different kinds exist, the allocation of subsidies behaves in a purely redistributive fashion. In Norway, Australia and Finland, the allocation disproportionately favours both groups, yielding near-neutral distributions in the first two and a clearly regressive one in the latter. In fact, the Finnish, Spanish and Italian (pre-1993) cases, all of them with severely skewed distributions, provide a convincing demonstration of the harmful effects on small parties of seat-based DSF allocation rules.

Table 1.10 shows that DSF can be, and frequently is, a means to improve the relative financial situation of small parties. Rather than attempting to freeze the relative positions of large and small parties, political finance reformers often improve the electoral chances of the latter and increase the dynamism of the party system. In some cases, the enactment of egalitarian allocation rules derives from systemic needs imposed by parliamentary regimes with proportional representation. In such regimes large parties may have an interest in keeping a pool of viable coalition partners. For instance, the decision to lower the threshold of eligibility for DSF to 2.5 per cent of the national vote in two consecutive elections in Sweden was largely the result of the interest of the Social Democrats in helping the Communist Party, whose support was often required to secure majorities in the *Riksdag*.[41] More importantly, the bargaining power enjoyed by small parties frequently turns *them* into political finance reformers. The crucial role of Germany's FDP in pushing for a myriad of generous redistribution schemes for small parties since the 1960s is well known.[42] It is also noteworthy that Canada, where first-

Table 1.10: *Proportionality of DSF distribution among eligible recipients in ten democracies*

| Country | Years | Eligible parties with <10% of votes | | | Two parties with largest share of votes | | |
|---|---|---|---|---|---|---|---|
| | | A | B | C | D | E | F |
| | | Share of total DSF (%) | Share of votes (%) | Difference (A-B) | Share of total DSF (%) | Share of votes (%) | Difference (D-E) |
| Mexico | 1997–98 | 14.3 | 4.6 | +9.7 | 65.0 | 70.0 | -5.0 |
| Germany | 1970–89 | 29.5 | 20.5 | +9.0 | 70.5 | 77.7 | -7.2 |
| Canada | 1993 | 17.4 | 11.0 | +6.4 | 47.9 | 60.0 | -12.1 |
| Austria | 1975–90 | 13.4 | 7.8 | +5.6 | 86.6 | 90.4 | -3.8 |
| Sweden | 1964–88 | 12.4 | 8.2 | +4.2 | 61.0 | 65.5 | -4.5 |
| Norway | 1981–88 | 28.5 | 25.7 | +2.8 | 71.5 | 69.0 | +2.5 |
| Australia | 1987 | 7.0 | 6.0 | +1.0 | 80.9 | 80.1 | +0.8 |
| Finland | 1967–89 | 7.6 | 6.7 | +0.9 | 56.7 | 45.5 | +11.2 |
| Spain | 1993–96 | 14.5 | 15.0 | -0.5 | 77.5 | 75.0 | +2.5 |
| Italy | 1983–89 | 19.0 | 22.0 | -3.0 | 72.6 | 61.9 | +10.7 |

Sources: See Appendix

Graph 1.2: *DSF dependence by party size (forty-three West European parties, 1970s–1980s)*

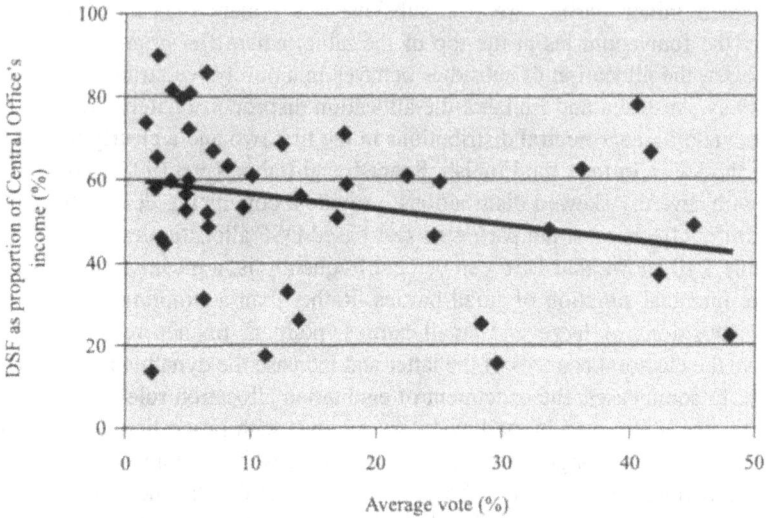

Sources: See Appendix

past-the-post renders coalition government an oddity, enacted flat electoral subsidies in 1974 as part of a comprehensive reform demanded by the New Democratic Party (NDP) as a price for its support of the Liberal Party's minority government.[43]

Other motives underpin the egalitarian adjustments made to the allotment of DSF in other countries. In South Korea and Mexico the enactment of DSF in 1981 and 1986, respectively, and the gradual move towards equitable allocation rules, can be traced to the imperatives of regime-opening processes. In Mexico, in particular, the long-ruling *Partido Revolucionario Institucional* (PRI) used DSF to nurture the development of opposition parties and thus strengthen its claim to democratic legitimacy. Interestingly, in both countries the empowerment of the opposition led to successive and ever-more-generous amendments to DSF rules, a process in which the challengers to the status quo gradually became an active force in the shaping of political finance arrangements.[44]

An analysis of the income sources of parties provides additional evidence of the benefits of DSF for minor groups. The latter tend to obtain a larger proportion of their income from DSF than is the case for large parties.[45] Data from forty-three West European parties during the 1970s and 1980s show that small parties received an average of 60.6 per cent of their central income from direct subsidies, well above the mean for mid-sized (49.8 per cent) and large (44.9 per cent) parties, a phenomenon previously detected by Nassmacher.[46] Graph 1.2 shows a negative correlation between electoral size and subsidy dependence.

Though the variance of the data is significant, the pattern appears clear: small parties are largely clustered around and above the 60 per cent dependence line, with only two parties falling below 40 per cent. Conversely, among large parties, only Norway's Labour Party shows a dependence rate exceeding 70 per cent. Two reasons may explain this phenomenon. First, with the exception of the Italian Communist Party, all large parties in the sample were clear government options during the period under consideration. These parties find it easier to attract contributions from members and private donors and thus develop more diversified funding structures. Second, the category of small parties includes all the parties founded after 1960, notably the Greens. These groups, born well after the struggle for universal suffrage and citizenship rights had ceased in Western Europe, have not developed the organisational features – especially mass membership – that were instrumental in an earlier phase. In an environment where incentives to become a party member are greatly diminished, new and small non-membership-based parties find subventions increasingly essential for their survival. In such an environment, those parties exist *because* DSF is available.

The unclear effects of subsidy eligibility thresholds, the complexity of the interests of political finance reformers and the competition-enhancing effects of certain subsidy arrangements cast doubts on the contention that DSF petrifies the party system. Several authors have found this claim unconvincing in view of the dramatic changes of government undergone by several heavily subsidised political systems and the numerous examples of electoral obliteration of once-mighty parties in such systems (e.g Italy's Christian Democratic Party, Canada's Progressive Conservative Party, Spain's Democratic Centre Union).[47] A simple analysis of changes in electoral volatility and party system fragmentation in West European and other developed democracies casts even greater doubts on the ossification hypothesis.[48] Graph 1.3 charts the evolution of electoral volatility in directly subsidised and non-directly subsidised elections in seventeen developed democracies (including eleven where DSF is currently in operation and six where it is not[49]) between 1945 and 1996.

Despite the increasingly common implementation of DSF, electoral volatility grew considerably, in particular during the 1990s. More importantly, the chart reveals that in three out of the four marked periods, as well as for the entire fifty-two-year span, volatility was *higher* in elections in which DSF was available. Throughout the period, average volatility was considerably lower in the six countries where DSF was absent (8.9 per cent) than in those countries where direct subsidies were used (11.4 per cent).[50] In order to minimise the distorting effect of electoral systems, a restricted comparison between countries that share analogous electoral systems (list-based PR) was also made. Once more, the results show the same tendency: DSF-free countries (Luxembourg, The Netherlands and Switzerland) displayed a *lower* average volatility (9.3 percent) than DSF-enacting ones (Austria, Belgium, Denmark, Finland, Germany, Israel, Norway, Sweden and pre-1994 Italy). For the latter group, the figure was 9.4 per cent if all elections were included and even higher (10.2 per cent) if only subsidised elections were considered.

Graph 1.3: *Average electoral volatility (seventeen developed democracies, 1945–96)*

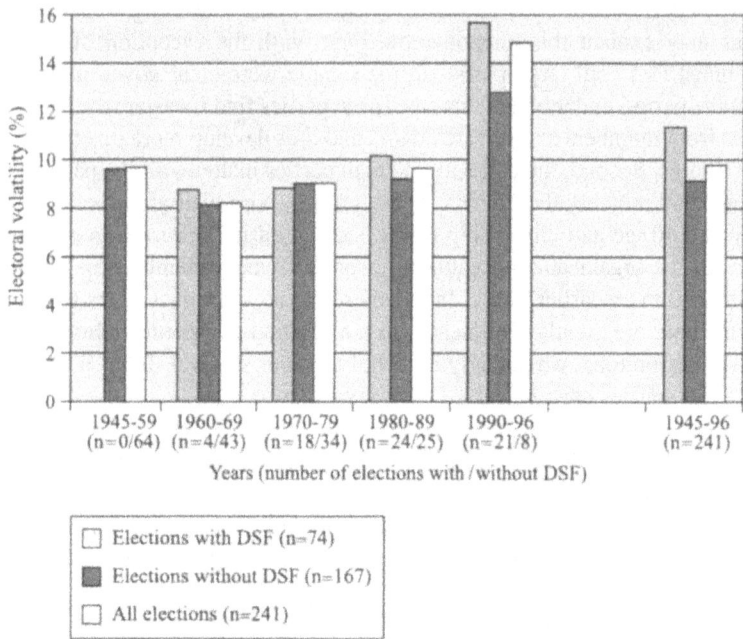

Sources: See Appendix

Comparing across time the behaviour of electoral volatility and party system fragmentation in countries where DSF have been introduced yields similar results, summarised in Table 1.11.[51]

In seven out of ten cases, volatility increased after the introduction of DSF. The evolution in the effective number of parties is equally striking: in all but two cases, the number grew after the enactment of direct subsidies. Clearly, any presumed intent by political finance reformers of freezing the party system by introducing DSF failed in the vast majority of cases. It is, of course, possible to argue that electoral volatility and the effective number of parties have both increased *in spite of* DSF and that changes would have been greater in its absence. However, the evidence from non-subsidised democracies – which exhibit lower levels of volatility – argues powerfully against this counterfactual, which, in any case, would only prove DSF's relative inability to influence the dynamics of the party system. Instead, the data shown in this section are suggestive of an alternative conclusion: due to the diminishing returns of electoral disbursements,[52] the greater importance of expenditure for electoral challengers (and, presumably, for emerging parties),[53] and the dearth of fee-paying members in new parties, the introduction of even small sums of DSF allows at least some minor groupings to survive and expand

Table 1.11: *Party system dynamics before and after enactment of DSF (ten developed democracies, 1945–96)*

| Country | Year of enactment of DSF | Mean electoral volatility | | | Mean effective number of elective parties | | |
|---|---|---|---|---|---|---|---|
| | | A | B | C | D | E | F |
| | | Before DSF | After DSF | Difference (B-A) | Before DSF | After DSF | Difference (E-D) |
| Austria | 1975 | 4.6 | 6.9 | 2.3 | 2.5 | 3.0 | 0.6 |
| Belgium | 1989 | 8.4 | 10.0 | 1.6 | 3.9 | 5.4 | 1.5 |
| Canada | 1974 | 8.8 | 16.2 | 7.4 | 3.1 | 3.1 | 0.1 |
| Denmark | 1986 | 10.9 | 10.1 | -0.8 | 4.6 | 5.3 | 0.7 |
| Finland | 1968 | 5.7 | 9.7 | 4.0 | 5.2 | 5.9 | 0.7 |
| Germany | 1959 | 15.3 | 7.6 | -7.6 | 4.5 | 3.3 | -1.2 |
| Israel | 1969 | 12.0 | 16.6 | 4.6 | 5.1 | 4.7 | -0.4 |
| Italy | 1974 | 10.9 | 10.2 | -0.7 | 4.0 | 4.6 | 0.6 |
| Norway | 1970 | 8.3 | 14.5 | 6.2 | 3.7 | 4.3 | 0.6 |
| Sweden | 1965 | 4.5 | 8.3 | 3.8 | 3.3 | 3.7 | 0.3 |

Note: Columns C and F may be affected by rounding.
Sources: See Appendix.

their electoral share. In other words, the enactment of DSF appears to *increase* electoral competition.[54]

**Socio-economic inequalities between parties.** The effects of DSF in redressing socio-economic disparities between parties remain unclear and difficult to generalise. As suggested by studies of party systems in different regions, the common notion that right-of-centre/bourgeois parties enjoy a secular funding head start over their rivals has proved, in fact, of limited use. In the traditionally class-based party systems of Western Europe, several factors reduce the significance of this presumed bias. First, deep public distrust of corporate political contributions has entailed the reluctance of bourgeois parties to depend upon their traditional income source in some countries, thereby minimising any potential financial advantage. Thus, studies have reported repeatedly that bourgeois parties voluntarily ceased to accept corporate donations in Sweden since the 1970s.[55] Though it is possible to see such reluctance as a result of the introduction of public subsidies, this phenomenon has pre-dated the enactment of DSF in some countries, such as Germany and Norway,[56] while it has also been observed in DSF-free systems, like The Netherlands (pre-1999) and Britain.[57]

Second, large left-of-centre political parties, traditionally based upon a numerous and disciplined membership, have generally faced less daunting threats to their finances, and managed to reduce the financial gap even in the absence of DSF.[58] Indeed, in some countries, notably Austria and Sweden, leftist parties have enjoyed a consistent funding edge over their bourgeois opponents.[59] It is therefore unsurprising that the former have often been critical of the attempt to introduce direct subsidies. Thus, while in Australia and the Nordic countries the Left pro-

moted DSF, it was the pressure of the bourgeois parties that prompted its enactment in Germany in 1959.[60] The Social Democrats remained largely aloof from
the proposal to enact DSF in Germany and Austria, as did the mostly member-
funded Communist Parties in Austria and France.[61]

Whether a long-term wealth disparity between parties exists, and whether DSF
does contribute to redressing it, is probably less important than the effect that DSF
seems to have of homogenising the structure of financial dependence in all parties.
The availability of DSF may gradually create a situation whereby all parties come
to rely on subsidies for a significant proportion of their income. Indeed, data from
seven West European countries in the 1970s and 1980s show bourgeois parties
receiving a larger share of their central income from DSF (55.4 per cent, on average) than either Socialist/Social Democratic (47.9 per cent) or Far
Left/Communist parties (50.8 per cent), thus confirming Nassmacher's earlier
findings.[62]

If long-term socio-economic disparities between parties are blurred in class-
based party systems, they are even less apparent where catch-all parties play a
dominant role, as in US, Canada, most of Latin America and, arguably, Israel.
Other than for incumbency reasons, there are no bases to expect a significant funding bias in those systems. Thus, the emergence of a bipolar party system in Israel
during the 1980s entailed a virtual equilibrium of electoral spending between the
multi-class blocs led by Labour and *Likud*.[63] Meanwhile, the traditional funding
advantage enjoyed by the Republican Party in US presidential elections had all but
disappeared by the early 1990s. In fact, the 1992 Democratic presidential campaign raised almost 50 per cent more funds than its Republican counterpart.[64]

Ultimately, as we will see with clarity in Chapter five, the dynamics of the
party system are too complex a phenomenon to be uniformly affected by DSF. The
evidence collected in this section hardly supports any neat, univocal conclusions.
Those propositions that have been better sustained by the available research tend
to disprove the critics' case: DSF can be, and frequently is, an egalitarian instrument; by allocating money to minor parties and challengers it may, and often does,
enhance electoral competition.

*Organisation and strength of political parties*
Do subsidies render political parties dependent on the state? Do they affect significantly the parties' membership base and internal power distribution? Do they distort the parties' ability to represent civil society, turning them into part of the state?
What is at stake here is whether DSF contributes to strengthening parties or to
their demise, if not literally, then at least in terms of their fulfilling their representative functions.

**Subsidy-dependence and party membership.** In most West European countries
parties largely depend on DSF. In Europe and beyond, public funding has been the
instrument of choice to bridge the gap between the sluggish growth of traditional
sources of party income and the rapid increase in the costs of politics.[65]

Table 1.12: *DSF in central income of all parties in eight West European democracies (%)*

| Country | 1967–71 | 1977–81 | 1987–9 |
|---|---|---|---|
| Denmark | -- | -- | 20.0 |
| Austria | -- | 29.8 | 30.1 |
| Italy | -- | 38.1 | 34.3 |
| Sweden | 55.3 | 60.7 | 52.0 |
| Finland | 78.3 | 69.1 | 56.9 |
| Norway | 47.8 (1) | 50.4 | 60.1 |
| Germany | 56.9 (2) | 49.5 | 71.5 |
| Spain | -- | -- | 76.7 (3) |

Notes: (1) 1971. (2) 1968–71. (3) 1989–96, only election figures included.
Sources: See Appendix.

Nonetheless, levels of dependence on the public purse vary significantly, even within Western Europe (see Table 1.12).

At the end of the 1980s the headquarters of Danish, Austrian and Italian parties were much less dependent on DSF than their equivalents elsewhere in Western Europe, though Italian estimates must be taken sceptically, given the low reliability of official statistics. Dependency figures were much higher in Sweden, Finland, Norway and Germany, and truly staggering in Spain, where they reached 95.1 per cent in the 1996 general election.[66] The evidence also suggests that, while dependence may remain at a high level, it does not necessarily evolve in a linear fashion towards ever-higher figures. It did so in Norway, but not in Finland, where it decreased markedly in the course of twenty years. Meanwhile, Sweden and Germany followed divergent paths, with DSF evolving non-linearly.

Do subsidies replace membership fees and reduce the parties' incentives to recruit new members? (See Table 1.13.)

Table 1.13: *Membership fees in central income of all parties in eight West European democracies (%)*

| Country | 1967–71 | 1977–81 | 1987–9 |
|---|---|---|---|
| Denmark | -- | -- | 62.5 |
| Italy | -- | 52.8 | 48.5 |
| Austria | -- | 43.2 | 40.5 |
| Germany (1) | 21.4 (2) | 29.6 | 19.8 |
| Norway | 5.9 (3) | 7.6 | 9.8 |
| Sweden | 9.5 | 7.9 | 8.2 |
| Finland | 1.1 (4) | 2.7 | 3.6 |
| Spain | -- | -- | 0.6 (5) |

Notes: (1) Includes party taxes. (2) 1968–71. (3) 1971. (4) 1970–71. (5) 1986.
Sources: See Appendix.

Table 1.13 is virtually the mirror image of Table 1.12. With the exception of Germany, relatively low levels of subsidy-dependence are clearly correlated with higher reliance on membership fees and vice versa. A strong negative correlation (-0.760) was found between both variables in a sample of forty-one parties in the same countries (minus Spain) during the 1970s and 1980s. The evidence suggests that the introduction of DSF causes more than a one-off fall in the reliance on fees due to a sudden inflow of public funds. In fact, once subsidies become available, subsidy-dependence and membership-dependence remain negatively correlated across time.[67]

Therefore, as claimed by critics of DSF, financial dependence on public subsidies replaces reliance on party members. Yet, this is merely a manifestation of a broader point. Unless the structure of incentives favours the collection of small contributions – either through legal changes, as in Germany, or through a strong social sanction against large donations, as in The Netherlands or Sweden – economies of scale dictate that membership fees will inevitably be crowded out by larger sources of income, public or private, which are easier to collect. This may happen in the absence of DSF, as the recent experience of Britain clearly shows. There, the share of membership fees in the central income of both major parties decreased from 49 per cent in 1975–9 to 25 per cent in 1993–7, while the proportion of donations grew from 46.3 per cent to 63.7 per cent. Moreover, in the Labour Party, a lower reliance on affiliation fees from trade unions has not implied a correlative increase in individual subscriptions but a sharp growth in private donations, some of them disturbingly large.[68] With or without DSF, members' financial dominance in modern parties is no more than a remembrance of things past.

Whether the parties' reduced financial reliance on members translates into decreasing membership figures is, however, a different matter. The available evidence suggests that this is not the case (see Table 1.14).[69]

Major differences appear in the evolution of party membership throughout Europe between 1960 and 1989, but they seem unrelated to the presence of DSF, to the relative size of the available grants, or to the rates of subsidy dependence amongst parties. Thus, precipitous declines in party membership rates took place in countries where DSF was absent (UK and The Netherlands) or very low (Denmark). In the latter case, moreover, the largest drop happened before the introduction of DSF in 1986.[70] Conversely, in Sweden and Norway, as well as Germany during the 1970s, membership rates grew in spite of notoriously generous subsidy systems and high levels of reliance on the public purse.[71] The evidence shows that there is simply no uniform covariance between the evolution of subsidy levels and membership rates.[72]

The weak correlation between DSF and party membership rates is not entirely surprising. First, the claim overestimates the relevance of financial incentives in the decision of the party elite to reach out for new members. Numerous incentives to attract new members remain in publicly funded parties, ranging from strengthening the core of loyal voters to increasing the organisation's democratic legitima-

Table 1.14: *Party membership trends in Western Europe, 1960–89*

| Country | Party membership as proportion of voting-age population (%) | | | Difference 1960–64/ 1985–89 (%) | Mean annual DSF per voter, 1975–89 (US$1990) | Mean annual (%) of DSF in central income of parties 1975–89 |
|---|---|---|---|---|---|---|
| | 1960–64 | 1975–79 | 1985–89 | | | |
| UK (1) | 10.0 | 5.9 | 2.6 | -73.7 | 0.00 | 0.0 |
| Denmark | 20.0 | 8.6 | 6.7 | -66.7 | 0.08 | 4.0 |
| Netherlands | 8.7 | 4.1 | 3.0 | -65.2 | 0.00 | 0.0 |
| Italy | 12.6 | 10.3 | 9.5 | -24.6 | 4.04 | 37.5 |
| Finland | 18.3 | 16.1 | 14.0 | -23.5 | 3.44 | 64.3 |
| Austria | 25.5 | 24.1 | 21.3 | -16.3 | 1.38 | 28.9 |
| Germany | 2.9 (2) | 4.2 | 2.6 | -7.7 | 1.36 | 61.3 |
| Norway | 13.2 | 14.2 | 13.2 | 0.6 | 2.24 | 55.0 |
| Sweden | 20.4 | 21.7 | 21.0 | 3.0 | 3.62 | 57.4 |
| Belgium | 5.7 | 8.0 | 7.6 | 33.4 | 0.00 | 0.0 |

Notes: (1) UK membership figures: 1960, 1974, 1989 only. (2) 1968-70.
Sources: See Appendix.

cy. Second, by assuming that membership is merely a function of the parties' recruiting efforts rather than the product of rational decisions by potential activists, the available literature embraces a lopsided notion of the dynamics that shape party membership. Indeed, DSF does *not* negatively affect the incentive structure for potential party members. On the contrary, comparing the relatively stable membership rates of Sweden, Norway and Finland and the plummeting figures of Denmark, Sundberg has argued that the absence of DSF in the latter and the correlative obligation of Danish party members to bear the cost of ever-more-expensive campaigns, severely increased the costs attached to active participation and led to a reduction in membership rates.[73] Third, the fall in party membership rates in Western Europe pre-dates the advent of public funding. Socialist and social democratic mass-parties, the mainstay of high membership rates, have seen their membership figures slide down since the 1950s in Sweden, Norway, Denmark and Germany.[74]

**Bureaucratisation and centralisation of power.** The assertion that DSF stifles the growth of party membership is usually conflated with the claim that public subventions magnify the size and role of party headquarters and hence incline the balance of power in favour of the party elite and against the rank-and-file. There is little doubt about the existence of a long-term increase in the resources commanded by party headquarters in Western Europe (see Table 1.15, column C). Moreover, most observers agree that the growth in party bureaucracy has been one of the clear-cut consequences of the introduction of DSF.[75] Indeed, as columns A–B show, low levels of subsidisation are clearly linked to relatively understaffed political parties (UK, The Netherlands and Denmark), Ireland being the only exception.

The table shows that, while the size of party bureaucracy may be related to DSF, neither the *trend* towards bureaucratisation nor its *speed* have much to do with the availability of public funding. This trend seems to occur regardless of DSF, as suggested by columns C–E. Central income grew significantly in non-directly subsidised party systems (Ireland, UK, The Netherlands and, nearly, Denmark), while it remained stable or even decreased in those countries where subsidies were most generous (Norway, Finland, Sweden and Italy). Meanwhile, countries with no or very low DSF occupy three of the top four positions in the growth in total party staff (Ireland, Denmark and The Netherlands) and headquarters' personnel (Ireland, Denmark and the UK). In the latter two categories, Finland and Sweden, with singularly expensive subsidy schemes, rank last. In most cases, the enactment of DSF thus seems to foster a rapid increase in the resources commanded by the party's central organisation, followed by a phase of relative stability.

If the link between DSF and party bureaucratisation is uncertain, the subsidies' impact on the centralisation of power in political parties is even less clear. Indeed, the assumption that bureaucratisation leads to centralisation of power must not be taken for granted. Table 1.15 (columns D–E) reveals that in seven out of nine countries the increase in the parties' central staff has been considerably lower than the overall growth in party personnel. This implies that the trend towards bureaucratisation has been more acute in other parts of the organisation, such as the parliamentary fraction and the sub-national branches, than at the party headquarters. Recent research has shown that the organisational evolution of West European parties can hardly be construed as a zero-sum power game between the party elite and the members. As Mair notes, most parties in developed democracies are best described as *stratarchical* rather than *hierarchical* organisations, i.e. structures in which the parliamentary fraction, the central office and the rank-and-file enjoy autonomous spheres of influence.[76]

The organisational critique of DSF seems to underestimate the enormous variety of factors that influence the degree of centralisation of power in each party. Factors such as the country's political structures (unitary/federal),[77] the locus and procedure of party nomination decisions[78] and the party's own historical evolution[79] may generate powerful centrifugal forces that no subsidy scheme is likely to offset. The introduction of DSF in Italy in 1974 is a case in point. By virtue of being channelled through the parties' headquarters, DSF was expected to reduce the endemic fractionalisation of Italian parties.[80] In the event, pre-existing institutional incentives proved too strong, and the decisive role of internal factions – notably in the Christian Democratic Party – remained virtually unchanged until the collapse of the post-war party system in the 1990s.[81] In addition, one should recall a point made earlier: several subsidy systems do *not* centralise the distribution of funds within parties, directing instead a share of the subvention towards sub-national layers of the organisation.

More fundamentally, in deploring the link between DSF on the one hand, and

Table 1.15: *Changes in party central income and staff in Western Europe, 1975–89 (1)*

| Country | A | B | C | D | E |
|---|---|---|---|---|---|
| | Mean annual DSF per voter (US$ 1990) | Voters per member of party staff, 1989 (1000s) | Growth in income of party central offices (%) | Growth in total staff employed by parties (%) | Growth in staff at the parties' central office (%) |
| UK | 0.00 | 50.8 | 46.0 | -23.0 | 24.8 |
| Netherlands | 0.00 | 16.4 | 41.0 | 81.6 | 10.0 |
| Ireland | 0.00 | 6.8 | 123.0 | 430.0 | 176.5 |
| Denmark | 0.08 | 13.6 | 50.0 | 228.7 | 131.5 |
| Germany | 1.36 | 10.0 | 350.0 | 231.7 (2) | 17.2 (2) |
| Austria | 1.38 | 10.1 | 286.0 | 36.0 | 15.8 |
| Norway | 2.24 | 7.7 | 14.0 | 25.3 | 28.8 |
| Finland | 3.44 | 7.1 | 6.0 | 22.0 | 7.3 |
| Sweden | 3.62 | 10.6 | -4.0 | 20.4 | 6.1 |
| Italy | 4.04 | n.a. | -25.0 | n.a. | n.a. |

Notes: (1) Except for A–B, only parties where a cross-time comparison was possible were included. B includes parties on which information was available, i.e. virtually all the relevant parties in all the countries. Figures in B are the product of dividing the total votes obtained by parties in the election nearest to 1989 for the number of party staff. (2) 1972–89.
Sources: See Appendix.

the fall in party membership rates, the increasing bureaucratisation and the centralisation of parties on the other, the critique of DSF betrays a longing for a particular type of party structure. The mass-party *à-la-Duverger* is thought of as the normal organisational paradigm for modern political parties, the equilibrium undesirably altered by public funding. Yet, as Katz and Mair rightly point out, the mass-party-model has clearly lost its relevance in Europe.[82] Already in the 1960s, well before DSF became widespread, Kirchheimer could confidently write that mass-parties were giving way to a new kind of organisation, the *catch-all* party, geared more towards electoral success than the exclusive representation of class interests.[83] Moreover, it is dubious that the model was ever relevant elsewhere. The 'empty' nature of US parties is well known, while catch-all parties, rather than mass organisations, have by and large substituted for traditional elite-centred parties in Latin America.[84] The implications for the present analysis should be clear: DSF cannot reduce high membership rates and financial reliance on members where the latter have never existed in the first place; nor can they lead to a relative loss of power by party members, where the latter have traditionally been powerless. If the proposed link between DSF and specific party features is ambiguous and increasingly irrelevant in Europe, it is largely meaningless in Latin and North America.

**Are parties merging with the state?** The claim that DSF stunts parties' ability to represent civil society and turns them into part of the state has received wide currency in Western Europe. The argument is at the heart of the influential 'cartel party' theory developed in the 1990s by Katz and Mair,[85] and has indeed had definite policy implications. In its 1992 landmark decision, the German Constitutional Court closed the door to a fully public system of political funding, arguing that it would jeopardise parties' freedom from the state. They defined parties as society's agents, which ought to be mainly funded by society and not by the state.[86]

The parties' shift from the orbit of civil society to that of the state has proved, however, much easier to pose than to demonstrate. Clearly, if this notion is to have the normative power attributed to it by the German judges, it should entail something else beyond the fact that parties receive money from the state. Instead, financial dependence should change the parties' behaviour in an observable way, depriving them of the power to decide autonomously and leading them to act closer to the interests of the state than to those of civil society. Even assuming, implausibly, that an objective identification of the state interest is possible, troubling issues remain. First, as Koole has argued, the very distinction between state and civil society is problematic in societies where corporatist practices are pervasive.[87] Second, the evidence suggests that even if this distinction could be made, it need not lead to a zero-sum game whereby a closer bond of the parties to the state implies their correlative dissociation from society. On the contrary, by allowing parties to enlarge the reach of their organisations – including their press – DSF has probably increased their social presence in Germany, Austria and Scandinavia, and ultimately contributed to stabilise membership rates in those countries (see Table 1.14). The hypothesis that publicly funded parties move away from civil society and merge with the state is bereft of any empirical evidence to support it. In the absence of such evidence, it is better to assume that publicly subsidised parties are no more a part of the state than a recipient of welfare payments is a public servant.

Moreover, this line of argument is based on two misconceptions. On the one hand, it displays an unwarranted faith in the power of private contributions and membership dues to secure the parties' links to society. Once more, the argument is underpinned by the mass-party-model with millions of small contributors, as in the German or British experience. Even in these cases, however, party members may constitute an unrepresentative sample not only of the general electorate but even of each party's own constituency, as the experience of Britain's Labour Party in the 1980s suggests.[88] In Canada, where the pool of political donors is comparatively large, the percentage of potential electors contributing to candidates and federal parties was a mere 1.78 per cent in 1984 and 1.77 per cent in 1988.[89] Meanwhile, research in the US has shown that donors contributing between US$201 and US$1,000 to pre-nomination campaigns, which accounted for close to 70 per cent of the money raised by presidential candidates during 1988 and 1992, are overwhelmingly white, university-educated and very affluent.[90] The supposition that private funding is essential to the parties' representative ability is controversial, at best.

On the other hand, the notion that DSF is the sign of a cartel of parties protected against the consequences of electoral failure, is based upon the questionable idea that DSF is less sensitive to electoral vagaries than private sources of income. It should be enough to recall that, with few exceptions, DSF is largely allocated according to seats or votes. In such a system, as pointed out by Wiberg, the financial consequences of electoral defeat can be dire.[91] In heavily subsidised systems the economic survival of parties depends fundamentally on their ability to attract voters, the critical test of the representativeness of parties.

Definite answers to the questions posed at the start of this section have once more proved elusive. The introduction of DSF has altered the financial structure of parties in Western Europe and beyond, and led them to various degrees of dependence on the public purse. Beyond that, little is known. Subsidies have reduced the financial weight of party membership fees, but this has also happened in their absence. Their effect on party membership figures is uncertain. They have probably fostered bigger party bureaucracy, but not the *process* of bureaucratisation of parties, which seems to be occurring even faster without them. The DSF-assisted centralisation of power within parties remains contentious: atomisation rather than centralisation seems to be the norm in developed democracies. Finally, the supposed conversion of parties into state organs still awaits being fleshed out empirically.

## CONCLUSION

Few general propositions can be advanced about the effects of DSF or, indeed, political finance rules. Of all the claims examined in the previous section only four seem safely sustained by the evidence: DSF tends to somewhat favour minor parties, has a limited effect on political-finance-related corruption, reduces the financial weight of membership fees and leads to comparatively large party bureaucracies. Even these assertions, however, convey mere tendencies and are subject to significant exceptions. The available evidence thus points towards a more sober evaluation of DSF than that envisaged by its advocates and critics. As all political finance instruments, DSF hardly seems to change dramatically or single-handedly the fate of any political system. Wiberg rightly notes that, 'the impact of the public financing of political parties has been widely overestimated in the political debate... Public financing is only one element in a complex network of relations.'[92]

The paucity and untidiness of these findings should not come as a surprise. This chapter has shown that public funding systems are not just extremely heterogeneous but also part of a wider regulatory framework that admits as many permutations as the subsidies themselves. The evidence given here cautions against general empirical claims that isolate specific regulation instruments from other parts of the PFS. Devoting attention to the policy combination is crucial if we are to predict with relative accuracy the effects of political finance rules. To do otherwise is a recipe for bad policy prescriptions and unpleasant consequences. The fate undergone by the contribution limits enacted in 1974 in the US reminds us of the empirical relevance of this point. There, the avowed intention of curbing the influence of large private donors, as seen in the enactment in 1974 of a US$1,000 limit on individual contributions, was undermined by the simultaneous enactment of a US$5,000 ceiling on donations by Political Action Committees (PACs)[93] in an attempt to create incentives for collective action. It soon became evident that PACs, and interest groups through them – including business and labour, formally banned from making direct contributions – were destined to become the new 'fat cats' of the US political finance landscape. Moreover, a combination of subsequent reforms and decisions by the Federal Election Commission (FEC), aimed at strengthening local party organisations, opened the way to the use in federal elections of largely unregulated contributions made at the state level. This phenomenon, known as 'soft-money', was, in turn, a product of a basic institutional feature of the US political system – federalism – which created a tapestry of funding rules, often at cross-purposes with the national legislation. The effects of contribution limits, as those of any other political finance instrument, are contingent on the surrounding institutional framework.

Factors such as regime type, electoral system, unitary versus federal structures, fragmentation of the party system, strength of party identities, range and depth of government intervention, and judicial prerogatives, to name but a few, mould the incentives and financial needs of political actors, the obstacles to monitoring the flow of political money, and, ultimately, the effects of any PFS. Thus, the parties' economic requirements and the political finance reform issues that will arise in a parliamentary system are naturally different from those in a presidential regime. While the strengthening of parties is a systemic need of the highest order in the former, in fixed-term presidential systems the permanent organisation of parties is far less crucial; much more so are the incentives for the parties' electoral orientation. Similarly, candidate-oriented electoral systems, preferential voting systems, federal structures and highly fragmented party systems increase the number of campaign structures and minimise the economies of scale that come with centralisation. By multiplying the inlets and outlets of political money and hence the obstacles to enforcing funding controls, decentralised electoral structures demand a different regulatory framework from that required by a system based upon closed party lists in a unitary country. Moreover, the size of the floating electorate, the electoral parity between parties and the power and resources commanded by the elected authorities conceivably have a bearing on the resources that parties and candidates are willing to invest in electoral pursuits, and therefore on the effects of DSF. Finally, the role of the courts and, in particular, the presence or absence of judicial constitutional review can make a critical difference in the route followed by political finance rules. This is shown conclusively by the post-*Buckley vs. Valeo* experience in the US and the repeated intervention of the German Constitutional Court in shaping funding legislation since the 1950s.

If one lesson is to be drawn from this chapter let it be that when it comes to establishing the effects of DSF or any other political finance instrument, we must *understand* before we can *predict*. We must grasp the linkages that bind political finance rules to their institutional and political surroundings. Predicting with relative accuracy the effects of DSF is possible, but only if the analysis is underpinned by a fine grasp of the context and by the awareness that most inferences will be considerably bounded. Compared with the exercise of formulating and testing grand generalisations about the effects of political finance rules, the option of weaving together in-depth case studies of political finance promises less glorious rewards, but a higher likelihood of success. This monograph will pursue this kind of analysis, using two small Latin American countries as case studies.

## NOTES

1 Heard (1960), p. 8.

2 'Kickbacks' are commission payments made to incumbents in return for government contracts. 'Toll-gating' is the system that extracts financial contributions to incumbent parties from the holders of government licences and concessions. 'Macing' is the practice of assessing public servants for political contributions in favour of incumbents.

3 *Buckley vs. Valeo* (1976). For a summary of the ruling see *Congressional Quarterly* (1992), pp. 59–86.

4 Tables 1.1–1.4 depict legal provisions as they stood, in most cases, at the end of 2002, based on a range of primary and secondary sources. Though an effort was made to corroborate and update the information, inaccuracies may have occurred. Moreover, these tables do not reflect factual realities, i.e. whether, and to what extent, political finance provisions are implemented . Their intention is simply to illustrate the diversity of political finance arrangements in contemporary democracies.

5 On the obstacles faced by the US Federal Election Commission (FEC) in enforcing the set of limits enacted by the 1974 Federal Election Commission Act, see Gross (1997); 'In political money game, the year of big loopholes', *The New York Times* (NYT), 26/12/1996; FEC (1998), pp. 31–4; Sorauf (1992), p. 185.

6 Levush et al (1991), pp. 90–2; Avril (1994), pp. 85–9.

7 Alexander et al. (1997).

8 The normative discussion on general spending caps has been intense in the US, where they were struck down by the Supreme Court in its 1976 ruling on *Buckley vs. Valeo*. See *Congressional Quarterly* (1992), pp. 59–86; Nicholson (1977), pp. 334–40; Shockley (1983), pp. 691–9; Dworkin (1997); Smith (2001).

9 A national spending ceiling operated for the first time in the 2001 General Election.

   Ewing (1992), pp. 220–25; Stanbury (1993a), pp. 97–9; Royal Commission on Electoral Reform and Party Financing (1991), pp. 327–8.

10 Pajares-Montolío (1998), pp. 137–45; Levush et al. (1991), pp. 89, 126, 155; Park (1994), pp. 181–2; Cepeda-Ulloa (1997), pp. 94–97; Walecki (2001), p. 410.

11 The issue has been discussed, for instance, in Chile, Panama and much of Eastern Europe. See Valdés-Prieto et al. (2000), pp. 420–37; *La Prensa Panamá*, 22/7/1995; *El Panamá*

12 *América* 14/8/2001; Walecki (2001), pp. 413–14.

This is the case in the US, Israel and Latin America, with the exception of Chile and, possibly, Brazil, where the value of broadcasting allowances is considerable. The situation is less
13  clear in Western Europe, due to the size of parliamentary subsidies in some countries.

The demarcation of different kinds of state funding is controversial, particularly in regard to the status of parliamentary grants. Paltiel (1981) and Nassmacher (1993) use the same cate-
14  gories – direct, indirect and specific subsidies – but classify parliamentary grants as direct subventions and in-kind subsidies as specific grants. Del Castillo (1985), Pedersen and Bille (1991) and Klee (1993) also consider parliamentary grants as direct subsidies. Pulzer (2001), Svasand (1991), Schefold (1995) and Alcántara et al. (1997) all consider parliamentary subventions as indirect subsidies. Finally, Nassmacher (2001c) seems to exclude parliamentary grants from state financing altogether, 'as long as subsidies are spent for intra-parliamentary business only' (p. 104).

This is clear in Britain, where debates on DSF continue to this day, despite the fact that various forms of political subvention have been in operation for decades.
15  In Belgium, the subvention is channelled through a surrogate non-profit organisation designated by the party. In the US, parties receive funds from the public purse in Alabama,
16  Arizona, California, Idaho, Indiana, Iowa, Kentucky, Maine, Minnesota, New Mexico, North Carolina, Ohio, Rhode Island, Utah and Virginia (Alexander, Goss and Schwartz [1992], pp. 5–8; FEC [1999]).

Müller (1994), pp. 54–5; Nassmacher (2001c), p. 103; Klee (1993), pp. 183–9; Gidlund & Koole (2001), p. 123.
17  Katz and Kolodny (1994).

This is, of course, a crude generalisation. Canada is an exception.
18  Hofnung (1996b), p. 138; Mendilow (1992), p. 109; Blechinger & Nassmacher (2001), pp.
19  168, 177–8.
20  Participation in the check-off scheme decreased from a high of 28 per cent of taxpayers in 1980 to below 18 per cent in 1992 (Federal Election Commission [1993], p. 2).
21  Smith (2001), p. 89.

'Soft-money' is, in essence, funds raised outside federal campaign finance regulations. Such
22  funds were banned by the Bipartisan Campaign Reform Act of 2002, signed by President
23  Bush on March 27, 2002. After a major legal challenge from its critics, the US Supreme Court upheld in late 2003 most of the bill's provisions, including the ban on 'soft-money'. Open Secrets (2002b).

Mendilow (1996), pp. 337.
24  Kinzo (1998), pp. 130–1.
25  Olivero (1994), Chapter 6; Cepeda-Ulloa (1997), p. 99; De la Calle (1998), p. 121; Cerdas
26  (1998), pp. 167–8; Ardaya and Verdesoto (1998), p. 190; Torres-Rivas and Aguilar (1998),
27  p. 278; Kinzo (1998), pp. 129–32; Aguiar (1994), p. 79.

The number of individual contributors to all Canadian parties grew from 84,610 in 1975 to 222,376 in 1993 (Stanbury [1993a], p. 83; Chief Electoral Officer of Canada [1993], p. 1).
28  Paltiel (1970), pp. 109, 112; Stanbury (1993a), p. 88 and (1993b), pp. 41516; Ewing (1992), p. 94.
29  Nassmacher (1993), pp. 256–59.

The reform created a system of matching-funds and tax-credits for individual donations of

30 less than DM3,000 ( 1,534), eliminated tax deductions for donations from legal persons and
31 decreased drastically the lower limit for the reporting of individual donations. Large political donations (>DM20,000 [ 10,226]) dropped from 375 and DM17.7 million ( 9.1 million)
in 1993 to 215 and DM8.6 million ( 4.4 million) in 1994 (Pulzer [2001], pp. 24–5).
With the exception of Germany and, probably, France, weak reporting procedures exist in
Western Europe. A large share of party income and expenditure in the region goes unreport-
32 ed (Nassmacher [1993], pp. 246–7).
See, amongst many: 'European politics plagued by funding scandals', *The Guardian*,
4/12/1999; Blechinger & Nassmacher (2001), pp. 178–80; Galiardo and Berbell (1995);
33 Rhodes (1997); Pujas & Rhodes (1998); Pulzer (2001), pp. 31–2.
Von Beyme (1985), p. 201; Mendilow (1992), p. 112; Hofnung (1996b), p. 138; Pedersen
and Bille (1991), pp. 163–6; Mayorga (1998), pp. 37–8.
34 Mendilow (1992), p. 112. See also Blechinger and Nassmacher (2001), pp. 179–80.
Corrado (1993), Chapter 2; Alexander (1989), p. 106; Sorauf (1992), p. 159.
35 Mendilow (1992), pp. 99–100. During the 1969–92 period, following the enactment of DSF,
36 11 breakaway parties achieved representation.
37 Pizarro-Leongómez (1997), p. 129; Fiallos (1998), pp. 384–5.
Figures calculated from Mackie and Rose (1991) and updates in the *European Journal of*
38 *Political Research (EJPR)*.
39 Jenson (1991), pp. 127–131; Andren (1970), p. 65; Wiberg (1991a), p. 66.
Klee (1993), p. 182.
40 Del Castillo (1985), pp. 88–9.
41 Ewing (1992), pp. 6–7.
42 Prud'homme et al. (1993), pp. 77–118; Alemán-Velasco (1995), Chapter 7; Woldenberg et
43 al. (1998), p. 324; Park (1994), pp. 173–182.
44 For the purpose of this analysis, small parties are those that average less than 10 per cent of
the vote in national parliamentary elections during the period under consideration, as distinct
45 from mid-sized and large parties (10–25 per cent, and > 25 per cent, respectively).
Nassmacher (1989), pp. 252–4; Nassmacher (1993), pp. 258–9.
Nassmacher (1989), p. 248 and (2001b), p. 25; Gidlund (1991b), pp. 184–5; Koole (1996),
46 pp. 516–17; Pierre, Svasand and Widfeldt (2000), pp. 20–1; Gidlund and Koole (2001), p.
47 130.
Electoral volatility is measured here using Pedersen's index, i.e. the sum of the net gains and
losses of all political parties within a system from one election to the next (Pedersen [1990]).
48 Party system fragmentation is measured by the effective number of elective parties (Laakso
and Taagepera [1979], p. 4).
The cases where DSF currently operates are Austria, Belgium, Canada, Denmark, Finland,
France, Germany, Israel, Italy, Norway and Sweden. The other cases in the sample are
49 Ireland, Japan, Luxembourg, The Netherlands, Switzerland and the UK. Given that the sample includes only Japanese and Irish elections prior to the introduction of DSF, both countries have been classified as DSF-free. For each country, elections with DSF include only
those held from the following year of DSF's enactment onwards.
The comparison includes only the seventy four directly subsidised elections held in the latter group of countries.

50 In order to minimise the effect of electoral system changes, particularly on the effective number of parties, the table only includes countries where the electoral system remained
51 basically stable throughout the period. Hence, France has been eliminated and Italian elections were included until 1992. Figures of elective parties may be affected by changes in electoral rules that lowered the representation threshold in Austria (1971) and increased it in Sweden (1970). Note, however, that figures in the table refer to elective rather than *parliamentary* parties. It is the latter figure that is directly affected by representation thresholds. Welch (1976); Jacobson (1985).

Research has shown that electoral funds tend to be more decisive for challengers than for
52 incumbents. See Jacobson (1978, 1979 and 1985) on campaign spending in US congression-
53 al elections. For similar analyses in Britain, France and Japan see, respectively, Johnston (1986) and (1987), pp. 184–5; Pattie, Johnston & Fieldhouse (1995); Palda and Palda (1998); Cox and Thies (2000).

Similar conclusions in Pierre, Svasand and Widfeldt (2000), p. 22; Nassmacher and Nassmacher (2001), p. 192.

54 Klee (1993), pp. 192–193; Gidlund (1991a), p. 46; Pierre and Widfeldt (1994), p. 347; Gidlund and Koole (2001), pp. 118–119.

55 Paltiel (1981), p. 145; Heidenheimer (1970), p. 9; Pulzer (2001), pp. 13–14; Heidenheimer & Langdon (1968).

56 Koole (1989), pp. 206–207; Gidlund & Koole (2001), p. 118. In 1979–80 corporate donations constituted 57 per cent of donations to the British Conservative Party's Central Office.
57 This figure fell to 41 per cent in 1983–84 and 28 per cent in 1987–88 (Pinto-Duschinsky [1989], p. 210). See also Johnston & Pattie (1993), p. 148.

Duverger (1988 [1951]), pp. 391–2; Heidenheimer (1963), pp. 792–5; Schleth and Pinto-Duschinsky (1970), p. 29.

58 In Austria (1975–90), the Socialist Party's central income was, on average, 153 per cent that of the Conservatives and Liberals combined. In Sweden (1965–89), the annual combined
59 income of the Social Democrats and Communists was, on average, slightly higher (101.7 per cent) than that of the Conservative, People's and Moderate parties combined. Data calculated from Katz and Mair (1992).

Chaples (1989), p. 76; Von Beyme (1985), p. 211; Pierre and Widfeldt (1994), p. 338; Gidlund (1991a), p. 18 and (1991b), pp. 178–179; Leonard (1975), pp. 11–12.

60 Del Castillo (1985), p. 89; Drysch (1993), p. 156; Von Beyme (1985), p. 211.

Data calculated from Katz and Mair (1992). These estimations are largely consistent with
61 those reported by Nassmacher (1989, p. 252–4) using data from Germany, Austria, Italy and
62 Sweden until 1984.

Mendilow (1992), p. 110 and (1996), p. 345.

Alexander & Corrado (1995), p. 115. The 2000 presidential election in the US saw, howev-
63 er, a return to the secular trend, with the Republican candidate heavily outspending his
64 Democratic rival (US$193 million to US$133 million). See Open Secrets (2002a).

Campaign expenditures doubled in Austria in 1975–90 and nearly doubled in Sweden in 1982–88 (Katz [1996], p. 130). In Britain, they experienced a fourfold growth in real terms
65 between 1983 and 1997, as did presidential and overall electoral expenditures in the US in 1960–92 (Committee on Standards in Public Life [1998], p. 43; Alexander and Corrado

[1995], pp. 6, 21). In Austria, Germany and The Netherlands the increase in the cost of party structures – notably staff salaries – has outpaced in recent times that of campaign disbursements. I owe this observation to Karl-Heinz Nassmacher. See also Nassmacher (2001b, pp. 21–22).

These estimations are largely consistent with those given by Klee (1993), p. 188; Wiberg (1991a), pp. 91–2; Gidlund (1991a), pp. 43–5; Svasand (1994), pp. 324–5; Müller (1994),
66   pp. 66–7; Poguntke (1994), pp. 196–7; Del Castillo (1992), pp. 157–8. They are, however, markedly lower than those provided by Bille (1994, p. 147) for Denmark, which include reliance on parliamentary subsidies. They are also much lower than estimates provided by Nassmacher (2001c, p. 96) for Germany 1987–89, that put reliance on subsidies at roughly one-third of total party income. It is not clear if Nassmacher's figures include all levels of the party or only the headquarters.

The correlation coefficients are: Finland 1967–89: -0.933; Italy 1974–89: -0.847; Germany 1968–89:-0.785; Denmark 1987–89: -0.631; Norway 1968–89: -0.590; Sweden 1965–89: -
67   0.551. Only Austria 1975–90 (0.177) deviates from the norm. Figures calculated from Katz and Mair (1992).

The proportion of trade union affiliation fees plummeted from 72.6 per cent in 1975–9 to 28.7 per cent in 1996–7. Meanwhile, individual subscriptions moved from 6.3 per cent to
68   8.8 per cent, and donations from 20.8 per cent to 54 per cent. See Pinto-Duschinsky (1985), pp. 330–3; Committee on Standards in Public Life (1998), pp. 30–1, 46; 'New Labour peer gave party £1m.' and 'Helping hand?', *The Sunday Times*, 16/11/1997.

A very similar analysis to mine may be found in Pierre, Svasand and Widfeldt (2000), pp. 16–18.
69   Pedersen and Bille (1991), pp. 156, 165–6.

Gidlund and Koole (2001), p. 129.

70   A test of correlation in the evolution of DSF per voter and party membership rates in six
71   countries yielded the following coefficients: Austria 1975–90: -0.637; Sweden 1965–89:
72   0.074; Norway 1968–89: 0.240; Italy 1974–89: 0.432; Germany 1968–89: 0.201; Finland 1967–89: -0.242. Data calculated from Katz and Mair (1992).

Sundberg (1987).

Bartolini (1983), pp. 185, 190.

73   Paltiel (1980), p. 367–368 and (1981), pp. 169–170; Nassmacher (1989), p. 250; Pinto-
74   Duschinsky (1981), p. 292 and (1991), pp. 228–229; Schefold (1995), p. 449; Del Castillo
75   (1993), p. 90 and (1994), p. 59; Mendilow (1992), pp. 100–102 and (1996), p. 346. See also Wiberg (1991a), p. 71 and Sundberg (1994), pp. 174–175 on Finland; Svasand (1991), p. 143 and (1994), p. 325 on Norway; Pedersen & Bille (1991), p. 168 on Denmark.

Mair (1994), p. 17.

Federal structures limit the centralisation of power within parties. See Poguntke (1994), p.
76   187; Paltiel (1970).

77   Sartori (1992), pp. 134–141.

Panebianco (1988).

78   Sassoon (1974), p. 98.

79   Bardi and Morlino (1994), pp. 244–70.

80   Katz and Mair (1995), pp. 6–15. See also Bartolini (1983), p. 213; Pizzorno (1990), p. 65.

81 Kirchheimer (1966).
82 Katz and Kolodny (1994); Dix (1989), pp. 27, 34–5.
83 Katz (1996); Mair (1994) and (1997); Katz and Mair (1995) and (1996).
84 González-Varas (1995), pp. 29–32; Gunlicks (1995), p. 109.
85 Koole (1996), pp. 509–15.
86 Bartolini (1983), p. 211.
87 Stanbury (1993a), p. 82.
88 Brown, Powell & Wilcox (1995), Chapter 3.
89 Wiberg (1991a), p. 115.
90 Wiberg (1991a), p. 115.
91 A Political Action Committee is a non-partisan committee that receives contributions from
92 more than fifty people and contributes to at least five candidates for federal office in the US
93 (Corrado et al. [1997], p. 124).

# chapter two | political finance and state funding in costa rica and uruguay: political and institutional background

## INTRODUCTION

The rest of this book offers a comparative study of the effects of DSF on campaign finance practices and party system dynamics in Costa Rica and Uruguay. As the introductory chapter pointed out, they are, arguably, the most institutionalised and consolidated democracies in Latin America. Moreover, they share obvious similarities that range from the nature of their political regime to their relatively egalitarian social structures. These parallels extend, in many ways, to the field of political finance. Both countries exhibit the oldest schemes of direct subvention of parties and candidates in the world, ranked amongst the most generous in Latin America and, on some accounts, the world. Remarkable as they are, these similarities co-exist with equally visible differences in each country's political history, electoral system, party system format and state funding scheme.

Building on the arguments put forward in Chapter one, this comparative exercise will first place the Costa Rican and Uruguayan DSF schemes in a larger politico-institutional context and map out the similarities and differences evinced by that context. As will become clear, both the shared and the divergent traits of the politico-institutional landscape are central to the understanding of the political effects of DSF in Costa Rica and Uruguay, and indeed help to explain why particular political finance rules are adopted or resisted, and why broadly similar DSF systems come to have peculiar features that shape their consequences in distinct ways.

This chapter will thus give a broad account of the characteristics of the political and electoral regime, the party system and the evolution of political finance rules – with particular emphasis on the state funding scheme – in Costa Rica and Uruguay. Each country will be treated separately, leading to a concluding section that will summarise and tease out the main political, institutional and historical elements that should be borne in mind throughout the remaining chapters.

## COSTA RICA

Costa Rica's political system displays a combination of institutional features that has proved highly functional for democratic stability and yet has received very little attention from political scientists. Presidentialism, a strong electoral system, electoral bipolarity and generous public subsidies for parties are some of the central traits of this institutional framework. The relative endurance of these features does not imply, however, an uneventful evolution. In fact, they have undergone relevant transformations time and again, in some cases gradually, in some cases dramatically as a result of critical historical conjunctures. The 1948 civil war, in particular, stands as the inevitable point of reference for much of the country's contemporary political history.

**Democratic consolidation, political regime and electoral system**

The exceptional political stability enjoyed by Costa Rica in the last fifty years, and its widely perceived uniqueness in the Central American context, have diverted attention from the country's political travails for much of the nineteenth century. Recurrent power disputes among the country's coffee-growing elite, helped by the presidency's wide prerogatives in electoral matters, gave Costa Rica's early political life a distinct Latin American flavour, with coups and electoral frauds as common occurrences. Carlos J. Gutiérrez has observed that, 'out of the governments that ruled the country between 1824 and 1890, seven seized power by means of force, six served only temporarily, eleven were designated through elections where choice was not possible, and only one claimed power by virtue of a contest worthy of the name'.[1] The gradual shift of powers from the presidency to a legislative branch where the opposition could enjoy adequate representation was an essential condition for the adoption of a pattern of free and regular – if not necessarily fair – elections from the late nineteenth century onwards.[2]

The full consolidation of democracy, however, came much later, and not without a major intervening crisis. For all its periodicity, at the dawn of the twentieth century, Costa Rican elections were largely intra-oligarchic tournaments, where the franchise accounted for a mere 11.5 per cent of the total population.[3] Two major electoral reforms in 1913 and 1925 expanded the franchise, introduced direct suffrage, created the National Election Council and adopted the secret vote.

Costa Rica's electoral institutions suffered new and dramatic changes during the 1940s. The decade was marred by a sharp intensification of political conflict that would eventually lead to a short civil war in 1948, and thus to the emergence of the cleavage that has defined the country's politics ever since. The 1940 election of Rafael Angel Calderón-Guardia, a populist physician, and his eventual alliance with the local Communist Party, signalled the twilight of the liberal-oligarchic political order and the start of an ambitious programme of socio-economic reforms that, as elsewhere in Latin America, would generate intense political loyalties and hostilities.[4] However, it was the struggle for the presidency, the deterioration of the electoral guarantees for the opposition and the widespread perception of fraud that were at the core of the decade's increasingly polarised political climate.[5]

In 1946, an Electoral Code was introduced as a last-ditch attempt to prevent a looming democratic breakdown. It included a thorough systematisation of electoral procedures, intended to clamp down on fraudulent practices. The 1946 Code proved, nonetheless, insufficient to quell the atmosphere of political confrontation. Two years later civil war ensued, ostensibly triggered by the annulment by the government-controlled Congress of the 1948 election, in which the opposition presidential candidate, Otilio Ulate, had defeated Calderón-Guardia. Led by José Figueres, a rural caudillo and small farmer, an assortment of anti-government conservative factions and middle-class reformers prevailed in the armed conflict. This gave way to a long season of political, social and economic change.

Figueres, the pre-eminent political figure of the second half of the twentieth century in Costa Rica, remained in power for eighteen months as head of a de facto government – *the Junta Fundadora de la Segunda República* – and then handed the presidency to Otilio Ulate in 1949. Figueres' administration – the first of three – preserved the social reforms introduced by Calderón-Guardia and established the bases of an activist state that would transform Costa Rica in the course of the next decades.[6] Many of these changes were enshrined in the 1949 Constitution, enacted in the wake of the civil war and still in operation.

Given the immediate causes of the civil war, Figueres and the framers of the 1949 Constitution went to great lengths to transform the country's electoral institutions. The most far-reaching reforms were the extension of suffrage to women and the creation of the Supreme Election Tribunal (TSE), an upgraded and much-strengthened version of the electoral authority created by the 1925 electoral law. The new constitution endowed the TSE with wide-ranging powers for the administration of elections and the resolution of electoral conflicts, turning it into a virtual fourth branch of the state. The new electoral arrangements proved remarkably successful: since 1949, the country has held thirteen free, fair and peaceful general elections, with an entrenched pattern of power alternation.

While the 1949 framers decided to preserve the long-standing presidential nature of the political regime, they nevertheless curtailed the electoral and legislative prerogatives of the presidency. They gave the president, for instance, no constitutional authorisation to legislate by decree and a rather reduced veto power, which cannot be invoked in budgetary matters.[7] This has led some authors to judge the Costa Rican presidency as a comparatively weak institution.[8] Even so, the president retained extensive appointment and patronage capabilities throughout the state. These capabilities allow him a good measure of control over his own political party and, through the latter, over the workings of the Legislative Assembly.[9] To this day, the presidency has remained, in practice, the main focus of politics in the country, and the biggest electoral prize.

Today, Costa Rican presidential elections take place every four years and are decided by a peculiar system of plurality voting in a national constituency. A 40 per cent majority is required for an outright victory. If no candidate achieves the threshold, a run-off between the two most popular candidates takes place two months after the first round. The 40 per cent clause, unique in comparative constitutional practice, was introduced in 1936 to modify the absolute majority required by the 1871 Constitution, which frequently left the presidential election in the hands of Congress, generating major constitutional impasses in the process. This apparently innocuous reform proved effective: no second-round run-off was necessary for nearly seventy years, until the 2002 election. It should also be noted that, currently, Costa Rican presidents are allowed to seek re-election after sitting out two terms. This is the result of a ruling of the country's Constitutional Court, which in April of 2003 struck down a long-standing absolute ban on presidential re-election.[10]

Costa Rica's small, unicameral fifty-seven-member Legislative Assembly, in turn, is elected simultaneously with the president in seven multi-member constituencies that overlap with the country's seven provinces. Though both elections are concurrent, vote-splitting is allowed. In congressional elections votes are given to closed party slates, with the seats being allocated according to a proportional representation (PR) system of quota and largest remainder, corrected by the use of a provincial electoral threshold (50 per cent of one quota). Since the country presents a mixture of large and small electoral districts – the average magnitude is 8.1 – the result is a moderate degree of proportionality.[11] These rules have remained stable for a long period. The most recent changes were the introduction of the provincial electoral threshold or *subcociente* in 1946 as well as the elimination of consecutive congressional re-election and the adoption of full electoral concurrence in 1949. The latter reform eliminated a long tradition of mid-term legislative elections.

Since then, only candidate-selection processes within parties have undergone significant changes. Parties have enjoyed the legal monopoly over candidacies since 1932. This monopoly, paired with the closed-list system and the low levels of party institutionalisation, conferred party leaders a high degree of control over political careers for a long time.[12] In general, historic leaders of the parties alternated the presidential nomination between them and then, as candidates, strongly dominated – and frequently coerced – the party organs in charge of making congressional nominations.[13]

This pattern remained largely unchanged until the late 1970s, when the erosion of historic leaderships, particularly in the dominant National Liberation Party (PLN), heralded a shift towards American-style open contests for the presidential nomination. By the mid 1980s, open presidential primaries had been established de facto as a rule in major parties, and were incorporated in the Electoral Code in 1988. They remain, according to the law, an optional rather than a mandatory mechanism and must not take place more than eight months before the presidential election. The use of open primaries, now also in the process of being adopted for congressional races, has had obvious and considerable implications for party finance in Costa Rica.

Costa Rica thus exhibits a co-existence of different electoral formulas – plurality for the presidency and PR for congressional elections – that should in principle pull the party system in opposite directions. The crucial detail to observe is that

Table 2.1: *Key features of political regime and electoral system in Costa Rica*

| Regime features | Type of regime | Presidential |
|---|---|---|
| | Assembly structure | Unicameral (fifty-seven members) |
| Electoral system | Presidential election | District: One, nationwide. |
| | | Formula: Plurality with 40% threshold (run-off between top two if no candidate achieves 40% of the vote). |
| | | Re-election: Yes (after sitting out two terms. Between 1969 and 2003 re-election was banned). |
| | | Candidate selection process: Usually, open primaries in major parties. In all cases selection ratified by party's National Assembly. |
| | Legislative election | Districts: Seven, multi-member. (Mean magnitude: 8.14, but San José = 21 [1998]). |
| | | Form of candidacy: Closed party list. |
| | | Formula: PR (Hare and largest remainder) with threshold (50% of provincial quotient). |
| | | Re-election: Yes (alternating, not consecutive). |
| | | Candidate selection process: Selected by party's National Assembly. Currently moving towards open primaries in major parties. |
| | Election cycle | Concurrent, every four years. Vote-splitting allowed. |

the presidential nature of the regime, coupled with full electoral concurrence since 1949, turns plurality – particularly if reinforced with the 40 per cent threshold – into much the more dominant force of the two.[14] Though, as we will see below, there is a visible difference in voting behaviour in both elections, and therefore in the format of the party system in each, it is widely accepted that congressional elections are dragged on the presidential race's coat-tails. The combination of presidentialism, a dominant *plurality-plus* formula, and closed party lists, bestows on the Costa Rican electoral system a restrictive influence over the voters. It is, to use Sartori's term, a 'strong' set of rules with definite effects on the party system.

**Party system**

The 1948 civil war also had far-reaching consequences for the development of the party system in Costa Rica. Though parties have existed in the country since 1889, the 1948 conflict created a new defining cleavage and, indeed, a new set of political actors. In the future, the country's political life would evolve under the shadow of the leaders of the two forces that had fought the war, Figueres and Calderón-

Table 2.2: *Electoral results in Costa Rica, 1953–2002*

| Election | Party | Presidential election (% of valid votes and elected president) | Legislative election (% of seats) | Abstention rate (%) |
|---|---|---|---|---|
| 1953 | **PLN** | **64.7 (José Figueres)** | **66.7 (1)** | 32.8 |
| | Democrat | 35.3 | 24.4 | |
| | National Union | -- | 2.2 | |
| | Other | -- | 6.7 | |
| 1958 | PLN | 42.8 | 44.4 | 35.3 |
| | **National Union** | **46.4 (Mario Echandi)** | **22.2** | |
| | Independent | 10.8 | 6.7 | |
| | Republican | -- | 24.4 | |
| | Other | -- | 2.2 | |
| 1962 | **PLN** | **50.3 (Francisco Orlich)** | **50.9** | 19.1 |
| | Republican | 35.3 | 31.6 | |
| | National Union | 13.5 | 15.8 | |
| | Popular Democratic Action | 0.9 | 1.7 | |
| 1966 | PLN | 49.5 | 50.9 | 18.6 |
| | **National Unification Coalition** | **50.5 (Jose Joaquín Trejos)** | **45.6** | |
| | Other | -- | 3.5 | |
| 1970 | **PLN** | **54.8 (José Figueres)** | **56.1** | 16.7 |
| | National Unification | 41.2 | 38.6 | |
| | Socialist Action | 1.3 | 3.5 | |
| | Other | 2.7 | 1.7 | |
| 1974 | **PLN** | **43.4 (Daniel Oduber)** | **47.4** | 20.1 |
| | National Unification | 30.4 | 28.1 | |
| | Socialist Action | 2.4 | 3.5 | |
| | Other | 23.8 | 21.0 | |
| 1978 | PLN | 43.8 | 43.9 | 18.7 |
| | **Unity Coalition** | **50.5 (Rodrigo Carazo)** | 47.4 | |
| | United People Coalition | 2.7 | 5.3 | |
| | Other | 3.0 | 3.4 | |
| 1982 | **PLN** | **58.8 (Luis Alberto Monge)** | 57.9 | 21.4 |
| | Unity Coalition | 33.6 | 31.6 | |
| | United People Coalition | 3.3 | 7.0 | |
| | Other | 4.3 | 3.4 | |
| 1986 | **PLN** | **52.3 (Oscar Arias)** | **50.9** | 18.2 |
| | PUSC | 45.8 | 43.9 | |
| | United People Coalition | 0.6 | 1.7 | |
| | Popular Alliance Coalition | 0.8 | 1.7 | |
| | Other | 0.5 | 1.7 | |
| 1990 | PLN | 47.2 | 43.9 | 18.2 |
| | **PUSC** | **51.5 (Rafael A. Calderón F.)** | **50.9** | |
| | United People Coalition | 0.7 | 1.7 | |
| | Other | 0.6 | 3.4 | |

Table 2.2: *(Cont)*

| Election | Party | Presidential election (% of valid votes and elected president) | Legislative election (% of seats) | Abstention rate (%) |
|---|---|---|---|---|
| 1994 | **PLN** | **49.6 (José M. Figueres O.)** | **49.1** | 18.9 |
| | PUSC | 47.7 | 43.9 | |
| | Democratic Force | 1.9 | 3.5 | |
| | Other | 0.8 | 3.5 | |
| 1998 | PLN | 44.6 | 40.3 | 30.0 |
| | **PUSC** | **47.0 (Miguel A. Rodríguez)** | **47.4** | |
| | Democratic Force | 3.0 | 5.1 | |
| | Other | 5.4 | 7.0 | |
| 2002 (2) | PLN | 31.1 [42.0] | 29.8 | 31.2 [39.0] |
| | **PUSC** | **38.6 [58.0] (Abel Pacheco)** | **33.3** | |
| | Citizen Action Party | 26.2 | 24.6 | |
| | Libertarian Movement | 1.7 | 8.8 | |
| | Other | 2.4 | 3.5 | |

Notes: (1) Bold indicates majority. Due to rounding, totals for each election may not add up to 100. (2) Figures in parentheses refer to second round run-off.
Sources: See Appendix.

Guardia. More importantly, the post-war Costa Rican party system would come to be defined by the presence of the PLN, a party that emerged from the ranks of the victorious *figuerista* forces.

Marked by the basic cleavage of the civil war, and shaped by the restrictive influence of presidentialism and its electoral rules, the post-1949 party system embarked on a long journey towards the consolidation of a two-party format. This can be seen in Table 2.2, which summarises electoral results in Costa Rica since 1953.

Five basic features of the post-1948 party system in Costa Rica can be inferred from the table. First, there is a persistent electoral bipolarity, particularly in the presidential race, only weakened in 1962, 1974 and 2002. Second, there is a high correlation between presidential and legislative majorities (either absolute or relative), with the same party achieving both in eleven out of thirteen cases. Third, the table shows a small but systematic difference between presidential and legislative results, which consistently favours minor parties in legislative contests. As will be explained in more detail in Chapter five, the coexistence of these three phenomena suggests, on the one hand, the strong effect of the combination of a plurality formula in the presidential election and full electoral concurrence, and, on the other hand, the countervailing influence of PR in legislative elections. Thus, while it is generally accurate to characterise the Costa Rican party system as a 'dissuasive bipolarity',[15] in which both rules and results have discouraged the development of third parties, it should nonetheless be stressed that the intensity of such dissuasion is not identical across different types of elections. Fourth, the chart displays a firm pattern of alternation of the presidency between parties, only broken by the PLN in 1974 and 1986, and by the Social Christian Unity Party (PUSC) in

2002. Fifth, the table makes clear the remarkable, if increasingly eroded, electoral strength of the PLN. Over the last half century, the PLN won seven presidential elections and reaped at least 42 per cent of the votes in all cases. Perhaps more significantly, it achieved a relative or absolute legislative majority in nine out of thirteen administrations since 1953, including a continuous twenty-five-year spell that ended in 1978.

Though founded in 1951, the origins of the PLN lie in the early 1940s, with the creation of the Centre for the Study of the National Problems (CSNP). Established in 1941 by a cohort of young urban middle-class intellectuals, the CSNP articulated through numerous publications a powerful critique of the prevailing liberal-oligarchic order, its exclusive political mores and its economic model dependent on primary exports. More importantly, the CSNP also elaborated an alternative development paradigm, loosely based upon social-democratic tenets, in which an activist state would have a chief role. The CSNP eventually merged with the small Democratic Action Party to form the Social Democratic Party (PSD) in 1945. Six years later, in the aftermath of the civil war and the 1948–9 de facto government, the SDP dissolved itself and became the PLN.

The emergence of the PLN gave the Costa Rican party system an ideological dimension that it had largely lacked before.[16] Based on the ideas of the CSNP and strongly influenced by the teachings of the UN-sponsored Economic Commission for Latin America (ECLA), the state interventionist project implemented by the *Junta Fundadora* and, later, by the PLN, soon led to a bitter rift with its wartime conservative allies, grouped around Otilio Ulate and his National Union Party (PNU). Indeed, this feud and, above all, the long electoral domination of the PLN after 1953 subtly modified the cleavage shaping the party system. Not long after the war, the basic dividing line had already ceased to run between liberacionistas (the followers of Figueres and the PLN) and calderonistas (the followers of Calderón-Guardia), and had begun instead to separate *liberacionistas* from *antiliberacionistas*, the latter including also the same conservative groups that had opposed Calderón-Guardia in the 1940s.

The crystallisation of this cleavage was, however, a singularly intricate task, hindered by historical, ideological and personal rivalries between the main *antiliberacionista* factions, the *calderonista* Republican Party (PRC) and the *ulatista* PUN. Their first attempt to collaborate came before the 1958 election, when Calderón-Guardia, exiled in Mexico after the war, directed his followers to lend their support to the PUN presidential candidate. This remarkable change of heart revealed the increasing anxiousness of both groups about the prospect of an impregnable PLN hegemony. Through successive electoral alliances and coalitions, these forces were able to capture the presidency in 1958, 1966 and 1978, in the first case aided by a formal division of the PLN.

By 1970 the PRC and the PUN had merged to form the National Unification Party (PU), an achievement that would prove short-lived. The new party soon descended into a bitter internecine war, which largely betrayed the different origin of its components. Weakened by a fragmented leadership structure and by the profound distrust between a vote-rich but financially strained *calderonista* sector and the electorally dwindling but economically powerful conservative groups, the PU disintegrated gradually throughout the 1970s until its demise after the 1978 election.

In the meantime, the PLN, which masterfully played upon the internal divisions of the opposition, reaped a rich electoral harvest. By the time the 1974 election was held the anti-*liberacionista* sector had splintered into a myriad of small and mid-sized parties, which were unable to coalesce to prevent a PLN victory. This was a humiliating blow for the opposition. It was not just that the PLN had broken for the first time the post-war pattern of alternation of the presidency, but that it had managed to do so with one of the lowest tallies in its history: a mere 43.4 per cent of the vote, barely above the electoral threshold. Just as the 1958 election had taught the PLN a powerful lesson on the costs of defection in a bipolar system, the 1974 election would come to exert a lasting influence on the behaviour of the anti-PLN forces.

The opposition managed to recreate a formal alliance before the 1978 election, the Unity Coalition (CU). It combined two groups that had abandoned the PU – the conservative Popular Unity Party (PUP) and the Calderonista Republican Party (PRC) – as well as the small Christian Democrat Party (PDC), and the Democratic Renovation Party (PRD), a group founded by PLN dissidents after the 1970 election. Helped by the charismatic candidacy of Rodrigo Carazo, a prominent PLN defector, and supported by Rafael A. Calderón-Fournier, the young political heir of *calderonismo*, the coalition inflicted a decisive defeat on the PLN, depriving it, for the first time, of its legislative majority. The success of the Unity Coalition restored the pattern of electoral bipolarity, and finally stabilised it. Despite frequent internal conflicts and a heavy electoral defeat in 1982, the coalition remained unchanged until 1983, when its components finally merged to create the Social Christian Unity Party (PUSC).

After that, a two-party system became solidly entrenched for nearly two decades. The 2002 election saw, however, a sharp change of fortunes for both major parties and the emergence of a significant electoral challenge from new groupings (notably the Citizen Action Party [PAC]) formed by their own defectors. Whether the ascent of these groupings heralds a permanent change in the Costa Rican two-party system it is, of course, too early to tell. At any rate, it should be noted that both major parties retained enough electoral strength in 2002 to qualify comfortably for the presidential run-off.

Equally eventful was the evolution of the Left, the third relevant, if consistently small, actor in the system. Having played a crucial political role in the 1940s, the Popular Vanguard Party (PVP) – the local Communist Party – lived through a long season of repression and proscription after 1948 that would formally end in 1975. In practice, however, the Left returned to electoral participation well before that, under different names and with limited electoral fortune. The lifting of the ban in 1975 spawned several small left-wing parties, which formed the United People Coalition (CPU) in 1978. After electing four deputies in 1982 – the best electoral showing of the Left since the 1940s – the coalition dissolved amidst acri-

Graph 2.1: *Party transformation in Costa Rica, 1948–2002 (1)*

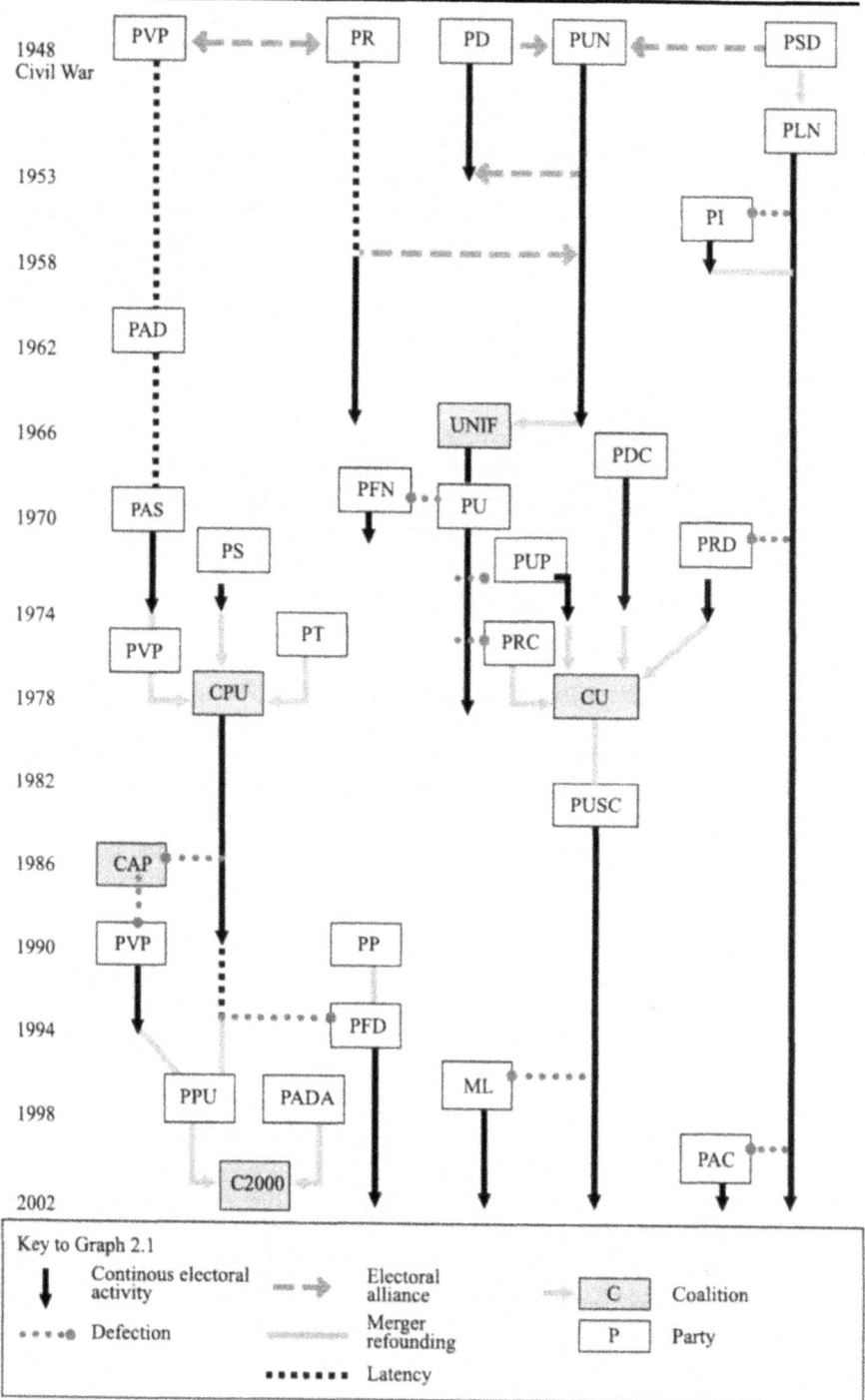

| | |
|---|---|
| 1948 Civil War | PVP ⇐⇒ PR PD ⇒ PUN ⇐ PSD |
| | PLN |
| 1953 | ⇐ |
| | PI |
| 1958 | ⇒ |
| 1962 | PAD |
| 1966 | UNIF ⇐ PDC |
| 1970 | PAS PFN · PU PRD |
| | PS PUP |
| 1974 | PVP PT PRC |
| 1978 | CPU CU |
| 1982 | PUSC |
| 1986 | CAP · · · |
| 1990 | PVP PP |
| 1994 | PFD |
| 1998 | PPU PADA ML PAC |
| 2002 | C2000 |

Key to Graph 2.1

| | | | | | |
|---|---|---|---|---|---|
| ↓ | Continous electoral activity | ⇒ | Electoral alliance | C | Coalition |
| · · · •● | Defection | | Merger refounding | P | Party |
| | | ■ ■ ■ ■ ■ ■ | Latency | | |

Key to Graph 2.1

C2000: Coalición 2000
CAP: Coalición Alianza Popular
CPU: Coalición Pueblo Unido
UNIF: Coalición Unificación Nacional
ML: Movimiento Libertario
PAC: Partido Acción Ciudadana
PADA: Partido Acción Democrática Alajuelense
PAD: Partido Acción Democrática Popular
PAS: Partido Acción Socialista
PD: Partido Demócrata
PDC: Partido Demócrata Cristiano
PFD: Partido Fuerza Democrática
PFN: Partido Frente Nacional
PI: Partido Independiente
PLN: Partido Liberación Nacional

PP: Partido del Progreso
PPU: Partido Pueblo Unido
PR: Partido Republicano
PRC: Partido Republicano Calderonista
PRD: Partido Renovación Democrática
PS: Partido Socialista
PSD: Partido Social Demócrata
PT: Partido de los Trabajadores
PUN: Partido Unión Nacional
PU: Partido Unificación Nacional
PUN: Partido Unión Nacional
PUP: Partido Unión Popular
PUSC: Partido Unidad Social Cristiana
PVP: Partido Vanguardia Popular
CU: Coalición Unidad

Notes: (1) Chart includes only those parties and events deemed relevant for the understanding of the text. The parties' place in the chart does not reflect their position in the ideological spectrum.
Sources: See Appendix

monious disputes, leaving its components to languish electorally until today. Outside the Left, other minor parties – normally regional and non-ideological – have played a largely insignificant role since 1948.

Graph 2.1 provides a sketch of the transformations undergone by the main political forces in the Costa Rican party system since the 1948 civil war.

Thus, since 1983 the Costa Rican party system has come to be dominated by two large, catch-all parties, loosely described as social-democratic (PLN) and christian-democratic (PUSC). The strongly bipolar electoral competition and the primarily historic nature of the basic cleavage have combined to blur the ideological identity of each party and the differences between them. As befits most two-party systems, both parties have long behaved as flexible coalitions of groups with diverse interests and ideological positions, located, roughly speaking, on the centre-left (PLN) and the centre-right (PUSC) of the ideological spectrum.

Moreover, the experience of the last fifty years has also diluted each party's reliance on its historic bases of social support. Traditionally, the stronger endorsement of the PLN amongst the middle classes and entrepreneurial sectors linked to industrialisation contrasted with the support for its rivals amongst traditional higher income sectors and poor strata left out by the PLN policies or faithful to Calderón-Guardia's legacy of social reform.[17] Recently, however, the sources of support of both parties have overlapped, with the PLN having only a slightly more educated and rural constituency than that of the PUSC. This is shown in Table 2.3.

As in Kirchheimer's[18] seminal characterisation, the catch-all quality of the PLN and the PUSC can also be seen in their strong electoral orientation. Both parties boast a complex permanent structure, partly imposed by Articles 60–1 of the Electoral Code – which put a national assembly and a three-member executive committee atop each party – and partly devised by the parties' own internal regu-

Table 2.3: *Analysis of support for major parties in Costa Rica, 1997 (% of supporters)*

| Category | | | PLN | PUSC |
|---|---|---|---|---|
| A | Gender | Male | 50 | 49 |
| | | Female | 50 | 51 |
| B | Residence | Metropolitan Area (1) | 47 | 49 |
| | | Rest of the country | 53 | 51 |
| C | Education | None / Primary | 48 | 52 |
| | | Secondary | 36 | 34 |
| | | Higher | 16 | 14 |
| D | Income (2) | Lower | 36 | 36 |
| | | Middle | 24 | 24 |
| | | Higher | 21 | 19 |
| | | n.a. | 19 | 21 |

Notes: (1) The Metropolitan Area comprises the capital city, San José, and the main cities in the Central Valley. (2) Lower income: <US$271(65,000 CR¢); Middle income: US$271-417 (100,000 CR¢); Higher income: >US$417. In October 1997: 239.67 CR¢ = 1 US$.
Sources: See Appendix.

lations. Through the latter, both groups have established powerful political directorates and a variety of ancillary organisations, notably youth and women movements. However, these formal structures remain largely dormant and under-funded up until the official start of the election campaign. Prior to the latter they are frequently swept aside by the parallel unofficial organisations established by the parties' presidential pre-candidates.

Once the nomination process has run its course, however, both parties become highly centralised and sophisticated electoral machines controlled by the presidential candidate and his closest advisors. The centralisation of electoral activities – a result of the country's small size and population, its presidential regime and, crucially, its electoral system – is a basic difference between electoral dynamics in Costa Rica and Uruguay and, consequently, between political finance practices in both countries.

## Political finance rules and state funding

For most of Costa Rica's democratic life, political finance rules have been defined by an enduring combination of features. The latter range from a nearly exclusive focus on the electoral activities of parties to a liberal approach towards the regulation of private sources of funding, electoral expenditures and financial transparency. However, it is the long-term presence of direct public subventions to parties that stands at the centre of the country's approach towards political finance.

Indeed, the idea that the state should economically support parties was accepted early and peacefully in Costa Rica. In 1956 Costa Rica became only the second country in the world, after Uruguay, to establish a direct subsidisation scheme for parties.[19] The roots of the state funding system, however, can be traced much further back. Already in 1910, the winning party issued an open letter addressed to all public servants, requesting their authorisation to deduct part of their salaries in order to cancel the party's debt after the election.[20] Over time, the practice of assessing public employees became a standard procedure in the system. The consent requested from the public servant was largely a formality. In practice, the 'payment of the political debt' (*pago de la deuda política*), as the mechanism came to be known, was simply a tax levied on public employees and, as such, a state subsidy to the winning party. Bar an interruption between 1928 and 1936, this system remained unchanged until 1948.

The framers of the 1949 Constitution did away with the routine 'macing' of public employees as part of the drive to establish an autonomous civil service. A sober text for Article 96 was thus sanctioned: 'The State will not do or permit any deduction to the salaries of public servants with the purpose of cancelling political debts'. The majority of the Constituent Assembly declined to create a state funding scheme to substitute for the old system. In the end, the plain formula approved by the Constituent Assembly left many of its members unsatisfied. For some, particularly the Social Democrats, it was a missed opportunity to liberate the parties from the control of wealthy contributors. For others, particularly the most conservative members of the PUN, the clause had a dangerous omission: it did not explicitly forbid the use of state resources other than the salaries of employees to fund political parties.

This omission did not go unnoticed for long, even by the groups that had warned against it. In 1950 a congressional majority authorised the payment of the debts accumulated by the ruling PUN with a budget appropriation, a practice that would be repeated four years later by the PLN.[21] In the latter case, however, the PLN extended the reimbursement to two defeated parties, allocating the funds according to their 1953 electoral results. In doing so, the 1954 laws introduced, de facto, a general system of subvention for parties.

The 1956 constitutional reform formalised the scheme and gave it a set of features that, with few changes, remains valid today:
a) The subsidy was conceived as a post-election reimbursement of expenses for parties. Neither candidates, nor pre-candidates, were granted direct access to public funds.
b) In order to have access to it, parties had to field candidates at the national or provincial level and also to overcome a certain threshold, initially fixed at 10 per cent of the vote.
c) The subsidy would be allocated proportionally amongst the parties that fulfilled those requisites. In order to claim their subsidy, however, eligible parties were required to document their expenditures before the General Comptroller of the Republic (CGR).
d) The TSE was bestowed with the power to define the sum of the subsidy, but the latter could not exceed 2 per cent of the average of national budgets in the

three years prior to the election.

The reasons invoked to justify the enactment of the subsidy prefigured those that would later underpin similar debates elsewhere: the subvention was needed – it was said – in order to offset the political influence exerted by large private contributors, and create a level playing field for all candidates and parties, regardless of their economic means. Neither these arguments, nor the features given to the subsidy, were the subject of a significant discussion either in Congress or the press.[22] This was not entirely surprising. By creating a purely post-electoral subsidy, the Assembly was bowing to the long tradition that had been established since the beginning of the century: it was simply the way in which things had always been done. Preserving this model and tying it to a neutral distribution of funds derived from the electoral result was an obvious way to render the approval of the subsidy as uncontroversial as possible. At the same time, by forcing parties to document their expenditures and leaving the amount-definition procedure in the hands of the respected TSE, the sponsors of the bill sought to increase its legitimacy before public opinion. Even the system's most conspicuous feature, the high access threshold, aimed at discouraging the formation of new parties, was not extraordinary for a system that had consciously moved towards electoral bipolarity in 1936.

Overall, the traits of the system look remarkably restrained. This is slightly puzzling since in 1956 the PLN enjoyed a large legislative majority and could have arranged the subvention system virtually at will. This apparent paradox may be explained by the combined effect of institutional inertia and, above all, by the PLN's need to attract as little criticism as possible in formalising the subsidy. The PLN's instrumental reasoning was less oriented towards devising a grossly favourable state funding scheme than to making sure that a subvention of some kind became entrenched in the rules.

By incorporating the subvention in the constitution, the 1956 reform eliminated the uncertainty from the system. Since constitutional norms need a two-thirds legislative majority in order to be reformed, it would be very difficult for any party to do away with the subvention in the future. Protecting the subsidy system was crucial for the PLN, whose nascent structure lacked both a large pool of active militants and the support of traditionally powerful economic sectors, which had already moved to the opposition. The PLN feared not just that it could end up depending on the whim of its opponents if it failed to win the elections, but also that, without stable rules, the subvention could lose all legitimacy and self-destruct through its spiralling costs.[23] The exceptionally generous subvention approved in 1954 had alarmed even the PLN, which had sponsored the 1954 bills and was now sponsoring the constitutional amendment.[24] In the event, the 1956 constitutional bill was approved virtually unanimously.[25]

The subsidy system created by the 1956 reform remained stable until 1971, when it underwent its first and crucial transformation: the introduction of pre-election financing for parties.[26] In the future, parties would receive 70 per cent of the subvention as a pre-election loan. The funds would be allocated according to the previous electoral result and only to those parties that had obtained more than 10 per cent of the votes. Parties had to guarantee the loan and pay it back with their eventual post-election subsidy.

Unlike the 1956 bill, the 1971 reform proved extraordinarily controversial. It unleashed a loud debate in which the PLN and the *calderonista* deputies of the PU supported the project against opposition from conservative sectors of the PU and the press.[27] For its sponsors, by allowing the state to provide parties with a steady flow of resources during the campaign, the project was a decisive step to free the parties from the influence of moneylenders. For the critics, by allocating the state funds according to the electoral past, the project was merely a spurious attempt to perpetuate the electoral success of the main parties and prevent the emergence of new political forces. From their perspective, the inescapable product of the amendment would be a frozen two-party system.

The system of pre-electoral financing was eventually enacted, but it never recovered from the heated exchanges that surrounded its introduction. In spite of a subsequent constitutional amendment that lowered the subsidy threshold to 5 per cent of the votes,[28] over the next two decades the 1971 reform became a prime target for the frustration of minor parties, sidelined by the system's inexorable move towards a two-party format. The explosive growth of the subsidy's nominal amount created the widespread perception that the rules had enshrined a protection for the two main parties, which consistently reaped the lion's share of the subvention. For many critics, the connection between pre-electoral financing and the consolidation of a two-party system was too obvious to be missed. Moreover, the cumbersome practical details of the system came to be viewed as a source of private gain and outright corruption within the parties. Not surprisingly, opinion poll figures released in 1988 showed 73 per cent of the Costa Rican public against pre-election financing of parties by the state.[29]

In spite of public hostility, a package of reforms approved by both major parties in 1988 reinforced the scheme by turning the provision of pre-electoral funds into a full-fledged permanent subvention.[30] This step was defended as a way to prevent the post-election lethargy of party structures, and therefore as an instrument to further the institutionalisation of the latter. However, the 1988 reform was never implemented. For then, when the consolidation of the state funding system looked complete, the courts intervened.

In 1991, the newly created Constitutional Court struck down the system of pre-electoral financing and most of the amendments made to it in 1988. Though the Court's decision was based on the procedural defects of the 1971 constitutional reform, the judges issued a stern rebuke to the principles of the system, warning that any future attempt to re-introduce pre-electoral financing could not solely rely on past results to allocate the funds.[31] The decision thus brought the state funding scheme back to its purely post-electoral nature and, in general, to the rules enacted in 1956.[32] The mechanism of pre-electoral state financing has not been re-enacted since.[33]

In 1997 and 2001 the state funding system underwent more transformations.

Table 2.4: *State funding to parties in Costa Rica. Quantitative evolution, 1953–2002*

| Election | Nominal amount in CR colones (millions) | Nominal growth (%) | Amount in US$ of 1995 (millions) | Real growth (%) | Subsidy per registered voter (US$ of 1995) | Real growth per registered voter (%) |
|---|---|---|---|---|---|---|
| 1953 | 9.9 | -- | 6.1 | -- | 20.7 | -- |
| 1958 | 5.4 | -46 | 3.1 | -49 | 8.7 | -58 |
| 1962 | 6.9 | +28 | 3.9 | +26 | 8.1 | -7 |
| 1966 | 10.1 | +46 | 5.5 | +41 | 9.9 | +22 |
| 1970 | 12.9 | +28 | 5.8 | +5 | 8.6 | -13 |
| 1974 | 22.3 | +73 | 5.5 | -5 | 6.3 | -27 |
| 1978 (1) | 77.7 | +248 | 13.1 | +138 | 12.4 | +97 |
| 1982 | 97.7 | +26 | 4.9 | -63 | 3.9 | -69 |
| 1986 (1) | 464.0 | +375 | 12.2 | +149 | 8.2 | +110 |
| 1990 | 943.8 | +103 | 12.6 | +3 | 7.5 | -9 |
| 1994 | 1982.7 | +110 | 13.6 | +8 | 7.2 | -4 |
| 1998 | 3065.3 | +55 | 11.5 | -15 | 5.6 | -22 |
| 2002 (2) | 4915.1 | +60 | 12.8 | +11 | 5.6 | 0 |

Notes: (1) In 1978 and 1986, subsidy figures include pre-election advances paid to parties that later failed to qualify for public reimbursement. Recipients were supposed to repay the funds, but in most cases never did, adding to the state's net outlays. Excluding these funds, the subsidy amounts to US$9.7 m. in 1978 and US$11.6 m in 1986. (2) Figures refer to allocated, rather than actually disbursed funds.
Sources: See Appendix.

Broad legislative agreements led to two consecutive constitutional reforms that lowered the amount of the subsidy to 0.1 per cent of GDP of the year before the pre-election year, a figure trumpeted as much lower than the 2 per cent of the government budget that had been the norm since 1956. The 1997 amendment also reduced further the state funding threshold to 4 per cent of the vote or one parliamentary seat.[34]

Both recent reductions in the amount of state funding responded to a long-term perception that state funding had grown exponentially and reached disproportionate sums. This perception, a recurrent theme in the press since the early 1960s, was indeed at the core of the criticism that held pre-electoral financing directly responsible for the consolidation of a two-party system in Costa Rica. However, Table 2.4 points towards a more complex reality.

The table suggests that the perception of disproportionate growth in state funding is, largely, an illusion derived from the evolution of nominal sums. When the sums are converted into constant currency, the subsidy's growth – though still sizeable – becomes much more moderate and unstable. But it is the evolution of the subsidy per voter that is striking. A large fall in 1958, in the wake of the enactment of the current system, was followed by a secular *descent* in the subsidy, even before the 1997 and 2001 amendments. Excluding the outlying figure of 1953, the subvention per voter has shown limited variance around an average of US$7.7

Table 2.5: *Key features of political finance system in Costa Rica*

| Policy instrument | | Details | Enforcement | Year |
|---|---|---|---|---|
| Input controls | Private funding controls | Foreign: Banned, except for party research and training | Uncertain | 1996 |
| | | Nationals: Limited (45 times the minimum wage per four years. Currently US$35,000 approx.) | Uncertain | 1996 |
| | Direct Subsidies | Recipient: Parties | Yes | 1956 |
| | | Timing: Post-electoral reimbursement | Yes | 1956 |
| | | Threshold: 4% of the votes or 1 seat in the Assembly | Yes | 1997 |
| | | Allocation: Proportional to votes | Yes | 1956 |
| | | Amount definition procedure: Fixed by the Constitution at 0.1% of GDP two years before the election | Yes | 2001 |
| | Indirect Subsidies | Institutional support for parties in Parliament | -- | -- |
| Output controls | General exp. ceilings | No | -- | -- |
| | Media advertising ceilings | No. (However, only a limited amount of advertising is to be covered with public funds.) | -- | (1988) |
| | Duration official campaign | Three-and-one-half months (Oct. 1–first Sunday of February, with an interruption between Dec. 16–Jan. 1) | No | 1988 |
| Transparency rules | Contributions | Parties: Report all contributions quarterly to the TSE and monthly during the official campaign | Uncertain | 1996 |
| | | Presidential pre-candidates: Report all contributions to the party's Treasurer | Uncertain | 2001 |
| | Expenditures | Parties: Eligible parties for subsidy must document their expenditures to the CGR after the election | Yes | 1950 |

(US$ of 1995).[35] The figures also show that whatever its intentions, the 1997 and 2001 constitutional amendments entailed, in fact, a modest reduction of the subvention, both in constant and per voter terms.

If the evolution of state funding in Costa Rica has been long and sinuous, that of other components of the political finance system has been rather uneventful. Other than institutional support for the parties in Congress, indirect state subsidies have been virtually non-existent.[36] Moreover, private sources of funding remained totally unregulated until 1996. Since then, foreign contributions have been banned – except those directed towards the strengthening of the parties' research and training capabilities – and private donations have been capped and made public.[37] The limit of the latter has been tied to changes in the minimum wage and currently stands at approximately US$35,000 per donor throughout a four-year period.

Currently, no limits to electoral expenditure are in place. Though the duration of the official campaign has been shortened to three-and-one-half months, in practice, pre-candidates and parties start their electoral expenditures long before that.[38] The 1988 reform set limits to media advertising by political parties but no sanction was attached to non-compliance. The state, however, will not reimburse a long list of expenses, including those advertising expenditures that flaunt the limits set by the Electoral Code.[39]

Financial transparency rules for parties have been traditionally weak. Since 1950 they were limited to the obligation imposed by the subsidy rules on eligible parties of fully documenting their expenses before the CGR if they were to receive state funds after the election.[40] This mechanism has only allowed a measure of control over the nature of electoral expenditures and the way subsidies are invested. Since 1996, however, all parties have been obliged to submit before the TSE a quarterly report (monthly during the official campaign) with all the contributions received, duly identified. A later ruling by the TSE extended these transparency rules to presidential pre-candidates.[41] Yet, as we will see in the next chapter, the enforcement by the TSE of this latter batch of controls remains uncertain at best.

Table 2.5 sums up the main traits of the Costa Rican political finance system.


## URUGUAY

If Costa Rica's political institutions have attracted limited attention from researchers, Uruguay's have long fascinated social scientists, an allure only heightened by the country's recent authoritarian experience and current democratic revival. The longevity of its democratic institutions, the centrality of its parties, and the bewildering complexity of its party system, have all endowed Uruguay's political life with a richness unparalleled in Latin America. Though the country retains most of the basic institutional traits sketched in its early democratic life – its presidential regime, its peculiar electoral system, and its longstanding, if overlooked, state funding scheme – the transformation undergone by its political system has been remarkable. The 1996 comprehensive electoral reform, which introduced open presidential primaries and a presidential run-off, is merely the last of a long list of far-reaching institutional reforms, which even include experiments with a collegiate executive. More importantly, the country's secular two-party system has experienced momentous changes in its format, dynamics and ideological profile in the past four decades. Amidst change, however, Uruguay's political life, strongly shaped, as we will see, by its unique system of preferential voting, remains as distinctive as ever.


### Democratic consolidation, political regime and electoral system

Branded a *partidocracia* by some authors,[42] Uruguay's political evolution is inextricably linked to the long history of its political parties.[43] In Uruguay, the secular weakness of the traditional power-constellation in Latin America – oligarchy, military and Church – and the belated constitution of viable state institutions helped to confer on parties a central social and political role.

Born in the wake of independence as little more than armed bands, the Colorado Party (PC) and the Blanco Party (later National Party, PN), went on to become more than conventional parties.[44] Sharing a liberal matrix, they indeed became parallel political traditions that cut across social classes and ideological positions. Their complex interaction made possible, as much as it impeded for a long time, the constitution of a democratic polity in Uruguay. If, on the one hand, the precocious politicisation of the Uruguayan population, and the early adoption of elections and political negotiation mores bear the mark of both traditional parties, on the other, the country's belated construction of statehood and nationhood are closely related to the entrenchment of partisan identities. Throughout the nineteenth century neither group was able to achieve a permanent political settlement that secured fair electoral practices, effective guarantees for the opposition and, crucially, the monopoly of legitimate coercion. Up until the dawn of the twentieth century, Uruguay's political history was a singularly turbulent one, in which two semi-sovereign entities – one, *Colorada*, based in Montevideo, one, *Blanca*, based in the hinterland – shifted between political stalemate and military conflict, often supported by complex international alliances. As in the case of Costa Rica, the first seventy years of Uruguayan political history may be summed up in very dire terms:

An inventory of seventy years of history shows: four or perhaps more visible foreign interventions, thirty-seven revolutions, three mutinies, two international wars, two tyrannies and two dictatorships. In those seventy years there were eighteen presidents, four dictators, one Triumvirate, one Council of State and your half dozen small indefinable interregnums. Of those eighteen presidents only eight completed their mandate. The other ten either fell to revolution or rose through insurrection.[45]

The election of the *Colorado* José Batlle y Ordóñez as president in 1903 marked a crucial departure from the past.[46] In 1904 the government crushed what would be the last rebellion launched by the *Blancos* and imposed the territorial unification of the republic. This opened the way to the final electoralisation of Uruguayan politics, the modernisation of parties and the consolidation of a pluralistic democracy. By 1919, a new constitution had established male universal suffrage and various electoral guarantees long demanded by the *Blanco* opposition, chiefly the secret vote and a pure form of proportional representation. This was followed, in 1925, by the creation of the Electoral Court (CE), a neutral body entrusted with the organisation of elections.[47] Moreover, between 1910 and 1942, both traditional parties developed complex electoral legislation, primarily aimed at protecting their external electoral unity in the face of significant internal diversity.

These, however, were hardly the only consequences of Batlle's triumph. Riding on his undisputed power after 1904 and aided by a favourable climate for Uruguayan exports, Batlle embarked on a long-range programme of social and economic reform. The legacy of his two administrations (1903–7 and 1911–5) is exceptionally broad and deep. Though the seeds of a dominant and autonomous state had already been planted in Uruguay in the 1870s, Batlle presided over an extraordinary expansion of the role and scope of the public sector. This was done through the creation of state monopolies across the economy as much as by establishing a wide welfare network and implanting the notion of the state as the natural moderator of class conflicts. The defence of state activism in the quest for social equity, a primary tenet of the *batllista* ideology, still remains a central feature of the Uruguayan identity.

Both the electoralisation of politics and the rapid growth of the state had crucial consequences for both traditional parties. Over time, a transversal division of the swelling state apparatus between *Colorados* and *Blancos* replaced the territorial divide of the nineteenth century.[48] The first sign of this phenomenon was the constitutional settlement of 1919, which enshrined numerous public institutions established by Batlle and created a dual executive with a president and a collegiate National Administration Council (CNA). The opposition had a minority participation in the latter. The dual structure was a compromise between Batlle and his adversaries, reluctant to accept one of Batlle's most controversial proposals: the adoption of a purely collegiate executive modelled upon the Swiss experience. Though government co-participation was not a new phenomenon in Uruguay – dating as far back as 1872 – the principles embodied by the semi-collective executive were nonetheless remarkable. Henceforth, and regardless of the electoral result, neither *Colorados* nor *Blancos* would be completely out of power, blurring in effect the dividing line between government and opposition. Moreover, the principle of proportional co-participation in the executive soon begot the proportional division of the entire public sector, which became thoroughly colonised by the parties. Over time, the demand and delivery of public resources became subject to a strictly political-electoral logic. Clientelism became the sap of life for the structures of both traditional parties and their numerous internal fractions.

Indeed, the extreme stability of the party system, in which both parties reigned supreme, albeit under the PC's continuous electoral supremacy,[50] moved the locus of political conflicts to the internal arena of each party, where widely divergent fractions co-existed. Pacts and counter-pacts, more often than not between fractions of both parties against their internal enemies, marked the evolution of electoral rules and co-participation practices. In the baroque world of Uruguayan politics, cross-party fractional alliances were not only the stuff of democratic politics, but of anti-democratic politics as well. In 1933, one such alliance supported the first breakdown of democracy in Uruguay in the twentieth century. Then, a coup led by conservative sectors of both parties paved the way for a decade of mild authoritarian rule and political exclusion of various sectors, notably directed against *batllismo*.

Neither the 1933 breakdown, nor the 1942 democratic restoration, nor the enactment of semi-parliamentary constitutions in 1934 and 1942 changed, however, the basic features of the Uruguayan political system: its electoral duopoly, the internal fractionalisation of its parties, and the entrenchment of the latter in the state. When in 1952 yet another cross-party alliance finally enacted Batlle's proposal of a collegiate executive and formalised the proportional distribution of public posts, it merely fastened a set of political practices that had come to be identified with the country's democracy and prosperity of the previous fifty years. As soon became evident, however, these practices, which played a crucial part in the consolidation of democracy in the first half of the twentieth century, were unable to process the political and economic reforms that the country came to require after 1950.

The adoption of the 1952 constitution coincided with the first signs of an economic downturn in Uruguay that, by the end of the 1950s, had turned into virtual stagnation.[51] The economic malaise was accompanied by a growing political restlessness that the cumbersome decision-making processes of the Uruguayan democracy were ill equipped to quell. Despite successive government changes – including a remarkable one in 1958, when the PN gained control of the presidency for the first time in ninety three years – by the mid-1960s the political and economic situation had worsened significantly. The collegiate executive was blamed for the stalemate, and was scrapped by a new constitution in 1966. Though the latter re-floated some of the semi-parliamentary features of the 1934 and 1942 constitutions, it created, in effect, the strongest presidency since 1919, not bereft of authoritarian overtones.[52]

A downward spiral towards democratic breakdown followed. Growing social tension, loss of credibility across the political system, and the perception of military and electoral threat from the Left[53] were met by increasingly authoritarian responses. In 1973, amidst political stasis and gradual encroachment of the armed forces on non-military functions, Uruguayan democracy collapsed.

A reactionary military government remained in power until the end of 1984. The process of recovery of Uruguayan democracy provided, however, a startling proof of the resilience of democratic and partisan identities in the country. Though the military regime outlawed and repressed all political organisations, it explicitly refused to decree the permanent dissolution of the traditional parties in 1976. This surprising concession was followed in 1980 by its decision to hold a referendum in order to legitimise the constitutional blueprint of a permanent civil-military regime. The referendum, held in a climate of intimidation of the opposition, resulted in an unexpected defeat for the regime.[54]

The latter paved the way for a protracted process of negotiation between military and political elites.[55] With few minor exceptions, the negotiation ended in the restoration of all the elements of the pre-coup political system. It included the same parties – including the leftist coalition Broad Front (FA), which had broken the electoral duopoly in 1971 – and even, largely, the same political leadership. It also reinstated the 1966 constitution, which remains in operation today. The constitution allows the bicameral legislature to censure and remove ministers, though risking presidential retaliation through the dissolution of parliament and the calling of new parliamentary elections (Article 148). The president, popularly elected for five years and armed with a vast array of discretionary powers (Article 168), cannot be removed by parliament. In fact, the semi-parliamentary features of the current constitution have gone virtually unused. As has been suggested by most analysts, in practice Uruguay behaves today as a pure presidential system.[56]

Since 1984, Uruguay has celebrated four free and fair general elections. Though the PC and the PN retain their electoral supremacy, the sustained ascent of the FA since the transition has significantly changed the country's political landscape.[57] Under different guises and modalities, coalition governments of both traditional parties have ruled the country for much of the post-transition period. The return of Uruguay's long tradition of political moderation and skilful negotiation has re-created the country's secular political stability. Today, little dispute remains as to the solidity of Uruguay's restored democratic institutions.[58]

If Uruguay's political regime underwent significant mutations during the twentieth century – from the various experiments with the presidency to the two authoritarian episodes – the main lines of its electoral system were laid down early in the century and remained stable for a long time. For much of the century, the following features defined the Uruguayan electoral system:

a) Plurality formula for the presidential election.
b) 'Integral' proportional representation formula for congressional elections. Based on a modified version of the D'Hondt method, the 'integral' quality of PR referred not only to its purity, but also to its use across the different levels of the party system: between parties, between sectors within parties, and even within those sectors.[59] The formula was applied both to the election of the thirty-member Senate – held in a single, nationwide district – and, in a more complex fashion, to that of the ninety-nine members of the Chamber of Representatives (ChR), elected in nineteen departmental constituencies.
c) Double Simultaneous Voting (DSV). This system of preferential voting allowed voters to simultaneously select a party as well as a specific sector within it.
d) Closed lists.
e) Vertical processes of candidate selection.
f) Absolute concurrence of all elections. This implied not only their simultaneity but also the impossibility of split voting: voters were forced to select the same party at all electoral levels.

All these traits were in place in 1942, though DSV had been introduced as far back as 1910 and most of the others had already been part of the 1919 constitution. Some aspects of the system deserve particular attention. First, the rules showed the same combination of plurality and proportional representation already seen in the Costa Rican case. However, though the Uruguayan variant of PR yielded some of the most proportional results in the world,[60] the impossibility of splitting the vote made the spillover effects of plurality not merely likely, as in Costa Rica, but mandatory. The distribution of votes between parties in the presidential election was thus automatically transmitted to Congress and local governments. It is striking that this restrictive electoral system could not prevent the transformation of the Uruguayan party system from its secular two-party format.

Secondly, contrary to the Costa Rican experience, the closed lists and vertical candidate selection processes were always relatively unimportant in Uruguay, due to the presence of DSV. Indeed, the latter became the defining feature of the entire system. It implied, essentially, simultaneous primary and presidential elections, with the candidate who obtained the most votes from the party that received the most votes becoming president. However, the *Ley de Lemas*, as the mechanism came to be known, entailed a complex electoral pyramid whereby multiple party fractions could compete with each other at a given level while pooling their votes at a higher level. Each party or *lema* could be divided in several *sub-lemas* supporting separate presidential candidates; a *sub-lema* could in turn group various competing lists of candidates for the Senate, each of which could be supported by multiple rival tickets for the ChR and even more lists at the local level. By choosing an option at the lowest level, the voter was in fact selecting an electoral alliance that cut the political system from top to bottom. Each vote was, thus, a *multiple* simultaneous choice. Furthermore, the mechanism was complemented by detailed legislation regulating the process of vote accumulation within parties. This legislation was repeatedly manipulated to deny the benefits of pooling to specific political sectors.

As we will see below, the use of DSV had profound effects on the Uruguayan party system. By allowing the parties' internal disputes to be resolved by the national electorate, DSV diluted the authority of their national leaders and the likelihood of break-ups. Since it was coupled with an extreme form of PR, DSV also made possible – if not actively stimulated – the fractionalisation of parties and an intra-party competition at least as important as the national inter-party competition.

Though the system increased the choices available to voters, it also complicated enormously their task and rendered unpredictable the outcome of their suffrage. Very often, voters had to watch in resignation how their votes, cast, say, for a progressive politician, actually helped to elect a conservative candidate of the same party by virtue of the accumulation mechanism. Moreover, during the 1960s the system saw the proliferation of 'electoral cooperatives', accumulation agreements between disparate lists of congressional candidates that were often unknown to the public. Juan V. Chiarino, an Uruguayan politician, summed up the system's consequences for the electors with a fine touch of irony: 'In Uruguay the vote is so secret, that not even the voter knows who he is voting for'.[61]

Some of the most intricate aspects of this electoral system were reformed in 1996, when a constitutional amendment introduced several key changes to it:

a) The plurality formula for the presidential election was abandoned in favour of a majority formula with *ballotage*. In the absence of an absolute majority in the first round, the two candidates with most votes advance to the second round, to be held one month later (Article 151).

b) DSV was eliminated in the presidential election, where parties were forced to field a single candidate (Article 151). DSV was kept, however, for congressional and local elections.

c) Open presidential primaries were made mandatory for all parties. The parties'

Table 2.6: *Key features of political regime and electoral system in Uruguay*

| Regime features | Type of regime | | Presidential (with some semi-parliamentary features) | |
|---|---|---|---|---|
| | Assembly structure | | Bicameral (Senate, thirty members + Vice-President)/Chamber of Representatives, ninety-nine members) | |
| Electoral system | Presidential election | | ------------------ | (1942–1996) | (1996–) |
| | | | District | One, nation-wide | |
| | | | Forms of candidacy and vote | Multiple candidates per party allowed | One candidate per party |
| | | | Formula | Plurality | Majority, with ballotage |
| | | | Re-election | Yes (not consecutively) | |
| | | | Candidate selection process | As prescribed by each party fraction | Open primaries |
| | Legislative election | Senate | District | One, nationwide | |
| | | | Forms of candidacy and vote | Closed lists. Multiple lists per party allowed. DSV applied. Accumulation alliances allowed | |
| | | | Formula | PR (D'Hondt modified) | |
| | | | Re-election | Yes | |
| | | | Candidate selection process | As prescribed by each party fraction. Not open | |
| | | Chamber of Representatives | Districts | 19 multi-member (Mean magnitude 5.21, but Montevideo = 44 [1999]) | |
| | | | Forms of candidacy and vote | Closed lists. Multiple lists per party allowed. DSV applied. Accumulation alliances allowed | Closed lists. Multiple lists per party allowed. DSV applied. Accumulation allianced banned |
| | | | Formula | PR (D'Hondt modified) | |
| | | | Re-election | Yes | |
| | | | Candidate selection process | As prescribed by each party fraction. Not open. | |
| | Election cycle | | | Concurrent every five years (four years before 1966). Vote-splitting between parties not allowed. | Presidential first round and congressional election are concurrent every five years (vote-splitting between parties not allowed). Presidential run-off one month after first round. Local elections six and one-half months after first round. |

primaries shall take place simultaneously six months before the presidential first round (Article 77.12 and Transitory Article W).

d) Electoral concurrence was partially broken. Congressional elections remain concurrent with the presidential first round, but local elections were separated in time (Article 77.9).

e) The formation of accumulation alliances or 'electoral cooperatives' between lists of candidates for the lower chamber was eliminated (Article 88). It is still allowed at the Senate level.

The reform, initially supported and later bitterly opposed by the Left, was approved by a narrow margin in a plebiscite held in December 1996. So far it has been applied only once, during the 1999–2000 electoral cycle.

Table 2.6 summarises the main traits of the political regime, as well as the previous (1942–96) and current (1996–) electoral systems in Uruguay.

**Party system**

As suggested above, Uruguay boasts some of the oldest parties in the world. The extreme resilience of the core components of its party system, the PC and the PN, which continue to rule the country after nearly 170 years, does not obscure, however, the momentous changes undergone by the system in the last half a century. Uruguay has gradually moved away from its secular two-party format and into a multi-party format in which the FA, a relative newcomer, has an increasingly important participation. Table 2.7 summarises Uruguay's general election results since 1942.

Table 2.7 displays the long itinerary of the transformation of the Uruguayan party system, which involved more than just the transit from a two-party to a multi-party format. To begin with, the country's secular two-party system was qualified, as noted above, by the PC's continuous electoral supremacy. The demise of the PC's predominance and the emergence of a truly competitive two-party system after the watershed 1958 election eased, but did not eliminate, the PC's long-term grip on the presidency. By showing the PC as the winner of nine out of twelve presidential elections since 1942, including five of the last six, Table 2.7 points towards a basic fact of Uruguayan political life: the PC has been *the* party of government in Uruguay. Though constrained by various co-participation schemes since the nineteenth century, the PC has controlled the presidency for 115 out of the last 139 years.

If the ushering in of a competitive two-party system in 1958 was already an important change, the real transformation of the party system did not arrive until 1971, when the FA broke the secular electoral duopoly, claiming nearly one-fifth of the national vote. The authoritarian interlude of 1973–85 did not reverse this change. If anything the post-transition years brought the gradual passage from the two-and-one-half party format of 1971 and 1984 to the full-fledged multi-party format exemplified by the 1989, 1994 and 1999 electoral results. Given the

Table 2.7: *Electoral results in Uruguay, 1942–99*

| Election | Party (1) | Presidential election (% votes) | Traditional parties vs. Left (% votes) | Abstention rate (%) |
|---|---|---|---|---|
| 1942 | **PC** | **57.2** | 91.7 | 33.1 |
| | PN | 22.8 | | |
| | Independent National Party (PNIU) (2) | 11.7 | | |
| | Communist Party (COM) | 2.5 | 4.1 | |
| | Socialist Party (PS) | 1.6 | | |
| | Other | 4.3 | -- | |
| 1946 | **PC** | **47.8** | 89.6 | 34.7 |
| | PN | 32.0 | | |
| | PNIU | 9.7 | | |
| | COM | 5.0 | 5.0 | |
| | Other | 5.4 | -- | |
| 1950 | **PC** | **52.6** | 91.2 | 29.5 |
| | PN | 30.9 | | |
| | PNIU | 7.6 | | |
| | COM | 2.3 | 4.4 | |
| | PS | 2.1 | | |
| | Other | 4.4 | -- | |
| 1954 | **PC** | **50.6** | 89.5 | 32.1 |
| | PN | 35.2 | | |
| | PNIU | 3.7 | | |
| | COM | 2.2 | 5.4 | |
| | PS | 3.2 | | |
| | Other | 5.0 | -- | |
| 1958 | PC | 37.7 | 87.6 | 28.7 |
| | **PN** | **49.9** | | |
| | COM | 2.6 | 6.1 | |
| | PS | 3.5 | | |
| | Other | 6.2 | -- | |
| 1962 | PC | 44.4 | 91.0 | 23.4 |
| | **PN** | **46.6** | | |
| | Left Liberation Front (FIDEL) (3) | 3.6 | 5.9 | |
| | Popular Union (UP) (4) | 2.3 | | |
| | Other | 3.1 | -- | |
| 1966 | **PC** | **49.4** | 89.8 | 25.7 |
| | PN | 40.4 | | |
| | FIDEL | 5.7 | 6.6 | |
| | PS | 0.9 | | |
| | Other | 3.6 | -- | |
| 1971 | **PC** | **41.0** | 81.2 | 7.3 |
| | PN | 40.2 | | |
| | Broad Front (FA) (5) | 18.3 | 18.3 | |
| | Other | 0.5 | -- | |
| 1984 | **PC** | **41.2** | 76.2 | 14.2 |
| | PN | 35.0 | | |
| | FA | 21.3 | 21.3 | |
| | Other | 2.5 | -- | |

Table 2.7: *(Cont)*

| Election | Party (1) | Presidential election (% votes) | Traditional parties vs. Left (% votes) | Abstention rate (%) |
|----------|-----------|-------------------------------|----------------------------------------|---------------------|
| 1989 | PC | 30.3 | 69.2 | 15.1 |
| | **PN** | **38.9** | | |
| | FA | 21.2 | 30.2 | |
| | New Space Party (NE) (6) | 9.0 | | |
| | Other | 0.6 | -- | |
| 1994 | **PC** | **32.3** | 63.5 | 12.9 |
| | PN | 31.2 | | |
| | FA-Progressive Encounter (EPR) (7) | 30.6 | 35.8 | |
| | NE | 5.2 | | |
| | Other | 0.7 | -- | |
| 1999 (8) | PC | 32.8 (54.1) | 55.1 | 11.8 |
| | PN | 22.3 | | |
| | FA-EPR | 40 1 (45.9) | 44.7 | |
| | NE | 4.6 | | |
| | Other | 0.2 | -- | |

Notes: (1) Bold indicates winning party. Due to rounding, totals for each election may not add up to 100. (2) The PNIU was a dissident fraction of the PN. (3) In 1962 the Communist Party ran under the *lema* FIDEL. (4) In 1962 the PS pooled its votes with another group and ran under the *lema* UP. (5)The FA was a coalition of FIDEL, PS, UP, Christian Democrat Party (PDCU) and dissident sectors of PC and PN. In 1971 and 1984, it ran under the *lema* PDCU. (6) The NE was a breakaway group of the FA. In 1989 it ran candidates under the *lema* People's Government Party (PGP) (7) In 1994 and 1999, the FA formed a coalition with two other small political groups, called the EPR. (8) Presidential first round and congressional election results. Results of the run-off are indicated in parentheses.
Sources: See Appendix.

remarkable stability of the electoral system, at least until 1996, the Uruguayan experience of the past sixty years thus provides a cautionary note on the limits of electoral rules to determine the format of the party system.

Table 2.7 also shows that the changes in the party system in the last forty years have been all in the same direction. The impressive electoral growth of the Left since the 1960s has been accompanied by a systematic erosion of electoral support for the traditional parties, which today comprise slightly more than half of the electorate, down from around 90 per cent forty years ago. As the results of the 1999 presidential election so clearly show, this phenomenon has changed the fault-line that defines the party system. The secular divide between PC and PN has become a mere sub-cleavage, secondary to the chasm between these two parties and the FA.[62]

This is no small change. *Sui generis* as it was, the traditional cleavage was profoundly ingrained in the Uruguayan population. In its early days the divide conveyed largely the loyalties to particular regional *caudillos* and the adherence to specific international alliances in the complex post-independence politics of the River Plate basin. Later, the civil war of 1839–51 and the decade-long siege of

Montevideo by the *Blancos* fixed the features of both parties in a lasting way. The *Guerra Grande* and the siege bequeathed a geographical dimension to the divide, creating, as noted above, a PC stronghold in Montevideo and a long-term predominance of the PN in the countryside. In doing so, the siege also begot the different relation of both forces to the institutionalised power and the outside world, with the PC establishing an early and enduring identification with the state and European influence.[63] None of this amounted to a neat ideological cleavage but it was enough to sustain the separation of two political traditions with a common liberal origin. Besides the geographical divide between both parties, the traditional cleavage did not reflect any significant difference in the bases of social support for both parties. As has been observed by Angel Cocchi, 'both parties represented all groups and their composition was a transversal cut of society'.[64]

Over time, each of these twin traditions came to resemble a self-contained party system, with diverse ideological positions, conflicting leaderships and multiple internal fractions. Despite their occasional virulence and tendency to generate cross-party alliances, internal conflicts rarely led to formal schisms in both parties. Here, the importance of institutional arrangements cannot be underestimated. The combined effect of the dominant presidential election, the plurality formula in place since 1830, the use of DSV, and the sheer electoral parity of both parties – particularly in the early twentieth century – was a strong centripetal force protecting their unity.

Formal schisms were not entirely absent, however. In the early twentieth century, resistance to the dominant leadership of José Batlle y Ordóñez in the PC and Luis Alberto de Herrera in the PN was at the root of various party break-ups, invariably costly in the electoral fray. Later, the 1933 coup and the position of different sectors of both parties vis-à-vis the authoritarian experience generated much deeper and lasting divisions, particularly in the PN. Indeed, after the 1942 democratic restoration, while the PC restored its unity once more under the dominance of *batllismo*, the *Blanco* vote remained split until 1958 between the *herrerista*-dominated PN and the Independent National Party (PNIU). It should be noted that none of these schisms, not even the prolonged dissidence of the PNIU, implied a challenge to the secular cleavage. They were merely expressions of internal dissent that could be contained within the boundaries of the two-party system. By the 1960s, however, it was the legitimacy of the latter that had come to be contested by various political actors, including, crucially, several fractions of both traditional parties. In this climate, the continuity of the secular party system could no longer be guaranteed.

Thus emerged the FA in 1971: as an unprecedented coalition of all the political groupings disgruntled with the status quo. Though attempts at uniting the political Left were not unfamiliar, the new coalition was clearly bolstered by the unification of the militant Uruguayan trade-union movement in 1966 and by the 1970 electoral victory of the leftist coalition Popular Unity in Chile. The alliance, in fact, extended well beyond the traditional Left to encompass, behind a common radical programme and a single presidential candidate, a tapestry of groups with diverse origins. The coalition included, mainly, orthodox Marxist forces (the Communist and Socialist parties), the Christian Democrat Party (PDCU) and various breakaway fractions from the PC and the PN. While hardly class-based, the FA's social support came mostly from highly educated, young and Montevideo voters.[65]

After its remarkable electoral performance of 1971, the 1973 military coup came as a harsh blow to the FA. During the next eleven years the Left bore the brunt of the repression. Notwithstanding this, the authoritarian interlude provided the FA with two opportunities that proved crucial for its long-term survival. First, as Caetano and Rilla argue, the struggle against the dictatorship endowed the Left with an epic experience, not unlike the ones that had long underpinned the political traditions of *Colorados* and *Blancos*. Second, the transition negotiations, in which the Left played a key role, gave the FA a venue to prove its unequivocal loyalty to democracy, an important change in the light of its ambiguous position of 1971.[66]

The FA was able to withstand military repression, but it proved less resistant to its own internal contradictions, frozen by the dictatorship. Before the 1989 election, the coalition split along clear ideological lines: while the radical Left remained with the FA, the moderate Left abandoned the alliance. The moderates, comprising the People's Government Party (PGP) – a group of *Colorado* origin – and the PDCU, formed the New Space Party (NE), an avowedly social-democratic option, which became the fourth significant actor in the party system.

Since then, the leftist vote has remained divided. The FA has avoided new schisms and has indeed accommodated new moderate leftist groups created in the wake of the PGP's departure. In fact, before the 1994 election, the FA re-established its alliance with the small PDCU under the guise of a wider coalition, the Progressive Encounter (EPR), which also embraced a new dissident fraction from the PN.[67] While the FA nearly doubled its vote in the decade after the division, capturing the government of the pivotal Montevideo department in the process, the NE fared considerably less well. It split before the 1994 election and again in 2001, and has polled 5 per cent of the vote or less in recent elections.

Graph 2.2 summarises the main party transformations that have occurred in Uruguay since 1942. This diagram depicts only changes at the party level. Yet, as suggested above, each Uruguayan party is, in turn, host to a variety of fractions and sub-fractions, whose conflicts, alliances and competition are at least as important as those that take place at the level of *lemas*. Though the internal fractionalisation of Uruguayan parties pre-dates and probably caused the adoption of DSV in 1910, there is little doubt that, at the very least, the latter contributed to perpetuating it. Since the early twentieth century, political parties in Uruguay have been amongst the most internally divided in the world, at least on a par with other paradigmatic cases such as Italy, Japan and Colombia. If the use of other systems of intraparty preference voting has been empirically linked to high levels of party fractionalisation, the system employed in Uruguay provides especially strong incentives for the latter. Luis E. González has argued that rather than nurturing

Graph 2.2: *Party transformation in Uruguay, 1942–1999 (1)*

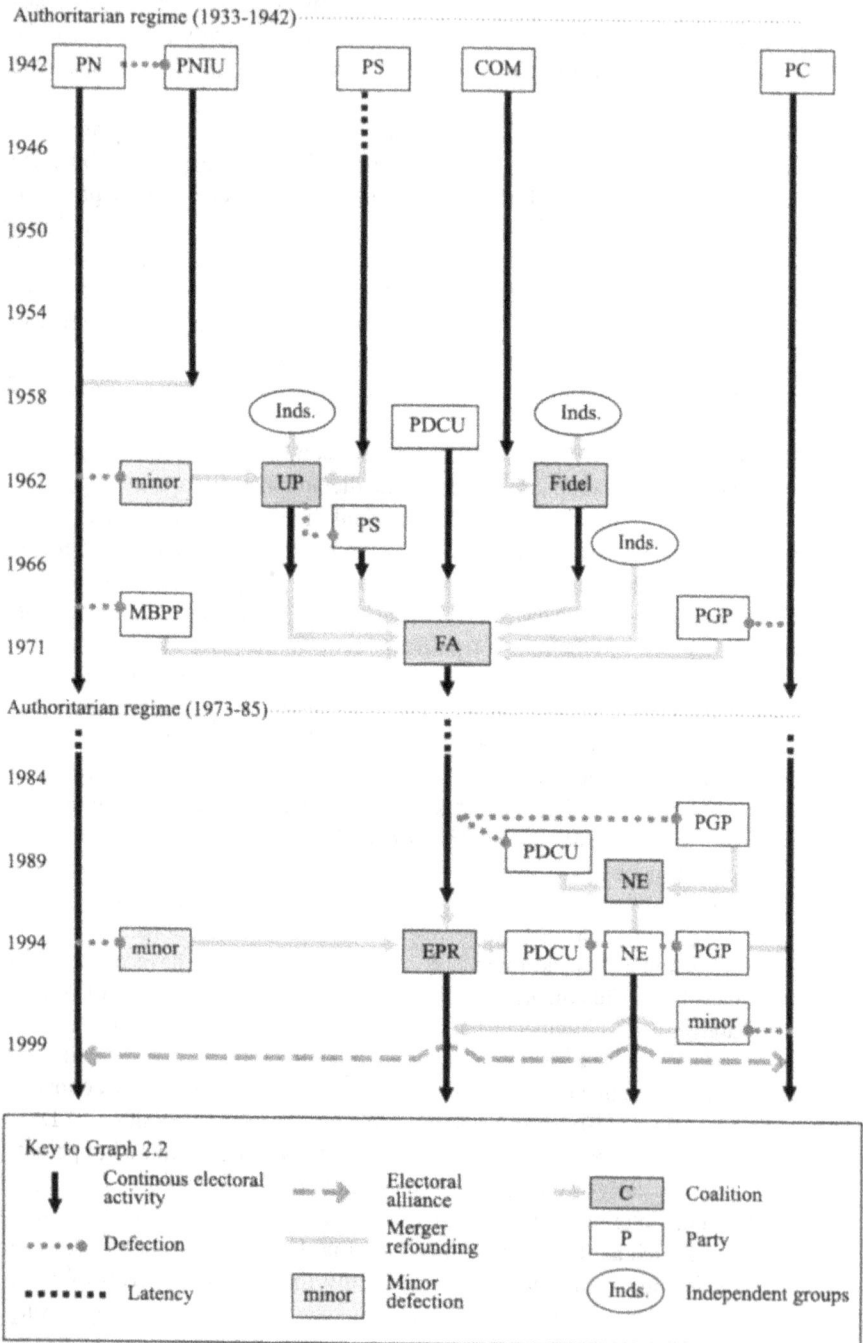

Key to Graph 2.2 *(Cont.)*

| | |
|---|---|
| COM: Partido Comunista | NE: Nuevo Espacio |
| EPR: Encuentro Progresista | PC: Partido Colorado |
| FA: Frente Amplio | PDCU: Partido Demócrata Cristiana |
| Fidel: Frente Izquierda de Liberación | PGP: Partido por el Gobierno del Pueblo |
| Inds: Independent groups | PN: Partido Nacional |
| MBPP: Movimiento Blanco Popular y Progresista | PNIU: Partido Nacional Independiente |
| Minor: Minor defections | PS: Partido Socialista |
| | UP: Unión Popular |

Notes: (1) Chart indicates only those parties and events deemed relevant for the understanding of the text. The parties' place in the chart does not reflect their position in the ideological spectrum.
Sources: See Appendix

individual rivalries, as other methods of preferential voting do, DSV fosters competition between organised *teams* that cut the political system from top to bottom.[68] Table 2.8, which reports the number of candidate lists assembled to compete in the election for the ChR, gives a hint of the organisational heterogeneity of Uruguayan parties and its evolution over time.

Intense as it is, fractionalisation does not affect Uruguayan parties uniformly. Graph 2.3 maps out the national fractions formally constituted in each party, as well as the distribution of national political posts between them according to the 1999 election.

The chart leaves little doubt that, both at the organisational and electoral levels, the EPR/FA is by far the most internally divided political force in Uruguay. Its sprawling internal map and fragmented electoral results, with four national fractions reaping above 10 per cent of the coalition's total vote, are in sharp contrast with the pure bi-fractional structure of the PC at the national level. In the latter, former President Julio M. Sanguinetti's *Foro Batllista* (FB) and current President Jorge Batlle's *Lista 15* (L15) are in equilibrium, with each sector harvesting 47 per cent of the party's vote in 1999. More ambivalent is the situation in the PN, where a picture of significant organisational diversity masks an overwhelming electoral dominance of the *Movimiento Herrerista* (MH). Finally, the small NE, conceived to be a one-piece party, suffered in 1999 its first internal division, which challenged the party's organisational mould, albeit not the dominance of its hitherto official sector, *Lista 99,000*.

Table 2.8: *Number of candidate lists for elections to Uruguay's Chamber of Representatives (major parties only), 1954–1999*

| Election→<br>Party↓ | 1954 | 1958 | 1962 | 1966 | 1971 | 1984 | 1989 | 1994 | 1999 |
|---|---|---|---|---|---|---|---|---|---|
| PC | 82 | 90 | 108 | 156 | 172 | 111 | 212 | 193 | 68 |
| PN | 75 | 98 | 142 | 166 | 183 | 117 | 189 | 211 | 93 |
| FA | -- | -- | -- | -- | 76 | 67 | 72 | 134 | 208 |
| Total | 157 | 188 | 250 | 322 | 431 | 295 | 473 | 538 | 369 |

Sources: See Appendix.

Graph 2.3: *Map of internal sectors and power distribution in Uruguayan parties, 2000*

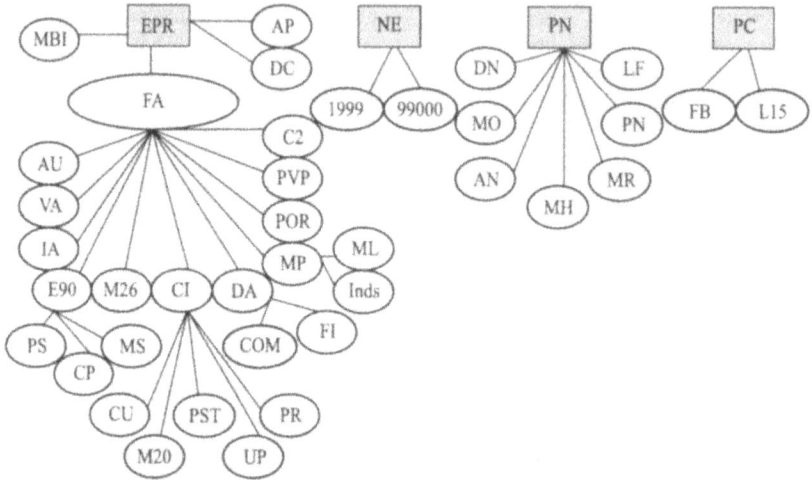

The complexity of the internal life in the Uruguayan parties and the central role of its fractions have prompted many observers to question the use of the 'party' label to describe the Uruguayan parties. Giovanni Sartori, in particular, has repeatedly referred to the latter as 'façade' arrangements where the real political actors are the internal fractions.[69] The direct implication of this argument is that Uruguay has had, in fact, a disguised multi-party system for most of its democratic history. Peculiar as the Uruguayan parties may be, this claim seems misguided, for at least four reasons. First, far from undermining their status as parties, the secular ideological looseness of Uruguayan parties is indeed one of the defining features of catch-all groups.[70] Second, recent research shows that all Uruguayan parties behave as surprisingly cohesive blocs in the legislature.[71] Third, copious evidence demonstrates that the loyalty of Uruguayan voters rests, primarily, with the party and only eventually with the fraction: breakaway sectors invariably suffer at the polls.[72] Fourth, bar few and minor exceptions, Uruguayan parties have not been defined by their ideas or organisational cohesiveness, but by the invocation of a distinct political tradition.[73] The latter, comprising foundational myths, historical landmarks and even martyrs, is typically suited to accommodate dissimilar interpretations. This is increasingly true even of the FA, which after thirty years of existence has become, in many ways, a traditional force. Despite their relative ideological looseness, Uruguayan parties are indeed parties to the extent that party identities in Uruguay are fundamentally 'epic.'

Notwithstanding the latter point, Uruguay's four relevant parties have developed increasingly defined ideological profiles in the recent past. Gone are the days of two overlapping all-encompassing ideological 'tents', with low levels of systemic polarisation. With the electoral advance of the FA and the emergence of a

Graph 2.3: *(Cont)*

| Party / Sector | Cabinet Min. | Senators | Deputies |
|---|---|---|---|
| **PC: Partido Colorado** | **7** | **10 (1)** | **33 (2)** |
| FB: Foro Batllista | 3 | 5 | 17 |
| L15: Lista 15 | 4 | 5 | 15 |
| **PN: Partido Nacional** | **6 (3)** | **7** | **22** |
| MH: Movimiento Herrerista | 3 | 5 | 17 |
| AN: Alianza Nacional | 0 | 1 | 3 |
| DN: Desafío Nacional | 1 | 0 | 1 |
| MR: Movimiento Nacional de Rocha | 0 | 1 | 0 |
| LF: Línea Nacional de Florida | 0 | 0 | 1 |
| MO: Manos a la Obra | 0 | 0 | 0 |
| PN: Propuesta Nacional | 0 | 0 | 0 |
| **EPR: Encuentro Progresista** | **0** | **12** | **40** |
| AP: Alianza Progresista | 0 | 1 | 5 (4) |
| DC: Partido Demócrata Cristiano | 0 | 0 | 1 (5) |
| MBI: Movimiento Batllista Independiente | 0 | 0 | 0 |
| FA: Frente Amplio (6) | 0 | 11 | 34 |
| E90: Espacio 90 | 0 | 4 | 14 |
| PS: Partido Socialista | | | |
| CP: Corriente Popular | | | |
| MS: Movimiento Socialista | | | |
| AU: Asamblea Uruguay | 0 | 2 | 8 |
| MP: Movimiento de Participación Popular | 0 | 2 | 5(7) |
| ML: Movimiento de Liberación Nacional | | | |
| Inds.: Independents | | | |
| VA: Vertiente Artiguista | 0 | 2 | 4 |
| DA: Democracia Avanzada | 0 | 1 | 1 |
| COM: Partido Comunista Uruguayo | | | |
| FI: Frente Izquierda de Liberación | | | |
| C2: Cabildo 2000 | 0 | 0 | 2 |
| CI: Corriente de Izquierda | 0 | 0 | 0 |
| CU: Corriente de Unidad Frenteamplista | | | |
| M20: Movimiento 20 de Mayo | | | |
| PST: Partido Socialista de los Trabajadores | | | |
| UP: Unión Popular | | | |
| PR: Pregón | | | |
| PVP: Partido por la Victoria del Pueblo | 0 | 0 | 0 |
| POR: Partido Obrero Revolucionario | 0 | 0 | 0 |
| IA: Izquierda Abierta | 0 | 0 | 0 |
| M26: Movimiento 26 de Mayo | 0 | 0 | 0 |
| **NE: Partido Nuevo Espacio** | **0** | **1** | **4** |
| 99000: Lista 99,000 | 0 | 1 | 3 |
| 1999: Lista 1999 | 0 | 0 | 1 |

Notes:(1) Since the Vice-President presides in the Senate, the PC has, in fact, eleven Senators. Currently, the Vice-President belongs to the FB. (2) Total includes one PC deputy that does not belong to FB or L15. (3) Total includes two ministers that belong to the PN but not to any specific party sector. (4) Includes one deputy jointly elected by AP and MPP. (5) Jointly elected by DC and MPP. (6) List does not include several regional movements within the FA. (7) Total does not include two deputies elected jointly with AP and DC.
Sources: See Appendix

Graph 2.4: *Mean ideological self-identification of party supporters in Uruguay, 1985–1999 (1)*

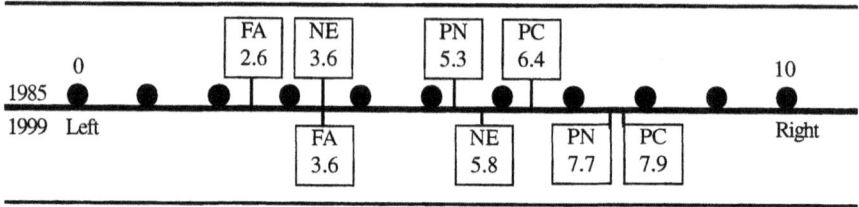

| | | FA 2.6 | NE 3.6 | | PN 5.3 | PC 6.4 | | | | |
|---|---|---|---|---|---|---|---|---|---|---|
| | 0 | | | | | | | | 10 | |
| 1985 | ● | ● | ● | ● | ● | ● | ● | ● | ● | ● |
| 1999 | Left | | FA 3.6 | | NE 5.8 | PN 7.7 | PC 7.9 | | Right | |

Notes: (1) Categories: Left (0–2), Centre-Left (2–4), Centre (4–6), Centre-Right (6–8), Right (8–10). Supporters of what González (1993) identified as the 'FA's right-wing' in 1985 have been equated to those of the NE in 1999.
Sources: See Appendix.

new political cleavage, both traditional parties have been pushed to cater to a neat centre-right electorate, with the PC's situated marginally further to the right, as seen in Graph 2.4.

The rightward shift of both traditional parties has been paralleled in the electorate of non-traditional parties, which has moved steadily closer to the ideological centre during the post-transition years. Today, the average supporter of the FA occupies the same ideological spot once held by the constituency of the groups that abandoned the FA to form the social-democratic NE in 1989. The FA is now firmly grounded at the centre-left of the spectrum. The NE has in turn migrated to the centre, once the basic recruiting space of both traditional parties. Overall, the ideological centre of gravity of the Uruguayan party system has moved noticeably to the right in the last two decades.

To be sure, the figures in the chart and the parties' increasingly delineated profiles conceal visible rifts between internal fractions in all three major actors. Yet, as suggested above, the levels of intra-party ideological diversity found in Uruguay are not exceptional in catch-all parties. Faithful to their historical tradition, Uruguayan parties, even the FA, continue to be catch-all organisations and to have multi-class constituencies.

Table 2.9 shows that with the exception of the NE, which relied disproportionately on lower-income groups in 1999, the other three parties had very heterogeneous social bases, with strong support from the middle income layer in all cases. The differences between the three major parties were relatively slight, with better-

Table 2.9: *Support for parties across socio-economic categories in Uruguay, 1999 (% of supporters)*

| Socio-economic category | PC | PN | FA | NE |
|---|---|---|---|---|
| High/higher-middle | 20.4 | 13.2 | 16.3 | 13.3 |
| Middle | 44.1 | 42.9 | 47.2 | 27.0 |
| Lower-middle/Low | 35.5 | 43.9 | 36.5 | 59.7 |
| Total | 100 | 100 | 100 | 100 |

Sources: See Appendix.

off groups enjoying greater electoral weight in the PC and middle and lower socio-economic strata doing the same in the FA and the PN, respectively.

In Uruguay, such a heterogeneous social support is not necessarily linked to the organisational features expected in catch-all parties. The link exists in both traditional parties, which, like their Costa Rican counterparts, have low levels of permanent institutionalisation. Such a trait is intensified in Uruguay by the weakness of the parties' central organisations vis-à-vis their internal fractions, and by the large autonomy enjoyed by the latter. Though the PC and the PN formally boast a comprehensive permanent organisation, topped by a national representative body and an executive directorate, in reality this structure commands limited power resources, least of all financial. The fractions – the undoubted organisational, electoral and financial centre of gravity in both parties – display poor levels of regular funding and permanent activity, interrupted every five years by intense bouts of fundraising and electoral action.[74] Despite the modicum of centralisation imposed by the adoption of single presidential candidacies, traditional parties in Uruguay remain, in essence, decentralised electoral machines.

The FA has partially escaped this fate. Though structured in a similar way as traditional parties and even more internally heterogeneous than them, it enjoys a much higher level of permanent activity and electoral centralisation, with more power bestowed on its *Mesa Política Nacional* (National Political Board). These features, which betray the organisational influence of the orthodox Left, have implications for the way in which financial resources, particularly state funds, are handled.

### Political finance rules and state funding

In Uruguay, one of the most liberal systems of political finance regulation has coexisted with a long-term participation by the state in providing the parties with resources for their electoral activities. Such participation started early *de jure*, through a state funding scheme, as much as *de facto*, through the symbiosis of both traditional parties with the state. No trait has been more enduring, however, than the conspicuous absence of political finance from the public debate. In a country with unrivalled interest in its parties, the topic has spawned virtually no academic literature and only passing mentions in the press.[75] Bar very specific and recent episodes, it has been non-polemic.

As with many other reforms in the country, it was José Batlle y Ordóñez who put forward the idea of state subsidies to parties. Writing in the pages of his newspaper, *El Día*, in 1924, Batlle argued that:

The constitution of government is as fundamental to the Republic as is the task of defence, and if the sacrifices demanded by the latter are allocated between all the citizens, the same must be done with those required by the former... (W)ith the goal of facilitating the exercise of the right to vote to all citizens, no matter how poor they may be, the electoral law should establish a State contribution for the electoral expenses incurred by the Colorado, Oribista, Socialist, Communist or Catholic parties, in proportion to the civic contingents achieved in the past election.[76]

For Batlle, the quest for political equality was not the only motive that justified the subsidy: also was the need to prevent the undue political influence of private donors. In a rather candid editorial, he drew an interesting picture of the political finance practices of the time:

> In effect, the funds obtained by the parties come from the discounts levied on the salaries of all the persons designated to occupy elective posts, and from the contribution of the party's sympathisers. With regard to the latter, it is worth observing that the State allocates salaries to the legislators, advisors and councillors according to the relevance of their tasks, so that, once properly paid, they devote all their efforts to those tasks. However, if the parties discount 20% or 30% of their salaries, they render impossible the fulfilment of this goal... Amongst the private contributors to the parties' treasury, some do it in an utterly selfless manner; yet, many, the vast majority, do it in return for a frank or implicit promise that they will be rewarded later with a public decision that will reimburse them from the expenses that they have incurred... (F)requently, the big contributors aspire to hold high-rank administrative posts, and it is not unusual to find their names amongst the candidates, with no other merit than that derived from their pecuniary contributions to the parties' benefit. Such immoralities would vanish from our democracy if a state contribution to party expenditures were established, with the express obligation to submit accounts...[77]

Batlle's proposal was adopted four years later, albeit in a somewhat oblique way. Instead of establishing a generic party subsidy, lawmakers introduced a limited post-electoral reimbursement scheme, whereby the Electoral Court (CE) would refund parties for the printing of their ballots or lists.[78] The CE would previously fix the price of each printed list and refund parties at a rate of twenty ballots per vote received.[79] The specificity of the refund was, however, a euphemism aimed at preempting the critique that parties would use the subvention to buy votes.[80] It was clear from the outset that printed lists were not the object of the subsidy, but rather the indicator of choice for its calculation.[81] The very rate at which ballots were to be refunded indicates that legislators were well aware that lists were not merely means for voting but also instruments of electoral publicity, and that it was the latter that the system would in fact subsidise. Voted as part of a wider electoral reform, the article that created the scheme received very little discussion in both legislative chambers and no press coverage at all.[82] The world's first direct state funding scheme for parties came about in the quietest possible way.

This was unsurprising. The electoral parity between both traditional parties in the 1920s and their transversal cut of society implied that the new subsidy would neither create nor even out – despite Batlle's rhetorical protestations – any significant funding disparity between the parties. No party had thus any incentive to oppose the system. Moreover, the protection of the parties' autonomy vis-à-vis the state – the ideological block over which many state funding proposals would stumble elsewhere – could hardly have been a consideration in a country where, quite literally, parties *were* the state.

Indeed, the subsidy created in 1928 was merely an extension of the myriad kinds of public support already extracted by the parties through their symbiotic relationship with the state. To begin with, in a system in which nearly every public employee was a party appointee, the 'party taxes' imposed on elected functionaries, as described in Batlle's long quotation, were more akin to a full-fledged 'macing' system, not unlike the one introduced in Costa Rica after 1910. Available evidence suggests that the coercive extraction of party contributions was a common occurrence at all levels of the public administration.[83] Yet, it was the politicisation of public services, the allocation of public employees to partisan tasks, and the institutionalisation of clientelism that undoubtedly constituted the basic forms of state support for parties.

The close electoral margins and the frequency of elections turned patronage into a crucial political lever in Uruguay, even before the formal division of all state positions between the parties in 1931.[84] The rapid growth of the state, the inefficient delivery of public services, and the entrenchment of party structures in the public sector, gradually turned parties into 'agencies of social distribution', to use the expression of Germán Rama.[85] The *Club Político* (Political Club), an innovation introduced by Batlle y Ordóñez in the PC in the early twentieth century, became the nodal point of the whole distribution network. Formally, the club was merely a neighbourhood association of supporters overseen by a party *apparatchik*, usually a public employee. In practice, it was the channel through which the citizens' particular demands were processed and transmitted to the state (or, rather, to party operators within the state) in return for their electoral support. Over time, the proliferation of clientelistic outposts linked to every conceivable party fraction reached prodigious levels: in 1966 approximately 8,000 political clubs could be found in Montevideo, a city with slightly more than 500,000 voters.[86] The inefficiency of the public sector provided the parties with a mechanism of extensive and permanent social penetration. Up until the breakdown of party structures in 1973, clientelism was the currency that allowed parties, sectors and lists to reach out for voters and sustain their organisation.

Nonetheless, albeit as a limited addition to the extensive forms of public support already available to parties, the direct subsidy became entrenched in the system. In 1946 the rate of reimbursement was increased from twenty to fifty lists per vote, and later, in 1950, to 150.[87] The latter modification was accompanied by a more substantive amendment to the 1928 scheme: the creation of a pre-election loan of up to 50 per cent of the public subsidy, to be distributed between the parties according to their vote shares in the previous election. Unlike the experience in Costa Rica, the introduction of pre-electoral financing in Uruguay was a thoroughly consensual affair: no discussion took place in either chamber and the reform was approved virtually unanimously.[88] This was probably a reflection of the limited importance of the subsidy for the parties, as much as of the extreme stability of electoral results. The idea that pre-election financing could ossify the results of presidential elections would have struck most Uruguayans as implausible: they were already frozen and had been for generations.

The pre-election loan was, however, short-lived. It was eliminated in 1954, when new reforms to the system were discussed in Congress. Irrelevant as the pre-election loan could be for parties, it could nevertheless be important for individual political 'entrepreneurs' of the kind encouraged by DSV. Sensing an opportunity and claiming that resources given to the parties' national authorities often stayed at the top, some representatives argued in favour of disbursing the loans to legislators rather than to party directorates. A draft of the reform, which would have granted access to pre-electoral funds even to breakaway party fractions, was discussed in a legislative committee of the ChR.[89] It was rejected amidst fears that it would foster the parties' internal fractionalisation. Instead, the committee, and later the ChR in full, decided to return the system to its previous post-electoral nature, while keeping the reimbursement circumscribed to the printing of lists.[90]

When the bill reached the Senate, no attempt was made to reinstate pre-electoral financing. However, the Senate's Commission of Finance modified the subsidy in two important ways. First, it did away with the mention of printed lists, choosing instead to fix a global subsidy amount (3.5 million Uruguayan pesos) and formally turning the scheme into what it had long been in practice, i.e. a general subvention fund. Second, it restricted the fund's operation to the forthcoming election, thus introducing a peculiarity into the Uruguayan subsidy system: its *ad-hoc* nature. Henceforth, the subvention would have to be renewed by a legislative act before each election. Today, alone amongst the world's state funding systems, the Uruguayan scheme is not underpinned by a permanent piece of legislation. It continues to be based upon a non-written political custom. Though the reasons for these amendments are unclear,[91] both had a direct precursor in a 1951 law that had created an *ad-hoc* fund to subsidise the parties' advertising expenditures, and not just their ballots, in the run-up to the constitutional plebiscite of that year.[92] In the event, the 1954 reforms were adopted peacefully by both chambers.[93]

The periodical revalidation of the subsidy meant that with every election new changes were introduced to the scheme, not least in the size of the budget appropriation. The latter grew steadily until 1971, more than doubling in real terms. While the proportional allocation and the post-electoral nature of the subsidy remained unchanged, its recipients did not. Indeed, in 1958, the subsidy ceased to run exclusively through the parties' national directorates, as had hitherto been the case. Henceforth, 75 per cent of the public funds (lowered to 60 per cent in 1966 and 1971) would be paid directly to the head of each list of candidates for the ChR. The change, already included in the bill sent by the executive,[94] was well received in parliament and approved, again, by large majorities.[95] Whatever concern about party divisions that had been voiced in 1954 was absent from the debate four years later. In a way, the 1958 reform simply brought the public funding system in line with the incentives created by the combination of DSV and pure proportional representation. Subsequently, the costs of internal dissidence would be even lower.

The 1958 changes were a sign of the growing agitation within the parties, and a portent of things to come. Eight years later, the parties' internal disarray, combined with the direct disbursement of the subsidy to internal fractions, was serious enough to frustrate the executive's attempt to re-introduce pre-election financing.[96] The 1966 bill met no opposition in the Senate, but proved controversial in the ChR. Some representatives noted that the internal situation in both parties was changing so fast as to make unthinkable any allocation based on the results of the previous election.[97] Amidst a barrage of objections, pre-election financing was dropped from the project.[98] Most probably, this was also a consequence of the perception by political actors that public pre-electoral funds were not essential for them. In fact, since 1954 subsidy recipients had been authorised by the law to use their eventual reimbursement as collateral in order to obtain bank loans.[99] Pre-electoral state funding, therefore, at most lowered the politicians' financial costs. As we will see in Chapter five, this realisation was echoed in Costa Rica during the 1990s.

After the uneventful discussion of a new subsidy law in 1971[100] and the suspension of party activities after the 1973 military coup, political finance issues were off the political agenda until the democratic transition. In 1982, with the transition underway, parties selected their national authorities in a countrywide poll that resembled, in many ways, a national election.[101] The long hibernation of their structures, the unavailability of appointees in the public sector from which to deduct 'party taxes,' and the demise of clientelistic exchanges, left the parties in a weak economic position. Recognising this, the military regime agreed to refund each list a token amount per vote, and cede free limited broadcasting space to the parties.[102] This was repeated two years later, before the 1984 restorative election, when the military regime re-enacted the subvention largely along pre-coup lines.[103]

The 1984 law reinstated the system of pre-election financing eliminated after 1954. Unlike in 1966, this time the proposal faced no opposition. Not only were parties banned from the discussion, but the conjuncture made the scheme particularly attractive to them. Six weeks before the election, one of the members of the financial commission of the PN remarked that:

We have great expectations about the measures that the government will take concerning election expenditures, namely the amount that will be given to each party, the eventual advances of funds, their timing, etc. The future action of each political organisation depends, to a large extent, on these and other factors.[104]

With feeble party structures and the country engulfed in a deep economic crisis since 1982, the early funds, as much as the reimbursement, proved essential for

Table 2.10: *State funding to parties in Uruguay. Quantitative evolution, 1950–2000*

| Election | Nominal amount in Uruguayan pesos (millions) (1) | Nominal growth (%) | Amount in US$ of 1995 (millions) | Real growth (%) | Subsidy per registered voter (US$ of 1995) | Real growth per registered voter (%) |
|---|---|---|---|---|---|---|
| 1950 | 1.7 | -- | 7.3 | -- | 6.3 | -- |
| 1954 | 3.5 | +106 | 9.4 | +29 | 7.3 | +16 |
| 1958 | 5.0 | +43 | 8.1 | -14 | 5.7 | -22 |
| 1962 | 20.0 | +300 | 13.1 | +62 | 8.6 | +51 |
| 1966 | 100.0 | +400 | 12.0 | -8 | 7.2 | -16 |
| 1971 | 1200.0 | +1100 | 19.5 | +63 | 10.4 | +44 |
| 1982–84 (2) | 116.1 | +9575 | 5.0 | -75 | 2.3 | -78 |
| 1989 | 5.2 | +4379 | 13.8 | +176 | 5.9 | +156 |
| 1994 | 83.4 | +1504 | 15.3 | +11 | 6.6 | +12 |
| 1999–2000 (3) | 256.7 | +208 | 20.5 | +34 | 8.5 | +29 |

Notes: (1) Due to high inflation rates, the Uruguayan currency was changed in 1975 and 1993, shedding three zeros in each case. The nominal growth figures in the table reflect these changes. (2) Includes the internal elections of 1982 and the national elections of 1984. In 1982 the subsidy was very small: US$0.3 million in total or US$0.16 per registered voter. Subsidy per voter of the whole cycle calculated on the number of voters for the 1984 election. (3) Includes the two rounds of the national election in 1999 and the 2000 local elections. Subsidy for the latter was US$4.1 million or US$1.71 per registered voter. Subsidy per voter calculated on the number of voters for the first round of 1999.
Sources: See Appendix.

the re-activation of parties. Pre-election state financing has been a part of the system ever since.

In 1989, the subsidy scheme underwent new adjustments that gave it most of its current features.[105] Legislators fixed a reimbursement per vote, this time measured as one half of a *Unidad Reajustable* (UR), an official indexible unit. Thus defined, the value of the subsidy was fixed at about US$6 per vote. As customary since 1958, this subvention was subject to a precise intra-party distribution between presidential candidates, parliamentary lists, and local aspirants. Moreover, following upon the practice re-established in 1984, each potential recipient was granted the right to claim before the state-owned Banco de la República (BROU) a pre-election interest-free advance of up to 50 per cent of the likely reimbursement, calculated according to the recipient's previous electoral result. The precise definition of the loan's amount was left, however, in the hands of the BROU. The bank was also authorised to take all legal actions necessary to retrieve any outstanding amount in case the recipient of pre-election funds failed to cover the advance with the eventual reimbursement.

By near unanimity and in record time, the Uruguayan Parliament enacted new subsidy laws before the 1994 and 1999 general elections, which closely followed the 1989 rules.[106] The demise of full electoral concurrence in the wake of the 1996

Table 2.11: *Key features of political finance system in Uruguay*

| Policy instrument | | Details | Enforcement | Year |
|---|---|---|---|---|
| Input controls | Private funding controls | None. | -- | -- |
| | Direct subsidies | Recipient: Presidential candidates (20%), lists of candidates for ChR (40%) and Senate (40%). Local candidates (100% of separate subsidy) | -- | 1999–2000 |
| | | Timing: Post-election reimbursement. (Recipients may receive from the BROU up to 50% of their likely reimbursement in advance, according to their previous electoral result) | -- | 1928 (1989) |
| | | Threshold: None | -- | 1928 |
| | | Allocation: Per vote | -- | 1928 |
| | | Amount definition procedure: Ad-hoc budget appropriation by Parliament. (Since 1989: 0.5 UR per vote in presidential election. Since 2000: 0.12 UR in local elections.) | -- | 1954 |
| | Indirect subsidies | Institutional support for parties in Parliament. Limited broadcasting in state-owned network.* | -- | 1998* |
| Output controls | General exp. ceilings | None | -- | -- |
| | Media advertising ceilings | None | -- | -- |
| | Duration official campaign | Primary and local elections: 40 days Presidential first round: 50 days Presidential run-off: 20 days | Yes | 1998 |
| Transpa-rency | Contributions | None | -- | -- |
| | Expenditures | None | -- | -- |

electoral reform, however, brought about an upgrading of the system. The intra-party distribution of funds (20 per cent to presidential nominees, 40 per cent each to Senate and ChR lists) was modified to the benefit of parliamentary candidates, reflecting the disappearance of multiple presidential candidacies and the separation in time of local elections. A specific, smaller, subvention was eventually enacted in the run-up to the latter.[107] Meanwhile, presidential primaries, also introduced in 1996, remained uncovered by the subsidy scheme.

Though the subvention for the presidential/legislative election stayed roughly constant, the separate subsidisation of the municipal contest implied that the overall subsidy for the 1999–2000 cycle was the largest ever. Table 2.10 summarises the quantitative evolution of state funding in Uruguay since 1950.

Unlike the Costa Rican experience, the quantitative evolution of state funding in Uruguay has been a thoroughly uncontroversial matter, although the subvention has nearly trebled in real terms over the past fifty years. It has done so through acute ups and downs, particularly before and after the fateful 1971 and 1984 elections. As in Costa Rica, the secular growth of the subvention per voter has been considerably more subdued, with a relatively low variance around a mean of US$6.9 per voter (US$ of 1995).

Besides the peculiar evolution of direct state subsidies for parties, little can be said about other elements of the Uruguayan political finance system. Setting aside clientelistic practices – which continue to exist to this day, albeit with much lower intensity than prior to 1973 – other indirect forms of state support for parties have been limited. The public provision of facilities and personnel for the parties' parliamentary activities is undoubtedly the most important of them.[108] Also, since 1998, presidential candidates have enjoyed free access to limited broadcasting on the state-owned television network. The very low ratings of the latter considerably limit the relevance of this benefit.

More importantly, the parties' private sources of income, as well as their expenditures, remain unregulated. Despite numerous attempts to curb private political contributions, no limits are currently in place.[109] Parties, sectors and candidates are allowed to spend unrestrictedly during electoral campaigns. Since 1998, however, the length of the latter has been limited.[110] Finally, no financial transparency rules have been imposed on parties or campaign structures. Subsidy recipients in Uruguay need not submit financial reports to the electoral, judicial, parliamentary or administrative authorities. Unlike the case of Costa Rica's TSE, Uruguay's CE plays no role whatsoever in political finance matters. The CE merely facilitates the BROU the official electoral results upon which the subsidy allocation is based.

Thus, with the exception of its direct subsidy scheme and the limited forms of indirect public support to parties, Uruguay's political finance system stands as close as any to a *laissez-faire* approach to political money. Table 2.11 sums up its main features.


CONCLUSION

This book began by describing Costa Rica and Uruguay as two small, relatively egalitarian societies with consolidated democratic institutions. This basic portrait has been replaced by a more textured image of both cases. Let us summarise some of the main politico-institutional affinities and contrasts that the previous pages have shown.

At the level of regime and electoral structures, Costa Rica and Uruguay share a central institutional trait: presidentialism. In both countries, the battle for the presidency is the vital electoral contest. This helps to explain not only crucial features of their state funding schemes – such as the tendency to privilege the parties' electoral moment rather than their permanent activity – but also many aspects of the dynamics of their party systems, such as Costa Rica's long-term electoral bipolarity. Indeed, although both countries have traditionally employed an electoral system that combines the use of plurality for presidential elections and PR for legislative contests, the centrality of the presidency and the concurrence of both elections have clearly turned plurality into the system's dominant electoral formula. Any analysis of the consequences of DSF for the long-term evolution of the party system must thus be seen against the background of the 'strong' or restrictive effects of plurality rules, particularly in their threshold-reinforced variant employed in Costa Rica.

Despite sharing pivotal features, the electoral systems of Costa Rica and Uruguay are separated by a glaring difference: the presence of DSV in Uruguay, as opposed to Costa Rica's conventional system of single party lists. The consequences of DSV for political finance are multiple and crucial. The presence of DSV has nurtured specific features in the Uruguayan state funding scheme – such as the decentralisation of subsidy disbursements – that are central to its long-term impact on the party system, as we shall see in Chapter five. More importantly, like other systems of preferential voting, DSV opens up a second dimension of electoral competition (i.e. within the parties) that imposes pressing economic needs on politicians. By allowing the open competition between party fractions, DSV breeds an organisational heterogeneity in Uruguayan parties that is simply unknown in Costa Rica. Though, of course, much the same could be said about Costa Rica's system of open presidential primaries, the fractionalisation effects of DSV are more permanent, more far-reaching, and more visible during campaigns. As we will see below, the plethora of parallel electoral structures hosted by each Uruguayan party during national campaigns sharply contrasts with the essential centralisation of electoral operations in Costa Rican parties. By thwarting the development of economies of scale, opening up multiple avenues for electoral mobilisation, and nurturing the atomisation of political power, the structural decentralisation of Uruguayan parties ultimately shapes the size and composition of electoral expenses, as well as the incentives for business donors.

The intense fractionalisation of Uruguayan parties is but one of the differences between party systems in Costa Rica and Uruguay. They also part in their ideological configuration and number of relevant actors. Whereas in Costa Rica, an increasingly eroded historic cleavage and a centripetal competition have yielded two major parties with extraordinary similarities on social, organisational, programmatic and ideological grounds, Uruguay's age-old cleavage between the PC and the PN has been replaced by a far more clear-cut divide between these parties and the FA. The contrast between both sides of the Uruguayan cleavage is ideological as much as organisational. More importantly for this research, by informing the perceptions and decisions of business donors, the cleavage has come to acquire a financial dimension. The Uruguayan case indeed allows for an interesting inquiry into one of the issues already raised in Chapter one: whether state funding affects conservative and leftist parties in a different way, and whether subsidies play an important role in protecting electoral equality and, ultimately, political pluralism.

Similarly, the presence of three major parties in Uruguay as opposed to only two in Costa Rica merits attention from a political finance standpoint. The reasons for this are not unlike those that make the parties' internal fractionalisation relevant. If centralised parties may be theorised to reap important economies of scale that are denied to more atomised electoral structures, two-party systems may be equally expected to have, *ceteris paribus*, lower fixed electoral costs than more fragmented formats. Both conjectures point in the same direction: given the existing differences in electoral and party systems, the cost of elections should be expected to be considerably higher in Uruguay than in Costa Rica.

The interplay between similarities and differences continues at the level of political finance rules. Both countries are united by a long tradition of direct state support to parties and a liberal approach to private contributions, only recently and ambiguously modified in Costa Rica. Moreover, their state funding systems share basic features, such as their purely electoral orientation, proportional allocation rules, and level of generosity. Indeed, while the Uruguayan DSF system is currently the more lavish of the two by some margin (Uruguay: US$8.5 per voter and election cycle; Costa Rica: US$5.6), the disbursements of both schemes display a similar long-term evolution and amount to some of the most generous electoral subventions in the world today.

These important coincidences should not obscure, however, several contrasts on political finance issues. Notable amongst them is the long-term interweaving between the Uruguayan state and its traditional parties, which has no parallel in Costa Rica. Besides its obvious consequences for the fairness of electoral competition, this trait helps to explain the largely quiet evolution of the Uruguayan subsidy system, bereft of the controversies that have beset and shaped the Costa Rican scheme. In the eyes of Uruguay's political actors, DSF has been but one specific form of state support to parties, and in many cases not the most relevant one.

This contrast is compounded by very concrete differences in the design of both subsidy schemes. The most important of them concern the use of an access barrier in Costa Rica as opposed to the unrestricted entry granted by the Uruguayan scheme; the decentralisation of subsidy recipients in Uruguay in contrast to the subsidy's centralised disbursement in Costa Rica; and the existence of pre-electoral advances of state funds in Uruguay and their current absence in Costa Rica. These divergences reflect in most cases the presence of surrounding institutional factors, ranging from DSV in Uruguay – to which the decentralisation of disbursements is clearly endogenous – to the power of constitutional review held by the Costa Rican Supreme Court, which has defined the timing of subsidy disbursements in Costa Rica and the limits of legislative prerogatives in this field. As we shall see below, these differences in the subvention's design shape in distinctive and important ways the political effects of otherwise broadly similar schemes.

In the next two chapters the politico-institutional traits illustrated here will provide useful signposts to understanding the campaign finance practices of parties and candidates in Costa Rica and Uruguay. To these practices we now move.

## NOTES

1 Quoted in Vega-Carballo (1982), p. 90. Translations from Spanish sources are the author's own.

2 Lehoucq (1998), pp. 56–7.

3 Vega-Carballo (1992), p. 205.

4 The main reforms were the creation of the Social Security system in 1941, the constitutional enshrining of various social rights in 1942, and the promulgation of the Labour Code in 1943.

5 Lehoucq (1998), pp. 95–123.

6 On the post-1949 socio-economic changes in Costa Rica see, amongst many, Vega-Carballo (1983) and Rovira (1988).

7 See *Constitución Política*, articles 125–8 and 139–40.

8 Shugart and Carey (1992), pp. 155, 165; Carey (1996), pp. 27–8 and (1997), p. 222; Lehoucq (1998), p.55–7, 133.

9 Urcuyo (1992), pp. 23–42.

10 Sala Constitucional de la Corte Suprema de Justicia (SCCR), Vote No. 2771 of 4/4/2003.

11 Using Lijphart's largest deviation index, Costa Rica's current electoral system for legislative elections ranks thirty-first in proportionality amongst seventy systems analysed in Lijphart (1994).

12 Shugart and Carey (1992, p. 176) give Costa Rica nine points out of ten in a five-variable index of party-leadership control over the rank-and-file in thirteen presidential systems. Only El Salvador scores higher.

13 See Casas-Zamora and Briceño-Fallas (1991).

14 Shugart and Carey (1992), p. 228–9; Jiménez-Zeledón (1996), pp. 1049–50.

15 Fernández (1991), p. 67 and (1996), p. 147.

16 One important exception was the presence of the Communist Party, founded in 1931.

17 Fernández (1996), p. 159; Vega-Carballo (1983), pp. 343–4, n. 29; Yashar (1995), pp. 85–9.

18 Kirchheimer (1966)

19 Law No. 2036 of 18/7/1956.

20 Chacón-Pacheco (1975), pp. 295–296; CEJUL (1989), p. 41.

21 LN, 9/11/1950; LPL, 15/11/1950; Laws No.1748 of 3/6/1954 and No.1780 of 30/7/1954.

22 Only the *ulatista Diario de Costa Rica*, opposed to the bill, devoted some space to the issue. See DCR, 17/5/1956; 31/5/1956; 12/7/1956; 14/7/1956; 17/7/1956 and 18/7/1956.

23 See President Figueres' statetement in Asamblea Legislativa de Costa Rica (ALCR) Exp. Ley No. 2667, p. 54. See also ALCR Exp. Ley No. 2036, p. 2.

24 Partido Liberación Nacional (PLN), (1971), p. 7. See also Daniel Oduber's comment in *La*

*República* [LR] , 23/11/1960. On the amount of the subsidy in 1954 see below Table 2.4.

25  ALCR Exp. Ley No. 2036, p. 59.

26  Law No.4765 of 17/5/1971.

27  The project attracted a lot of press coverage, particularly in the conservative daily La Nación, which opposed the amendment. See, in particular: LN, 2–14/2/1971; LN, 7–13/5/1971; LN, 23/5/1971; LR, 5/5/1971.

28  Law No. 4973 of 11/5/1972.

29  *La Prensa Libre* [LPL], 12/2/1988.

30  Law No. 7094 of 27/4/1988.

31  SCCR, Vote No. 980–91of 24/5/1991, p. 28.

32  With the exception of the subsidy threshold, lowered to 5 per cent of the vote in 1972.

33  Law No.7675 of 23/6/1997 reintroduced the constitutional principle of pre-electoral public financing, but left its application in suspense until the approval of a regulating law. The latter has yet to be sanctioned.

34  Law No. 7675 of 23/6/1997.

35  Throughout this chapter and the rest of the book, all figures denominated in US$ refer to US$ of 1995 unless otherwise indicated. For Costa Rica, conversion made using deflators and exchange rates from BCCR. For Uruguay, conversion made using deflators and exchange rates from BCU and INE.

36  The Costa Rican state provides support for the parties' legislative activities, in terms of goods and services, as much as paid personnel. Each deputy is entitled to at least one secretary, one advisor and one assistant. Large parliamentary blocs also have a department of paid advisors, under the purview of the party's legislative leader. These items add up to a significant amount of the legislative budget. Other forms of indirect support include free use of postal services and public buildings, such as schools, for party activities.

37  Law No. 7653 of 28/11/1996.

38  Law No. 7094 of 27/4/1988.

39  Electoral Code, article 177; Tribunal Supremo de Elecciones, Costa Rica [TSE] (1997), articles 1–5.

40  *Constitución Política*, article 96.4; TSE (1997); Contraloría General de la República, Costa Rica [CGR] (1997).

41  TSE, Vote No. 1548 of 31/8/1999.

42  Caetano, Rilla and Pérez (1988) and (1989).

43  On the history of the Uruguayan parties see Pivel-Devoto (1994); Rial (1984); Caetano et al. (1985); Caetano, Rilla and Pérez (1988) and (1989); Caetano and Rilla (1990) and (1999); Cocchi (n.d.).

44  Both parties already existed in 1836. Their names originated in the Carpintería Battle, when they identified themselves by wearing red (colorado) and white (blanco) ribbons. Hence their names. See Pivel-Devoto (1994); Cocchi (n.d.), p. 3; Sotelo-Rico (1999), p. 144; Pérez (1990), pp. 42–3; Franco (1985), p. 55.

45  Rodríguez-Fabregat, as quoted in Weinstein (1975), p. 144.

46  On Batlle and his reforms see Vanger (1968) and (1983); Caetano and Rilla (1999), pp. 105–140.

47  The CE has never been entirely neutral in its composition. Currently it has nine members:

six party representatives allocated proportionally, and three non-partisan members appointed by a qualified congressional majority. See Franco (1985), pp. 22–25.

48  Weinstein (1975), pp. 50–84; Solari (1988), pp.19–28; Costa-Bonino (1995), pp. 122–127.

49  Rama (1971); Solari (1988), pp. 15–40; Panizza (1990), pp. 69–77.

50  In all the elections conducted between 1925 and 1966, both parties (including their dissident factions, which occasionally participated separately) polled an average of 93.4 per cent of the votes. The PC, however, controlled the presidency uninterruptedly between 1865 and 1958. See Franco (1985), pp. 77–81; Venturini (1989), pp. 14–15; Cocchi (n.d.), p. 3.

51  In 1955–60, GDP per capita growth averaged –1.5 per cent. See Finch (1981), pp. 220–45.

52  González and Gillespie (1994), p. 157; Costa-Bonino (1995), pp.161–171; Cocchi (n.d.), p. 36.

53  In 1968, the National Liberation Movement Tupamaros, a left-wing insurgent group, began operating in earnest. The Army defeated it in 1972. Meanwhile, in the 1971 election the Left made an unprecedented electoral showing, obtaining 18.3 per cent of the national vote and close to one-third in Montevideo. On the Tupamaros see Panizza (1990), pp. 151–79; Costa-Bonino (1995), pp. 197–217.

54  57.2 per cent of the voters rejected the military project. See Gillespie (1995), pp. 84–91; Solari (1988), pp. 236–7.

55  See González (1991b), pp. 53–68; Gillespie (1995), pp. 125–228.

56  Gillespie and González (1994), pp. 153–159; González (1991b), pp. 22–23; Buquet et al. (1998), p. 58; Nohlen (1986), p. 257, and (1995), p. 262.

57  On October 31st 2004, as this book was going to press, the FA finally put an end to the long electoral supremacy of both traditional parties. A comfortable and widely predicted victory gave the Left not only control of the presidency for the first time, but also a congressional majority, something that had not happened in Uruguay in nearly four decades.

58  Linz and Stepan (1996), pp. 151–65.

59  Bottinelli, as quoted in Buquet et al. (1998), p. 10 n. 12.

60  Using the largest deviation index of disproportionality for the period 1984–99, Uruguay's electoral system would rank as the second most proportional (0.55 per cent deviation) in a sample of seventy electoral systems. See Lijphart (1994).

61  Quoted in Bottinelli (1999), p. 27.

62  The second round of the 1999 presidential election indeed posed a formal electoral alliance of both traditional parties against the FA.

63  Pérez (1984), p. 77. See also Rama (1987), pp .19–20; Caetano and Rilla (1999), p. 43.

64  Cocchi (n.d.), p. 10.

65  Rama (1987), p. 114; González (1993), pp. 174–175.

66  Caetano and Rilla (1999), pp. 279–280; Dutrénit (1996); Gillespie (1995), pp. 45, 169–71.

67  The weight of the FA in the EPR is such that, in practice, they are the same entity. For the sake of simplicity, I will refer to the FA throughout this volume, unless it is necessary to do otherwise.

68  González (1991a), p. 20 and (1993), p. 56.

69  Sartori (1992), p. 102 n. 11; (1986), p. 67 n. 20; and (1997), p. 177.

70  González (1991b), pp. 15–16.

71  Using roll-call data for seventy-seven important laws voted by the Senate in 1985–95,

Buquet et al. (1998) calculated Rice's Index of parliamentary discipline for each party, with values oscillating between 0 (minimum discipline) and 1 (unanimity). The PC's figures were 0.91 (1985–90) and 0.87 (1990–95). The PN's values were 0.94 and 0.90. The FA had a perfect score of 1 for both periods as did the NE in 1990–95, suggesting airtight discipline.

72  Franco (1985), p. 98; Buquet at al. (1998), p. 29.

73  Bottinelli (1993), p. 110; Mieres (1992), pp. 70, 74; Panizza (1990), p. 52; Trías (1990b), p. 84. Uruguayans, tellingly, distinguish between traditional parties and 'parties of ideas'. The latter comprise cases such as the *Unión Liberal*, *Partido Radical* and *Partido Constitucional* in the nineteenth century, and the orthodox Left and the small Catholic *Partido Unión Cívica* in the twentieth century.

74  Neither the *Foro Batllista* nor the *Lista 15* in the PC, nor the *Movimiento Herrerista* in the PN, the largest internal sectors in both parties, have membership records. Between elections they are largely sustained by contributions levied by the sector on the salaries of elected officials. Political training and education activities are virtually non-existent in any sector.

75  To this day, there are only four academic works on Uruguayan political finance: Rial (1998), Caetano et al. (2002), and Casas-Zamora (2002) and (2003). Beyond occasional newspaper notes only three press reports offer a general overview of the topic: 'Pasando el sombrero', *El Observador* (*EO*), 22/10/1994; 'El millonario carnaval electoral', *EO*, 7/3/1999; 'En Uruguay hay una absoluta libertad', Revista Tres [TRES], 9/4/1999.

76  *El Día* (*ED*), 26/10/1924. See also editorials in *ED*, 30/10/1924, 7/11/1924, 9/11/1924 and 13/11/1924.

77  *ED*, 13/11/1924.

78  In Uruguay, suffrage is exercised by inserting a printed ballot with the number and symbol of one list in an envelope provided by the CE. Each political sector must make sure that its ballots get distributed to all its potential voters: otherwise they will not be able to support it at the polls.

79  Law No. 8312 of 17/10/1928, article 30.

80  See Cámara de Senadores del Uruguay (CSU), DS 208, p. 201.

81  See Cámara de Representantes del Uruguay (CRU), DS 328, pp. 132, 136; DS 208, p. 201; Carp. 1711/1953, p .23–4.

82  Not even legislative committees discussed the article. Proceedings in the Senate committee only indicate that it was the product of a 'political agreement'. In the Chamber of Representatives, only four deputies in seventy voted against it (CRU, DS 328, pp. 414, 514). Only the PN-leaning daily *El País* mentioned the new subsidy, without further comment (*EP*, 14/10/1928).

83  See an interesting discussion on forced assessment of public employees by the PC in 1928 in CRU, DS 328, pp. 370–375.

84  Weinstein (1975), p. 67.

85  Rama (1987), p. 50.

86  Rama (1971), p. 13.

87  Laws No. 10789 of 23/9/1946 and No. 11603 of 18/10/1950.

88  CRU, DS 484, p. 767; CSU, DS 194, p. 237.

89  CRU, Carp. 1711/1953, pp. 28–35.

90  CRU, Carp. 2464/1954.

91  According to the proceedings, an ample debate took place in the Senate's Committee. Unfortunately, the proceedings do not include the transcript of the discussion.

92  Law No. 11762 of 19/11/1951.

93  Law No. 12145 of 19/10/1954. See CSU, DS 208, p. 203; CRU, DS 499, p. 655.

94  CRU, Carp. 2222/1958.

95  Law No. 12561 of 21/10/1958. See CRU, DS 528, p. 129; CSU, DS 223, p. 351.

96  CRU, Carp. 3085/1966.

97  CRU, DS 578, p. 314–315

98  See Law No. 13574 of 26/10/1966; CRU, DS 578, pp. 378–379.

99  Law No.12145 of 19/10/1954, article 2.

100 Law No.14012 of 3/9/1971.

101 See Gillespie (1995), pp. 112–22; Franco (1984), pp. 125–44.

102 Law No.15320 of 31/8/1982; CEst., DS 34, pp.78–86; EP, 31/3/1982; EP, 1/9/1982; EP, 14/10/1982; EP, 3/11/1982; ED, 19/10/1982; ED, 31/10/1982; ED, 8/11/1982.

103 Law No.15673 of 9/11/1984; CEst., DS 47, pp. 224–231.

104 *La Mañana* [LM], 14/10/1984.

105 Law No.16103 of 10/11/1989.

106 Laws No.16567 of 26/8/1994 and No.17157 of 20/8/1999. See CSU, DS 361, pp. 252–255; CRU, DS 692, pp. 250–256; CSU, DS 28/7/1999, pp. 338–351; CRU, DS 4/8/1999, pp. 21–25; UN, 27/7/1994; EP, 28/7/1994; BUS, 29/7/1999.

107 Law No.17237 of 14/4/2000. The subsidy was fixed at 0.12 UR per vote, or slightly less than a quarter of the rate for presidential elections.

108 Members of Parliament are entitled to basic office infrastructure. They may also request the services of up to five public employees from any State agency, through a mechanism called *pases en comisión* (commissioned licenses). These personnel may be employed in parliamentary or purely partisan activities. Parties are exempt from taxes other than the value-added tax (VAT). They enjoy free access to postal services. See Bottinelli (1993), pp.129-130; [TRES], 9/4/1999, p.18; Ifrán and Gallegos (1999).

109 The Fundamental Law No.2 of 7/6/1982, a military-enacted organisation law for parties, is the only piece of legislation to have regulated political donations in Uruguay. It banned anonymous, foreign, corporate, and trade union contributions, while establishing a sanctioning regime for parties and donors. The law was annulled soon after the return of democracy in 1985. See CEst, Carp.201/1981, pp. 255–283.

110 The limits are forty days for primary and local elections, fifty days for the presidential first round, and twenty days for the presidential run-off (Law No.17045 of 14/12/1998).

# chapter three | state funding and campaign finance practices: the case of costa rica

## INTRODUCTION

The following two chapters provide a systematic and empirically grounded account of the way in which election campaigns are financed in Costa Rica and Uruguay. Their aim is, however, more than descriptive. The chapters will highlight the key similarities and differences between campaign finance practices in both countries, and examine the extent to which political and institutional phenomena surveyed in the previous chapter explain them. The Costa Rican experience is explored first.

As in most of Latin America, discussions on political finance in Costa Rica have proceeded so far largely along normative lines. A long-standing preoccupation with the features of political finance regulation – particularly the rules and amounts of state funding – has not been matched by an effort to scrutinise the realities of campaign finance. Despite the availability of detailed information regarding the uses of direct state subsidies and the introduction in 1996 of transparency rules regarding private funding, our knowledge has not advanced much beyond the comments made by analyst Oscar Fernández in 1993:

> The electoral ritual, in the way it is practised by Costa Ricans, is a costly and, in some aspects, pompous ritual.... Where do all the resources that make possible such expenses come from?.... It has been suggested...that more than one half of that funding is made possible thanks to the legal contribution made by the State to the parties, while the rest comes from private funding.[1]

This chapter will show that the conventional wisdom about campaign finance in Costa Rica is only partially accurate. We will see that if it is true that state funding enjoys a dominant – albeit increasingly eroded – financial role in national campaigns, it is, on the other hand, far from certain that Costa Rican elections have become ever more expensive tournaments driven by massive expenditures on television advertising. Also, if it can be safely said that subsidies have mitigated the dependence on private sources of capital, it is by no means clear that they have eliminated their prominent role, the occurrence of questionable fundraising practices, and the strong social bias that pervades the election financing process.

The chapter will be divided into two sections dealing, first, with campaign expenditure, its amount and breakdown, and, second, with campaign income sources, the weight of state funding, and the intricacies of fundraising processes. The reason for such a sequence should be reasonably obvious: gauging the relative weight of alternative funding sources, and the extent to which state funds substitute for private contributions, becomes an impossible exercise in the absence of an estimate of the total cost of campaigns. Finally, the chapter's conclusion will identify the crucial implications of the Costa Rican system of state subsidies for campaign financing and democracy.

## CAMPAIGN EXPENDITURE: AMOUNTS AND ITEMS

One of the few academic works on campaign finance in Costa Rica notes that, '(t)he creation of norms to regulate (political finance) has proceeded very slowly vis-à-vis the parties' increasing necessity of resources in order to face ever more expensive election campaigns, due to the use of the media'.[2] This sums up the prevailing consensus about the trend of campaign expenditure and the driving force behind it. The truth of this assertion is, however, far from certain. A closer look at the evidence on campaign expenditure yields surprising results, particularly about the distribution of electoral spending per items and the relative importance of television advertising.

### The cost of elections

No reliable estimate exists of the cost of elections in Costa Rica. This is unsurprising, given the limitations in the available data. First, no spending ceiling exists in the country. Second, expenditure reports submitted by the parties to the TSE and the National Comptroller (CGR) cover, in principle, only those expenditures that are to be paid with state funds. The purpose of these reports is not to establish the level and content of each party's spending but to verify whether the state subsidy is spent in those items expressly authorised by the electoral law. Whatever disbursements the parties cover with private sources of funding are of no consequence for the existing legislation. By the same token, expenditures made by non-subsidised parties remain beyond the scope of the rules in operation. Third, and crucially, reporting only covers expenses made by the parties in the course of *national* elections. This implies that neither presidential nomination contests nor sub-national elections – notably legislative races – are subject to expenditure reporting rules.

However, leaving aside for now the issue of presidential nomination and legislative contests, a by-product of the existing reporting procedures allows us to have a relatively precise idea of the parties' outlays during national election cam-

Table 3.1: *Total campaign expenditure per party in Costa Rica, 1978–1998 (US$m of 1995)*

| Election →<br>Party ↓ | 1978 | 1982 | 1986 | 1990 | 1994 | 1998 | Mean<br>1978–98 |
|---|---|---|---|---|---|---|---|
| PLN | 8.66* | 5.19 | 9.26* | 6.68* | 8.72 | 6.55* | 7.51 |
| Unidad/PUSC | 7.99 | 2.43* | 8.38 | 7.63 | 11.16* | 9.12 | 7.78 |
| Other | 4.49 | 0.96 | 0.68 | 0.23 | 0.63 | 1.20 | 1.37 |
| Total (1) | 21.14 | 8.58 | 18.32 | 14.53 | 20.51 | 16.79 | 16.65 |

Notes: * Denotes incumbent party at the time of election. (1) Though only parties that reported to the CGR are included, 1978 and 1986 include parties that received pre-electoral state funding but subsequently failed to qualify for the post-election reimbursement and therefore did not submit expenditure reports. It has been assumed that the PU and the PNI in 1978, as well as the CPU, CAP and PADA in 1986, spent *at least* the sum received in pre-election funding. This situation did not arise in other elections.
Sources: See Appendix.

paigns. Indeed, as a result of their bureaucratic shortcomings as well as their wish to forestall the partial rejection of their expenses by the Comptroller, Costa Rican parties (those entitled to the subsidy, that is) invariably submit spending accounts for a sum well in excess of their subsidy entitlement according to their vote share. Evidence from the CGR's audits and extensive interviews with party officials strongly suggest that these reports comprise the near totality of the expenditures incurred by the parties in the course of the national campaign.[3] Albeit it should be taken as a minimum, the total amount of the receipts submitted to the CGR is the best available proxy to the parties' total campaign outlays.[4] Using this proxy, Table 3.1 summarises campaign expenditures per party in presidential elections between 1978 and 1998 in constant currency.

Table 3.1 shows the secular parity between both main parties. However, the spending advantage of the PLN in the first three elections of the sample has been more than offset by a PUSC domination in the last three, particularly in 1994 and 1998. This sequence coincides with the consolidation of the PUSC as a polar opposite to the PLN, and its absorption of the previously diverse anti-PLN forces, including some with roots in economically powerful groups. The table also shows the lack of a consistent spending advantage for the incumbent party: in three cases it outspent the opposition, in three cases it trailed the latter.

The behaviour of total and per-voter expenditure, as shown in Graph 3.1, is more interesting. The graph shows that, contrary to common perception, total electoral expenditure has not grown constantly, or even at all. In fact, the 1978 election marks the peak of the period, with more than US$21 million. Expenditure fell dramatically in 1982 and then followed a jagged pattern until 1998. With the exception of the 1990 election, the behaviour of total expenditure coincides with changes in the availability of state funding. Since reimbursement rules make it impossible for Costa Rican parties to accumulate the subvention, i.e., they must spend whatever state funds are available, it is reasonable to expect that an increase in public funding will lead to higher electoral outlays. Less obvious, however, is

Graph 3.1: *Total and per voter election expenditure in Costa Rica, 1978–1998*

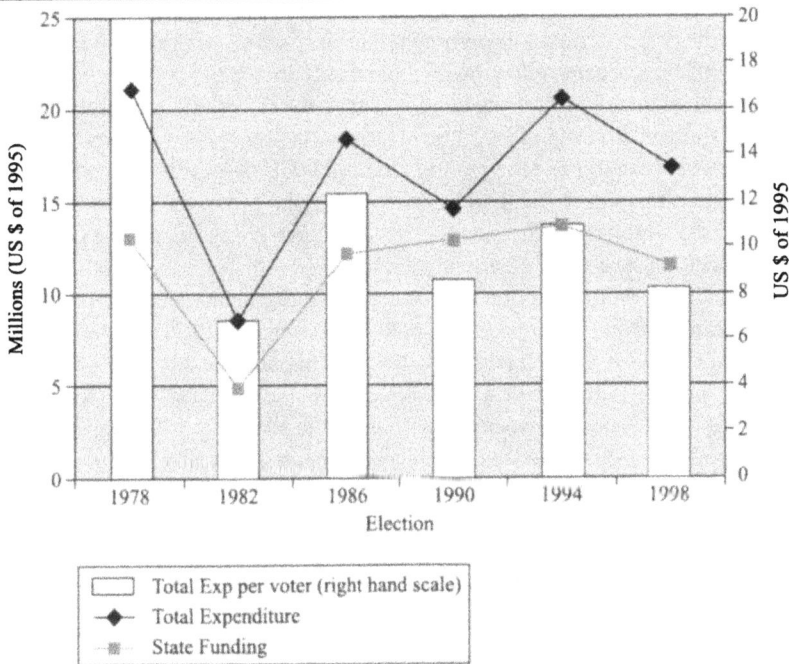

Source: See Appendix

whether expenditure should decrease when public funds fall: conceivably, private funding could replace public funds, thus keeping total expenditure constant. Yet, the two cases (1982 and 1998) in which state funding declined coincided with parallel drops in total outlays. More importantly, throughout the period (bar 1990), the rate of dependence on state funding of the party system as a whole seems impervious to changes in levels of subsidisation: increases in subsidies do not crowd out private funds, nor do decreases in the former open the way for an increased dependence on the latter. This evidence weakens the case in favour of higher levels of subsidisation in Costa Rica on two accounts. First, more generous subsidies do not automatically translate into less reliance of the parties on private funds. Second, lower levels of subvention seem to make for more thrifty elections.

Besides the availability of state funding, other factors seem to drive the level of total expenditure. Thus, the spending peak of 1978 is related to the presence of third parties armed with abundant financial resources, mostly provided by the state. In 1978, the PU and the PNI, having achieved 30.4 per cent and 10.9 per cent of the vote in the previous election, were entitled to hefty pre-elections loans. The fact that they both suffered at the polls and ended up heavily indebted to the state matters less than the fact that, in 1978, for once, the election campaign was not, financially speaking, a bipolar race. The precipitous decline in total expenditure in 1982 is, in turn, explained by at least three factors. First is the severe economic crisis that engulfed the country in 1981–2, which conceivably reduced the resources available for electoral purposes.[5] Second, the crisis led to an agreement between the deficit-stricken government and the parties, whereby the latter agreed to a one-off 30 per cent reduction of the subsidy in return for receiving the funds in cash rather than government bonds.[6] Third, the economic downturn made the result of the forthcoming election a foregone conclusion, in which the only open question was whether the ruling Unity Coalition (CU) – largely blamed for the crisis – would remain as a viable political force. In the event, the PLN won the election with the largest majority since 1953. Any fundraising imperatives entailed by a tight electoral race were clearly absent in 1982.

Expenditure more than doubled four years later, aided by a sharp increase in state funding and a close presidential contest between the PLN and the PUSC. The perceived closeness of the result also helps to explain the steep hike of electoral spending in 1994 – the tightest race since 1966 – and the drop in expenditure in 1998. With less than four weeks to go before the February 1994 election, a CID-Gallup poll put the difference between both main candidates at 4 per cent, just above the margin of error, a gap which shrank to just 1.9 per cent in the actual result.[7] This is in sharp contrast with a similarly timed poll four years later, which recorded a PUSC advantage of more than 12 per cent.[8] The mistaken perception that the ruling PLN would be heavily defeated in the 1998 presidential election contributed decisively to the party's acute fundraising and spending problems throughout the 1997–98 campaign.[9]

This leaves only the 1990 election as an anomaly. The somewhat severe fall in total spending in the run-up to the 1990 election cannot be accounted for by a drop in the availability of state funds – which went up slightly – nor by the perception that one of the candidates was on course to an ample victory.[10] The explanation for the behaviour of electoral expenditure in 1990 must be sought elsewhere. Indeed, the 1989–90 campaign was dominated by a string of revelations about questionable fundraising practices employed by both parties during the 1985–86 campaign, including their acceptance of contributions from several characters eventually linked to drug-trafficking and money-laundering activities.[11] These allegations proved damaging for both parties and made them unusually wary of raising money from private sources. This would also explain their abnormal dependence on state funds in 1990, which exceeded 85 per cent of total expenditure in both parties, a figure that has not been reached before or since.

The evolution of spending per registered voter in the graph is equally noteworthy. Here, the long-term decrease is striking: from US$19.9 per voter in 1978 to US$8.2 twenty years later, a drop of nearly 60 per cent. Even the relatively expensive 1994 contest stood barely above one half the per capita cost of the 1978 election. While the secular descent of state funding per voter is, probably, an important force behind this trend, there is little doubt that the stability of the party system (i.e. the absence of significant third parties between 1978 and 1998) and the spatial concentration of the Costa Rican electorate also helped to reduce the marginal cost of each new vote.

Table 3.2: *Estimated expenditures of presidential nomination campaigns in Costa Rica, 1987–2001 (US$m of 1995) (1)*

| Pre-campaign →<br>Party ↓ | 1987–89 | | 1991–93 | | 1995–97 | | 1999–01 | |
|---|---|---|---|---|---|---|---|---|
| | Cand. | Exp. | Cand. | Exp. | Cand. | Exp. | Cand. | Exp. |
| PLN | Castillo | 0.3 | Figueres | *0.9–1.5* | Corrales | 0.2 | Araya | *1.6* |
| | | | Corrales | *0.3* | | | Corrales | *1.1* |
| | Araya | 0.5 | Penón | *0.9* | Coto | 0.2 | Alvarez | *1.0* |
| | | | Araya | *0.5* | | | | |
| PUSC | Calderón | *1.3* | Rodríguez | 1.5 | Rodríguez | *0.4* | Pacheco | 0.4 |
| | Rodríguez | *2.0* | Trejos | 0.8 | (2) | | Méndez | 1.6 |

Notes: (1) Since pre-candidates are not required to report their expenditures the figures provided are rough estimates, based on a number of reliable sources. Only major pre-candidates are included. Within each pre-campaign and party, pre-candidates are arranged according to primary election results. Figures in italics denote opposition party. (2) Rodríguez ran unopposed.
Sources and method: See Appendix.

Although national elections in Costa Rica may be less expensive now than a generation ago, does this imply a decline in the cost of electoral activity *as a whole*? Here the story grows in complexity, for the 1978–2002 period also saw the emergence of new electoral arenas – notably, open presidential primaries – with significant costs of their own. These costs are notoriously difficult to calculate, partly because the public subvention scheme and the reporting requirements that are attached to it do not explicitly cover them.

Open presidential primaries were introduced in Costa Rica during the late 1970s. It soon became evident that their costs were substantial and would weigh heavily on the prospects of many political careers. During the 1977–8 cycle, the four primary candidates in both parties were said to have spent between US$1.8 million and US$2.6 million in total, the bulk of it in the CU nomination contest between Rodrigo Carazo and Miguel Barzuna.[12] Barzuna, a wealthy industrialist, reputedly spent US$1.2 million in his unsuccessful presidential bid.[13] Meanwhile, Carazo claimed to have invested in his 1977 nomination campaign nearly US$0.7 million.[14] By the time of the primary election, however, several pre-candidates in both parties had abandoned the race, crippled by their lack of financial resources.[15]

The situation has changed little since then. The consensus among politicians – including presidential pre-candidates – and the scattered evidence available from past contests suggests that the cost of a serious nomination bid in any of the major parties is normally in the region of US$1 million (see Table 3.2).

While exceptions to this rule are numerous, they are not entirely unpredictable. The table suggests that the level of expenditure in nomination contests is directly related to each party's perceived chances of victory in the forthcoming presidential election. Given the entrenched tradition of power alternation in Costa Rica, primary campaigns in opposition parties are consistently more expensive than those in incumbent parties. Table 3.2 also shows that whatever the number of pre-candidates and the distribution of expenses between them, and with the exception of atypical cycles such as that of 1995–7, presidential primaries add at least US$4 million to the cost of national elections in Costa Rica.

The last two decades have also seen transformations in the financial dynamic of legislative elections. Though the system of party lists employed for the national election remains in place to this day, the procedures to select the candidates in the major parties have changed considerably, raising the costs attached to legislative races. The first milestone in the process came during the 1980s with the introduction of open local elections of party authorities. These elections were conceived to trigger a pyramid-like three-stage mechanism that would lead to the appointment of the party's seventy-member National Assembly. Since the parties' internal bylaws bestowed the task of selecting the party's legislative candidates on the National Assembly, it soon became clear that controlling the election of authorities at the local level was almost a pre-requisite to further a congressional aspiration through all the echelons of the party structure. Prospective legislative candidates were thus dragged into an electoral dynamic that demanded more than merely vying for the attention of party leaders, as had been traditionally the case.

This system would remain largely unchanged until the 1998 election. The total expenditure of a successful legislative aspirant, i.e., one who passed through all the internal stages of the party structure and was placed at or near the top of his party's list of candidates, has been estimated at between US$30,000 and US$50,000. This sum was partly allocated to strict nomination costs, and partly to complement the party's campaign in each constituency. Since no more than twenty five candidates per major party were in such a situation,[16] those figures would take the total expenditure in legislative races to somewhere between US$1.5 million and US$2.5 million, and more probably to the region of US$2–3 million if unsuccessful candidates were included. These numbers, however, almost surely increased during the 2001–2 election cycle, due to the introduction of full-fledged open congressional primaries in both main parties. No reliable estimates of the cost entailed by the new system are available yet.[17]

It should be noted that once the nomination is achieved, and in the absence of intra-party competition at the national election, the congressional candidate's race in their multi-member constituency becomes indistinguishable from their party's campaign. Other than a limited mobilisation effort by each candidate in their own region, not bereft of costs, the party normally runs all legislative campaigns as part of a *single* national effort, driven by the presidential contest. A curious episode during the 1997–8 campaign illustrates the point well. In December 1997 it became public that some of the PLN's traditional financial backers had offered to finance the party in the forthcoming election only if their contributions were earmarked for legislative races. The reaction of José Miguel Corrales, the party's standard-bearer and twice a congressional candidate himself, was one of anger and astonishment: 'I don't want such a funding. It's outrageous! How could there be separate funding for legislative candidates?'.[18] He went on to state, categorically, that no parallel accounts would be open for legislative contests and that the cost of the latter would be subsumed into the general expenses of the national campaign.[19] Despite the presence of fundraising and spending practices at the local level, national campaigns in Costa Rica remain, in essence, centrally controlled efforts, where the overwhelming majority of the resources are centrally disbursed.

The expansion of electoral arenas, and the correlative weakening of the public subsidy system, has not been confined to presidential and legislative contests. The recent adoption of direct elections for the country's eighty-one mayors has now expanded the process to the municipal level. Uncovered by state funding, the costs of the first election of this kind, held in December of 2002, are hard to estimate. While a leading candidate to the mayoralty of San José – far and away the country's most important – publicly claimed to have spent about US$75,000 in his campaign, aspirants in lesser constituencies typically disbursed US$2,500–12,500.[20] Assuming a minimum of two competitive candidacies per mayoral race, it is almost certain that the cost of this new electoral dimension reached well above US$1 million.

In sum, the adoption over the past twenty-five years of open presidential primaries and less vertical congressional nomination procedures in the PLN and the PUSC, as well as direct mayoral elections, has added considerably to the cost of politics in Costa Rica. Though precise figures are elusive, it can be safely assumed that since the 1980s these arenas have added approximately US$7–8 million to the cost of each national electoral cycle. Plainly, the broadening of democratic procedures has come at a significant economic cost. The central point to bear in mind is that, as opposed to the resources used by the parties during national campaigns, the funds for intra-party and mayoral contests come, almost entirely, from private sources. Whatever substitutive effect may be attributed to state funding in Costa Rica, it goes to benefit a set of competitors generated by procedures in which private funding reigns unfettered.

**The structure of expenditure**

'The state does not subsidise the parties: it subsidises television stations.'[21] Thus spoke the leader of a minor party in Costa Rica, pointing to the presumably overwhelming and growing dominance of television advertising in the parties' campaign expenditures. His opinion is hardly unique. The perception that TV outlays are the quintessential 'electoral spending trigger', to use Daniel Zovatto's expression,[22] has become an article of faith in Costa Rica and beyond. The reality, however, looks different, as shown in Graph 3.2.

The chart shows that television advertising only consumed a very limited proportion of the parties' electoral budget, 10 per cent on average in 1990–8. Not just that: this proportion *declined* over the three elections: from 11.7 per cent in 1990, to 9.7 per cent in 1994, to 8.7 per cent in 1998. Disbursements on TV advertising amounted to merely one-third of the parties' expenditure on salaries and professional fees, by far the largest item in their electoral budgets. Moreover, during 1990 and 1994 TV advertising absorbed a mere 38.3 per cent and 34.6 per cent of

Graph 3.2: *Campaign spending per items in Costa Rica, 1990–98 (1)*

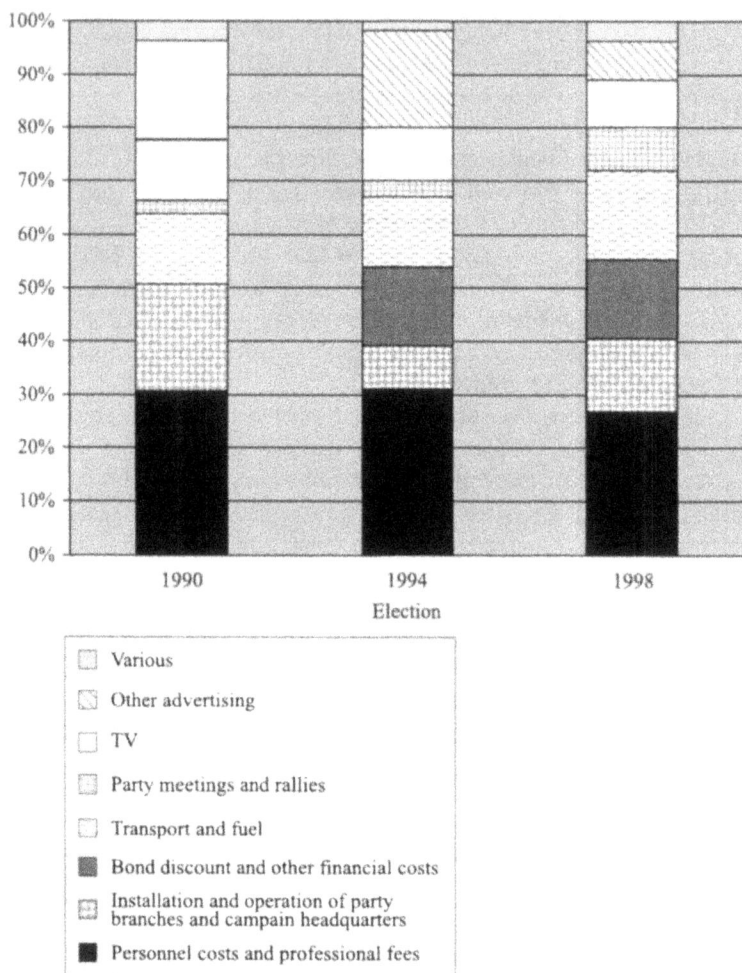

Legend:
- Various
- Other advertising
- TV
- Party meetings and rallies
- Transport and fuel
- Bond discount and other financial costs
- Installation and operation of party branches and campain headquarters
- Personnel costs and professional fees

Notes: (1) 1990: PLN, PUSC and PUAC only; 1994: PLN, PUSC and PFD only; 1998: PLN, PUSC, PFD and PUAC only.
Sources: See Appendix

total publicity outlays. This share climbed to a still surprisingly low 54.4 per cent in 1998, in the wake of the elimination of party flags from the list of reimbursable expenditures.

These figures may be criticised by noting that *reported* TV spending – as opposed to *real* spending – has not increased due to constant law-imposed limits to reimbursement of advertising expenses, which may create a bias towards stability. This is, however, an insufficient objection. First, the media expenditure receipts submitted by the parties to the CGR are not constrained by the reimbursement limits imposed by the EC (Article 85f). Major parties invariably produce receipts for TV spending that clearly exceeds those ceilings, notably the daily ones (ten minutes of advertising per party per TV station).[23] Second, even if parties surpass on occasion the *daily* reimbursement limits, the *overall* reimbursement ceiling remains well above the documented presence of the parties on the screen. Let us see. With five major open-air TV channels operating in Costa Rica, each party is theoretically endowed with fifty minutes of advertising per day. Since a TV campaign spot typically lasts for thirty seconds, each party would have to air above 3000 advertisements per month before it exceeds the monthly limit. Between 1986 and 1998, no party programmed more than 2336 advertisements in any month during the campaign.[24] Thus, there seems to be no need for any party to under-report its television outlays. If anything, the incentive is the opposite: to over-report them in order to claim subsidies. Third, there is no evidence to suggest that the parties' use of television during campaigns has systematically increased. In 1986–98, the combined number of TV spots placed by the two major parties during the last month of the campaign exhibited no particular trend, though it grew substantially before the 1998 election.[25] The assumption that reported TV outlays closely correspond to actual TV expenses, and therefore that the latter have not increased in the recent past, is thus at least as plausible as the alternative.

If not to television, where, then, does the money go? Chart 3.2 suggests that the answer lies largely in party structures and, more precisely, in the need to recreate a national party organisation before every national election. Salaries, payroll costs and professional fees – often paid for services such as polling or strategic advising that are routinely performed by regular structures in most West European parties – consume the largest share of campaign resources (30.5 per cent in 1990, 30.9 per cent in 1994 and 26.6 per cent in 1998). Chronically starved of funds for most of the electoral cycle, the feeble regular structures of the major Costa Rican parties undergo a dramatic transformation in the months prior to the national election. A sudden glut of resources fuels not only an explosive growth in their personnel, but also heavy disbursements on the installation and operation of party branches and campaign headquarters (20 per cent, 8.3 per cent and 13.9 per cent, in 1990, 1994 and 1998, respectively). Together, these items took the share of 'organisational' outlays to more than 50 per cent in 1990 and around 40 per cent in 1994 and 1998. Clearly, if Costa Rican national campaigns have any 'spending trigger' at all it is hardly the excess of television advertising, but the *lack* of permanent party structures.

Two other items, which are direct upshots of the particularities of electoral and party funding legislation in Costa Rica, also play a central role in electoral expenditure. The first of them, transport, is a result of the rule that obliges Costa Rican voters to exercise their suffrage in the same precinct where they were registered by the electoral authority. Since the latter may not correspond with the voter's current place of residence, both major parties have traditionally organised parallel nationwide transportation networks to mobilise their supporters on the election day. The cost of these networks grew to reach nearly 17 per cent of total expenditure in the 1998 election, up from slightly more than 13 per cent in 1990 and 1994.

Equally substantial are the financial costs incurred by parties in order to fund their campaigns. This item is overwhelmingly dominated by costs attached to the parties' traditional method of issuing bonds against the eventual receipt of state funds. This practice has a long history in Costa Rica, linked to the subsidy's secular conception as a post-electoral reimbursement. Already in 1953, before the constitutional consecration of the modern subvention system, the PLN sold at least US$0.9 million in bonds to finance its electoral efforts.[26] The practice provided the parties with most of their campaign funds until 1971. The introduction in 1971 of a public pre-election loan of up to 70 per cent of the eventual subvention did not end the mechanism, but it diminished its importance. With the new rules, parties entitled to the loan would receive ten monthly instalments of interest-paying, immediately tradable state bonds, thereby reducing their need to issue their own financial instruments. The Constitutional Court's annulment of this system in 1991 brought party-issued bonds back to the centre of the parties' financial strategy. These bonds are only rarely sold at face value, normally bearing hefty discounts that amounted to nearly 15 per cent of total spending in the 1994 and 1998 campaigns. Since bond discounts are only partially reimbursed by the state,[27] the system re-introduced in 1991 has entailed a net reduction in the amount of state funding effectively received by the parties, to the benefit of a handful of financial operators.

While it thus seems safe to say that organisational, transport and financial costs absorb the lion's share of electoral expenditure in Costa Rica, this generalisation conceals relevant differences between parties, particularly between major and minor ones. Table 3.3 compares the structure of expenditure of the two main parties and the small, regional Cartaginesa Agricultural Union Party (PUAC).

Table 3.3 displays relevant contrasts between both major parties. A larger allocation of resources to organisational (items 1–2) and logistic (items 4–5) tasks in

Table 3.3: *Campaign expenditure per items in Costa Rican parties, 1990–1998 (%)*

| Item | Party | PLN 1990–8 | PUSC 1990–8 | PUAC 1990–8 (1) |
|------|-------|-----------|------------|----------------|
| 1 | Personnel costs and professional fees | 27.8 | 29.8 | 13.1 |
| 2 | Installation and operation of party branches and campaign headquarters | 13.0 | 15.5 | 16.2 |
| 3 | Bond discount and other financial costs | 10.0 | 10.2 | 5.1 |
| 4 | Transport and fuel | 13.4 | 15.8 | 6.7 |
| 5 | Party meetings and rallies | 3.9 | 5.2 | 2.1 |
| 6 | TV | 11.6 | 8.6 | 0.0 |
| 7 | Other advertising | 16.8 | 12.3 | 46.8 |
| 8 | Various | 3.5 | 2.7 | 10.0 |
| | Total | 100 | 100 | 100 |

Notes: (1) 1990 and 1998 elections only.
Sources: See Appendix.

the PUSC (66.3 per cent to 58.1 per cent in the PLN) is compensated with a heavier proportion of advertising outlays (items 6–7) in the PLN (28.4 per cent to 20.9 per cent in the PUSC). While these differences may in some ways reflect the PLN's greater expertise in organising campaigns since 1953 and its slightly more solid permanent structure, they probably point to a more concrete issue: the fact that the PLN was the incumbent party in 1990 and 1998. As we will see below, advertising providers consistently reward the opposition party – expected to win the presidential election – with much more favourable rates, thus helping it to liberate resources for other expenditure items. During 1990–8 this rule operated to the PUSC's advantage and skewed its expenditure towards non-advertising items.

Differences are much greater between both major parties and the PUAC. For the latter, personnel and transport disbursements, in particular, are considerably less relevant than for major parties. Moreover, the PUAC did not spend *any* resources on TV advertising, relying heavily on other forms of publicity instead. The relative weakness of personnel costs (item 1) in the PUAC points to a general phenomenon: minor and new parties rely much more on voluntary activity than major parties. The words of a former campaign official at the Democratic Force Party (PFD), a left-wing minor party, convey the point well:

The last time around we made an effort, and between January and June of 1997 we had three party militants (on the payroll). By June they were still there, but working for free. And we went on like that till the election. Only one militant, working at the Party's Secretariat, did stay on a more permanent basis, though facing salary problems. The rest was pure voluntary work.[28]

Such a description is common. An intensive use of voluntary work allowed the small Agrarian Labour Action Party (PALA) to elect one deputy in 1998 after a campaign virtually bereft of economic resources. Meanwhile, the core of the campaign structure of the urban-based National Integration Party (PIN), which also managed to elect one representative in 1998, consisted of a cadre of young professionals – doctors, lawyers, dentists, etc. – willing to visit communities and offer free professional advice on behalf of the party. These stories contrast sharply with the way in which the top manager of the PLN's 1994 campaign explained the success of the organisation under his care:

Everybody was earning money. I was paying fees. No one was working for free… Nobody would come to me and say, 'I'll do this for free'. I would take none of it. I would tell them, 'How much are you worth? I'll pay you but you have to do a professional job.' That was the reason behind our success: pure entrepreneurial sense.[29]

The evidence seems to bear out the remarks of former President Rodrigo Carazo, twice a presidential candidate and a long-standing critic of the public subsidy system:

Graph 3.3: *Advertising investment by major parties in Costa Rica: Primary vs. national campaigns, 1986–98*

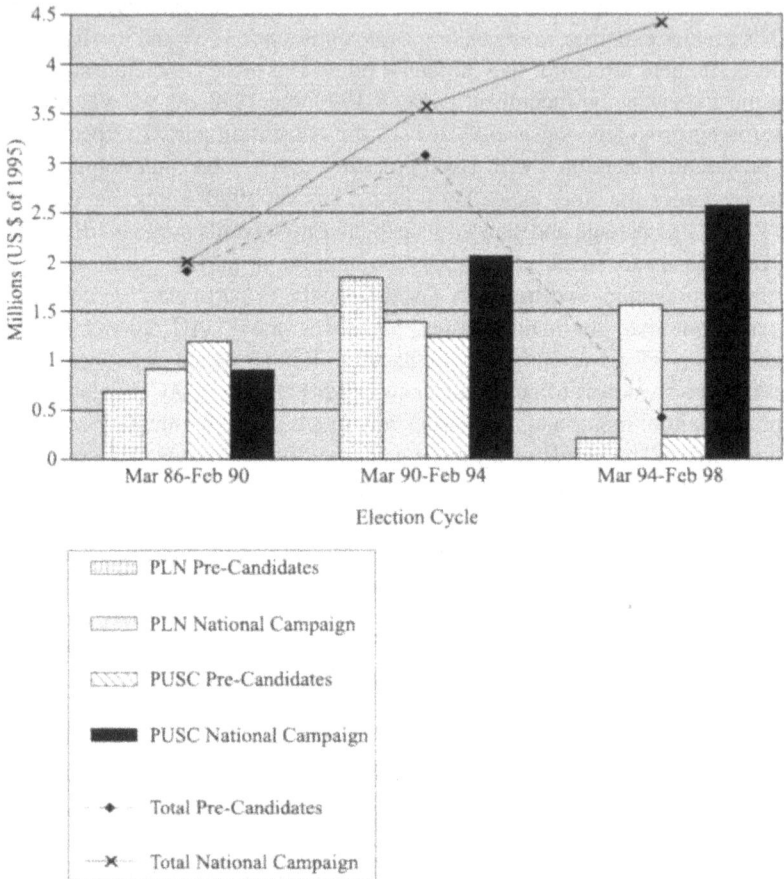

Election Cycle

PLN Pre-Candidates

PLN National Campaign

PUSC Pre-Candidates

PUSC National Campaign

Total Pre-Candidates

Total National Campaign

Sources and method: See Appendix

The more money there is in a campaign, the less voluntary support it attracts. When political parties start distributing money, people do not want to do anything for free. When parties lack resources, people combine civic resources to try and help their party.[30]

The PUAC's low transportation and media advertising expenses are, on the other hand, directly related to its regional nature, which facilitates the spontaneous mobilisation of its constituency and makes irrational the use of advertising in national TV networks. The low priority of TV does not hold true, however, for minor parties that operate on a national scale. For parties such as the PFD, the PIN and the Libertarian Movement (ML), television is an indispensable tool to balance the overwhelming name recognition enjoyed by both major parties at the national level. Not surprisingly, television outlays tend to represent a significant proportion of their campaign budgets, with other forms of advertising absorbing a large share of the rest.[31]

The quest for name recognition also explains the relatively large proportion of advertising expenses in presidential nomination campaigns. Graph 3.3 compares the media advertising outlays incurred by presidential pre-candidates and their parties in the three election cycles leading to the 1990, 1994 and 1998 elections, according to official tariffs.

Graph 3.3 shows that the value of media advertising by presidential hopefuls may on occasion surpass that of their own party or run on a par with it. This happens despite the fact that total expenditure in nomination campaigns is a fraction of that for national campaigns. This is consistent with estimations drawn from the final months of the PLN's 2001 nomination campaign, during which media expenditures absorbed between 39 per cent and 54 per cent of the pre-candidates' budgets.[32]

The reasons behind the intensive use of the media in nomination campaigns are not hard to fathom. Name recognition is paramount in presidential primaries. While party labels offer voters a crucial 'information shortcut' in national campaigns – thus reducing the major parties' need to 'position' themselves in the electoral market – they are meaningless in the context of intra-party races. Moreover, as Table 3.2 attests, the quest for the presidential nomination in the PLN and the PUSC is usually a drawn-out process in which the winning candidate is expected to 'pay his dues' in the way of one or more previous unsuccessful bids. Many nomination campaigns thus have no other objective than increasing the pre-candidate's name recognition through hefty media expenses, with an eye on future presidential races. Finally, primary campaigns are addressed to a limited and politically active section of the electorate, which demands less extensive organisational resources for its mobilisation.

Even with the caveat entailed by the relatively large media expenses of some minor parties and presidential pre-candidates, a basic conclusion is safe: the level of electoral expenditure in Costa Rica is not determined by an uncontrollable, self-propelled trend towards greater television spending, as commonly assumed. The reasons behind current levels of electoral expenditure are more complex and more linked to specific features of the country's electoral and party funding legislation, ranging from registration rules for voters to the timing of the disbursement of public subsidies. Moreover, as shown above, overall spending trends in Costa Rican elections defy facile interpretations.

## CAMPAIGN INCOME: SOURCES AND PRACTICES

A more pressing set of questions concerns how parties and candidates meet the costs examined above. We know by now that a significant part of the answer lies in the country's generous state funding system. However, the precise extent of its relevance and, even more, the origin and implications of non-public electoral funds, have long been clouded by the lack of political finance transparency in Costa Rica. Let us examine what the evidence has to say about these issues.

**State funding and its relative weight**

One crucial claim made by advocates of state funding concerns the role of subsidies in curbing the dependence of parties on private sources of income. We saw in Chapter one that the generosity of state funding has indeed helped to homogenise the financial structure of West European parties, inducing their heavy reliance on the public purse. Is this the case in Costa Rica?

The answer is yes, but not without qualifications. It is certainly the case in the context of *national* campaigns (i.e. excluding intra-party contests), in which direct state subsidies cover a very high proportion of total outlays. According to Graph 3.4, throughout six campaigns between 1978 and 1998 this proportion has remained consistently around 60–70 per cent, ranging from a low of 57 per cent

Graph 3.4: *State funding as a proportion of total expenditure in national campaigns in Costa Rica, 1978–1998*

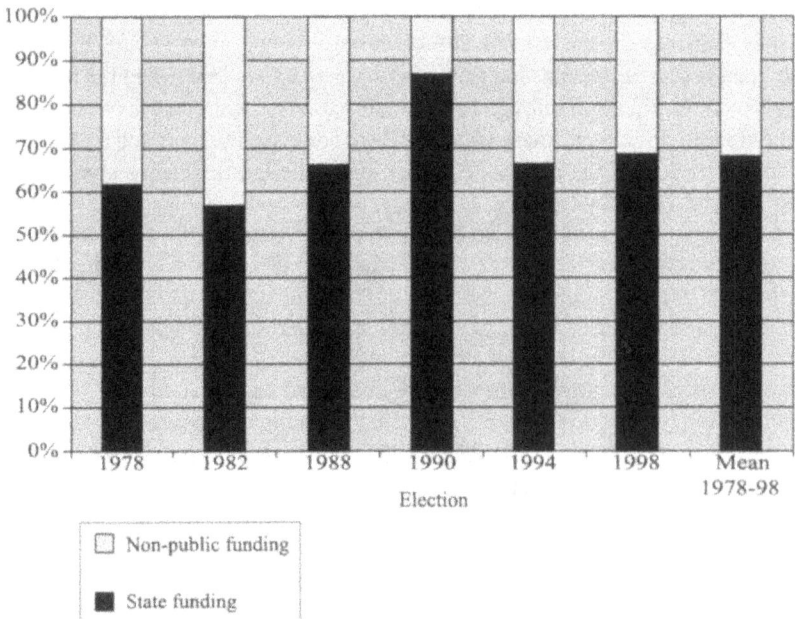

Sources: See Appendix

in 1982 to a peak of 86.9 per cent in 1990. As explained above, variations in this rate are normally related to changes in the availability of state funding.

The information in the chart is consistent with the perception of every campaign manager, financial officer and presidential candidate from both major parties interviewed in the course of this investigation. Not *one* of them put the proportion of state funding in their own party's national campaigns below 50 per cent, and most indeed provided much higher estimates. This evidence suggests that rather than state support playing an *additive* role vis-à-vis private funding in national campaigns, as observed by Rodolfo Cerdas,[33] the opposite is true: it is the latter that is an addition to the former.

This is true for the party system as a whole, as much as for its components. Table 3.4 reports the rates of subsidy dependence of the PLN and the PUSC, as well as the average rate for minor parties, during national campaigns.

While the average rate of subsidy dependence of both major parties is very similar, their behaviour across time differs. PLN campaigns grew consistently more reliant on the subsidy over the six elections analysed, while those of the PUSC followed a more stable path. In both cases the 1990 election stands out as an oddity. As suggested above, such a steep hike in subsidy dependence across the party system is probably linked to the peculiarities of the 1989–90 campaign, strongly dominated by the fundraising scandals of the previous election cycle. Leaving aside this deviation, the divergent secular paths of the PLN and the PUSC point to a more relevant issue. When coupled with its considerably larger expenditures in the 1990, 1994 and 1998 national campaigns, the PUSC's lower subvention dependency rates during the 1990s are suggestive of a sizeable fundraising advantage over the PLN. This trend coincides with the PUSC's consolidation as the major centre-right political force in Costa Rica from the 1980s onwards.

The levels of subsidy reliance of minor parties are less clear. Table 3.4 puts them below those of major parties, a somewhat counterintuitive finding. As shown in Chapter one, minor parties in Western Europe display a high reliance on public funds, due to the dearth of fee-paying members and their limited access to instrumentally motivated donations, which flow largely into the major parties' coffers. Both conditions apply to minor parties in Costa Rica. The answer to the puzzle

Table 3.4: *State funding as a proportion of total expenditure in national campaigns in Costa Rican parties, 1978–1998 (%)*

| Party      Election | 1978 | 1982 | 1986 | 1990 | 1994 | 1998 | Mean 1978–98 |
|---|---|---|---|---|---|---|---|
| PLN | 47.5 | 56.7 | 66.5 | 89.1 | 77.7 | 78.8 | 69.4 |
| Unidad/PUSC | 59.3 | 65.9 | 64.3 | 85.1 | 58.4 | 65.8 | 66.5 |
| Other minor subsidy recipients (average) | 73.6 | 66.9 | 57.3 | 82.5 | 55.4 | 39.5 | 62.5 |

Sources: See Appendix.

lies, largely, in the features of the subsidy system. Levels of subsidy dependence amongst minor parties are affected by the subsidy's nature as a post-election reimbursement – which deprives them of public resources during the campaign – and, above all, by the cumbersome reporting process required in order to claim the subsidy. Small parties often find this exercise well beyond the capabilities of their weak administrative structures. This combination of factors results in lower subvention rates than would otherwise flow from their vote share.

Although the figures reported in Graph 3.4 and Table 3.4 give a reasonably accurate idea of the level of reliance on state funding of Costa Rican parties in national campaigns, they should be qualified in two important ways. The first of them concerns the presence of unofficial forms of state support for the incumbent party. For a long time the most conspicuous of them was the use of the so-called *partidas específicas*, small pork-barrel budget appropriations targeted at specific communities, frequently used for local infrastructure projects.[34] Though a small proportion of the government's budget,[35] these appropriations, virtually monopolised by the deputies of the incumbent party and delivered by them to their communities, represented an average of US$23.3 million per year in 1986–97.[36] The system was long criticised as a form of patronage, and revamped in 1998, trying to subject the allocation of funds to technical criteria and eliminate the overt inter-

Graph 3.5: *Television advertising by government agencies in Costa Rica, 1995–99*

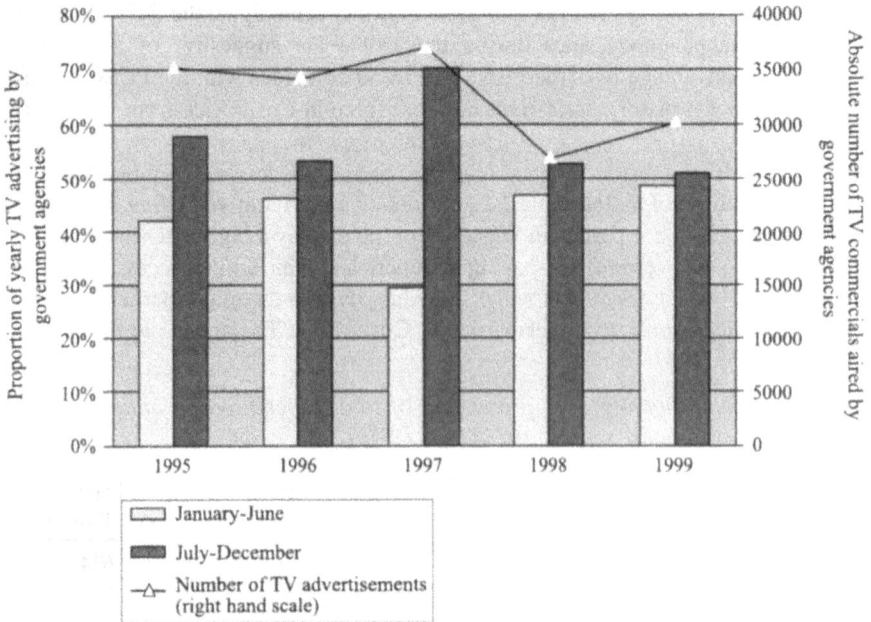

Sources and method: See Appendix

vention of deputies from the process.[37] The success of this reform in curbing the manipulation of the specific appropriations by the incumbent party is dubious. The allocation of these funds is now largely under the purview of the executive, climbing again to nearly US$14 million in 1999[38] after a total truce in 1998.

Media advertising by government agencies is another form of support for the party in power. Though legislated against and relatively subdued when compared to the Uruguayan experience, to be examined below, the electoral manipulation of official advertising persists in Costa Rica. Graph 3.5 shows the number of television commercials placed by ministries and key government agencies over a five-year period, including the pre-election year of 1997.[39]

Graph 3.5 suggests that while the election cycle seems to have exerted only a moderate influence over the total amount of official publicity, it clearly affected its timing. The high allocation of publicity during the second semester of 1997 – just before the February 1998 election – is conspicuous. Not only was it concentrated in only three months[40] but also in some institutions with obvious electoral relevance, such as the Ministry of Public Works and Transport (MOPT).[41] In 1997, an advertising blitz by the government preceded the launching of the campaign of its own party. Though the available data does not allow for any long-term inference, the occurrence of government advertising manipulation *despite* the legal controls introduced against it before the 1998 election probably attests to the continuation of a procedure routinely used by previous administrations.

The second qualification to the subsidy dependence figures given above concerns their scope: high as they may be, they only apply to *national* campaigns. They exclude intra-party and mayoral races, which, as seen above, absorb an important share of electoral spending in Costa Rica. Due to the subsidy's restrictive regulation and to the parties' reluctance to reduce the pool of resources available for the national campaign, both major parties have shied away from overtly allocating a share of state funds to presidential nomination races. Bar few exceptions, any allocation has been done on an *ad-hoc* basis after the primary, allowing the winner to cover a small proportion of his nomination expenses with public funds.

While still high, the subsidy dependence rate of the Costa Rican party system falls sharply, in some cases below 50 per cent, if the presumed costs of intra-party elections are included in the calculation (see Table 3.5).

Though the expenditure figures for intra-party elections should be taken with caution, a clear point stems from the table: private funding continues to play a central role in campaign finance in Costa Rica. Private funding has been replaced to a significant extent in national campaigns, where it arguably matters most. Indeed, no matter how much the generosity of public subsidies may have pushed major Costa Rican parties to increase unnecessarily their electoral expenses, it is hard to see how these parties could wage a full-blown national campaign equipped only with the amounts of private funding that they currently raise.[42] In all likelihood, thus, the absence of state funding would simply intensify their quest for private contributions. Yet, the replacement effect of state funding has been visibly eroded

Table 3.5: *State funding dependence rates in Costa Rica (including intra-party elections), 1986–1998*

| | A | B | C | D | E | F | G |
|---|---|---|---|---|---|---|---|
| Election | State A/(B+C+D) | Spending in | Spending in | Spending in | A / B | | A/(B+C) |
| | funding (US$m) | national campaign (US$m) | presidential primaries (US$m) | intra-party legislative contests (US$m) | (%) | (%) | (%) |
| 1986 | 12.2 | 18.3 | 2.4 (1) | 2.5 | 66.4 | 58.7 | 52.4 |
| 1990 | 12.6 | 14.5 | 4.1 | 2.5 | 86.9 | 67.8 | 59.8 |
| 1994 | 13.6 | 20.5 | 5.9 (2) | 2.5 | 66.2 | 51.4 | 47.0 |
| 1998 | 11.5 | 16.8 | 0.8 | 2.5 | 68.4 | 65.3 | 57.7 |
| Mean | | | | | | | |

Notes: (1) No direct or indirect estimate of the 1982–5 pre-campaign is available. Since the total cost of open primaries in each election cycle has been estimated at around US$4 million, the cost of the PLN's 1984–5 open contest was estimated in the table at US$2 million, while the PUSC's primary-less pre-campaign was calculated at US$0.4 million, following the party's experience in the 1994–7 cycle, when no primary took place. (2) There are two estimates in Table 3.2 for the cost of the Figueres nomination campaign in 1990–3. The lower, more reliable figure (US$0.9 million) has been used in the table.
Sources: See Appendix.

by the role that private funds now play in nomination contests. The absence of subsidies in primary elections poses a serious obstacle to potential candidates and puts a small group of private contributors in a vital position. The case of primary elections in Costa Rica shows an important point: the effects of state funding in curbing the parties' dependence on private contributions are strongly contingent on the peculiarities of the electoral system and of the subsidies' own regulation (their timing and recipients, for instance), rather than on the sheer presence or generosity of subsidies. In this matter, the Devil is clearly in the details.

If private contributions are still at the centre of campaign finance in Costa Rica, how do parties and candidates raise them? What are the implications of the fundraising process?

## Fundraising processes: Mechanics and implications

The process whereby Costa Rican parties raise campaign funds involves two closely related but analytically distinct activities. It includes, first, the complex mechanisms used by parties to translate state subsidies into actual cash. Second, it features the set of procedures whereby parties collect private donations from domestic and international sources. While these activities may significantly differ in major and minor parties, they are virtually identical in the PLN and the PUSC, which attract an overwhelming proportion of public and private funds in Costa Rica. Since the realisation of state subsidies is the more important of the two activities from a quantitative standpoint, let us begin there the analysis of fundraising practices.

*The activation of state subsidies*
Far from curtailing private fundraising activities, the availability of state funding in Costa Rica crucially depends upon them. Indeed, the subsidy's design as a post-election reimbursement leaves the parties with the task of raising the cash needed for the campaign from non-public sources. For this purpose parties have traditionally issued bonds backed by the expectations attached to the eventual reimbursement of their election expenses.

The bonds' issue procedure has remained virtually unchanged since the 1970s, and probably before that. The system relies on the parties' knowledge of the amount of state funding that will be made available for the forthcoming election, based on the estimation rules defined by the constitution (Article 96.1). With this knowledge in hand, each party estimates the proportion of the vote that it is likely to get in the election according to its electoral history and prospects. Since the allocation of subsidies follows proportional rules, vote estimations translate automatically into financial prospects. Subsequently, the party's fundraising committee issues two or three series of bonds. The first series ('A' bonds) comprises the sum of the subsidy that the party deems of virtually certain retrieval. For both major parties, this amount has normally stood around 40 per cent of total state funding, i.e. the vote share which main parties are unlikely to fall under. A second series ('B' bonds) covers a further proportion of the subsidy, whose attainment by the party is uncertain. A third one ('C' bonds) adds yet another sum which is known in advance to be of nearly impossible recuperation. The retrieval of these sums does not depend solely on the party's achievement of a given electoral result. It presupposes a second condition: that the party will properly report its electoral expenses to the CGR.

Party bonds, even those classified as 'A', are hardly ever bought at face value. Price discounts allow buyers to cover not only the risks involved in the operation, but also their financial costs until the moment of payment of the bonds, well after the election. Indeed, it is not until the CGR determines the sum that each party is entitled to receive from the state that bondholders may exchange their party-issued documents for proper interest-earning state bonds. Investors retrieve the face value of their titles insofar as the party's subsidy entitlement is enough to cover each bond issue in its entirety. Otherwise, the shortfall is distributed pro-rata between bondholders (EC, Article 191). These rules apply to successive bond issues, which are paid only after the first issue has been liquidated and therefore entail a much higher risk. In fact, while the second issue is usually considered a high-risk investment, the third one operates, in practice, as a means to attract donations.

Table 3.6, shows the bonds put in circulation by the financial committees of major parties during the 1994 and 1998 campaigns, and clarifies the system's workings:

With the exception of Class 'C' titles, the logic underpinning the transaction of

Table 3.6: *Bond issues by major parties in Costa Rica, 1994–1998*

| Election ⟶ | | 1994 | | | 1998 | | |
|---|---|---|---|---|---|---|---|
| Party ↓ | Bond issue ↓ | Amount (US$m) | Issue as % of state funding | Face value retrieved (%) | Amount (US$m) | Issue as % of state funding | Face value retrieved (%) |
| PLN | A | 6.6 | 43.0 | 100 | 6.3 | 45.0 | 83.2 |
| | B | 1.2 | 8.0 | 53.0 | 1.0 | 7.0 | 0 |
| | C | 1.4 | 9.0 | 0 | -- | -- | -- |
| PUSC | A | 6.1 | 40.0 | 100 | 6.5 | 46.7 | 90.8 |
| | B | 2.2 | 15.0 | 28.0 | 1.6 | 11.7 | 0 |
| | C | -- | -- | -- | 1.0 | 7.0 | 0 |
| | Total (1) | 17.6 | 114.9 | -- | 16.3 | 117.4 | -- |

Notes: (1) Due to rounding, total sum may not coincide.
Sources: See Appendix.

party bonds is much closer to that of a risky commercial loan than to that of a political contribution. If the system is, in essence, a means to attract loans, it is unsurprising that prime party bonds are sold, largely, amongst banks and financial intermediaries.[43] Four major private financial operators purchased 94.9 per cent of the US$5.5 millions sold in bonds by the PLN in the run-up to the 1998 election.[44] A further US$0.6 million was used by the PLN as collateral for loans obtained at yet another private bank, a procedure extensively employed by the PUSC. Remaining 'A' bonds were sold amongst individual investors and service providers, who continue to be the main outlet for subsequent bond issues, as well as for the few titles put in circulation by minor groups.

Although the system has operated for several decades, the parties' heavy reliance on *private* banks is a recent phenomenon. Since the 1950s and until 1994, state-owned banks figured prominently in the parties' financial strategy, not least due to their near-monopoly over Costa Rica's financial sector. However, the stringent banking regulations put in place in the wake of the collapse of the state-owned Banco Anglo-Costarricense (BAC) in 1994 have made it more difficult for state banks to trade in party-issued bonds.[45] Private financial operators have thus become an inescapable option for parties in need of campaign cash.

The dangers derived from the new situation, as well as the irony of having a state funding system largely dependent on private investors, have not gone unnoticed by parties. As a former PLN's Secretary-General noted, 'a few "fat cats" who own the banks and the financial trading houses are profiting with the money of the Costa Rican people. Yet, they are essential under the scheme we have'.[46] Though most party officers insist on the primarily financial nature of bond transactions, a former party treasurer did not rule out other motivations:

...this system somehow betrays and defeats the (subsidy's) fundamental purpose of making the parties more independent from strong financial or economic groups… The system allows some people to earn important money with (the discounts). Possibly, the ability to purchase those bonds also gives them in some cases…chances to enjoy access and influence.[47]

Several examples suggest that bond purchases, a cheap alternative to full-fledged contributions, have indeed been used in the past to further particular political interests. During the 1970s it became known that EHG Enterprises, a Puerto-Rico-based company, had bought US$400,000 in PLN bonds in the run-up to the 1970 presidential election, which resulted in a victory by José Figueres. Prominent amongst the firm's main shareholders was Clovis McAlpin, a controversial businessman indicted in the US for his participation in various fund-diversion scams. In the early 1970s, McAlpin fled to Costa Rica where he became a close associate of Figueres.[48] Two decades later, early in the Calderón-Fournier administration, Lloyd S. Rubin, a Panama-based financier, was appointed as Costa Rica's commercial attaché in Panama, a post serviced with diplomatic immunity. His appointment, preceded by nearly US$140,000 in bond purchases during Calderón-Fournier's 1985–6 and 1989–90 presidential bids, was soon cancelled when it became known that Rubin was implicated in money-laundering activities.[49]

Thus, while it is probably true that the bond-trading system is mostly guided by financial considerations on the part of bondholders, these examples suggest that, by forcing parties to seek private investors in order to make state funds effective, the mechanism harbours a dangerous potential. Exchanges between politicians and bond purchasers may simply be a watered down version of the troubling links that often bind politicians and plain political donors.

*The quest for non-public sources*
Though less economically significant than bond trading, the mechanisms put in place by the parties to raise private donations are more intricate and politically relevant. Their dynamics unveil interesting aspects of the internal life of Costa Rican parties and the social environment in which they operate.

**Candidates, committees, and social networks.** As opposed to party bond transactions, which take place in the months immediately prior to the national election, the pursuit of private contributions starts up early in the election cycle. In the absence of state subsidies for nomination processes, the creation of a fundraising committee is one of the first decisions made by any presidential aspirant. This group, typically formed by five to ten members, is recruited amongst the candidate's innermost circle, and will provide, in case of victory, some of the key members of his cabinet. Its selection, particularly that of its chairperson, is done with two criteria in mind: social connections and reputation for trustworthiness. In the words of a high-ranking PUSC politician, which presage the social bias that pervades the private fundraising process:

Members of the financial committee normally have professional prestige in the business realm. They are well-known, wealthy people who will inspire trust in other wealthy people, trust that their contributions will be well kept and well spent.[50]

Though appointed during the pre-campaign, the role of this financial committee extends beyond the latter. The onset of the pre-campaign heralds a shift of the party's financial centre of gravity from its headquarters to the pre-candidates' fundraising committees. This displacement becomes ever more visible as the election cycle proceeds. Indeed, once the nomination contest has run its course, the winning pre-candidate's financial committee largely supersedes the party's official financial structures. This is as much a result of the candidate's trust in her own team, as of her nearly absolute dominance over the party, a phenomenon that permeates all spheres of party life. A long-term member of fundraising committees in the PLN observed:

> Any duality (of funding structures) disappears from the moment the candidate says 'this is the campaign's treasurer'... Sometimes there is a party treasurer who refuses to collaborate, but even then the weight of the power expectation, which lies with the candidate, dictates the rules of the game and thus his own structure ends up in control.[51]

This is merely one of the ways in which the presidential candidate dominates the fundraising process. In both main parties his direct involvement is deemed vital for the success of the financial effort. His participation often takes the shape of a substantial economic contribution to his own campaign, notably during the nomination struggle. At the very least it entails his presence at a myriad fundraising activities – from private meetings with potential donors to public fundraisers – which normally absorb between 20 per cent and 30 per cent of his time schedule, and up to 40 per cent at certain moments of the campaign. According to the financial chairman of the PLN's 1994 campaign, 'the candidate becomes *the* fundraising figure. Without the candidate you cannot raise any funds'.[52]

As the financial committee's own members, Costa Rican political contributors are recruited within a remarkably restricted social circle and through a process in which personal connections are vital. The nucleus of this circle is found amongst each candidate's own connections – relatives, business partners and friends – as well as their party's traditional financial backers. The latter, a small cadre of prominent businesspersons of known political affiliation that a former party treasurer compared to a 'gentlemen's club',[53] not only contribute routinely to their party's campaigns but also feature, consistently, in its fundraising commissions. This 'hard core' of contributors is expanded by the social networks provided by the members of the candidate's fundraising committee. The latter are expected to contact their friends and acquaintances and are frequently given contribution quotas that they are relied upon to raise amongst them.[54] The strategy of tapping social contacts often results in a sector-based organisation, whereby a co-ordinator in each main business activity – industrial, financial, coffee-growing, banana-export-ing, etc. – spearheads and legitimises the candidate's quest for funds in the sector.

Familiarity, reputation and trust are thus the lubricants that oil the fundraising process. As an important entrepreneur noted, fundraising in Costa Rica is about 'businessmen asking businessmen for money... You know who you're giving your money to, otherwise you don't give anything'.[55] Moreover, it is the ability to exploit these long-term links that largely defines the prowess of the fundraising co-ordinator. A former financial chair of the PUSC observed that 'there are some people to whom you can't say no. This is part of the secret: to send an emissary that can obtain a contribution'.[56]

The presence of a trusted envoy is not always enough, however. In fact, a sub-tle code operates whereby visits to potential donors are reinforced with the pres-ence of members of the candidate's immediate entourage, or, ultimately, the can-didate himself, according to the size of the expected contribution. In the search for large contributions the candidate's attendance is indeed a must, as remarked by Alberto Dent, the financial chairman of PUSC's 1997–8 campaign:

> If you want someone to sign an 8 million colones cheque, then the candidate has to be there. At the beginning of the campaign the candidate had to devote two afternoons per week, and three when the campaign was already in full swing, to such visits... If we can fit five or six appointments per afternoon, it means that the candidate will be able to visit roughly ten donors per week, which translates into roughly eighty people during the official campaign. Amongst those eighty people you have to raise 500 million colones, more or less.[57]

Somewhat perversely, fundraising mores guarantee that the political operators that will potentially wield the greatest influence in any future administration are precisely those expected to establish direct contact with the largest potential donors.

**Types of contributions.** Up-front cash donations are merely one way to con-tribute. Indeed, even with the presence of the candidate, an eight million colones cheque (about US$33,000), of the kind mentioned by Dent, is probably an oddity in Costa Rican campaigns. Though single donations of US$100,000 and even US$150,000 have been known,[58] large private contributions are often split into smaller ones, either to comply with the ceilings introduced in 1996, or, simply, to reduce the economic impact on the donor. An increasingly common option, par-ticularly preferred in nomination contests, is the monthly contribution over long periods. These contributions vary from US$30 for an average liberal professional to US$1,000–2,000 in the case of wealthy entrepreneurs, and add up to sizeable sums in the course of a protracted campaign. This may be compounded by other kinds of help, including, as seen above, bond purchases (particularly type 'B' bonds) or contributions in kind, ranging from providing paid personnel to the par-ties to providing free transportation or food during election day.

However, rather than through in-kind options, which, with the exception of television time, are strongly discouraged by the parties, additional contributions are normally channelled through participation in the myriad special activities organised by the candidates' fundraising committees. These include raffles – often of cars or artworks donated by the committee's own members – and periodic fundraising gatherings attended by the candidate. The latter may take the shape of a structured programme of meetings over breakfast, lunch or dinner, often targeted at specific business and professional sectors. These activities facilitate the candidate's contact with various economic sectors and help to attract people to their campaign structure. Yet, crucially, they are also a means to activate a vital fundraising tool: social pressure. A prominent businessman described the dynamic at a typical social gathering attended by the candidate:

> A former president told me the strategy that he used at these occasions: 'I deliver a speech, but before I do that, I have already agreed with someone that after the speech he will stand up and say "This is the man that the country needs and I want to invite you all to contribute". This person would then pledge publicly, say, 500,000 colones. He would say so, though he may not give me anything in the end. The important thing is to say it, so that everyone stands up and does the same.' This is exactly the point: it is social pressure... Costa Ricans, and human beings in general, act like this: if you are in the group and everyone gives money, then you have to give money as well.[59]

Fundraising meetings are a common occurrence throughout the campaign and increase in frequency and price as the campaign heats up. As with private audiences with contributors, the candidate's presence at these activities comes at a price:

> In our case, the candidate's time was valued as follows: a breakfast was worth one million colones, a lunch was worth two-and-one-half million, and a dinner was worth five million. If you wanted to have a dinner in your house, and less than five million were expected from the guests, then the candidate would not attend. Those were the initial rates. Later on they went up, of course.[60]

Fundraising gatherings reach the apex in the days before the national election, when both major parties traditionally hold a 'Victory Dinner'. The price of one seat at the latter is measured in the thousands of dollars, having reached US$20,000 per guest on at least one occasion.[61]

**The case of nomination campaigns.** Fundraising processes are laborious and disheartening, and never more so than in nomination campaigns. Though the fundraising work in the latter does not differ significantly from that carried out during national campaigns, the number of potential donors and the size of the largest contributions shrink considerably. 'The possibility of obtaining private donations in a national campaign exceeds by a factor of five, six or seven times that in a pre-campaign', observed a former campaign manager.[62] Another fundraiser remarked that, 'pre-campaigns rest upon the shoulders of a very limited number of people that truly want to promote the candidate... Normally 100 or 200 people put down 2 or 3 million colones each, and the pre-campaign gets done with that.'[63]

The explanation for this is related to the larger number of aspirants at the nomination stage – which reduces the number of potential financial backers for each pre-candidate – and to the absence of party-issued bonds during the primary season. The latter allow supporters the chance to retrieve at least a share of their contribution. More important, however, are other reasons grounded on the instrumental value of contributions. One entrepreneur remarked that 'businessmen are very reluctant [to contribute in pre-campaigns] because the odds of victory for pre-candidates are much more uncertain. Normally, you don't contribute unless you have a personal commitment with the candidate'.[64] Another one added, 'entrepreneurs are interested in the final campaign, the presidential campaign... People say "if I contribute to the pre-campaign, then I will later have to do it again in the campaign", and money does not stretch for everything'.[65] Ultimately, 'contributors are interested in supporting the prospective president, rather than the prospective candidate'.[66] Not surprisingly, candidates and donors uniformly regard private contributions in pre-campaigns as less interest-driven than those doled out during national campaigns.

The reluctance to support pre-campaigns has a critical implication: it forces presidential pre-candidates to contribute heavily to their own campaigns, thereby raising a formidable obstacle to many potential aspirants. A current pre-candidate in the PLN noted that 'if you don't have your own economic base, don't even go into a nomination contest, for contributions in the latter are exceedingly low'.[67] Pre-candidates are indeed *expected* to bear the cost of their campaign by their followers. A former PUSC Secretary-General noted that, 'the candidate must necessarily have a certain sum and say "in order to be the candidate I'm willing to put down this money"... As the person with the greatest interest in the post, he must have a certain sum in order to jump-start the activities'.[68]

Most candidates take this expectation seriously. A former aspirant in the PUSC estimated his family's support to his own nomination bid at nearly 80 per cent of its total cost.[69] Moreover, the dire fate undergone by former President Miguel A. Rodríguez' once large personal fortune, mostly spent during the 1987–8 and 1992–93 pre-campaigns, is well known.[70]

**Domestic business elites and the case of media owners.** The pre-candidates' economic 'dues' are but one symptom of the elitism that bedevils fundraising processes in Costa Rica. The latter's most noticeable feature is the unqualified bias in favour of the participation of a small social elite. With the limited exceptions entailed by the involvement of professional strata in certain fundraising activities and in the free provision of specific services, private resources raised domestically by the PLN and the PUSC come exclusively from the same social group that collects them: wealthy businesspeople. The acute dearth of fee-paying members,[71] the secular weakness of the country's trade unions,[72] the interlocking of political and economic elites and the deeply ingrained notion that non-public funds *must* be sought amongst business circles, have resulted in similarly lopsided and unimaginative fundraising practices in both parties. The expectation that pre-candidates must largely fund their own electoral efforts is, hence, but a corollary of the basic assumption that underpins fundraising processes in Costa Rica: if top entrepreneurs are not willing to support campaigns financially, no one else will. Former President Rafael A. Calderón-Fournier articulated this presumption with disarming clarity:

> Only entrepreneurial sectors can contribute economically. Popular sectors contribute with their voluntary work, with their labour and their vote, but obviously it is the wealthy sectors of the country that can give money.[73]

A former campaign manager of the PUSC noted that,

> Contributions are not sought amongst the middle classes. Mass contributions are not sought. It is industrial and commercial sectors that contribute... Basically the country's big traders and big industrialists; big interests and that's it.[74]

In a small country, big interests are few and known to all. Unsurprisingly, the same big political donors feature, largely, in every election cycle. Thus, many significant financial backers of the PLN's standard-bearer in 2002, Rolando Araya, were already prominent contributors to Oscar Arias' candidacy in 1985–6.[75] Moreover, given the restricted social circle within which fundraising takes place, many contributors – particularly the wealthiest amongst them – are approached by both major parties during the national campaign and support both of them. One entrepreneur observed that, 'the big people will contribute to both... Not everyone is like that, only the "big fish"'.[76] Crucially, the small circle of donors helps to raise the average private contribution to levels that are far from insignificant. The evidence of high-priced fundraising dinners and Alberto Dent's above-quoted admission that presidential candidates must raise nearly US$2 million amongst not many more than eighty donors clearly point in this direction. Though *overall* private funding rests at relatively low levels in Costa Rica and is more than counterbalanced by state subsidies – at least in national campaigns – the *concentration* of private funds in a small circle of contributors remains a real concern.

However, the concentration of private contributors neither presupposes nor leads to any co-ordinated effort on the part of donors. Another central feature of fundraising practices in Costa Rica is the extent to which they are defined by *individual* links between donors and politicians, rather than by the *collective* participation of social or economic sectors. Within a close-knit circle, long-term familiarity and direct contact between contributors and politicians override the intermediary role of organised lobbies. 'If you contribute,' noted an influential businessman, 'you do it in a rigorously personal manner, because you are a good friend of the candidate, because you've known him for a long time, because he is a good candidate and you want to help him'.[77] Miguel Schyfter, a former president of the country's industrial lobby, gave an interesting account of the prevalence of individual over corporative interests:

> When I was a member of the directing board of the Chamber of Industry, I felt that we were not sufficiently organised in this aspect. We don't use the strength of our contributions, because they are not felt as though they go together. Contributions are made according to (each person's) political preferences, and this makes no sense if you want to maximise your influence. But no, in Costa Rica each of us wants to be *the strongest one*... I always felt that we could have been much stronger and say, 'Look, here are 200 million colones', rather than giving 1 million or half-a-million each...[78]

Corporate co-ordination is hindered by familial relations between entrepreneurs and candidates, as much as by the fact that corporate bodies invariably include members of both major parties. Prospects for collective action are further undermined by the ideological and programmatic overlap between both major parties. The experience of the last two decades clearly shows that, despite rhetorical disputes, the PLN and the PUSC are both solidly grounded on pro-business platforms and that for nearly every business sector the policy outcomes to be expected from a government of either party are marginally different at most. In a context of convergent public policy options, corporative contributions may well be a futile instrument. 'Being the strongest one', i.e. construing contributions as *individual* pursuits aimed at securing personal benefits, is probably the most efficient way to secure any pay-off from a political donation in Costa Rica.

Though donors may be found across all business activities – with variations between them largely explained by circumstantial personal links – specific features can nevertheless turn entrepreneurs in certain economic sectors into big political contributors. When asked about the funding role of specific business sectors, the head of one of the country's business chambers identified some conspicuous cases:

> The strongest (contributing) sector is the mass media, especially television. These are very, very strong contributors, particularly in kind: by cutting the price of their service or even giving it freely. Also public works contractors. This is a slightly more complicated and understandable case, for this sector has only one client: the State... Hence, contributing to both parties is standard practice for them... All other business contributions cannot be explained by sectorial motives, but rather by personal bonds with the candidate or his campaign.[79]

The importance of television stations as political contributors is well known and far exceeds the relevance of television disbursements in election spending.

Indeed, television outlays are relatively low in Costa Rica precisely because television stations are heavy political contributors. Though electoral laws formally compel media firms to publicise their official rates and grant equal treatment to all parties, this does not prevent media owners from making donations in kind to specific parties, thereby overruling in practice the desired effects of the norms. Thus, significant price differences exist and no party or candidate pays the official rate.[80] A presidential aspirant remarked that, 'owners of television stations in the 90s are the equivalent of bank owners in the 40s... Who reaches a good agreement with Channel 7 and Channel 6, will enjoy great advantages'.[81]

Though rate discounts and additional benefits are a normal component of relations between media firms and large advertisers, there are additional reasons that account for the flexibility that surrounds political advertising dealings. The weight of government advertising, and, more importantly, the fact that radio and television frequencies are ultimately owned by the state and conceded to particulars for negligible annual fees, no doubt act as incentives for the liberality of media owners towards future state authorities.[82] State ownership of wireless frequencies helps to explain the greater rigidity with which newspapers, spared of licensing requirements, treat their advertising rates.[83]

By comparing the value of campaign advertising according to official rates with the parties' reported media disbursements, Table 3.7 allows us to appreciate the remarkable generosity of television stations, in particular, during national campaigns.

Table 3.7 shows that, with the exception of the PLN in 1990, major parties received significant price breaks from media providers in recent campaigns. While discounts by radio stations and newspapers seem to have played an important role in 1990, total media discounts (column C) in the 1994 and 1998 elections were almost entirely attributable to price breaks granted by TV stations (column G). Moreover, deals with media firms have become increasingly favourable for major parties. The absolute difference between the value of media advertising at official prices and the parties' effective disbursements moved from a net *overcharge* of US$0.15 million in 1990 to a net *discount* of US$0.34million in 1994 and US$2.34 million four years later (column C). Column H shows that dealings with TV channels, in particular, became consistently more favourable to *all* parties over the three elections examined. In the case of the PUSC in 1998, reported television outlays stood at less than one quarter of the official price of the purchased advertising time, a discount amounting to a net donation of US$1.7 million. This was, in all probability, the largest contribution by any economic sector in the entire election cycle.

The table also shows that the largesse towards major parties has not been extended to the small PFD, punished with relatively high rates in all media outlets. This finding, partially due to the much smaller volume of publicity purchased by the PFD, is consistent with evidence that suggests that media donations are underpinned by instrumental motives. A comparison of media and TV contribution indexes for both major parties (columns D and H), i.e. the relative price paid

Table 3.7: *Media advertising by parties according to official prices vs. reported media expenditures in Costa Rica, 1990–1998 (US$m of 1995)*

| Party | Election | Television + radio + press | | | | Only television | | | |
|---|---|---|---|---|---|---|---|---|---|
| | | (A) Advertising value at official rates | (B) Reported expenses | (C) Absolute difference index (A-B) | (D) Media contribution (A/B) | (E) Advertising value at official rates | (F) Reported expenses | (G) Absolute difference index (E-F) | (H) TV contribution (E/F) |
| PLN | 1990 | 0.91 | 1.19 | -0.28 | 0.76 | 0.61 | 1.08 | -0.47 | 0.56 |
| | 1994* | 1.37 | 1.06 | 0.31 | 1.30 | 1.01 | 0.73 | 0.28 | 1.38 |
| | 1998 | 1.53 | 0.89 | 0.64 | 1.72 | 1.27 | 0.83 | 0.44 | 1.53 |
| PUSC | 1990* | 0.89 | 0.76 | 0.13 | 1.17 | 0.58 | 0.72 | -0.14 | 0.81 |
| | 1994 | 2.04 | 2.00 | 0.04 | 1.02 | 1.38 | 1.34 | 0.05 | 1.03 |
| | 1998* | 2.54 | 0.84 | 1.70 | 3.04 | 2.26 | 0.56 | 1.70 | 4.03 |
| PFD | 1994 | 0.002 | 0.028 | -0.026 | 0.07 | 0.002 | 0.013 | -0.01 | 0.15 |
| | 1998 | 0.13 | 0.21 | -0.08 | 0.62 | 0.11 | 0.13 | -0.02 | 0.84 |

Notes: * Denotes main opposition party at the time of election.
Sources and Method: See Appendix.

by both major parties for their publicity, systematically yields a larger benefit (lower relative rates) for the opposition party, routinely expected to win the presidential election in Costa Rica. As depicted in Table 3.8, in 1990–98 the media

Table 3.8: *Contributions in kind by media and television firms in Costa Rica, 1990–1998 (ratio major opposition party/incumbent party)*

| Election | Ratio of media contribution index | Ratio of television contribution index |
|---|---|---|
| 1990 | 1.54 | 1.45 |
| 1994 | 1.27 | 1.34 |
| 1998 | 1.76 | 2.63 |
| Mean 1990–8 | 1.52 | 1.81 |

Sources and method: See Appendix.

contribution index on average was 52 per cent larger for the opposition (PUSC in 1990 and 1998, PLN in 1994) than for the incumbent party. This figure grows to 81 per cent in the case of television advertising. Although these figures cover only a limited number of elections, they do suggest that media generosity is a finely targeted commodity.

**Foreign sources.** Though the heavy reliance on social networks inevitably puts national business sources at the centre of fundraising processes, foreign sources (those based abroad as much as those based in Costa Rica but of foreign origin) have long played a prominent and controversial role in Costa Rican elections. Their participation dates back to the 1940 election, when US-based oil multinationals were said to have made contributions targeted at the elimination of the state monopoly over fuel distribution.[84]

Notwithstanding the ban imposed by article 19 of the 1949 Constitution on the political participation of foreigners, the practice of attracting funds of foreign origin continued unabated long after that, gaining a new salience in the 1970s, when the presence of Robert L. Vesco, a US financier, loomed large over the country's political system. Fleeing from prosecution in the US on embezzlement charges, Vesco arrived in Costa Rica in 1973 at the request of President José Figueres, as the country was gearing up for the 1974 presidential election. Until his expulsion from Costa Rica in 1978, Vesco became the focus of acute political controversy and an irresistible magnet for politicians. He, after all, was no stranger to seeking political protection, having contributed generously to Richard Nixon's 1972 re-election campaign in the US. Years later, Figueres would publicly accuse his own party, as well as others, of using Vesco's money to pay for a large part of their 1974 campaign, prompting a legislative inquiry on party funding practices.[85] Though it was suggestive of widespread foreign involvement in Costa Rican elections, the probe produced inconclusive results, having descended into party bickering in the run-up to the 1978 election.

The issue of foreign contributions resurfaced in a more dramatic fashion between 1987 and 1992. Then, a series of legislative inquiries into drug-trafficking activities in Costa Rica[86] evinced that during the 1985–86 campaign both main parties had sought or, at any rate, accepted contributions from a number of questionable foreign sources. The probes covered a long list of cases – from purchases of PUSC bonds to substantial donations personally handed to PLN Presidents Oduber and Arias – involving foreign businessmen eventually linked to illicit activities in the US and Europe. The core of the allegations concerned, however, the purportedly large donations received by both parties in 1985 from General Manuel A. Noriega, neighbouring Panama's strongman at the time.[87] When the accusations surfaced, in 1989, Noriega was already in the eye of an international row over his own alleged drug-trafficking operations, which eventually led to his forceful ousting from power by a US military intervention.

The parties' links with Noriega were only partially proven.[88] Yet, the investigation clearly showed that both parties had been profusely engaged in fundraising amongst foreign sources. Not only had the candidates collected money amongst foreign businessmen based in Costa Rica, but they had also attended several fundraising activities abroad and resorted extensively to a time-honoured source: contributions from like-minded, 'sister' organisations or governments.[89] This source was particularly important for the PLN, that had long benefited from the generosity of fellow members of the Socialist International (SI), notably Venezuela's *Acción Democrática* (PAD), Mexico's *Partido Revolucionario Institucional* (PRI), and Panama's *Partido de la Revolución Democrática* (PRDP), as well as from trade unions in the US.[90] The PLN had also profited greatly from a close relationship with the *Friedrich Ebert Foundation*, linked to Germany's SDP, which occasionally spilled over into specific forms of in-kind support during the electoral season. The amounts involved were substantial: the PLN claimed to have received nearly US$250,000 before the 1986 election from PAD, the PRI and the PRDP, or politicians closely linked to them.[91] In fact, Noriega's only contribution to the PLN turned out to be a US$90,000 donation from Panama's then official PRDP, readily admitted by Oscar Arias as the continuation of a tradition of inter-party support which could hardly have been suspicious at the time.[92] The PLN was not the only party that had taken advantage of international links: the PUSC had received financial aid from Venezuela's Christian Democratic party COPEI,[93] not to speak of the local Communist Party (PVP), routinely bankrolled by the Soviet Union. In the latter case, support before the 1982 election amounted to as much as US$200,000.[94]

Since then, funds of foreign origin have become, in general, less relevant for Costa Rican parties, not least because they were legally banned in 1996, weak as the enforcement of this rule may be.[95] The post-1986 period saw a sharp decline in contributions from like-minded organisations or governments, following a change in geo political circumstances as much as in the fortunes of some of the parties involved. Today, with the possible exception of the government of Taiwan – a continued contributor to both major parties due to pressing geo-political reasons[96] – related parties or governments merely lend marginal support, typically allowing Costa Rican parties to organise fundraising activities in their countries. Similarly, while private funds of foreign origin continue to be collected – as shown by revelations about the 2001–02 campaign – the parties' fundraising efforts have been generally scaled down to what the individual connections of the presidential candidate in specific countries may allow, and what some prospective foreign investors may channel through domestic sources.[97] Meanwhile, multinational corporations – bound, in some cases, by restrictive legislation in their home country and torn by the divergent political allegiances of their local executives – are by all accounts modest contributors to national campaigns.

Ultimately, by driving home the greater relative perils inherent in courting foreign contributors rather than the small, well known circle of domestic donors, the experience of 1986 made Costa Rican fundraisers generally wary of the former. As noted emphatically by the PUSC's chief fundraiser in 1998, a well reputed banker: '[Seeking foreign contributions] is simply asking for troubles that may land you in jail…'.[98]

At this point the analysis of fundraising leads to an obvious question: Why do members of the domestic business elite – the largest source of political donations – care to contribute at all? What motives and retributions, if any, are involved?

**Motives and retributions.** There are multiple and overlapping motives for contributing to a party or candidate. Political and ideological identification with the recipient undeniably play a role, particularly in pre-campaigns and amongst each party's traditional contributors. So does exposure to social pressures. However, the evidence offered above suggests the obvious relevance of instrumental motives amongst donors. This is visible in the dearth of private contributions in nomination contests as much as in the tilt of media contributions towards the opposition party. Moreover, the 1982 and 1998 elections provide examples of the fundraising difficulties that plague any party with only a long shot at victory. In 1982, non-public funding sources raised by the CU amounted to 37 per cent of those collected by the PLN, the overwhelming winner. In 1998, it was the PLN's non-public sources that trailed the ample favourite PUSC's by more than two to one, and by a much larger difference if only reported donations are included.[99]

As suggested above, the quest for an individual rather than a corporative or collective pay-off, stands at the centre of the decision to contribute. Expected benefits vary significantly, not least according to the size of the contribution made and the institutional levers controlled by politicians. Given the intense control exerted by Costa Rican presidential candidates over their own parties and the president's extensive appointment powers, political appointments – either in the party's congressional slate or the administration – are obvious means of reward for large donations. Are they routinely used in Costa Rica?

To some extent they are, but not at the highest political level. The above-mentioned case of Lloyd S. Rubin suggests that diplomatic appointments may have been frequently at the core of exchanges between donors and politicians. The records of the 1991–2 congressional investigation into party funding contain repeated admissions by campaign managers of both main parties that diplomatic posts had been routinely eyed and often bought by large political donors. The following exchange between a PLN deputy and a high financial official at the PUSC is telling:

> Deputy Aiza-Campos: And were there enough contributions to pay (the foreign media consultant) US$10,000 per month?
> Mr Luis Manuel Chacón: Yes, you can't imagine how many people want to be consul.[100]

During the 1990s the Costa Rican diplomatic service was subject to repeated reforms aimed at rooting out its traditional role as a prime electoral bounty. However, the account made by Alberto Dent, the chief fundraiser of President Rodríguez (1998–2002), suggests that old habits persist:

> I have been in meetings where some people said: 'Dr. Rodríguez, here's the

money... But I would like you to consider that if you are elected president, I would like to be ambassador in such and such place.' And one would write down: Mr. So-and-so, ambassador in such and such place... We had a list.[101]

What happens with the diplomatic service also happens with the directing boards of a myriad state agencies and firms controlled by the presidency. Donors particularly covet appointments at the top of the three state-owned banks, which continue to manage a large share of credit operations in the country.

Yet, coveting a post and making a large contribution are by no means a guarantee of appointment. Dent was quick to point out that donors with an eye on a post merely 'open themselves the door in order to be considered, insofar as they may be professionally competent'.[102] The limited and unreliable evidence available – circumscribed to the 1998–2002 administration – tends to back his words. A comparison of 367 appointments made by the Rodríguez administration during its first twenty months in office (May 1998–December 1999) and the largest contributors reported by the PUSC during the 1997–8 campaign shows that, out of fifty-two donors of more than US$10,000 to the PUSC, thirteen received appointments in the new administration.[103] However, the majority of these designations can be explained by plain political or familial motives.[104] Indeed, when it comes to the highest echelons of political power, hefty contributions may be of limited value. Congressional lists reflect a complex decision in which political and electoral criteria – notably the candidates' local popularity and their loyalty to the party's standard-bearer – are far more consequential than financial considerations. Meanwhile, if cabinet appointments may sometimes be preceded by large contributions, the causal link between the two is unclear. Cabinet members are normally recruited amongst the president's closest circle, where some of his largest donors are also likely to be found. Any connection between contributions and cabinet designations may well be spurious.

Causal links between campaign contributions and other kinds of post-election pay-offs are equally muddled. Though some party officials attest to instances in which donors articulate an interest in specific public procurement contracts, exchanges between donors and politicians remain implicit and unspecific in the vast majority of cases. Even public works contractors, whose funding role has already been mentioned, seem driven by a subtler set of motives, in which the prevention of disadvantage vis-à-vis competitors and the oiling of a generic good will from state authorities are central.

As confirmed by a large number of interviewees, the pivotal benefit sought by most political donors is indeed access to decision-makers and their good will. Rather than as a blunt instrument to buy public decisions in advance, Costa Rican contributors and politicians largely conceive political donations as an *insurance policy* aimed at ensuring that the donor's interest will get a closer consideration by decision-makers in specific instances. Two entrepreneurs put the matter clearly:

What people want to get out of contributing is, firstly, access... This access need not be to the president. When do you need the president? Hardly ever. What you need is access to the ministers. Generally, the people that are in the financial committee will be ministers. Later, you call them up and ask for an appointment. That's very important. It is not about influence, is about access, which not everyone has. To be able to explain a problem to someone, that's a big advantage.[105]

What (the contributor) expects is a certain access: the facility to get an audience, to put across his point of view, and that the politician may help insofar as it is legally possible, nothing else. That's the way the vast majority of businessmen understand this. To go and *demand* something in return because you contributed to the campaign is very dishonourable.[106]

As both quotations imply, with access come specific requests. Yet, as the second quotation shows, these requests are carefully framed in the understanding that after the electoral moment the bargaining power shifts heavily in favour of politicians and against donors. Both a close-knit social milieu where reputation is paramount and the ban on consecutive presidential and congressional re-election help to weaken the links between contributions and policy outputs. In doing so, they undermine the rationality of exceedingly large donations. In the absence of additional pressure factors, such as a pre-existing personal bond between donor and recipient, a contribution becomes, in some ways, a gamble. As noted by Constantino Urcuyo, a former deputy and presidential advisor, the direct link often assumed between political contributions and outputs is a misconception:

This is very haphazard, because... if someone gives 20 million colones and then asks something from the president, very often people don't respond. He who contributes with the idea that he will have... absolutely favourable decisions, is radically mistaken. [A contribution] creates, of course, a more favourable attitude towards that person, so that if he asks for an audience he will get one soon, if he asks to be listened to by certain officials he will be listened to, but none of this necessarily guarantees that decisions will be favourable.[107]

If certain evidence does suggest conspicuous links between political contributions and policy outputs, some of the best documented cases show the contingency of the connection, emphasised by Urcuyo. The affairs of Ricardo Alem and 'Ocean Hunter', examined by the legislative inquiries of 1987–92, both of them involving former President Oscar Arias, provide examples of significant contributions whose pressure went largely unheeded by elected officials.[108]

Alem, a young entrepreneur and political newcomer, became a large contributor to the Arias campaign throughout 1984–85.[109] Though his contributions led to his designation in an important campaign post, his name was conspicuously bypassed by Arias at the time of appointing his cabinet, in the wake of his 1986 electoral victory. Alem, who had clearly hoped to land a key post in the administration, preferably the Ministry of Public Works and Transport, resorted to the PLN's newly elected legislative caucus, which lobbied in his favour before the president-elect. Though Arias eventually yielded to the pressure of his party, Alem's reward was meagre: nearly one year into the administration he was appointed to an obscure diplomatic post, devoid of power, from which he would be swiftly dismissed ten months later, when his suspicious financial activities became known to the president. In the second case, a US$20,000 contribution from 'Ocean Hunter', a Miami-based company with large business operations in Costa Rica, was personally handed to Arias in 1985 and deposited in a campaign account. Years later, the company would be linked to drug trafficking by the US government. A copy of the donation cheque only surfaced when the company's indicted owners expressed their displeasure at Arias' refusal to support the Nicaraguan 'Contras' or grant them business favours. Their attempt to 'earn indulgences', to quote their own words, had plainly proved a fiasco.

These examples illustrate well the indeterminacy of political funding exchanges in Costa Rica, and the risks that beset donors and not only politicians. These cases, of course, do not belittle the risk of corruption inherent in large political contributions, which have indeed been borne out in other instances. However, they do suggest that links between donations and policy decisions are not automatic. While contributions certainly allow specific actors to buy good will, the evidence shows that this will still rests with the politicians.

However, if these cases are reassuring in one sense, they are deeply disturbing in another. They point towards grave lapses of control in the fundraising procedures of the Arias 1984–86 campaign. Have things evolved since then?

**The issue of control.** Private fundraising activities in Costa Rica were free from legal interference until 1996. Well before that, however, the 1977 and 1987–92 legislative probes into party funding had made clear the risks attached to the country's *laissez-faire* approach and the limited effectiveness of public subsidies in the prevention of campaign finance greed.

If the probes failed to show – or refused to acknowledge – that any party authority had *knowingly* accepted contributions from questionable sources, they did reveal a disturbing lack of selectivity on the part of fundraisers and the absence of mechanisms to filter out suspicious contributions.[110] In 1985–6, the economic strain of a close election, the parties' imperviousness to the threat of drug trafficking, and the lack of regulation, proved a dangerous cocktail. Arias later admitted that '[in 1985], in a convulsed Central America, where drug traffickers wanted to infiltrate themselves to buy influence… we simply did not notice that reality had changed and kept applying the traditions of the past: to accept contributions in good faith if we did not have any suspicion about the contributor's moral quality'.[111] In the absence of a legal framework, money – he said –was 'sought everywhere'.[112] Parties paid dearly for their adherence to the 'traditions of the past': Alem was merely one of several political donors later linked to the drug trade, who were enthusiastically welcomed by major parties and, in some cases, even given fundraising responsibilities.

Though the breakdown of fundraising self-control mechanisms had been diagnosed since the 1970s, the 1986 experience was a turning point, not least due to the immense embarrassment inflicted on high-ranking politicians – notably Presidents Arias and Calderón-Fournier – called to testify in a drug-trafficking probe. A PLN's former treasurer noted that the 1986 campaign, 'awoke our awareness that we couldn't hurry along with fundraising mechanisms'.[113] The available evidence supports his words: private contributions to the PLN fell precipitously during the 1989–90 national campaign, remained low four years later, and plunged to an all-time low in 1997–8, due, partly, to the PLN candidate's profound distrust of private donors.[114] Changes have been far less enduring in the PUSC, though a profound drop also occurred in 1989–90, in the wake of the 1986 revelations. Moreover, the findings of the 1987–92 investigations also led to a revamping of political finance rules in 1996, which included the introduction of a ban on foreign contributions, contribution ceilings, and the parties' obligation to periodically report their income sources. The latter rule was later extended to presidential nomination contests.

Nonetheless, the changes in the post-1986 fundraising climate should not be overestimated. Intra-party transparency remains weak, and, as suggested above, campaign fundraising remains the province of a select group of collaborators of the presidential candidate, largely beyond the control of the parties' formal organs. When asked about the PUSC's fundraising practices during the 1993–4 election, current President Abel Pacheco, the party's chairman at the time, was quick to state that not only did he not have anything to do with his party's finances, but that, indeed, this had been one of his conditions before accepting the post.[115] Another high-ranking party official at the PUSC clearly hinted that many donations flow directly into the presidential candidate's hands and, though used in the campaign effort, remain outside the party's coffers and hence unreported.[116] Moreover, parties and pre-candidates continue to engage in the time-honed habit of creating parallel corporations conceived to attract donations and pay electoral expenses on their behalf. This practice allows parties to be protected against creditors, while keeping contributions largely anonymous. Finally, several politicians conceded the risks posed by any fundraising carried out by legislative and mayoral aspirants, which remains beyond the control of the parties' headquarters.

More importantly, pervasive obstacles bedevil the enforcement of the rules introduced in 1996. Though the reform formally obliged party treasurers to submit quarterly contribution reports to the TSE (monthly during the national campaign), most do not, even after repeated warnings from the electoral authorities.[117] While the PLN and the PUSC regularly submit their reports, their contents, however, are merely glossed over by the authorities, only keen to make sure that reported contributions abide by the existing ceilings.[118] Since no attempt is made to corroborate the information provided by the parties, their reports should be taken quizzically. One party official confided that 'though the law specifies a maximum contribution, these are "siren's songs": we somehow abide by the law while in fact, there may be a single source for several contributions.'[119] Ultimately, as bluntly admitted by Oscar Fonseca, the TSE's current chairman, legal controls over private contributions in Costa Rica remain 'cosmetic'.[120]

The 2001–2 campaign brought all these points home. Already in the final days of the campaign, the press documented several contributions under false names in the reports submitted to the TSE by the PLN.[121] Later, in September 2002, another press investigation revealed that the campaign of President Pacheco had engaged in a wide-ranging effort to circumvent party and legal controls over fundraising activities. Through a complex parallel structure, involving several corporations and bank accounts, including one in Panama, Pacheco's campaign channelled several million dollars in private donations that were never reported to the TSE and that, in many cases, flaunted the legal ceilings and bans.[122]

Unlike the scandals of the late 1980s, the recent controversy has yet to yield evidence of reception of funds from questionable sources. However, it has bluntly exposed the shortcomings of the prevailing normative framework. The latter not only proved unable to prevent the transgressions. In fact, it also proved insufficient to punish the responsible financial officers once the violations became public. Faced with a criminal indictment against the financial managers of Pacheco's campaign, the courts concluded that the badly drafted norms of the EC did not allow for the individual attribution of criminal responsibilities for political finance abuses.[123] The detection of the abuses triggered, nonetheless, other institutional controls with potentially far-reaching consequences. The scandal brought about yet another congressional probe on party funding matters – the fifth in thirty years – which has yet to report on its findings. More importantly perhaps, it led to a crucial intervention by the country's Constitutional Court, which has recently lifted bank secrecy rules in all matters pertaining to political finance.[124]

Amidst the weakness of party and legal controls, the protection of the soundness and integrity of private fundraising in Costa Rica continues to hang from the finest of threads: the post-1986 wariness of most fundraisers, the curiosity of the press, and the decisive role of reputation in the fundraising process. Within the small circle of the country's political contributors, the name of the chief fundraiser and the long-standing bonds of trust between members of the financial committee and targeted donors are still decisive in attracting economic support. It is not accidental that in recent times major parties and their candidates have routinely chosen very respected entrepreneurs to manage their financial affairs. Strong social connections come with them, but also reputations to protect and lines that are not to be crossed, at least not often or systematically. The risks inherent in this mechanism are obvious and its sustainability in a time of intense electoral competition precarious at best, as shown by the 2001–2 experience. Legal controls notwithstanding, when it comes to protecting the integrity of fundraising in Costa Rica, self-control continues to rule.

After this detailed exploration of the highly similar fundraising procedures followed by the PLN and the PUSC, it is worth looking briefly at the very different and much harsher reality of minor parties.

### The case of minor parties
Despite their heterogeneity, daunting fundraising obstacles unite minor parties in Costa Rica. Their ability to attract private donations remains negligible, as do their chances of taking advantage of the existing public subvention.

In most cases, state funding is, in fact, a distant and largely theoretical instrument for minor parties. Though the latter often issue campaign bonds, the uncertainties surrounding their electoral result and their ability to justify their expenses before the CGR undermine decisively the economic value of these titles. Public and private financial operators systematically reject them, leaving minor parties heavily dependent on the willingness of service providers – particularly television stations – to receive them as part of their fees.[125] A high official at the small PFD described the obstacles faced by his party:

> We did not go to the private banks, because they are not willing to finance us. There is no history to tell them that we stand a chance of reaching (the subsidy threshold of) 5%... State funding thus turns into something theoretical. It is not like that for the PLN and the PUSC... One issues the bonds hoping that they will be sold: you may or may not succeed. We were lucky that the television ran the risk and accepted. Otherwise the bonds would have remained in our hands.[126]

The generosity of service providers towards minor parties is neither predictable nor particularly generous, as seen in the case of television stations. Yet, it is vital for these parties. The current subsidy legislation – with its subsidy threshold and its post-election accounting ritual – has dealt minor parties a poor hand to play. Virtually unable to borrow resources against the expectation of reimbursement, minor parties must limit their campaign to what private donations may allow. This, in turn, constrains the expenses that may be submitted to the CGR, and thereby the amount of funding that they will ultimately receive from the state.

Problems are, if anything, worse when it comes to raising private donations. While ideological reasons may prevent some minor groups – such as the left-leaning PFD – from tapping into business sectors, ideological identification with the latter offers little succour. Otto Guevara, the leader of the ML, a small libertarian party, expressed his bitter disappointment with the country's top entrepreneurs, who refused to support financially his party in 1998, in spite of its strenuously pro-business platform. 'They simply preferred', he noted, 'to keep investing in the PUSC and the PLN... rather than having a couple of representatives in Congress to defend wholeheartedly and as a matter of principle the ideas that, in theory, they support'.[127] Within a set of institutions strongly geared towards the dominance of two large parties or coalitions, minor actors stand a slim chance of attracting instrumentally motivated contributions.

Thus, hampered by subsidy rules, by-passed by business contributors, and largely disconnected from international funding sources, the situation of minor groups is not unlike that of nomination movements in major parties: they must rely disproportionately on the contributions of their candidates and immediate associates. The case of the PFD is probably typical. There, a group of ten donors – including the party's presidential candidate, his predecessor, the candidates at the top of the party's legislative and municipal lists, and various relatives of the former – provided more than three-quarters of the party's reported donations during the 1997–8 campaign.[128] The concentration was even higher in the case of the ML in 1998, where legislative candidates bore the cost of the campaign almost entirely, as was also the experience of the United People Coalition (CPU) and the Generaleña Union Party (PUGEN) in 1990.[129]

If one of the objectives of political finance rules is to create a level playing field where the emergence of new political options is not trampled by gross economic disparities then the Costa Rican political finance legislation shows no signs of having succeeded. Fundraising disparities between major and minor parties remain vast.

CONCLUSION

This chapter has put together the pieces of a complex and not always visible jigsaw puzzle. The image that emerges defies the simplicity of conventional knowledge of campaign finance in Costa Rica, as much as it refuses to yield an unequivocal assessment of the country's state funding rules, of the kind that has dominated debates on party subsidies elsewhere.

These pages have shown, first, that contrary to expectations, Costa Rican national elections have *not* grown more expensive over the last two decades, either in real or per capita terms. In fact, a sharp decline in per capita costs is visible since 1978. Real electoral expenditure, in turn, has followed a jagged evolution in recent elections, which reflects in no small measure the availability of state funding. This raises interesting questions about the potential role of generous state subventions in driving up electoral expenses.

However, while national elections may not be dearer now than a generation ago, Costa Rican politics *as a whole* certainly is. This has less to do with the presence or availability of state funding than with the opening up of several layers of electoral competition within major political parties, notably, open presidential primaries. The emergence of the latter has unbound a second electoral dimension that qualifies the essential centralism of the major parties' electoral structures, a trait that nevertheless remains in place during national elections.

Bereft of public support, this second dimension has come to absorb a significant and probably growing proportion of electoral expenses, altering in fundamental ways the consequences of state funding. It reduces markedly the parties' otherwise very high reliance on state funds and mitigates the subsidies' ability to create a level playing field for presidential aspirants. Open nomination contests pose an increasingly formidable economic barrier in Costa Rica, which is largely conquered by the pre-candidate's own resources as well as those of his relatives and immediate associates. Disturbing for democracy as it may be, this finding indeed offers a powerful counterfactual of what could happen in national campaigns in the absence of state funding. Though difficult to demonstrate, it is highly likely that without the current subvention system several contemporary candidates who lacked large personal fortunes and especially close links to domestic business elites – from Rafael A. Calderón-Fournier in the PUSC to Luis A. Monge and José M. Corrales in the PLN – would simply have stayed out of the presidential race, a perception shared by key political actors.[130]

The presence of open intra-party contests is merely one of the ways in which electoral rules and the subsidies' specific traits shape campaign finance practices and, ultimately, the effects of state funding. The chapter's second section has demonstrated that instead of accruing, as expected, to television outlays, the lion's share of the parties' electoral expense flows into items directly derived from the institutional framework. This applies to the parties' hefty organisational disbursements – related to the weak party structures nurtured by Costa Rican presidentialism – and, even more clearly, to their transportation and financial outlays. Bond discounts, in particular, simply reflect the state subsidy's nature as a post-election reimbursement and the uncertainties that stem from the subsidy's eligibility threshold and reporting process. These traits, which are not inherent in state funding systems, raise the parties' electoral expenses and undermine the subsidy's effectiveness in curbing the parties' dependence on private money. As it stands, the Costa Rican system of electoral subventions rests upon a paradox: parties are forced to depend on private sources of funding – notably private banks – in order to activate the mechanism that is precisely meant to reduce their reliance on those sources.

The subsidy system's specific features also determine its consequences for minor parties. If the combination of reimbursement, threshold and meticulous reporting procedures poses problems to major parties, it virtually dooms minor ones to benefiting only marginally from state funds. The minor parties' relatively low reliance on state funds is more related to the subsidy's features than to the party's access to alternative sources of funding, which remains, in fact, extremely limited. As we will see in Chapter five, somewhat ironically, the current rules – which exclude pre-electoral advances of state funds – leave minor groups worse off than the much-maligned loan scheme that operated during 1971–91, struck down by the Constitutional Court largely at those groups' insistence.

In line with several West European examples, the Costa Rican experience shows that the generosity of state subsidies does not by itself guarantee that politicians will relinquish their aggressive courting of private contributors. This is due not just to the fact that intra-party elections remain uncovered by subsidies or to the role bestowed on private lenders by the post-election reimbursement mechanism. The truth is that neither in national elections – where the weight of state resources has always been palpable – nor in the pre-1991 period, when private lenders were far less indispensable than they are today, parties abandoned their indiscriminate and often reckless quest for private funds, as the 1986 experience so clearly shows. To be sure, and despite the setbacks experienced in 2002, things have improved slightly since then and, though still reliant on self-control, the parties' financial officials are generally more careful and selective in their private fundraising procedures today. This evolution, however, has hardly been caused by changes in the availability of state funding or in the country's political finance regulations. It derives, instead, from the activation of powerful control mechanisms in Congress and the press, and, ultimately, from the rise of drug-trafficking and money-laundering activities in the region as a threat to fundraisers and fundraising procedures. In the cosy world of the Costa Rican business elite – where reputation- and trust-based practices reign supreme – fear of being publicly linked to drug-traffickers continues to act as a powerful deterrent for most fundraisers. This points towards an important caveat: though the active cause of these changes may lie elsewhere, the availability of state funds has been, certainly, a facilitating condition for them. Fear of public embarrassment and the greater selectivity that comes with it are, after all, luxuries that Costa Rican fundraisers can afford.

The amount of private funding still present in Costa Rican elections is less troubling than its concentration in a small, socially homogeneous circle of donors, which happens to be the same for both major parties. This matters not so much because donors may consistently buy general state policies or even specific political benefits. We have seen, in fact, how the link between contributions and political decisions is far from straightforward. If, on the one hand, the lack of co-ordination between Costa Rican donors diminishes the risk of state policies being hijacked by special interests through political contributions, on the other, even particular pay-offs are highly contingent on the goodwill of public officials not troubled by consecutive re-election. The central problem of private fundraising in Costa Rica should be posed differently: we do not know for sure – and it is probably impossible to know – if political decisions are purchased in Costa Rica, but it is more than clear that through political contributions the interests of an exceedingly small group get a privileged chance to be considered by decision-makers. In other words, rather than for reasons related to the integrity of the political system, exchanges between Costa Rican donors and politicians matter primarily for reasons related to political equality.

Thus, when it comes to campaign finance the record of state funding in Costa Rica is mixed and strongly shaped by the institutional and social milieu. While subsidies are undoubtedly dominant in national elections, they are less relevant for Costa Rican politics as a whole; while they have probably contributed to create a more level playing field for presidential aspirants in major parties, they have certainly failed to do so for minor parties; while they have allowed parties to refine their private fundraising practices, they certainly have not eliminated either the prominent role of private contributions in Costa Rican elections or the political bias that comes with it. Let us examine how this experience compares to that of Uruguay.

## NOTES

Fernández (1993), p. 297.
1   White (1997), p. 162.
2   Since parties find it difficult to follow the cumbersome formalities required by the CGR, they
3   simply discharge on the auditors *all* the receipts collected in the course of the campaign, whether suitable for reimbursement or not, and let the CGR do the sorting work. See Vargas-Aguilar (1995).
    This excludes expenditures by non-subsidised parties. Due to the relatively low threshold of
4   eligibility (4 per cent or one MP), the parties that are left out of the reporting procedure are invariably very small.
    GDP contracted 2.2 per cent in 1981 and 7.3 per cent in 1982.
5   *La Nación* [LN], 28/12/1980; Cruickshank (1984), pp. 213–7.
6   CID-Gallup, January 1994.
7   CID-Gallup, January 1998.
8   Unexpectedly, the gap between the main parties in the presidential election narrowed to 2.2
9   per cent in the actual result.
    The gap between both major parties stood barely above 4 per cent in November 1989, with
10  nearly three months to go before the polls (CID-Gallup, November 1989). The actual result was: PUSC 51.5 per cent, PLN 47.2 per cent.
    See pp. 140, 144-5.
11  *LN*, 1/2/1977; *The New Republic*, 16/4/1977.
12  *The New Republic*, 16/4/1977.
13  Carazo [29/9/1999]; Asamblea Legislativa de Costa Rica [ALCR], Exp.7898 (Informe de
14  Minoría Dip. Salas), p. 24.
    LN, 9/1/1977.
15  Until 2002, both main parties typically elected between twenty-five and twenty-nine
16  deputies each. Both enshrined in their internal bylaws the right of the presidential candidate to handpick a certain number of candidates at the top of the party list in the San José Province (see Partido Unidad Social Cristiana [PUSC] 1999, article 70). Thus, the expenditure figures given in the text normally apply to a lower number of deputies than those actually elected by each party.
    In January 2001, some of the PLN's congressional pre-candidates projected their total
17  expenses until the June 2001 primary at US$30,000–US$60,000, strictly for nomination costs. Both parties were said to have more than 160 legislative pre-candidates. See LN, 15/1/2001; *LN*, 22/1/2001.
    *LN*, 19/12/1997.
18  *LN*, 23/12/1997.
19  *LN*, 14/10/2002.
20  Muñoz [21/10/1999].
21  Zovatto (1998), p. xlix.
22  Contraloría General de la República, Costa Rica [CGR], Departamento de Estudios
23  Especiales, Informes No.158–90, 167–90, 70–94, 92–94, 99–94, 95–98, and 97–98.
    Servicios Publicitarios Computarizados [SPC] (various years)
24  Both parties aired 3922 commercials in January 1986, 2664 in January 1990, 2458 in

25 January 1994, and 4474 in January 1998. See SPC (various years).
DCR, 7/7/1956.

26 The state reimburses up to 20 per cent of the bonds' face value (TSE [1997], article 20).

27 Depending on each party's electoral prospects, discounts may be much higher.
Montero [21/12/1999].

28 Vargas [28/10/1999].

29 Carazo [29/9/1999].

30 According to ML's leader, Otto Guevara, approximately 65 per cent (US$50,000) of the

31 party's campaign budget was used to purchase TV slots during the last two months of the
1998 campaign [24/9/1999]. The proportion was even higher for the PIN (Muñoz
[21/10/1999]).
Both figures were projections made by the PLN pre-candidates' campaign managers for the

32 period January–June 2001 (*La República* [*LR*], 31/1/2001).
Cerdas (1998), pp. 148, 167.

33 Carey (1996), pp. 107–13, 120–7; White (1997), pp. 181–5.

34 In 1974–90, they averaged 1.8 per cent of total government appropriations (Carey [1996], p.

35 112).
Calculation based on White (1997), p. 183 and CGR figures for 1997.

36 Law No.7755 of 16/2/1998.

37 Budgeted figure.

38 Graph 3.5 includes the entire executive branch and seven government dependencies and

39 state-owned firms: ICAA, ICE, CCSS, IMAS, INVU, RECOPE and CONAVI.
Government agencies are not allowed to advertise during the campaign, which officially

40 begins on October 1st of the year before the election (Electoral Code [EC], article 85j, as
reformed by Law No. 7653 of 10/12/1996).
67 per cent of the MOPT's 4438 TV advertisements during 1995–99 were aired during the

41 second half of 1997. Based on SPC (various years).
A comparison should clarify the point. Since 1986, non-public sources in the PLN have aver-

42 aged US$1.8 million per national campaign. Meanwhile, as shown in Table 3.2, during the
last election cycle *each* PLN pre-candidate spent on average US$1.2 million for a much
smaller campaign effort geared towards a limited share of the electorate.
*LR*, 16/11/1993; *La Prensa Libre* [*LPL*], 8/10/1997; *Al Día* [*AD*], 6/4/1998.

43 Data calculated according to the PLN accounting books, generously provided to the author

44 by Antonio Burgués and Eduardo Morera, the PLN's Treasurer and Chief Accountant at the
time of writing, respectively.
Note, however, that during the 2001–2 campaign the PLN negotiated a US$4.4 million loan

45 with the state-owned Banco de Costa Rica, using party bonds as collateral (*LN*, 2/10/2001;
*LN*, 5/12/2001; *LN*, 15/12/2001; *LN*, 21/3/2002).
González [17/9/1999].

46 Weisleder [23/9/1999].

47 *LN*, 15/4/1974; *LN*, 15/7/1977.

48 Asamblea Legislativa de Costa Rica [ALCR], Exp.Leg.10934, pp. 4120–7, 4264–4304,

49 4851–67, 4891–2, 6993; *LN*, 21/1/1992.
Tovar [1/11/1999].

50 Constenla [20/9/1999].

51 Vargas [28/10/1999].

52 Altmann [28/9/1999].

53 ALCR, Exp.Leg.10934, p. 4446.

54 Schyfter [9/12/1999].

55 Luis M. Chacón in ALCR, Exp.Leg.10934, p. 1871.

56 Dent [22/12/1999]. In 1998, approximately 8 million colones was the maximum contribu-
57 tion allowed by the law.
   See ALCR, Exp.Leg.10934, pp. 4447, 4460, 4475; *LN*, 13/8/2003.

58 Ruiz [10/12/1999].

59 Dent [22/12/1999].

60 The price of one seat at the PUSC's 'Victory Dinner' in 1998 was US$5,000 (Dent
61 [22/12/1999]). The occasion quoted was a PLN dinner during the 1985–6 campaign, attended by twenty guests. See ALCR, Exp.Leg. 10934, p. 4470.
   Constenla [20/9/1999].

62 Dent [22/12/1999]. The list of contributors made public in January 2001 by Rolando Araya,
63 then a PLN pre-candidate, included ninety-seven names (*LN*, 29/1/2001).
   Chávez [22/10/1999].

64 Yankelewitz [20/10/1999].

65 Vargas [28/10/1999].

66 Alvarez [7/12/1999].

67 Palma [15/10/1999].

68 Trejos [25/10/1999].

69 See Rodríguez' own remarks in *LN*, 17/5/2001.

70 According to the contribution reports submitted by both major parties to the TSE during
71 December 1996–September 1997 and February–May 1998, i.e., just before and after the
   national campaign, the number of fee-paying members averaged 405 per quarter in the
   PUSC and seventy-five in the PLN.
   Yashar (1995), pp.80–1; Castro-Méndez (2001). Not *one* of my interviewees mentioned
72 trade unions as potential, let alone actual, sources of political funds.
   Calderón-Fournier [16/9/1999].

73 Fishman [1/12/1999].

74 Other than his own family, Araya's largest contributors to his 1999–2001 nomination bid
75 included Calixto Chávez, Alberto Esquivel-Volio, Emilio Baharet, Moisés Fachler and
   Tomás Batalla, all of them wealthy entrepreneurs. They can all be found in a set of documents produced in the course of a congressional investigation on party funding, which
   includes several attendance lists to fundraising activities during the PLN's 1984–6 campaign. Chávez and Esquivel-Volio, both of them cabinet members in PLN administrations,
   were amongst the twenty guests to the PLN's 1986 'Victory Dinner'. Attendants to the latter also included Víctor Mesalles-Cebriá, another top industrialist, who was an important
   contributor to José M. Figueres 1992–4 presidential campaign. See *LN*, 12/9/1999; *LN*,
   29/1/2001; *El Financiero [EF]*, 8–14/1/2001; ALCR, Exp.Leg.10934, pp. 4463–4472.
   Schyfter [9/12/1999]. A congressional probe on the funding of the 2001–2 campaign, still on
76 course, has yielded many examples of this phenomenon. A particularly controversial one

involved the Panama-based trader Waked International Inc., which donated US$55,000 to the PUSC and US$25,000 to the PLN in the final months of the last campaign (*LN*, 20–21/9/2002; *LN*, 1/11/2002).

Yankelewitz [20/10/1999].

77  Schyfter [9/12/1999].

78  Chávez [22/10/1999].

79  See *LN*, 13/9/1999; *LN*, 29/1/2001; *LR*, 29/3/1998; *EF*, 8–14/1/2001.

80  Alvarez [7/12/1999].

81  See *Constitución Política*, article 121, 11c. Costa Rican TV networks pay no annual licence
82  fee for the use of their frequency. Radio stations pay less than US$8 per year.

For instance, the country's main daily, *La Nación*, is renowned for not giving special rates
83  or payment facilities to parties or candidates.

D. Oduber, quoted in ALCR, Exp.7898 (Informe de Minoría Dip. Ferreto Segura), p. 10.

84  On the allegations see *The New Republic*, 23/4/1977; *LN*, 5–7/7/1977; *LR*, 11/5/1977. On the
85  inquiry see ALCR, Exp.Leg.7898; *LN*, 11/7/1977; *LN*, 28/7/1977; *LN*, 30/7/1977; *Excelsior* [*EXC*], 14/8/1977.

ALCR, Exp.Leg.10200–10684–10934.

86  The scandal received extensive press coverage. See *LN*, 4/11/1988; *LN*, 10/11/1988; *LN*,
87  19/1/1989; *LN*, 27/1/1989; *LN*, 15/4/1989; *LN*, 1/6/1989; *LN*, 9/6/1989; *LN*, 13/6/1989; *LN*, 23–25/6/1989; *LN*, 25/7/1989; *Extra* [*EXT*], 15/4/1989; *EXT*, 19/4/1989; *EXT*, 21/7/1989; *EXT*, 27/7/1989; *LPL*, 17/10/1988; *LR*, 15/4/1989.

ALCR, Exp.Leg.10934, pp. 6987–6989.

88  ALCR, Exp.Leg.10934, pp. 1865–6, 1673–5, 1687–88, 1695–8, 4102, 4447–58, 4854,
89  4987–8, 5001–2, 5047.

ALCR, Exp.Leg.10934, p. 5047; *LN*, 23/6/1989.

90  ALCR, Exp.Leg.10934, pp. 1673, 1697–8.

91  ALCR, Exp.Leg.10934, pp. 4987–8; *LN*, 23/6/1989; *LN*, 31/1/1992.

92  ALCR, Exp.Leg.10934, p. 1866.

93  *El País* [*EP*], 14/3/1999.

94  EC, article 176 *bis*. It should be noted that according to the Code (article 152), the violation
95  of the ban carries a prison sentence of two–six years for all the involved.

Fishman [1/12/1999]. Costa Rica is one of only twenty-nine countries that maintain diplo-
96  matic relations with Taiwan. Recent evidence seems to have confirmed Fishman's assertion. In 2003, it was revealed that the campaign of President Abel Pacheco received US$500,000 in illegal donations from two Taiwan-based companies, reputedly linked to the Taiwanese government (*LN*, 20–22/8/2003; *LN*, 3/10/2003; *LN*, 14/10/2003). Although the latter reject- ed any involvement in this case, the existence of a secret fund to support 'friendly' politi- cians and parties around the world has been publicly admitted by Taiwanese diplomats (*The Washington Post*, 5/4/2002).

The evidence from the 2001–2 campaign evinces that in some cases the amounts involved
97  are still very significant. For instance, during the 2001–2 campaign, Credomatic, a local financial operator, contributed US$250,000 to both major parties. Credomatic is owned by Casa Pellas, a Nicaraguan conglomerate with financial and commercial interests all over Central America (*LN*, 13/8/2003; *LN*, 5/9/2003).

Dent [22/12/1999].

98  Between December 1996 and February 1998, the PUSC reported US$1.28 million in pri-
99  vate contributions. Meanwhile, the PLN reported donations for less than US$62,000, and
none between October and December 1997 when the campaign was in full motion. While
there are many reasons to be sceptical about the accuracy of these reports, they suggest an
obvious fundraising difference between the parties. The PLN figure was confirmed by several sources.

ALCR, Exp.Leg.10934, p. 1864. See also ALCR, Exp.Leg.10934, pp. 1677, 1695; *LR*,
100  1/2/1992.

Dent [22/12/1999].

101  Dent [22/12/1999].

102  Only appointments of ministers, vice-ministers, chief administrative officers, directors of
103  autonomous institutions and a few other state agencies, and diplomatic personnel down to
the level of ambassadorial first secretary, were included. Information taken from *LG* (May
1998–December 1999). Information on donors taken from PUSC contribution reports, covering the period December 1996–February 1998.

The list includes two ministers (out of thirteen), three presidential advisors (out of seven),
104  three ambassadors (out of thirty-three), two presidents of autonomous institutions (out of
twenty-four), one member of the directive board of a state-owned bank (out of twenty) and
two directors of minor public-private agencies. Three of the appointees had previous political experience directly related to their posts, two were close relatives of the new president
and at least four were long-standing collaborators of his. This, of course, does not preclude
the presence of close associates and relatives of the donors in the list of appointees.

Schyfter [9/12/1999].

105  Chávez [22/10/1999].

106  Urcuyo [23/11/1999].

107  On Alem's case see ALCR, Exp.Leg. A45-E8008, pp. 216–28; ALCR, Exp.Leg. 10934, pp.
108  1664–1700, 4973–5053; *LN*, 4/11/1988; *LN*, 10/11/1988; *LN*, 25/7/1989; *EXT*, 19/4/1989.
On 'Ocean Hunter', see *LN*, 27/1/1989; *LN*, 5/6/1991; *LN*, 31/1/1992; ALCR,
Exp.Leg.A45-E8008, pp. 206–15; ALCR, Exp.Leg.10934, pp. 4976–5053, 6990–92.

His contribution to the Arias campaign was estimated at nearly US$85,000 (ALCR,
109  Exp.Leg.10934, pp. 1680, 5033; ALCR, Exp.Leg.A45-E8008, p. 225).

ALCR, Exp.Leg. 10934, pp. 6996–7.

110  ALCR, Exp.Leg. 10934, p. 5051.

111  *LN*, 23/6/1989.

112  Burgués [11/11/1999].

113  See Table 3.4 and note 99.

114  *LN*, 31/7/1995.

115  Palma [15/10/1999].

116  A TSE internal memo dated 22/3/1999 notes that fourteen parties failed to submit contribu-
117  tion reports for the February–April 1998 quarter, a figure that climbed to twenty-one, twenty-four and twenty-five in each of the following quarters.

*LN*, 1–3/10/2001.

118  Tovar [1/11/1999].

119 Fonseca [24/11/1999].

120 *LN*, 29–30/1/2002; *LN*, 12–15/2/2002; *LN*, 24–26/3/2002.

121 See, amongst many, *LN*, 20–25/9/2002; *LN*, 30/9/2002; *LN*, 9–10/10/2002; *LN*,

122 14–19/10/2002; *LN*, 5/11/2002; *LN*, 4/4/2003; *LN*, 9/5/2003; *LN*, 23/5/2003; *LN*, 30/5/2003; *LN*, 7/6/2003.

*LN*, 12–13/11/2002.

123 Sala Constitucional de la Corte Suprema de Justicia, Costa Rica [SCCR], Vote No.3489-

124 2003 of 2/5/2003.

Before the 1998 election, the country's largest bank, the state-owned Banco Nacional, for-

125 bade any operations involving bonds issued by new parties or parties that failed to qualify for reimbursement of their electoral expenses. BNCR (1997); *LN*, 27/9/1997; *LPL*, 10/10/1997. As we shall see in Chapter five, the experience of the emerging Citizen Action Party (PAC), which successfully negotiated a large amount of bonds during the 2001–2 campaign, is not really an exception to this rule.

Montero [21/12/1999].

126 Guevara [24/9/1999].

127 The party's reported contributions during the campaign barely surpassed US$15,500 (party

128 contribution reports to the TSE from December 1996 to January 1998).

Guevara [24/9/1999]; *LN*, 20/1/1991.

129 Laclé [7/9/1999]; Urcuyo [23/11/1999].

130

# chapter | state funding and campaign finance
*four* | practices: the case of uruguay

## INTRODUCTION

If the funding of campaigns is far from transparent in Costa Rica, it is a decidedly arcane matter in Uruguay. Despite several legislative attempts to regulate them since the return of democratic rule in 1984, the fundraising activities of the Uruguayan parties and their myriad internal sectors remain bereft of any external control. The features and amounts of the long-standing electoral subsidy scheme stand as the only publicly known traits of Uruguay's political finance system. Even state funding of parties is, however, devoid of the accounting and transparency controls that are so pivotal an element of the Costa Rican experience with campaign finance. It is not entirely surprising, thus, that the topic has failed to spawn any academic literature or even extensive journalistic coverage.

This chapter attempts to piece together the available information on the funding of Uruguayan elections, including that derived from numerous interviews with politicians, party officials, and political donors. As in the Costa Rican case, campaign finance practices and the effects of electoral subsidies in Uruguay are decisively shaped by institutional, historical and social realities, which tend to be overlooked in political finance discussions. The chapter will suggest that Uruguay's system of Double Simultaneous Voting (DSV) and, in particular, the format of its party system, significantly raise the cost of elections and limit the proportional weight of state funding on campaign finances. The analysis will demonstrate the differences that exist in this regard, and many others, between the country's right-of-centre traditional parties and their left-leaning rival, the FA. It will also suggest that specific features of Uruguay's electoral legislation have a direct bearing on the structure of campaign expenditure, making it considerably more media-oriented than in Costa Rica. Finally, the chapter will convey the remarkable similarities that unite private fundraising processes and mores in Uruguay and Costa Rica, especially the overwhelming dominance of domestic business donations collected within a small social circle.

To an even greater extent than in the Costa Rican case, the dearth of political finance information in Uruguay limits the scope of the analysis. The following pages focus primarily on Uruguay's campaign finance experience in the immediate past (the 1994 and 1999–2000 election cycles, mostly), and in presidential contests. They offer a snapshot of political finance practices in Uruguay, rather than a long-term account of their evolution and change. Even this snapshot is strongly focused on political finance realities in Montevideo, the country's nearly exclusive locus of political and economic power. As in the previous chapter, the analysis starts by establishing the approximate cost of Uruguayan presidential elections and the structure of electoral disbursements and moves on to the study of fundraising processes. The latter section tries to gauge the significance of the country's generous state funding system on the parties' finances, while giving a textured and comprehensive account of the activities, incentives, constraints and expectations of fundraisers and donors. The concluding section matches the chapter's findings with the inferences drawn from the Costa Rican experience in campaign finance. This comparison raises key normative questions about the justification of public funding of parties in Latin American democracies.

## CAMPAIGN EXPENDITURE: AMOUNTS AND ITEMS

'It is heard in all political circles, no one questions it, and there seems to be a great agreement on it: election campaigns are more expensive every day.'[1] The words of a respected Uruguayan columnist echo similar views already quoted in the analysis of the Costa Rican case. Long ago, conventional wisdom in Uruguay also settled on the twin notions that election campaigns grow dearer every day and that television advertising costs are the main culprits of this trend. The former perception was strongly reinforced by the electoral reform of 1996, which turned a single electoral act into a four-stage process spread over more than one year. Does this consensus bear any resemblance to the realities of campaign spending in Uruguay?

### The cost of elections

Estimating the cost of Uruguayan elections is a difficult endeavour. The lack of reporting procedures and the extreme decentralisation of electoral structures fostered by DSV enormously complicate the task of keeping track of electoral expenditure throughout the country. Before the onset of the long 1999–2000 election cycle, the only academic work available on Uruguayan political finance loosely estimated the total cost of the country's elections at US$30 million, a sum that the author conceded to be merely a 'possible indication'.[2]

Though based on pure guesswork this figure may be, however, close to the mark. A more thorough reconstruction of electoral expenditure based upon extensive interviews, the parties' disbursements on television advertising and the invaluable set of figures released by the New Space Party (NE) yields roughly similar results (Table 4.1).

Table 4.1: *Campaign expenditure per party in Uruguay (excluding selected legislative races), 1994–2000 (millions of US$ of 1995)*

| Election → Party ↓ | A November 1994 | B April 1999 (1) | C October– November 1999 (2) | D May 2000 (3) | E 1999–2000 Election cycle (B+C+D) |
|---|---|---|---|---|---|
| PC | 10.08 | 3.13 | 7.97 | 1.31 | 12.41 |
| PN | 10.35 | 2.00 | 5.03 | 1.17 | 8.20 |
| FA | 5.46 | 0.67 | 7.36 | 1.63 | 9.66 |
| NE | 0.85 | 0.08 | 1.54 | 0.04 | 1.66 |
| Other | 0.13 | 0.00 | 0.05 | 0.01 | 0.06 |
| Total | 26.87 | 5.88 | 21.95 | 4.17 | 31.99 |

Notes: (1) Primary elections. (2) Presidential first and second round. (3) Municipal elections.
Sources and method: See Appendix.

My estimation shows a relatively subdued increase of 19 per cent in electoral expenditure between 1994 and 1999–2000. The introduction in 1996 of open internal elections and the presidential *ballotage*, as well as the separation of national and local elections, seem not to have caused an exponential growth of electoral spending but largely its reallocation between the different moments of the election cycle.

However, if changes in total expenditure were relatively limited, alterations to its distribution between parties clearly were not. The fall of more than one-fifth in the expenses of the PN contrasts sharply with increases for the PC (23 per cent) and, above all, for both parties of the Left (77 per cent for the FA and 95 per cent for the NE). These changes were largely a reflection of the perceived chances of electoral success for each party in the October 1999 election. Indeed, in the wake of a highly conflictual dispute for the presidential candidacy, opinion polls consistently indicated that the PN was on course for a heavy electoral defeat in the presidential first round. The same surveys suggested that the FA would win the first round handily and therefore reap the largest share of the proportional public subsidy.[3] This expectation explains the disappearance in 1999 of the sizeable spending gap between both traditional parties and the FA in 1994. At the same time, the NE, basking in its unexpected electoral success of 1994 and betting over-optimistically on the possibilities offered to minor parties by the new electoral system, nearly doubled its election disbursements.

The Uruguayan experience shows that electoral prognoses decisively influence spending levels in two distinct ways: first, by affecting the instrumental value attached to donations to each party, and therefore the behaviour of private donors; second, and more importantly, by allowing political actors to estimate their post-electoral subventions. As confirmed by politicians across the spectrum, the calculation of the latter remains a crucial element in the definition of the parties' and internal sectors' campaign budgets, particularly amongst groups with limited possibilities of attracting private donations. This mechanism makes overall expendi-

Graph 4.1: *Total campaign expenditure in Uruguay, 1994–2000*

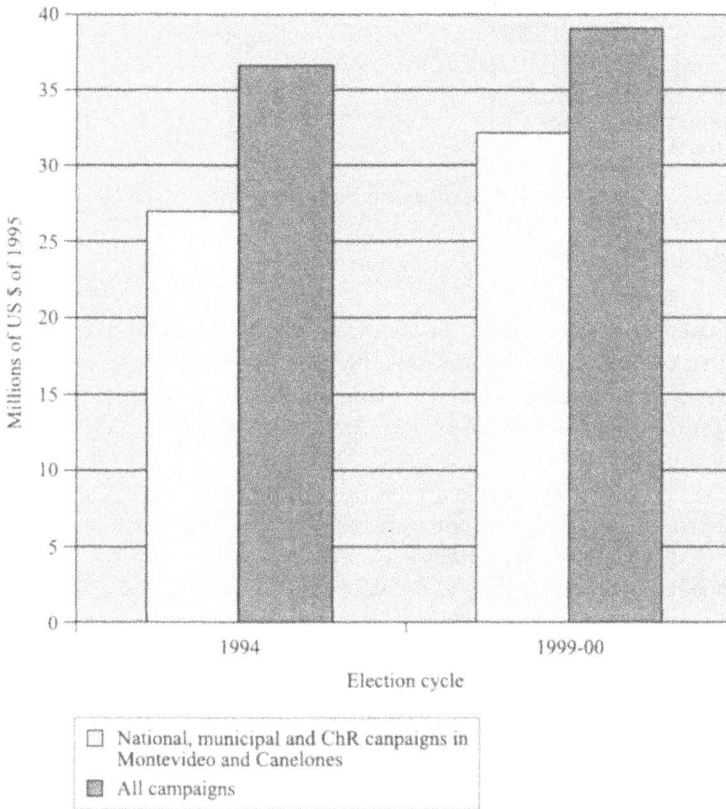

Sources and method: See Appendix

ture levels very sensitive to changes in the availability of state funding, a phenomenon also observed in Costa Rica.

The figures in Table 4.1 require extensive qualification, however. Due to limitations in the available information, they only cover elections that make extensive use of national TV networks. These include nationwide campaigns, such as presidential, primary and Senate races, as well as races for the Chamber of Representatives (ChR) in the urban conglomerate formed by the neighbouring departments of Montevideo and Canelones.[4] The table thus excludes ChR races in the Uruguayan hinterland, about which very little is known. Based on informed estimates of the average expenses incurred by a competitive list of candidates to the ChR, conservatively calculated at US$50,000 for 1994 and US$60,000 for 1999,[5] a rough estimation of the cost of local legislative races in all the departments of the Uruguayan interior can be made. Since 'competitive' and 'non-competitive' lists have been distinguished, and only the former (178 in 1994 and 104

Table 4.2: *Total expenditure per voter by two largest parties in Uruguay and Costa Rica, 1990s (US$m of 1995)*

| Election ——————➤<br>Country ▼ | 1990 | 1994 | 1998–2000<br>(1) | Mean 1990s |
|---|---|---|---|---|
| Uruguay | – | 12.4 (2) | 11.1 (3) | 11.8 |
| Costa Rica | 12.4 | 14.5 | 9.3 | 12.0 |

Notes: (1) Costa Rica: 1998 election; Uruguay: 1999–2000 election cycle. (2) PC and PN. (3) PC and FA.
Sources: See Appendix.

in 1999) included in the estimate, the following results should be taken as a bottom line that underestimates significantly the real cost of campaigns in the country's interior.[6] The procedure employed suggests that these races added *at least* US$9.65 million to the cost of Uruguayan elections in 1994 and nearly US$7 million five years later.

This estimate moves the likely total cost of all Uruguayan elections much closer to US$40 million, flattening in the process the differences between the 1994 and 1999–2000 election cycles (Graph 4.1). This estimation is nearly twice as high as the cost of all processes leading to the 1998 election in Costa Rica, which stood at US$20.1 million.

Once all elections are included in the calculation, campaign expenditure in Uruguay during the 1990s stands at US$15.9 per registered voter and election cycle, i.e. 26 per cent above the comparable Costa Rican figure (US$12.6). While Uruguay's decentralised party structures, as opposed to Costa Rica's centralised ones, may explain part of the difference, it is the contrasting format of their party systems[7] that appears to hold the key to the spending gap between both countries. Table 4.2 shows that in the absence of a third major party, campaign disbursements per voter in Uruguay during the 1990s would have been virtually identical to those in Costa Rica. If, as argued by Sartori, the structure of the party system mediates decisively the effects of electoral formulas,[8] it also seems to play a crucial role in shaping the consequences of political finance rules.

**The structure of expenditure**

While the allocation of campaign expenses bears little resemblance to popular myths in Costa Rica, it conforms better to stereotypes in Uruguay. Despite the introduction of free advertising slots for parties in the national TV networks during the 1999–2000 election cycle, television advertising consumes a much higher proportion of electoral disbursements in Uruguay than is the case in Costa Rica. Yet TV outlays vary across the multiple levels of the heterogeneous campaign structures in Uruguay. Moreover, as in Costa Rica, TV expenses coexist with equally heavy disbursements on other forms of advertising.

Graph 4.2: *Electoral expenditure per items, New Space Party 1994–99*

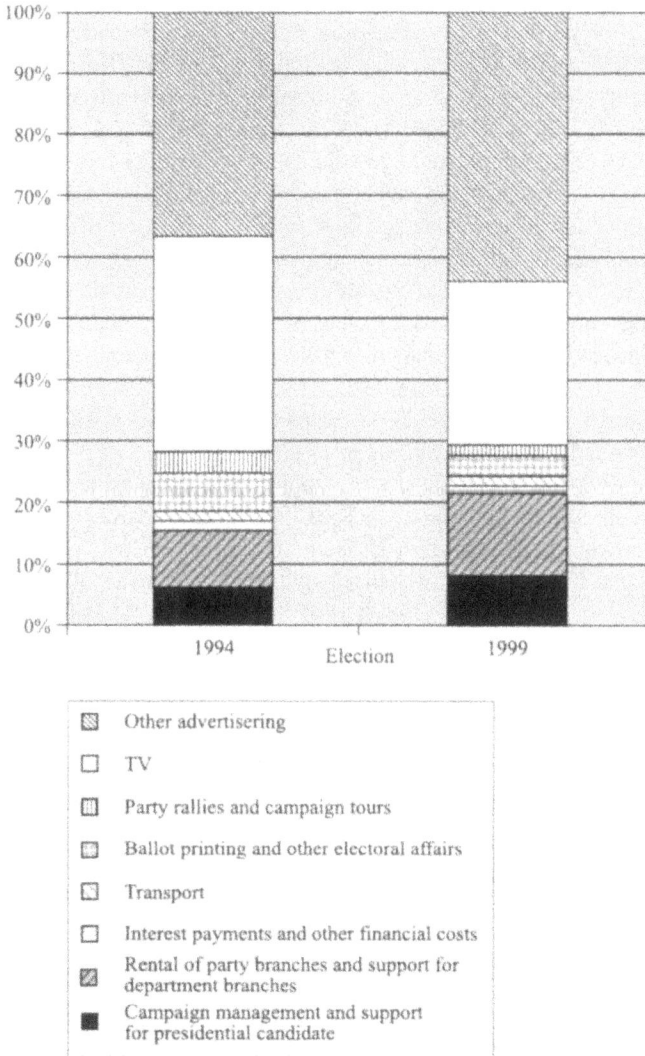

Sources: See Appendix

Graph 4.2 summarises the only publicly available account of the allocation of expenditures by a national political party or sector in Uruguay during the last two campaigns. The graph shows that in the New Space Party's [NE] case, the purchase of TV advertising slots amounted to 35.2 per cent of total expenditure in 1994 and 26.7 per cent five years later. Although the NE is largely a Montevideo-based organisation, these figures are, in all likelihood, a good proxy for the expenditure patterns of most other political sectors in their national and metropolitan (i.e., in the Montevideo metropolitan area) campaigns. Important caveats should be stressed, however. The proportion of TV advertising is probably much lower in campaigns in the interior of Uruguay (which are largely excluded from the NE's numbers), whose presence on television relies, if at all, on local stations with advertising rates well below those of national networks. The same applies to political sectors on the far Left, whose electoral efforts are largely based on traditional canvassing techniques executed by disciplined activists, rather than media advertising.[9] On the other hand, by all accounts, television outlays go up markedly in the case of the central campaign in all the major parties, where they probably exceed 50 per cent of all disbursements. Largely relieved from the organisational efforts carried out at the local level by the parties' internal sectors and their lists, presidential campaigns can afford a more intensive presence in the mass media. Taking into account these qualifications, and using the NE's figures as an approximation, the evidence suggests that advertising in national television networks by all parties amounted to US$8.2 million in 1994 and climbed to US$10.3 million in 1999.

If not overwhelming, the reliance of Uruguayan campaigns on television is significant and much higher than in Costa Rica. This is unsurprising, given the extraordinary penetration of television in Uruguay, which, at 531 sets per 1000 people, boasts the same TV density as Sweden and more than double that of Costa Rica (229 per 1000).[10] The relevance of TV advertising in Uruguayan campaigns is, however, less striking than the importance of advertising *in general*. One of the most remarkable features of Graph 4.2 is the very high proportion of publicity outlays in the NE's total electoral disbursements: above 70 per cent in both election cycles. These numbers coincide with evidence on the spending behaviour of some political sectors of the FA, which, during their campaign for the May 2000 municipal elections, allocated over 70 per cent of their budget to media expenses.[11] The purchasing of TV advertising slots is merely one part, and often a surprisingly limited one, of a broader picture in which media production costs, radio publicity, leaflets, campaign billboards and publications in the written press also feature prominently.[12] Thus, for instance, TV expenses absorbed less than half the total advertising budget of PN's leading presidential candidate in 1994, Alberto Volonté, a phenomenon also observed in the NE's campaigns of 1994 and 1999.[13]

The dominance of publicity outlays in Uruguay serves to highlight the other noticeable feature of Graph 4.2: the low proportion of organisational expenses, i.e. those of campaign management, logistical support for the presidential candidate, rental of party branches, and financial transfers to the NE's departmental branches outside Montevideo. These disbursements comprised 15.3 per cent and 21.7 per cent of the NE's total spending in 1994 and 1999 respectively, a much lower proportion than that absorbed by comparable items in major Costa Rican parties (40–50 per cent). Particularly striking are the very limited resources allocated to salaries (1.3 per cent in 1999) and rental of party branches (4.5 per cent on average in 1994–9), which comprise the largest share of organisational outlays in Costa Rica.

These differences have deep roots in the Uruguayan political tradition as much as in various institutional incentives. Although rigorous evidence is hard to come by, the legendary level of politicisation of the Uruguayan population probably translates itself into an uncommonly high willingness to engage in unpaid party activities, relieving parties from otherwise weighty organisational expenses. Already in 1919, in the wake of an election, the *Batllista* daily *El Día* reported that the PC's local branches in Montevideo boasted nearly 20,000 affiliates, an extraordinary number for a movement that had obtained 26,000 votes in the capital.[14] If extended campaign activism probably traces its roots to early forms of popular mobilisation activated by the numerous *caudillos* in both traditional parties, the adoption of DSV in 1910 added a strong institutional incentive to it. The multiplication of party lists and fierce intra-party competition mobilised a large number of political activists with a direct or indirect stake in the election. To this day, registered candidates at all electoral levels in Uruguay reach into the several thousands, way above their number in Costa Rica, where orthodox single party lists remain the rule.[15]

This incentive would be reinforced by the patronage structures put in place by the traditional parties in the first half of the twentieth century. The citizens' active engagement in the campaign was often the counterpart of a bargain that involved, at the other end, the parties' delivery of particularistic benefits to their followers. Patronage allowed parties to mobilise a large pool of free campaign labour and create a permanent capillary structure sustained by the taxpayers. This structure existed through the parties' multiple 'political clubs', manned and controlled by politicised public servants.

Widespread voluntary participation survived the demise of traditional clientelism and the authoritarian interlude and, indeed, reached extraordinarily high levels during the campaigns leading to the 1984 and 1989 elections. Even today, voluntary activism remains at relatively high levels: nearly one-sixth of the electorate claimed to have carried out voluntary tasks during the 1999 campaign.[16] This proportion is significantly higher amongst self-described centre-left (20 per cent) and left-wing (27 per cent) voters, a phenomenon that goes a long way towards explaining the NE's and FA's very low salary expenses. The FA, in particular, relies almost entirely on voluntary campaign workers, as noted by several interviewees, even from rival parties. The use of free campaign hands is merely one of the ways in which civic engagement slashes the parties' organisational costs. Indeed, a survey of the expenses incurred by Uruguayan political sectors in the opening of branches in Montevideo during the 1994 campaign, concluded that more than 90 per cent of the premises had been borrowed from the candidates' friends and supporters.[17] The irrelevance of rent payments in the NE's outlays, as seen in Graph 4.2, is, thus, far from atypical.

As with organisational outlays, so with financial and transport costs. The former, so important in recent election campaigns in Costa Rica, appear to be irrelevant in Uruguay. In the NE's case, they amounted to 2 per cent of total expenditure in 1994 and 1.2 per cent in 1999. As in the pre-1991 experience in Costa Rica, the presence of a system of interest-free pre-electoral advances of state funds in Uruguay may help to explain the irrelevance of the parties' financial burden. Yet the evidence also suggests that, with or without pre-election subsidies, Uruguayan political actors make very limited use of bank loans, preferring instead to contract debts, often extensive, with service providers. The reluctance of Uruguayan political actors to resort to bank credit has a very simple explanation: the extremely high real interest rates prevailing in Uruguay, hovering around 50 per cent in 1994 and 1999.[18] Rather than borrowing cash during the campaign, as Costa Rican parties do, Uruguayan political actors prefer to 'borrow' services at conditions that are usually more favourable than those offered by commercial banks.

Transport costs are just as low: 1.6 per cent as an average in the last two NE campaigns, or less than one-tenth their relative magnitude during the 1998 campaign in Costa Rica. As opposed to Costa Rican parties, Uruguayan parties do not develop large-scale operations in order to mobilise their voters on the election day. The approximately US$25,000 spent by the PC's presidential campaign on hiring 300 taxi-cabs to transport voters to the polls in October 1999 was a mere 3 per cent of the budget allocated to the same purpose by Costa Rica's PLN in the February 1998 election.[19] While sheer confidence in Uruguay's intense civic engagement may help to explain this difference, basic institutional traits are probably more relevant. In particular, Uruguay's mandatory suffrage, backed, unlike in Costa Rica, with effective fines, makes sure that citizens turn out to vote, even when faced with obstacles to doing so.[20]

The past paragraphs suggest that the importance of advertising outlays in Uruguay is not haphazard. Their weight is connected to, and probably the natural consequence of, the very limited non-advertising demands faced by Uruguayan parties. The irrelevance of their organisational, financial and logistical requirements allows Uruguayan parties to liberate resources that are largely allocated to advertising campaigns. As in Costa Rica, the structure of electoral expenditure in Uruguay appears to be more a reflection of the wider institutional framework than of an inexorable trend towards higher TV expenses.

## CAMPAIGN INCOME: SOURCES AND PRACTICES

So far, this chapter has given an estimate of the cost of Uruguayan election campaigns, analysed the spending structure of the latter, and established the relationship of both with the country's institutional make-up. What follows is a reconstruction of the fundraising practices of Uruguayan parties, largely based on extensive interviews with first-hand participants and their occasional public remarks on the topic. The analysis will begin by looking into the financial relevance of Uruguay's subvention system.

### State funding and its relative weight

An inquiry into the relative importance of Uruguay's state funding system should

Table 4.3: *State funding dependence rates in Uruguay, 1994–2000*

| Election Cycle | A State funding (US$m) | B Spending in national campaigns (US$m) | C Spending in presidential primaries (US$) | D A/B (%) | E A /(B+C)(%) |
|---|---|---|---|---|---|
| 1994 | 15.3 | 36.5 | – | 41.9 | 41.9 |
| 1999–2000 | 20.5 | 32.9 | 5.9 | 62.3 | 52.8 |
| Mean 1994–2000 | 17.9 | 34.7 | – | 52.1 | 47.3 |

Sources: See Appendix.

start by recalling a point made in Chapter two: amongst the purely election-oriented schemes, the Uruguayan subvention is one of the most lavish in the world. During the 1999–2000 election cycle, the system allocated US$8.5 per registered voter, far above the US$5.6 distributed by the Costa Rican scheme after the 1998 election.

However, greater generosity does not translate automatically into greater financial impact. The higher cost of Uruguayan elections in relation to Costa Rican ones restricts the country's subsidy system to covering a far-from-overwhelming proportion of campaign expenses. Table 4.3 shows the proportion of campaign expenses covered by the Uruguayan subsidy over the last two election cycles.

Subsidy dependence in national campaigns stood at just above 40 per cent of total campaign spending in 1994 and climbed sharply to 62.3 per cent during the 1999–2000 election cycle. The hike in the latter reflects a significant increase in the subvention as much as a contraction in the private sources available to presidential campaigns, which partially dried up in the course of the non-subsidised primary campaign of early 1999. Once the cost of party primaries is incorporated, the subsidy's relative weight drops 10 points to about 53 per cent of total campaign expenditure in 1999–2000. At 47.3 per cent, the average subsidy dependence rate of both election cycles stands well below the mean rate in Costa Rica for the period 1986–98 (54.2 per cent). Despite its remarkable lavishness, Uruguay's election subsidy has covered an inferior proportion of campaign expenses than the more modest Costa Rican subvention.

Systemic rates of subsidy dependence only tell one part of the story, however. In fact, reliance on state funds differs dramatically across Uruguayan parties (Table 4.4).

To an extent unknown in Costa Rica – where ideological distinctions between major parties are as small as their funding differences – or Western Europe – where the parties' income structures are similar, even across ideological families – the Uruguayan experience lives up to the preconception that left-wing parties are more heavily dependent on public subsidies than their conservative opponents. The average proportion of state funds in the expenses incurred by the left-leaning FA and NE in the last two election cycles is not just very significant in itself: it is also between

Table 4.4: *State funding as a proportion of total campaign expenditure by Uruguayan parties, 1994–2000 (%)*

| Election cycle → Party ↓ | 1994 | 1999–2000 | Mean 1994–2000 |
|---|---|---|---|
| PC | 34.6 | 46.7 | 40.7 |
| PN | 32.9 | 45.9 | 39.4 |
| FA | 71.5 | 66.6 | 69.1 |
| NE | 83.2 | 47.7 | 65.5 |
| Other | 76.9 | 73.8 | 75.4 |

Sources: See Appendix

twenty five and thirty points higher than the average for the PC and the PN.

While traditional parties continue to rely heavily on private donations, the public subsidy is the Left's veritable financial cornerstone. Despite a near doubling in the FA's campaign expenses between 1994 and 1999–2000,[21] public funds still covered two-thirds of the party's outlays during the latest election cycle, with a combination of small donations, post-election debts, and accumulated financial surpluses accounting for the rest. Moreover, this proportion climbs to practically 90 per cent in the national and metropolitan campaigns of the party and its internal fractions, and to well above 100 per cent in the case of some sectors. Indeed, financially thrifty sectors in the FA occasionally reap a large *surplus* from the public reimbursement, which is usually accumulated for future elections.

If the importance of public subsidies to the FA admits no shadow of doubt, the situation is less obvious in the NE. The dominance of public funding in its 1994 campaign turned five years later into a funding structure primarily reliant on nonpublic sources. Such a sudden transformation is attributable to a sharp and unexpected increase in the party's debts rather than to a larger inflow of private contributions. Excluding the party's heavy post-election liabilities, public funds still covered 65 per cent of the disbursements made by the NE during the 1999 campaign, with the rest coming, mostly, from the special contributions made by party members.

A note of caution should be sounded. Rates of reliance on 'official' party subsidies underestimate the support that traditional parties receive from the state. Although the heyday of their patronage structures is long gone, Uruguayan parties continue to benefit from public resources that, in many ways, ease their organisational burden. Eroded by the decade-long hibernation of party structures after 1973, and by the long-term reduction of state prerogatives and functions, blatant forms of patronage are now confined, mostly, to local governments and state-owned firms.

More visible, however, is the political cycle of television advertising by Uruguay's government agencies. While evidence of manipulation of official advertising in Costa Rica points towards a subtle change in the timing of government publicity during the election year, data from Uruguay suggests the govern-

Graph 4.3: *Television advertising by public agencies in Uruguay, 1999*

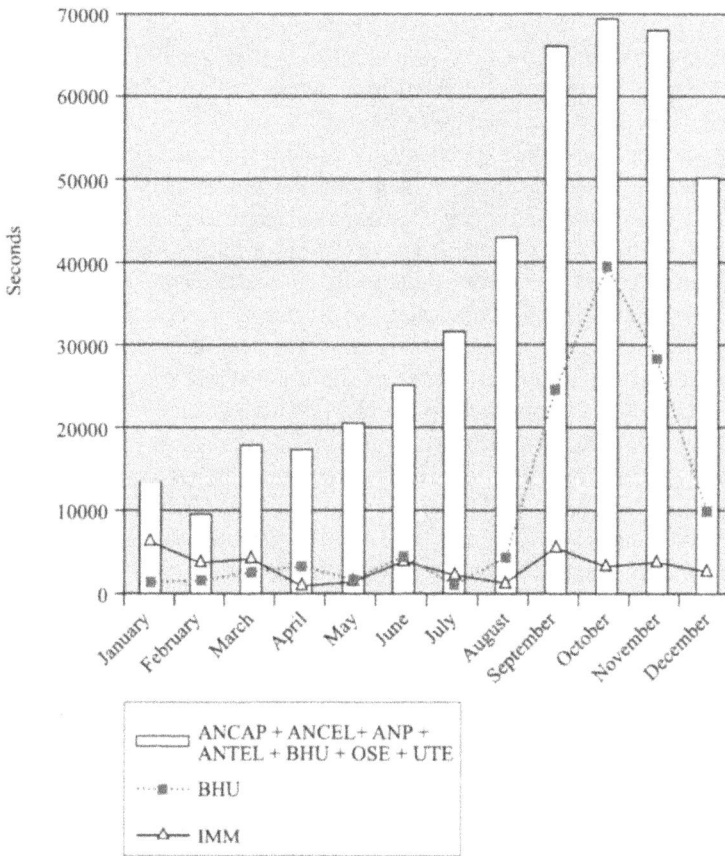

Sources: See Appendix

ment's intent to back the incumbent party's campaign with a veritable advertising barrage. Graph 4.3 charts the evolution of TV advertising by the state's seven largest firms and autonomous institutions in the run-up to the last presidential election, held over two rounds at the end of October and November of 1999. Moreover, it compares this evolution with the advertising behaviour of the *Intendencia Municipal de Montevideo* (IMM: Montevideo's municipal government), the one public body controlled by the FA, in many ways analogous to a large state firm.

Although only limited inferences can be made from the evidence of a single year, the chart is suggestive of a government advertising blitz that peaked in the weeks before the election. This is especially true of the Banco Hipotecario del Uruguay (BHU: Mortgage Bank of Uruguay), by far the largest government advertiser during the 1999 campaign: 75 per cent of its annual TV publicity was aired in the three months prior to the *ballotage*. The comparison of the BHU with the IMM could not be more telling: while both institutions had roughly similar advertising patterns during the first eight months of 1999, their behaviour during the final electoral push parted dramatically: while the publicity of the BHU soared, that of the IMM remained essentially stable.

The allocation of government publicity in the printed press has also been the subject of acute controversy. As noted by Danilo Arbilla, one of the country's leading journalists and most outspoken critics of government advertising in Uruguay, the latter's sharp increase during the campaign season has a fourfold objective: buying favourable coverage for the traditional parties in the mainstream newspapers, neutralising the attacks of critical media outlets, improving the parties' bargaining position in their negotiation with media owners, and bailing out fledgling party newspapers.[22] The advertising allocation figures of the state-owned and politically controlled BROU are indeed conspicuous. During 1999, the amount of publicity allocated by the bank to two PN-owned weekly publications (*Patria* and *La Democracia*), with a combined circulation of less than 700 copies, was virtually identical to the sum received by the country's most respected independent weeklies, *Búsqueda* and *Brecha*, with a circulation of more than 15,000 copies apiece.[23]

These isolated examples suggest that the traditional parties' relatively low reliance on state funds may be, after all, an appearance. In fact, their long-term entanglement with the Uruguayan state translates itself into considerable public support for their electoral efforts. As in 1928, when it was quietly enacted, Uruguay's state funding system is only a limited component of an extensive phenomenon of government support for parties.

This caveat notwithstanding, the main point remains: the collection of private funding sources remains *crucial* in Uruguayan election campaigns, particularly for the PC and the PN. Let us now turn to the analysis of fundraising processes.

## Fundraising processes: mechanics and implications

As shown by the analysis of the Costa Rican case, fundraising processes involve a complex set of practices that reveal central traits of the parties' internal life and their interaction with society. In Uruguay, these processes display the effects of DSV, but also of the peculiar marks left by each party's history on its organisation and political practices. Let us examine, first, the process of realisation of state subsidies.

### The activation of state subsidies
Since its inception Uruguay's state funding system has been conceived as a reimbursement of electoral expenses. However, the recent democratic transition saw the return of the practice, briefly used during the 1950s, of disbursing part of the subsidy before the election. Ever since, presidential nominees, heads of lists of candidates for the Senate and the ChR, and aspirants to the country's nineteen

governorships have been authorised to claim from the BROU, a state-owned commercial bank, an interest-free advance of up to 50 per cent of the funds that they may receive from the public purse. The loan is re-paid after the election once the public reimbursement is distributed, with any eventual surplus accruing to the recipient.

While the system of pre-electoral loans that operated in Costa Rica between 1971 and 1991 was the object of endless controversy – due to its presumed role in fossilising the party system and stimulating financial fraud – the Uruguayan provision has not elicited any criticism at all. This contrast is related to the specific features of the Uruguayan subsidy. The Uruguayan subsidy laws have not established any electoral barrier to benefit from the funds. Combined with norms that allow intra-party actors to claim the funds directly, the lack of an electoral threshold guarantees that even very minor political groups enjoy access to pre-electoral funding. One hundred and eleven ChR lists received funds from the BROU before the 1994 election, some of them on the basis of electoral shares of less than 300 votes in 1989.[24] Albeit in a slightly oblique way, subsidy rules allow the BROU to disburse funds even to new political actors (see Table 4.5, column E). As leading PC politician Washington Abdala noted, 'the BROU advances funds to every actor that demonstrates a certain presence in the electoral market'.[25]

Just like the Uruguayan subsidy's own existence – entirely reliant on non-written political practices – the allocation of pre-election state funds depends on the discretion of bank directors, rather than on fixed criteria of past electoral performance. If the system harbours the risk of political manipulation, not least because BROU directors have long been appointed by both traditional parties, it also offers a mechanism to fine-tune the allocation of funds to current political realities. The electoral prognoses made by the BROU directors before disbursing the funds are, in fact, remarkably accurate: out of the approximately US$8 million distributed by the bank in the run-up to the October 1999 election, only US$70,000 failed to be covered by post-election reimbursement payments. Even these minor lapses are virtually without consequences for the public purse: the recovery rate of pre-electoral state funding in Uruguay is virtually 100 per cent. The flexibility of the loan's allocation criteria and the practice of guaranteeing the advance with the recipient candidates' own assets and income, prevent the recurring losses that decisively undermined the Costa Rican loan scheme.

While the design of Uruguay's pre-electoral loans pre-empts potential criticisms, the scheme's lack of controversy also stems from its rather limited financial relevance (see Table 4.5, columns B–C).

However important as 'seed capital' for the campaign, in 1994 subsidy advances covered substantially less than half of the available state funding for parties, and less than one-sixth of total campaign expenditure. This is a far cry from the Costa Rican experience: for two decades Costa Rica's pre-electoral loan scheme distributed 70 per cent of the subsidy in advance, enough to routinely cover nearly one-half of the expenditures made in national campaigns.

The limited financial role of subsidy advances is compounded by the funds'

Table 4.5: *Distribution of pre-election state funds in Uruguay, 1994*

| Party | A | B | C | D | E |
|---|---|---|---|---|---|
| | Pre-electoral funds received (US$m of 1995) | Pre-electoral funds as proportion of total state total funding(%) | Pre-electoral funds as proportion of campaign expenditure (%) | Number of recipients | Number of new recipients (1) |
| PC | 1.99 | 40.1 | 13.9 | 43 | 11 |
| PN | 2.37 | 49.6 | 16.3 | 91 | 28 |
| FA | 1.32 | 28.1 | 20.1 | 8 (2) | 3 (2) |
| NE | 0.05 | 6.2 | 5.2 | 1 | 1 |
| Other | 0.05 | 50.0 | 38.5 | 5 | 0 |
| Total | 5.79 | 37.8 | 15.9 | 148 | 43 |

Notes: (1) Includes lists of candidates for the ChR only. (2) Refers to the EPR as a whole. For the FA, which comprises the vast majority of sectors within the EPR, the number of recipients is three, with no new recipients.
Sources and method: See Appendix.

decentralised disbursement. By granting party fractions direct access to pre-election funds, Uruguayan subsidy laws help to atomise the funding and erode its importance for any single campaign. In the absence of pooling mechanisms created by the parties, Uruguay's pre-election funding becomes a prime example of the 'shot-gun' effect: too little subsidisation for too many candidates for too many offices.

Mechanisms to pool pre-election subsidies do exist, however. Recipients at lower levels of competition are routinely encouraged, and often compelled, to transfer their subvention entitlements to their sector or the party's central structure in advance. The extent and effectiveness of subsidy-pooling mechanisms vary widely, but not randomly, across parties. Table 4.5 (column D) highlights the visible divide between the PC and the PN, and, once more, an even deeper one between both traditional parties and the Left. The decentralisation of pre-election funds (i.e. a higher number of recipients) is highest in the PN, where former President Luis A. Lacalle described the attempts to pull subsidy entitlements away from ChR lists as 'trying to wrest a bone from a dog'.[26]

The situation is very different in the PC. Having already displayed a lower number of loan recipients in 1994, the PC reduced it to a bare minimum five years later. In 1999, both Foro Batllista (FB) and Lista 15 (L15), the national sectors that dominate the party, centralised the reception and distribution of state pre-election funds at all levels. Moreover, despite the overwhelming superiority achieved by the FB in the previous election, both fractions agreed to an equal distribution of the available state loan. Such a contrast in the way in which both traditional parties handle pre-election funds reveals deeply rooted differences in their organisational culture. Romeo Pérez has pointed out the PC's secularly higher levels of party discipline and organisation, greater adherence to institutional authority, and 'contractual' political style.[27] These traits stand in contrast to the PN's notoriously unruly internal life, manifested in the long list of defections that plagued it throughout the twentieth century, its historically high number of candidate lists, and, most recently, its deeply divisive primary campaign in 1999.[28] The dispersion of pre-electoral funds in the PN is, thus, no more than the reflection of an equally wide and entrenched dispersion of power within the party.

As Table 4.5 shows, the concentration of pre-election funds in the party national structure is much more intense on the Left than in either traditional party. In the FA, all internal sectors and party lists traditionally cede their subsidy entitlement to the president of the conglomerate, entrusting him with the task of claiming the party's pre-election loan and eventual reimbursement.[29] The cession is the product of a hard-wrought agreement between the sectors represented at the party's National Political Board. The Board determines not only the allocation of the public advance between sectors but also, and crucially, the distribution of both pre- and post-electoral public funds between the sectors and the FA's central structure. The centre routinely keeps between 40 per cent and 50 per cent of the public funds received by the FA during and after the campaign, and distributes the rest to the national authorities of the party's myriad internal fractions. The distribution of pre-electoral funds amongst the FA sectors is done by the party's National Political Board on the bases of their previous electoral results, current prospects, and performance in the processes of selection of party authorities. Eventual post-election losses leave the recipient group indebted to the FA, rather than to the BROU.

Such a procedure is as revealing of the FA's history and organisational mores, as are the methods employed by traditional parties. The large proportion of resources traditionally retained by the FA's central campaign is a consequence of the party's foundational commitment to single presidential candidacies, a symbolic rebuke of the secular electoral practices of traditional parties. More importantly, the negotiation process reveals the much greater power enjoyed by central organs within the FA than in any of its conservative rivals. This centralism is a prerequisite for the survival of an extraordinarily heterogeneous alliance. It is also a product of the FA's long-term weakness outside Montevideo, and an organisational legacy of the orthodox Marxist parties that formed its core in its early days. The formality and regularity of the FA's subsidy transaction process, as opposed to the ad-hoc procedures used by the PN and even the PC, suggest a higher level of party institutionalisation, a remarkable achievement in view of the FA's bewildering internal complexity.

The process of securing state electoral funding in Uruguay involves more than the negotiation and reception of subsidy advances. Uruguayan political actors also use their eventual post-election subsidy entitlement as a financial lever to collect cash or credit from private sources during the campaign. Subsidy cessions in favour of third parties were expressly authorised by the law in 1954, and were already a common occurrence by the time of the 1958 election. Today, the practice is intensively – even recklessly – used by all parties, granting them access to goods and services during the campaign.

*The quest for non-public sources*
The largest share of funds in Uruguayan campaigns – particularly in both traditional parties – is obtained through a time-honed set of procedures defined, as in
Costa Rica, by the dominance of business interests and the prevalence of social
networks. An historical example illustrates the long tradition of such practices.

**Committees, social networks and candidates.** On December 5, 1942 Dr
Ricardo Butler and Dr Abalcazar García, members of the PN, submitted a
detailed report of their fundraising activities to the national authorities of their
party and sector. Drs Butler and García were part of one of the several fundraising teams assembled by the party's Finance Commission in the run up to the
November 1942 general election. Months before, the team had received from the
Commission a stack of 'party bonds'[30] and a mandate to 'sell them amongst their
numerous and valuable connections'.[31] Their report provides a list of collected
donations and a detailed account of their communications and meetings with
approximately twenty prospective patrons. Amongst the latter there were several
cattle ranchers and industrial firms – including some that, to the team's dismay,
flatly refused to make political contributions in general – two donors that had
contributed to smaller lists within the party, one who claimed to have already
given money to the PN as well as other parties, and one who was a candidate in
the lists of arch-rival PC. The militancy of the latter was not, apparently, a self-
evident obstacle to the team's approach: the report observes, with resignation,
that after several visits, 'we have the conviction that he does not want [to contribute to the PN] and will not do so. It is not possible to put more pressure on
him'.[32] This memorandum, and a broader list of bond purchasers prepared by the
party's Finance Commission immediately after the election, report 196 contributions for a total of 49,200 Uruguayan pesos (US$374,838 of 1995). Less than
one-sixth of the donations amounted to 500 pesos or more (>US$3,809), includ-
ing three of 3,000 pesos (US$22,854), the largest in the group. Only eleven were
corporate donations, most of them very small. Luis Alberto de Herrera, the
party's undisputed leader at the time, features in the list with a contribution of
2,000 pesos (US$15,236).[33]
    It is difficult to know how comprehensive or representative these pieces of his-
torical information are. They reveal, however, the remarkable longevity of some
defining traits of political fundraising procedures in Uruguay, particularly in both
traditional parties. The first of such features concerns the make-up and activities
of fundraising committees. To this day, a few months before the start of the campaign, every national political sector appoints a Finance Commission of between
fifteen and twenty members, largely comprised, as sixty years ago, of businessmen with 'numerous and valuable connections'.
    Social prestige and trustworthiness are vital features in the profile of
Uruguayan fundraisers. With words uncannily similar to those quoted in the Costa
Rican study, a PN politician noted that finance commissions are formed 'by people who are very prestigious in our circles, very well known in the business world,

so that whoever contributes is reassured by their presence and their signature on the party bond'.[34] The group is usually chaired by someone from the innermost circle of the sector's presidential candidate or leader.

As in 1942, the workings of the committee cast a wide net. Fundraisers approach scores of entrepreneurs and business executives, starting with those that have supported the sector or its candidate in previous electoral ventures and then stretching the quest well beyond the party's boundaries. As in Costa Rica, the key to the process is familiarity. One of the committee's first and crucial tasks is, in fact, deciding who talks to whom: a friend or acquaintance invariably contacts potential donors. A current ChR member noted:

> The quest for funds is strongly based on personal affinities. It is about getting in touch with all the people you know, from relatives to entrepreneurs with whom the candidate or deputy may have had contact.[35]

In the vast majority of cases, the contributor agrees to meet a member of the committee, doles out a cheque of a few thousand dollars and receives, in return, a numbered party bond or official receipt.[36] The transaction is usually smooth and gentlemanly, devoid of coercive language and overt indications of the size of the expected contribution. 'There is a lot of respect involved, a lot of culture,' observed a prominent construction entrepreneur.[37] Fundraising visits are indeed laden with subtle codes. High-ranking politicians occasionally attend meetings with potentially large donors, ostensibly as a sign of respect towards them but also as a hint of the committee's financial expectations. In a few cases, after an initial interview with fundraisers, large contributors request an audience with the presidential candidate or, more commonly, a candidate visit to the donor's firm or factory, during which a long list of anxieties is invariably communicated.

This time-honoured method of fundraising is merely one of the tools employed by finance committees, albeit the most important one by far. Alternative methods of money collection – such as the organisation of fundraising breakfasts, dinners and raffles – remain, in general, under-used in Uruguay, except at lower levels of competition, where fundraising activities that are intended to raise small sums have become a common occurrence.[38] The relative weakness of such alternative methods is related to the intense intra-party competition for private funds. The internal race multiplies the pressure from all quarters on potentially large contributors, thus limiting the chances of financial success for any fundraising event. Moreover, the country's deep-rooted tradition of un-conspicuous wealth possession and the entrenched habit of Uruguayan donors of contributing to more than one party combine to create strong negative incentives for public giving. 'In Uruguay nobody wants to be seen when he gives,' remarked former President Lacalle.[39]

If the tasks of fundraising committees are intense and complex, the role of presidential candidates in the process appears remarkably limited. Compared to their Costa Rican colleagues, Uruguayan presidential aspirants are largely sheltered from fundraising activities and, more importantly, from the duty of contributing heavily to their own campaigns. 'The candidate is not involved *at all* in the fundraising process. This is delegated to people of his utmost trust,' noted the long-term financial manager of the current President, Jorge Batlle.[40] A financial aide of Tabaré Vázquez, Batlle's left-wing rival in the 1999 presidential run-off, spoke in exactly the same terms: 'The candidate does not touch money *at all*. It's part of his personal characteristics'.[41]

Personal proclivities notwithstanding, the delegation of fundraising responsibilities to businesspeople reflects subtle but important distinctions between political and economic elites in Uruguay. To a degree unknown in Costa Rica, Uruguayan politicians are professionals who live *for* politics as much as *off* it, enjoying relatively weak interlocking mechanisms with the economic elite and a historically high degree of autonomy from it.[42] The reasons for this are deeply rooted in the country's history. A century of civil wars – and, in particular, the long siege of Montevideo during the *Guerra Grande* – bequeathed a class of 'impoverished patricians', forced to trade their destroyed estates for a public career, normally in the PC ranks.[43] Later, the professionalisation of politicians and their relative detachment from the business community would be compounded by the extraordinary expansion of the Uruguayan state, the adoption of unlimited re-election clauses and generous pension entitlements, and the emergence of political careers as avenues of social mobility in a stagnant economy. Simply put, Uruguayan politicians are rarely men of fortune or part of the business community. 'The presence of entrepreneurs [in the finance committee] allows us to translate the codes of the business system,' noted, tellingly, a high-ranking PC politician.[44]

The reluctance of Uruguayan candidates to engage wholeheartedly in fundraising amongst business elites should not be overstated, however. It weakens significantly at the lower levels of the political system, where candidates can ill afford to stay aloof from the money chase. Such is the case in small parties, hindered by weak fundraising structures and a diminished allure for donors. The NE's chief financial manager during the 1994 campaign remarked:

> Fundraising commissions are non-existent, except in major parties, like the Colorados, that had a commission that worked very well, because a phone call on behalf of [former President] Sanguinetti is very heavy indeed. In small parties such as ours, the activity of the candidate is fundamental.[45]

Similarly, at the legislative level – notably ChR elections – candidates are actively involved in the quest for funds. A former PN deputy and senator noted:

> When we talk about collecting important contributions in cash, the support normally depends on the candidate and her connections... It is the head (of the list) who collects, because the person who puts the money wants to go for something safe. She wants to have a friend on whose door she can knock.[46]

These words reveal more than the fundraising involvement of legislative candidates. They also point towards a crucial feature of fundraising processes in Uruguay: their strong decentralisation.

**Decentralisation, contribution fragmentation and multiple giving.** Weakened by DSV, central party organs have traditionally remained at the margins of electoral fundraising in Uruguay. As noted by donors and politicians alike, the quest for private funds is largely spearheaded by the parties' national fractions and their numerous ChR lists, locked in a struggle for resources that mirrors their competition for votes. Genuine disbelief thus met a 1996 judicial injunction to the PN's National Directorate, demanding the disclosure of campaign donations to the party. Faced with the request, former Vice-President Gonzalo Aguirre noted that '[The Directorate] is alien to the activity (of collecting private donations), which internal groupings carry out separately'.[47]

The subsequent imposition of single presidential candidacies changed the situation only marginally. While it provided a clearer rationale for the fundraising involvement of central party organs, the reform hardly weakened the pre-eminent role of the presidential candidate's own financial structure or of the party's internal groupings. Central party organs thus collected less than 5 per cent of the PN's total private funds during the 1999 campaign, according to one estimate.[48] However, even an increased campaign role for party headquarters would do little to tame the decentralisation of fundraising structures. As the above mentioned example of the PN in 1942 suggests, the active fundraising role of central party organs simply adds *another* participant to the fierce intra-party competition for funds, a situation neatly replicated by the FA's recent experience. The chief financial officer of the Socialist Party (PS), the FA's largest internal grouping, summed up the basic architecture of private fundraising efforts in the leftist alliance, and, ultimately, in all Uruguayan parties:

> Every sector carries out its own fundraising campaign and 100% of the proceeds go to the sector. Yet, the FA's central structure also has its own special financial team, that makes its own campaign to attract donations, which go in their entirety to the central campaign of the *Frente*.[49]

The implications of fundraising decentralisation for the effectiveness of political finance controls are obvious and will be examined below. Less evident, however, are its consequences for the size and fragmentation of private contributions. Just as the competition between hundreds of party lists stimulates widespread political activism, it appears to mobilise a comparatively high number of donors. Eight per cent of Uruguay's voting-age population claimed to have contributed money to parties or candidates during 1999, more than four times the comparable rate for Canada and only slightly lower than that of the US, probably the most broadly based system of political contribution in the world.[50]

Such a high participation figure translates into an average contribution of US$60.[51] Yet this average is misleading. Participation rates are considerably higher amongst self-described leftist sympathisers, which probably comprise a significant proportion of donors in Uruguay, albeit with very small amounts.[52] On the contrary, traditional parties attract, in all likelihood, a much smaller number of business donors, some of them remarkably generous. Although far from common, contributions of US$50,000 and even US$100,000 to PC and PN presidential aspirants are not unheard of. Donations of US$5,000–10,000 are considered average at the presidential level in both traditional parties, while rather exceptional at lower levels of competition.

Large or not, the important thing about private contributions in Uruguay is that in a different political environment they would probably be *larger*. Uruguay's electoral rules and party system generate powerful incentives towards the fragmentation of contributions and their scattering throughout the political system. Business donors, in particular, are *expected* to lend their support simultaneously to several fractions and parties. If Butler and García's report shows that the practice of multiple giving was already present in 1942, the recent case of Igor Svetogorsky provides a neat example of its endurance. In 1996, Svetogorsky, head of a holding linked to the Uruguayan state through several purveyance contracts, was accused of alleged high-level bribing and influence peddling by a journalistic investigation.[53] In the course of the inconclusive political and legal wrangle that ensued it became clear that Svetogorsky was, at least, a very generous and open-minded political donor. His known contributions during the 1994 campaign had amounted to US$110,000, widely distributed across parties, sectors and competition levels: US$50,000 and US$30,000 went to the presidential candidacies of Juan A. Ramírez and Alberto Volonté in the PN, respectively; US$10,000 to the *Lista 15* of PC's presidential aspirant Jorge Batlle; US$3,000 and US$7,000 to two Senate and ChR lists supportive of one of Batlle's internal rivals, Jorge Pacheco; and, finally, US$10,000 to the campaign of the NE and its presidential standard-bearer, Rafael Michelini. While his connections and munificence may have been atypical amongst businessmen, Svetogorsky's unselective contributing habits certainly were not. A young entrepreneur told the author:

> The norm is contributing to all the sectors, unless the entrepreneur has a very direct involvement with one of them. To begin with, it's not convenient to be in bad terms with one of the parties. Of course, one may decide not to contribute to any of them or to give a little bit to all of them, but the latter option is friendlier.[54]

The reasons for the prevalence of this practice, which surpasses anything seen in Costa Rica, are not hard to fathom. As mentioned above, DSV nurtures an intense struggle for funds between multiple political actors, which compels them to look for donations well beyond the boundaries of their own constituency. As the 1942 example already evinces, Uruguayan fundraisers – with the partial exception of the FA's – pay only limited attention to the political affiliation of their prospective patrons. The relentless pressure on prospective donors creates, to use the term of our previously quoted young entrepreneur, a *less friendly* atmosphere for those who systematically refuse to collaborate. Another businessman justified his decision to contribute moderately to all parties as follows:

> The rationale is, simply, not to say no. Since I know that they will come around, if I say no, I isolate myself in a context where everybody contributes... If I contribute with something, even if it's only a little, I join the group of those who collaborated, and then they may or may not forget who contributed with what. But if I don't contribute, they will surely remember that.[55]

Any tacit compulsion felt by contributors merely compounds, however, the effect of an underlying institutional incentive. In a fragmented party system, with highly fractionalised parties and a multiplicity of relevant actors, the share of power enjoyed by any given political agent is severely curtailed. In such an environment, a single contribution stands a slim chance of securing any real political influence. For Uruguay's instrumentally motivated donors, the diversification of political contributions is a highly rational strategy. As Svetogorsky's example so clearly shows, Uruguay's acute power diffusion forces donors to split oversized contributions into smaller parcels distributed at all political levels. Faced with a basic resource allocation dilemma, Uruguayan donors have chosen to sacrifice the *intensity* of their influence over any given political actor, in order to enlarge the *scope* of their pressure across the political system. Moreover, if the fragmentation of the party system limits the decision power enjoyed by any single actor, the country's secular political mores dictate, at the same time, that no fraction within the traditional parties is ever deprived of political power. The colonisation of the state apparatus by both parties and their sectors – which survives, if subdued, to this day – and the long tradition of power co-participation between them, turn even potential electoral losers into future power brokers, worthy of financial support. 'Even if a candidate can't win,' remarked a business leader, 'he is, almost always, an influential person whom you can call and who can lend you a hand to unfetter a file or procedure at any public institution'.[56]

No matter how entrenched multiple-giving behaviour may be, the last election cycle put its limits to the test. The break-up of the electoral process into several stages and, particularly, the introduction of presidential primaries by the 1996 electoral reform, increased enormously the burden of fundraisers and donors. The sheer cost of lending support across the board *twice* – at the primary stage and again during the national campaign – made business donors, as in Costa Rica, highly reluctant to contribute to the April 1999 primaries. Other than those with intense partisan or personal commitments, most offered very limited financial support to pre-candidates or chose to invest their resources only in national elections.

The higher partisanship of the contributors' behaviour during Uruguay's 1999 primary campaign confirms two points already raised by the Costa Rican case. First, private contributions to nomination campaigns appear less driven by instrumental motives than by political and personal loyalties. Second, coupled with the absence of public funding, the limited involvement of business donors leaves pre-candidates dependent on the economic might and willingness of a restricted group of supporters, when not on the aspirant's own financial resources. Out-spent by former President Lacalle by an 8-to-1 factor in the course of the PN's 1999 nomination campaign, Juan A. Ramírez, the defeated candidate, raised an alarm well known by now to many Costa Rican politicians:

> We have created in Uruguay the absurdity that in order to reach an election in which one enjoys more or less sufficient economic capacity through the state subvention, one must first go through a stage where there is no subsidy and therefore the inequalities derived from [the candidates'] economic power are blatant.[57]

**Domestic business elites and the case of television networks.** That the reluctance of businesspeople to fund primary races has become a source of concern for politicians is a reflection of business' pivotal involvement in all other campaigns. In spite of Uruguay's relatively broad base of political contributors, the overwhelming majority of non-public resources in Uruguayan campaigns come from large domestic entrepreneurs and firms. This dominance is most intense at the higher levels of the parties' electoral structures. The smaller amounts spent in local races, especially outside the metropolitan region, allow for a certain diversification of income sources and for the financial participation of Uruguay's extended professional strata.

If the social bias of private fundraising efforts in Uruguay falls short of their obvious elitism in Costa Rica, the extent to which Uruguayan politicians – notably those in traditional parties – regard visits to wealthy businesspersons as the nearly exclusive source of non-public funds is nonetheless conspicuous. The very composition of fundraising commissions, heavily dominated by business figures, reflects as much as it reproduces this entrenched notion. A former PC senator remarked that 'there are no resources from party members. Therefore, what happens? The fundraising commissions of the sectors and the party go and tour the firms, and the entrepreneurs give money'.[58] 'When a time of extraordinary expenses comes,' confirmed a colleague from rival PN, 'we all have to go out and tour the big firms and factories'.[59] Such inevitability is equally accepted by those at the receiving end of the request. As an important construction entrepreneur put it, matter-of-factly, 'in this country, the call asking you for political contributions is something that you assume from the moment you own a business'.[60]

Despite the institutionalisation of these links, they amount in practice to what a business leader called 'a very primitive system', devoid of sectoral co-ordination.[61] Like their Costa Rican counterparts, Uruguayan entrepreneurs regard the idea of pooling their contributions to maximise sectoral impact as 'absurd' and 'unthinkable'. The familiarity between fundraisers and donors, the status of contributions as a taboo topic amongst entrepreneurs, and the political fault-lines that have secularly criss-crossed business interests in Uruguay – a trait as old as the existence of *Colorados* and *Blancos* – combine to create a system entirely defined by individual exchanges.

While the system involves the vast majority of the country's entrepreneurial elite – from large industrialists to cattle ranchers and big traders – the intense participation of specific business groups is noteworthy. As the Costa Rican experience and Svetogorsky's above-quoted example suggest, the vulnerability of a business operation to the whims of public officials makes for eager political contributors. The *Banca de Cubierta Colectiva de Quinielas de Montevideo*, a private consortium that administers Uruguay's lottery and football pools under government control, retaining a set percentage of the sales, offers an interesting example. Monopolising a business with more than US$260 million in revenues during the 1997–78 period only, the *Banca* is more reliant on the goodwill of the political system than most firms are. Through a variety of means – chiefly the operations of the National Direction of Lottery and Football Pools – the government determines by fiat the *Banca's* profit margins and the very extent of its monopoly, being able to authorise by executive decree new gambling options outside the consortium's control. Not surprisingly, the *Banca* is a particularly generous and indiscriminate political contributor, as pointed out by sources across the party system.

A more relevant and controversial example is that of private television stations. Like the *Banca*, TV networks have peculiar and obvious incentives to make political donations. Through the National Direction of Communications, the government controls the authorisation of new TV frequencies and the revocation of those in place for reasons as vague as the disturbance of public tranquillity and the harming of the prestige of the republic.[62] In effect, however, the interaction between politicians in both traditional parties and the owners of Uruguay's main television networks has evolved into a complex web of mutual dependence, with crucial implications for political finance.

Closely connected to both parties from the outset, the family-controlled groups that own the country's three private TV networks have come to operate, with the acquiescence of public authorities, as a powerful business cartel. The groups' early domination of national airwaves merely preceded their control – sanctioned by government decisions – over emerging sectors of the TV market, notably regional channels and cable networks. By the 1990s, the three groups, acting as an oligopoly under the guise of various joint ventures, had consolidated a virtual stranglehold over the Uruguayan TV market.[63]

If the channels' successful lobbying against the development of the state-owned television network, SODRE, had long evinced their capacity to extract concessions from the political authorities, by the 1990s the situation had become extraordinarily blatant. The government's controversial 1994 decision to turn Montevideo's cable TV market into a closed shop jointly controlled by the three private networks was followed six years later by the Sanguinetti administration's order to *ban* the importing of satellite TV de-coders, unless done by the existing cable operators.[64] In the meantime, the 1997–8 attempt to legislate the TV channels' obligation to allocate free broadcasting time to parties in the run-up to the elections – an effort originally endowed with cross-party support – was thwarted in the Senate when the media lobby, National Association of Uruguayan Broadcasters (ANDEBU), made known to lawmakers its intense displeasure with the bill.[65] With the FA's opposition, the bill was subsequently limited to the state-owned channel in exchange for the private networks' *voluntary* commitment to allocate a number of free TV and radio slots to parties represented in Congress.[66] 'Formidable!' exclaimed on the occasion a left-wing deputy. 'Never have I seen any corporation so effectively twisting the Senate's arm.'[67]

Arm-twisting is only a partial explanation, however. In fact, the relationship of channel owners with traditional parties features sticks and carrots in roughly similar doses. Foremost amongst the latter is the TV networks' practice – already seen in the Costa Rican case – of charging wildly different advertising rates to the various parties and sectors, granting some of them heavy discounts over the official prices. In doing so, TV stations become *de facto* large political contributors, armed with an unmatched ability to bias the electoral playing field. Former President Julio M. Sanguinetti framed the issue with admirable clarity:

> In Uruguay, a donor who gives US$50,000 or US$60,000 to a campaign is a big donor, a really big donor. Yet US$50,000 in terms of television advertising is very little, almost nothing. What this tells us is that the television rate is, ultimately, the biggest sponsor. Here lies one of the most decisive factors in campaign funding. I would say that the number one factor.[68]

In the absence of any regulation, the networks' discretion to charge the parties is as complete as the opacity with which such discretion is exercised. While no political actor ever pays the official rates, the discounts reaped by certain PC and PN fractions may reach 95 per cent of the price.[69] These remarkable rebates are compounded by the networks' frequent practice of condoning the campaign debts accumulated by the sectors. A former PC senator described the system's standard procedure as follows:

> You go and buy publicity for US$200,000. The channel is interested in cashing in a part of that, say half of it. Later, you win or you lose. If you lose, the channel forgives the debt. If you win, given the new circumstance you are in, they forgive you the debt as well. Either way, the political system is always eternally grateful.[70]

Such munificence is hardly ever extended to the Left. While an important television executive claimed that his channel made no difference between the parties' central campaigns, he admitted that at the level of their internal fractions – which carry out their own independent negotiations – network executives normally grant a better treatment to those sectors 'closer to their hearts'.[71] And the heart, in this case, beats on the Right. Before and after their second-round defeat in 1999, FA officials complained bitterly about the TV networks' blatant discrimination against the Left, visible in the unfair pricing and programming of advertising as much as in the lopsided coverage offered by news programmes.[72] Their complaints were not unfounded. The advantage of the PC's presidential candidate, Jorge Batlle, over his left-wing rival, Tabaré Vázquez, in terms of TV presence during the run-off campaign was indeed sizeable: 65.2 per cent to 34.8 per cent in advertising and, more significantly, 59.7 per cent to 40.3 per cent in news coverage.[73] An advertising executive with a long experience in handling media campaigns for both the PC and the FA noted:

> The mass-media normally give away a certain number of slots to the parties... Television owners... are far more benevolent and open-handed with these slots in the case of the traditional political groupings... and particularly in the case of the *Partido Colorado*, that has been the party of government since well before I remember. The *Partido Colorado* receives the largest benefits in kind from the mass media...[74]

While the secrecy of the negotiations between TV networks and the parties precludes any conclusive confirmation of his words, available data on the parties' allocation of advertising time between TV networks during 1999 suggests that the PC may have received preferential treatment from key media firms (Graph 4.4).

At first glance, the graph displays the same basic allocation for each party: a very low proportion of advertising on the poorly-rated state-owned Channel 5 (3.3 per cent average), a much higher and similar percentage on private Channels 4 and 10 (28.3 per cent and 31.4 per cent average, respectively), and a still larger share on Channel 12 (37 per cent average), the strongest of the private networks. However, while the distributions of the FA, NE and PN deviate only marginally from each station's average, the PC's allocation – and specially that of its presidential campaign – is visibly skewed in favour of Channel 12. If the PC certainly had a greater presence in all private networks than any of its rivals, its advantage was truly overwhelming when it came to Channel 12: on the latter, its advertising time was virtually on a par with that of all the other parties *combined*. While such an allocation may be just the result of a strategy devised by the PC's media advisors – one not replicated by any other party – it is reasonable to suppose that it simply reflects the greater generosity of Channel 12 executives towards the party and its presidential candidate.

Remaining at an arm's length from the country's entrepreneurial elite, and treated with relative harshness by media owners, where, then, does the Left turn to in its quest for non-public resources?

**The Left and minor parties: peculiarities.** '*Al Frente lo financia el pueblo*' ('The FA is financed by the people'), decreed one of the foundational cries of the left-wing alliance in 1971, describing its policy of tapping a large number of members and sympathisers for minimal donations. If 'popular contributions' ever were the financial backbone of the FA's electoral efforts, they are certainly not now.

Graph 4.4: *Electoral advertising by parties in Uruguay. Time distribution per national television networks, January–November 1999*

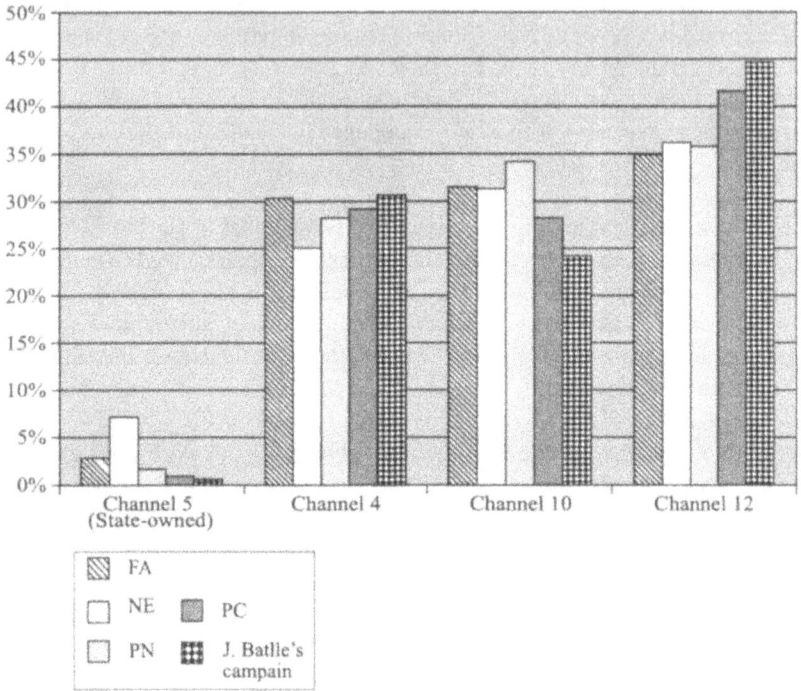

Sources: See Appendix

While the policy maintains much of its original significance between elections, during the electoral season the FA and its sectors also engage in special campaigns to attract large private donations.

However, they do so in a much more limited and discriminating way than their traditional adversaries, and with far less success. With few exceptions, such campaigns are geared towards high-earning donors who already contribute to the FA on a regular basis or have a well-known identification with it. 'Ninety-five percent of our contributors, I would say, are people with some kind of historic link to the party, even in the case of successful professionals or entrepreneurs,' noted a Socialist financial official.[75] Their contributions are, in most cases, an extraordinary membership fee levied during the electoral campaign and, as such, tend to be rather low. Donations obtained through this mechanism by the FA and its sectors are normally in the US$500–5,000 range and only exceptionally above the latter sum.

This phenomenon is echoed in minor parties. Thus, while keen on the orthodox method of touring firms and factories, the NE has been far more successful in carrying out several original campaigns to attract significant contributions from its closest sympathisers. The party raised approximately US$200,000 in the run-up to the 1999 election through the auctioning of paintings and photographs previously donated by Uruguayan artists, at a price of US$300–2,000 per ticket.[76] These activities – largely aimed at the party's top activists – were part of the NE's commitment to financial transparency in the wake of the damaging evidence of Svetogorsky's contributions to the party during the 1994 campaign.[77]

The irrelevance of private donations in the FA's campaign coffers is the result of ideological choice, as much as of the FA's acute lack of fundraising knowhow and troubled relationship with Uruguay's business community. The alliance's largely successful decade at the head of the Montevideo mayoralty and its increasingly strong electoral position have made some business donors more willing to extend their liberality to the FA's central campaign and even some of its moderate sectors, notably the Vertiente Artiguista (VA). Yet, they have hardly generated a change of heart: even in cases of multiple giving, left-wing groups tend to be rewarded with much smaller figures than their conservative rivals. Moreover, business's limited involvement has not been balanced by the financial participation of trade unions, which, while ideologically close to the FA, have doggedly clung to their age-old formal autonomy from political actors, and enjoy no organic links – financial or otherwise – with the leftist alliance. Amidst Uruguay's low unionisation rates[78] and the unions' chronic economic feebleness, labour's financial contribution to the FA is, by all accounts, non-existent.

As shown previously in this chapter, rather than 'financed by the people', the FA is simply funded by the state. The overwhelming dominance of public resources in the FA's election coffers is, however, a relatively new phenomenon for key sectors in the alliance. The experience of the Uruguayan Communist Party (COM) suggests that the notion of 'popular contribution' may have been a mystification from the outset, and that other non-public resources were probably crucial for the FA up until the early 1990s. Hermes Millán, a former COM Secretary of Finance, now distanced from the organisation, provided the author with a detailed account of the party's financial life during the Cold War, which started by throwing into question the financial relevance of mass contributions:

> Once every year, approximately, there was a financial campaign where raffles and bonds were sold, and special collaborations raised.... This campaign was...more important for its contribution to the party's organisation and agitation, than for its concrete financial results....[79]

According to Millán, mass contributions were, in fact, dwarfed by two largely concealed funding sources. The first, the COM's business ventures, constituted a complex operation that spanned several countries: from various commercial firms in Uruguay, to tour operators linked with Cuba, to minority shares in West European firms set up by the Soviet Union to commercialise products from the Socialist bloc, notably diamonds and precious woods from Angola. These ventures were a well kept secret. Due to legal and political reasons, chiefly hiding from the rank-and-file the fact that the party was reproducing its income through the workings of the capitalist system, they were never registered under the COM's name. These activities were complemented, and in many cases nurtured, by external subsidies:

> The other source of funding, which is very difficult to prove, but one which I can attest to from direct personal experience, was the concrete money – not through firms and corporations – that arrived from the Soviet Union…(N)one of that money was ever registered anywhere…there were no formal reports, no receipts, nothing. All this constituted a money merry-go-round, where you could never know how much money would get lost in each hand. And something would get lost. Moreover, since it was money sent from the USSR, it was also linked to the Soviets' own merry-go-round.[80]

Such an account is consistent with information released by the Russian authorities in 1992. According to the latter, between 1969 and 1990, the Soviet government's official aid to the COM amounted to slightly above US$5 million, including US$350,000 as late as 1990.[81]

Ironically, the system, described by Millán as 'ever prone to generate conflicts, and very related to the development of internal corruption in the party', collapsed as the COM was finally consolidating its dominant position within the FA. While the demise of the USSR spelled the end of external funding in the early 1990s, the internal fissures precipitated by the international crisis translated into acrimonious disputes over the COM's firms. Most of the latter simply accrued to their legal owners, leaving the party empty-handed. Today, the COM is a relatively minor sector within the FA, and, unlike yesteryear, its funding mores are only of limited relevance to the alliance's financial situation.

**Foreign sources.** The Soviet subsidies channelled to the COM are hardly the only known instance of financial participation by outsiders in Uruguay's electoral campaigns. Born as a 'buffer' state between Argentina and Brazil, Uruguay's political and economic life has been inextricably linked to both since independence. This closeness generates numerous manifestations of electoral support across borders.

The phenomenon has benefited the Left as much as traditional parties. As recently as November 1999, it was reported that the leftist *Partido dos Trabalhadores* (PT) and *Partido Socialista Brasileiro* (PSB) in the Brazilian border state of Rio Grande do Sul were collaborating with the FA in the mobilisation of thousands of voters with double nationality.[82] Such collaboration was not a novelty. Back in the transitional election of 1984, the leftist governors of the states of Rio de Janeiro and São Paulo allegedly offered free transportation to Uruguayan immigrants willing to return home and cast their votes for the FA.[83] This was a remarkable change of fate. In the previous election campaign, held in the ideologically charged days of 1971, the FA had bitterly denounced the Brazilian military authorities for printing large amounts of anti-Communist propaganda and having it smuggled into Uruguay.[84]

While the days of the National Security Doctrine are now gone, Uruguay's traditional parties continue to benefit, nonetheless, from the nervousness of conservative interests across the border. Both parties regularly collect campaign contributions from business in Argentina and, to a much lesser extent, Brazil. 'Economic groups and banks from Argentina', noted the campaign manager of one of the leading candidates in 1994, 'collaborate strongly with the Uruguayan parties. And it's reasonable that they do so, for all of them have business here or, at least, the expectation of investing in Uruguay in the short or medium term'.[85] Investment opportunities may or may not be part of the explanation, but the preoccupation with the stability of Uruguay's financial system – endowed with some of the world's strictest bank secrecy rules and long seen as Argentina's safety deposit box – certainly is. Available figures suggest that in September 2001 Argentines owned approximately US$8.8 billion in bank deposits and real estate investment across the River Plate.[86] Uruguay's political stability is crucial to Argentina's business interests.

The substantial participation of Argentine firms contrasts sharply with the rather subdued involvement of other foreign business interests. It was not always thus. In 1971, when US firms were deeply implicated in the funding of conservative political movements in Chile, Uruguay's left-wing press repeatedly denounced the participation of multinationals in the funding of both traditional parties, in some cases exhibiting the documents to prove it.[87] Two decades later, however, the situation had probably changed, due to the easing of the ideological atmosphere as much as to the enactment of the 1977 Foreign Corrupt Practices Act, which banned US multinationals from making political donations abroad. Indeed, ahead of the 1994 election, Uruguayan subsidiaries of US-based multinationals jointly and publicly stated that they would not contribute to parties or political sectors.[88]

If their statement merits some scepticism, it is yet to be refuted by any evidence to the contrary. When in 1999, the FA leader, Tabaré Vázquez, publicly accused both traditional parties of being funded by multinationals 'that have won or pretend to win public bids', he failed to provide any specific examples after being challenged to do so by his opponents.[89] More importantly, the statement above is consistent with the recent experience of Costa Rica, where foreign firms have been dismissed as a limited source of political funding, in spite of the far greater dynamism of foreign investment.[90] Today, with the possible exception of the controversial South Korea-based Unification Church,[91] multinational consortia are, in all likelihood, restricted funding sources for Uruguayan parties.

The same holds true for Germany's international political foundations. While the role of the liberal Friedrich Naumann Foundation – linked during the crucial transition years to the late PN leader Wilson Ferreira – may have raised a few eyebrows during the 1980s, the truth is that German foundations have remained on the margins of the electoral efforts of Uruguayan parties. Bound by restrictive legislation in their home country, which prevents them from making direct financial contributions to any party, even the Naumann Foundation's support of Ferreira was carefully channelled through the Centre for the Study of Democracy in Uruguay (CELADU), a research institute linked to his political sector *Adelante con Fe*. This behaviour was not restricted to the Naumann Foundation, nor has it changed significantly since the days of the transition. Today, as in Costa Rica, the foundations' role largely consists of shoring up with ever-smaller grants the activities of the frail education endeavours set up by the parties, mostly during the non-electoral season.

Even these indirect links have failed to reach in Uruguay the intensity that they once displayed in Costa Rica. Fractionalised and heterogeneous, Uruguayan parties – with the exception of the social-democratic NE – defy the neat ideological categories embodied by the foundations. This poses significant obstacles to the establishment of stable co-operation bonds. It is hardly surprising that no German foundation has implemented any collaboration scheme with the PC, whose ideology was once defined by one of its leaders as 'anti-dogmatic, anti-Marxist, rationalist yet anti-positivist'.[92] The complex games of ruptures and alliances that have shaped the Uruguayan party system have left the German foundations without natural partners and forced to walk on a political minefield, where large-scale co-operation is risky even when feasible. The head of the local branch of the social-democratic Friedrich Ebert Foundation, which lends occasional support to FA-related institutes, observed:

> It would be very difficult to establish an organic, permanent relationship with the FA, beyond the support of specific activities, because the diversity of sectors that are part of it makes co-ordination very, very difficult.... In fact, it is likely that some sectors within the FA would not accept a closer relationship with the Ebert Foundation.[93]

Amidst political complexity and financial strictures, the large funding role occasionally ascribed to German political foundations is, in Uruguay as in Costa Rica, simply a myth.

**Motives and retributions.** The involvement of domestic business interests in funding campaigns is, conversely, very real. The Uruguayan case indeed provides a good example of the combination of motives that drive most business donors. The large difference in the weight of private contributions in the finances of traditional parties, on the one hand, and the FA, on the other; the widely different treatment granted to both by TV channels; and the limited impact that the FA's electoral success has had on both phenomena, suggest that for most private donors in Uruguay the decision to contribute is laden with ideological considerations. 'In the first place, you contribute because you believe in the convenience of certain ideas for the country,' opined a prominent entrepreneur.[94] Believe they may, but many private businessmen also, and perhaps fundamentally, *fear* the inconvenience of certain ideas and contribute accordingly. The idea 'I'll put money on this candidate because I do not want the other one to be elected' describes just as plausibly the basic rationale of most business donors in Uruguay.

This is, however, merely the first stage of their decision. Beyond the ideological choice between Left and Right, instrumental motivations rule. As shown above, the pervasive habit of contributing across parties, sectors and competition levels, embodies a fine instrumental calculation framed by the prevailing institutional rules. As in Costa Rica, this calculation is only rarely geared towards securing an appointment in the future administration. In a country where political elites have long enjoyed a significant degree of autonomy and political careers are still patiently constructed through party ranks, demands for political appointments – from top legislative candidacies to directorial posts in state firms – stand a slim chance of succeeding. This rule may admit exceptions, nonetheless, at the local level, where age-old clientelistic practices remain unabated. Ultimately, as former presidential candidate Juan A. Ramírez sharply put it: 'The businessperson does not demand posts. The businessperson requires influence'.[95]

Influence may come in many different shapes, from very abstract to very concrete. The most common of them is, as in Costa Rica, a rather abstract one: the influence to be heard *in case of necessity*. Asked about her objectives whenever she made a political contribution, a construction entrepreneur fired a concise reply: 'To be known by them!'.[96] Another businessperson clarified the purpose of this introduction rite: 'The entrepreneur collaborates so that she doesn't get hurt, so that in case of *any problem* they remember her as someone who collaborated. I think the exception is she who contributes with a concrete deal or benefit in mind'.[97]

In the business world problems arise and phone calls arrive. As shown by the following remarks from Gonzalo Aguirre, a former vice-president, sooner or later the abstract turns into the specific:

> It once happened to me, when I was Vice-President of the Republic, that I received a phone call from a firm that had collaborated with the fundraising campaign of my Senate list.... The firm had important liabilities with the tax authority, had an immediate deadline on an important sum, and was asking for an extension. I arranged the extension and they got it. It is not immoral, but neither is it the most convenient practice.[98]

The specific *quid pro quo* is hardly ever articulated expressly; it is merely understood. The moment of contribution indeed calls for considerable delicacy on the part of the donor, generally unarmed with credible coercive devices and uncertain about the recipient's reaction. A PN senator noted that an explicit demand in return for a donation entails the 'risk that one can simply break off the meeting, say no, and be offended. [Donors] don't want to provoke such an awkward situation... That would shut them a door'.[99] Some things are better left unsaid.

Yet, unsaid does not mean unfathomed. As in Costa Rica, donors and fundraisers in Uruguay seem well aware of the contours of their implicit covenant. Rather than specific policy outcomes, always subject to the whims of decision-makers and the vagaries of political circumstance, the typical donor knows themself to be purchasing lesser goods: a special right of petition before the politician and a favourable environment for their request. At the same time, as Gonzalo Aguirre's example clearly shows, politicians understand that receiving such requests and acting upon them is part of their job. At the highest level, the bargain includes the politician's implicit commitment to appoint campaign fundraisers in key positions of the administration, where donors' generosity might be remembered and their petitions warmly looked upon. Such expectation operates as a powerful entice-ment to contribute. Not surprisingly, the directing board of BROU – the state-owned bank that, to this day, controls a large share of credit in Uruguay – has been a traditional province of campaign fundraisers.

The closer a party, sector or politician is to power, the clearer this agreement becomes. And in post-transition Uruguay no politician has been closer to power than former President Sanguinetti. He has, indeed, shown a remarkable eagerness to fulfil his side of the fundraising bargain. In 1985 and 1995, in the early days of his two administrations, businessmen Julio Kneit and Salomón Noachas – two of Sanguinetti's key fundraisers – were appointed at the top of the state-owned Mortgage Bank of Uruguay (BHU).[100] By allocating credit to a myriad housing projects all over Uruguay, the BHU is a nodal point in the activities of the coun-try's construction firms, believed to be – as elsewhere – significant political donors.[101] Equally conspicuous was the case of Osvaldo Risi, another important fundraiser in Sanguinetti's second presidential bid in 1994.[102] Risi, twice given low-profile posts in the Presidential House, became notorious in the course of a journalistic probe into an alleged high-level bribery scam in 1999. The probe, and the legislative investigation that followed, failed to implicate Risi in any wrongdo-ing. Nonetheless, they made clear that, contrary to what his obscurity suggested, Risi was an important figure in the President's entourage and had been in close contact with a variety of public authorities and private firms – including Svetogorsky's – involved in public bidding processes. Whatever the outcome of their phone calls, bidding firms had, at the very least, a friendly ear in the Presidential House.

*Friendliness* is, in fact, the key word, above and beyond *access*. In the small, egalitarian 'city-state' of Montevideo, access to politicians is generally swift and uncomplicated, as businesspeople and politicians were keen to note and the author fortunate to experience. 'Ours is such a small country,' remarked former President Lacalle, 'that I would receive any important person who calls me, as surely would any political leader ... It is not like in other parts of the world, where (a contribu-tion) opens a door. It doesn't open any door, just as no door is closed if you don't contribute'.[103] Yet, plain access does not bring goodwill; contributions do. Goodwill can be a decisive business advantage, coveted as much as feared by most entrepreneurs. The value of such an edge and the lack of transparency of the fundraising process concur to create a co-ordination failure that subtly forces most businesspeople to contribute. The owner of a large construction firm observed:

One contributes with all because it's always been like that, and also because one doesn't want to be the only one in the sector who doesn't contribute. And that you never know. Nobody knows if the other contributes, but if they came knocking on my door there's no reason to suppose that they haven't knocked on the others' doors.[104]

Either to secure a business advantage for the donor or, as in this case, to prevent someone else's from arising, campaign donations display once more the features of an *insurance policy* of sorts. The benefits of this policy may or may not become tangible, and, in any case, only reach the donor *personally*. Opposed to any form of contribution co-ordination and forced to split their money across the party system, the vast majority of Uruguay's campaign donors, with the glaring exception of television networks, realistically pay for political help rather than policy decisions, for a resource rather than a result. In the exchange between donors and politicians the currency is complex and contingent.

**The issue of control.** Yet, dangers abound, more so given the weakness of fundraising controls in Uruguay. As noted above, neither domestic campaign donations, nor international contributions, nor expenses, are subject to *any* kind of regulation or disclosure requirement in Uruguay.

Such a void is compounded by the virtual absence of control mechanisms within the parties. Sectors in both traditional parties and the FA operate with complete financial autonomy, free from any obligation to submit their accounts to party authorities.[105] In turn, lists are only rarely accountable to their own political sector. The internal competition for resources is, thus, not merely unrelenting, but untrammelled. Only the NE partially deviates from this pattern. In 1997, in the wake of the disclosure of Svetogorsky's donations to the party, the NE enacted a Code of Ethics to regulate its fundraising procedures. The Code calls for ceilings on anonymous donations (currently >US$190), institutional approval of large contributions (>US$12,500), and an outright ban on corporate funding.[106]

The NE's experience suggests an important point. As with so many traits of Uruguay's political finance system, the feebleness of legal and party controls over fundraising activities is largely endogenous to the country's electoral system. It is hardly accidental that, alone amongst Uruguayan parties, the NE has turned political finance transparency into part of its platform and practice. Small and endowed with a far higher level of centralisation than any of its rivals, it is, arguably, the only party capable of enforcing a measure of regulation over its finances. On the contrary, long conditioned by the centrifugal influence of DSV and counting their internal lists in the hundreds, the three major parties – and the national electoral authority – would find it very difficult to impose and enforce a unified set of fundraising practices.

In lieu of the latter, only self-control remains. Limited forms of it are indeed exercised. Fundraising committees at all levels make an effort to document every contribution through the handing over of receipts or party 'bonds' to donors, a practice that can be traced back to the 1920s. Contribution bonds are, however, merely an instrument of *internal* control, a mechanism of accountability for fundraisers geared to reassuring donors and political authorities that contributions will reach the coffers of the party, sector or list. Moreover, they are routinely given to donors who wish to remain anonymous. Party bonds notwithstanding, the contributions' origin may remain undisclosed even to the sector's political leaders.

Ultimately, to a much greater degree than in Costa Rica, the probity of Uruguay's campaign finance practices has come to rely on the willingness of fundraisers to protect the reputation of their political bosses – to which they are invariably very close – and their own business name. In Uruguay's close-knit business community, evidence of ghastly fundraising practices or campaign finance mismanagement would probably spell disaster for any fundraiser in their regular business activities.[107] Yet the effectiveness and sustainability of reputation-based checks is open to serious questions when coupled with a conspicuous lack of political, journalistic and academic interest in probing the topic. Unlike in Costa Rica, not a single Congressional probe on political finance has taken place in Uruguay. The press has shown virtually no interest in the topic, which has been publicly discussed only as a peripheral element in some corruption scandals, notably the Svetogorsky affair. Amidst such indifference, the increased fundraising pressure entailed by the post-1996 electoral rules may pose the ultimate test to Uruguay's *laissez-faire* approach to private campaign donations.

## CONCLUSION

This chapter has shown the myriad ways in which campaign finance practices and the effects of state funding rules in Uruguay are moulded by the institutional, historical, social and political context in which they operate. The preceding pages confirm some of the findings of the Costa Rican case, notably in the area of private fundraising dynamics. However, as expected, the picture that emerges also dvierges, in some cases dramatically, from that yielded by the previous chapter. It is also a richer and more nuanced picture, coloured by a deep ideological cleavage – laden with political-finance consequences – that has no parallel in Costa Rica.

We have seen how the internal fractionalisation of parties – nurtured by the electoral system – and, above all, the greater fragmentation of the party system push electoral costs in Uruguay well above their level in Costa Rica, despite the striking similarities between both countries, not least in the size of their electorate. However, contrary to expectations, Uruguay's 1996 electoral reform generated only a moderate increase in electoral costs. Rather than by soaring expenses, Uruguay's last election cycle was characterised by a visible redistribution of spending across electoral stages and parties.

Even more visible is the impact of electoral rules – including the subsidy's own design – on the structure of campaign expenditure in Uruguay. The dominance of television expenses and, more generally, of advertising outlays in the parties' budgets, is the reflection of an institutional framework that eases considerably the organisational, financial and logistic costs that weigh so heavily on the finances of Costa Rican parties. The roles of DSV in mobilising voluntary campaign activism, of compulsory suffrage in slashing transportation costs, and of public pre-election loans (along with sky-high interest rates) in keeping Uruguayan parties away from financial intermediaries, go a long way towards explaining the stark qualitative difference of campaign disbursements in both countries. The comparison of Costa Rican and Uruguayan campaigns suggests that, rather than governed by ineluctable international trends, electoral expenditure is largely a local phenomenon that defies easy generalisation.

The preceding pages have also demonstrated that despite its far greater generosity, Uruguay's state funding system covers, overall, a smaller proportion of campaign disbursements than its Costa Rican pair. This assertion, obviously related to the higher cost of Uruguayan elections, conceals, however, a central finding of this chapter: the striking variation of the subsidy's impact across parties and party levels. Indeed, while the official subvention represents a somewhat limited income source for both traditional parties – and increasingly so at the lower levels of electoral competition – it is, on the contrary, vital for the Left. Excluded from unofficial forms of state electoral support, deprived of once-important international funding sources, kept at an arm's length by the business community, and endowed with scant financial help from trade unions, the FA has come to depend almost entirely on public funds. The most important effect of Uruguay's state funding system is, arguably, providing a left-wing alliance with a fighting chance against two traditional rivals overwhelmingly favoured by the country's business donors. Limited as its overall financial weight may be, the public subvention system is, nonetheless, a crucial instrument for the protection of electoral equality and pluralism in Uruguay.

Compared to its pivotal consequences for electoral equality, the effects of state funding on the prevention of corruption appear more limited and uncertain. It should be enough to recall that the parties that have secularly monopolised political power in Uruguay are precisely those that rely least on electoral subsidies. Moreover, we have also seen how the subsidy's own design nurtures a tendency towards the atomisation of state funds and, hence, towards the erosion of their ability to replace private income sources. As the chapter's final section showed, the financial life of both traditional parties during the election season is defined by a relentless multi-layered competition for business donations, which is yet to be regulated by the law or the parties. This struggle for private funds is less affected by the presence of state funding than by other institutional devices, notably DSV. By dispersing power between numerous political sectors and nurturing an intense financial race between them, DSV encourages the less-than-discriminating behaviour of fundraisers and donors that has come to define campaign fundraising in Uruguay. The chapter has shown how, outside the Left, party and sector boundaries are of little consequence when it comes to raising and contributing campaign money. More importantly, we have also seen how this institutional set up tends to fragment and spread private donations thinner across the political system. Above and beyond state funding, it is such fragmentation, the lack of co-ordination between donors, and the crucial role of trust and reputation in fundraising process- es within Uruguay's business elite, that provide real – albeit far from ideal – coun- terweights to the country's overly liberal approach to private campaign donations. Dangerous as it is, the slope of Uruguayan campaign finance is less slippery than it seems.

With the exception of the disturbing relation between traditional parties and television networks, exchanges between donors and politicians in Uruguay appear infused with the same subtlety and contingency that they display in Costa Rica. They are underpinned by the widespread understanding that while campaign donations open the door to favourable political treatment, they fall short of guar- anteeing desired outcomes. Even in the most conspicuous of such exchanges, campaign donations emerge as merely one element in a complex matrix that includes other, frequently more powerful, pressures upon decision-makers, rang- ing from pre-existing personal links with contributors to outright bribing. The Costa Rican and Uruguayan cases suggest that, while the power of private cam- paign donations to subvert political equality is beyond doubt, their ability to per- vert the public interest is more debatable.

Finally, by featuring a reduced business elite as the overwhelming source of non-public campaign funds, the Uruguayan case confirms the Costa Rican expe- rience and raises an important normative issue. Uruguay and Costa Rica are small, democratically conscious societies, endowed with stable parties, large middle classes and high levels of political mobilisation. Yet, even in the case of the Uruguayan Left, both countries have clearly failed to generate mechanisms of party affiliation or popular contribution capable of bearing a significant part of the cost of campaigns. This is hardly the effect of public funding availability: non- subsidised elections in both countries – presidential primaries, for example – seem, if anything, particularly impervious to forms of popular fundraising. To par- aphrase the famous song, if alternative sources of non-public funding can't make it here, they surely can't make it anywhere in Latin America. If our two cases are anything to go by, the absence of state funding for parties in the region would sim- ply translate into a much heavier financial reliance on large business interests, legitimate or worse. The idea that public funding inhibits the use of alternative, more democratic sources of campaign funds exudes an unmistakably West European scent. Whatever normative objections may seem reasonable elsewhere, some kind of state subvention for political parties looks like a democratic neces- sity in Latin American countries.

Let us now shift the focus of the analysis and return to one of the issues briefly explored in Chapter one: the effects of direct state funding on electoral equality and the behaviour of the party system.

NOTES

1 J.M. Posadas, in *El Observador* [*EO*], 25/07/1999.
2 Rial (1998), pp. 553–4.
3 Three weeks before the first round, voting preferences were: PN 22 per cent, PC 27 per cent, FA 35 per cent (*EO*, 9/10/1999). The actual result was 22.3 per cent, 33.8 per cent and 40.1 per cent, respectively.
4 These are the races covered by the set of figures released by the NE, upon which much of the calculating procedure is based. In 1999, 58 out of 99 ChR members were elected in Montevideo and Canelones.
5 The 1999 figure was suggested separately by Heber [26/5/2000] and De Cuadro [13/6/2000]. For 1994, the lower end of Heber's range (US$50,000–70,000) has been used. The figure is consistent with other estimates given in *La República* [*LRU*], 24/7/1994 (US$50,000–200,000) and *Semanario Crónicas* [*CRO*], 19/7/1996 (US$25,000–100,000). The rationale behind the lower 1994 figure is related to the elimination by the 1996 reform of the so-called 'electoral co-operatives' for the ChR. This change generated a consolidation of the electoral market in fewer, wealthier lists for the 1999 election (Guerrini, in Cribari et al. [1999], p. 108).
6 Competitive lists were those with a reasonable probability of obtaining representation. The method for identifying these lists is described in detail in Casas-Zamora (2002).
7 The text refers to the Costa Rican party system as it stood until the 2002 election. As we know, it underwent major changes in 2002.
8 Sartori (1986).
9 The obvious case is the Popular Participation Movement (MPP), an FA sector with roots in the *Tupamaro* guerrilla of the 1960s, which reaped nearly 122,000 votes in 1999. Its TV use was minimal: Fifty-three commercials throughout 1999 and none in 1994 (Mediciones y Mercado [1999]; *CRO*, 19/7/1996).
10 World Bank (2001), 1999 figures.
11 This was the case of AU, VA and the FA's central campaign. See, for instance, Vertiente Artiguista [VA] (2000).
12 See *EO*, 22/10/1994; *EO*, 7/3/1999; *Semanario Demos* [*DEMOS*], 19/9/1994; *LR*, 24/7/1994.
13 See *EO*, 22/10/1994. However, in other campaigns on which information is available, the media mix is more skewed towards TV. The FA's central campaign in 1999 and the VA's municipal campaign in 2000 allotted nearly two-thirds of their publicity budgets to television.
14 *El Día* [*ED*], 9/6/1919.
15 In 1999, the number of titular and substitute candidates for the ChR reached practically 3,000 only in the Montevideo department. In Costa Rica, the comparable number in the entire country for the 2002 election was 1,036.
16 *EO*, 18/12/1999.
17 *La Mañana* [*LM*], 12/4/1995.
18 Calculation based on active interest rates for loans in Uruguayan pesos at private banks, taken from BCU (various years), and inflation figures taken from Comisión Económica para América Latina y el Caribe [CEPAL] (2001).

19  *EO*, 20/10/1999; Contraloría General de la República, Costa Rica [CGR] Departamento de Estudios Especiales, Informe No. 95–98; Pacheco [20/1/2000].
20  In 1999, the unjustified failure to vote carried a fine equivalent to US$16.
21  According to my estimation, the FA's total electoral expenses amounted to US$6.6 million in 1994 and US$12.4 million in 1999–2000.
22  Arbilla [3/7/2000].
23  Figures based on BROU's advertising budgets (kindly provided by Danilo Arbilla). March 2002 circulation figures from Equipos-MORI, kindly provided by Ignacio Zuasnábar.
24  Figures based on República Oriental del Uruguay [ROU] Ministerio de Economía y Finanzas (4/7/1996).
25  Abdala [25/4/2000].
26  Lacalle [4/7/2000].
27  Pérez (1984), pp. 69, 77.
28  On the 1999 primary see Moreira (2000), pp. 3–6; Cribari et al. (1999), pp. 33–5.
29  This does not apply to political sectors that belong to the EPR but not to the FA, such as AP and PDCU (See Graph 2.3).
30  The term 'party bond' denotes different things in Uruguay and Costa Rica. While in Costa Rica the document embodies a debt of the party with the holder, in Uruguay it is a plain money receipt.
31  PN, AHD 1942, doc. A195.
32  PN, AHD 1942, doc. A925.
33  All figures from PN, AHD 1942, doc. A925, A987–989.
34  Heber [26/5/2000].
35  Da Silva [29/6/2000].
36  *Semanario Búsqueda [BUS]*, 15/4/1993; *EO*, 22/10/1994; *EO*, 7/3/1999.
37  Businessperson No. 3 [24/5/2000].
38  According to one of its members, the FA's central financial committee did not organise a single fundraising dinner throughout the 1999–2000 campaign (Macedo [9/6/2000]).
39  Lacalle [4/7/2000].
40  Batlle [2/6/2000].
41  Castro [18/5/2000]. Four important entrepreneurs, interviewed in the course of the research, confirmed that it is very rare for the candidate to attend meetings with potential donors. Juan A. Ramírez, a PN presidential candidate in 1994, claimed to have met at most twenty significant donors through this mechanism [28/6/2000].
42  Costa-Bonino (1995), p. 65; Solari (1988), pp. 28–34.
43  Real de Azúa (1981), p. 49; Costa-Bonino (1995), p. 65; Caetano and Rilla (1985), pp. 14–5, and (1990), p. 114.
44  Abdala [25/4/2000].
45  Barandiarán [25/4/2000].
46  Gandini [12/4/2000].
47  *Semanario Opinión [OPI]*, 19/7/1996. See also *LRU*, 9–10/7/1996; *LM*, 10/7/1996; *Ultimas Noticias [UN]*, 10/7/1996.
48  Gandini [12/4/2000].
49  Nunes [10/4/2000].

50 *EO*, 18/12/1999; Stanbury (1993a), p. 82; Smith (2001), p.46.

51 Figure calculated by deducting direct state funds (US$16.3 million) from total expenditure in April and October-November 1999 (US$27.8 million), divided by 8 per cent of Uruguay's registered voters in 1999 (192,000 voters).

52 Contribution rates for left-wing and centre-left sympathisers are 16 per cent and 14 per cent, respectively. Rates are 5 per cent, 4 per cent and 2 per cent for centre, centre-right and right-wing partisans (*EO*, 18/12/1999). Left and centre-left sympathisers comprise approximately 25 per cent of the voters (Cribari et al. [1999], p. 85).

53 See *Este Diario* [*ESTD*], 21/6/1996; *Revista Posdata* [*POS*], 23/6/1996; *BUS*, 27/6/1996; *LRU*, 2–3/7/1996; *EO*, 3/7/1996.

54 Businessperson No. 4 [5/7/2000].

55 Businessperson No. 3 [24/5/2000].

56 De Cuadro [13/6/2000].

57 Ramírez [28/6/2000].

58 Flores-Silva [14/4/2000].

59 D. Ortiz in *LRU*, 24/10/1989.

60 Businessperson No.1 [15/5/2000].

61 De Cuadro [13/6/2000].

62 Pallares and Stolovich (1991), pp. 117–23.

63 See Pallares and Stolovich (1991) and García-Rubio (1994) for a detailed account of this process.

64 Later in 2000, the Batlle Administration repealed this decree. At the same time, however, it issued a parallel one reducing drastically the taxes paid by cable firms (*EO*, 31/5/2000; *POS*, 30/6/2000).

65 Cámara de Senadores del Uruguay [CSU], Carpeta No. 943/1997, pp. 4–6; Repartido No. 2299/1998. See also *BUS*, 24/12/1997; *EO*, 26/2/1998; *El País* [*EP*], 22/10/1998.

66 Law No. 17045 of 14/12/1998; CSU, Carpeta No. 943/1997; Repartido No. 2299/1998, pp. 5–6; *EO*, 19/11/1998.

67 J. Mujica, in *CRU*, *DS* 18/11/1998, p. 63.

68 Sanguinetti [12/4/2000].

69 Just for negotiating an advertising package, any client gets a 50 per cent discount over the official price. Discounts of between 11 per cent and 16 per cent are generally available on top of it if the service is paid in cash. However, the calculation made by the head of an advertising agency closely linked to the campaign of President Batlle goes well beyond those figures: 'The channels charge you for 100 slots. For those 100 slots you get another 100 as a bonus in non-peak periods. And those 100 that you are charged for you pay at the price of 10' (Advertising Executive [10/5/2000]).

70 Flores-Silva [14/4/2000].

71 Lassús [14/6/2000].

72 *EO*, 24/11/1999; *BUS*, 9/12/1999.

73 *EO*, 24/11/1999.

74 Visillac [23/5/2000].

75 Nunes [10/4/2000].

76 *EO*, 13/6/1998; *POS*, 3/7/1998.

77 *ESTD*, 21/6/1996; *LRU*, 2/7/1996.

78 In 1993, Uruguay's trade unions covered 11.6 per cent of the non-agricultural labour force. This figure is below the Costa Rican one (13.1 per cent) and the average for Latin America (14.7 per cent). See International Labour Organisation [ILO] (1997).

79 Millán [26/5/2000]. The following paragraphs are largely based on the account of his experience up until his resignation from the party in 1992. The author tried repeatedly and unsuccessfully to interview Senator Marina Arismendi, the COM's current Secretary-General.

80 Millán [26/5/2000].

81 *EP*, 14/3/1999.

82 *EP*, 6/11/1999.

83 *EP*, 8/11/1984.

84 *El Popular* [*ELP*], 17/9/1971; *ELP*, 29/9/1971.

85 Quoted in *EO*, 22/10/1994.

86 Montenegro (2002).

87 *ELP*, 28/10/1971; *El Eco* [*ECO*], 17–18/11/1971.

88 *BUS*, 19/5/1994 and 27/6/1996.

89 *BUS*, 25/2/1999 and 4/3/1999; *EO*, 26/2/1999.

90 In the period 1993–2000, foreign direct investment averaged US$414.5 million per year in Costa Rica as opposed to US$165.8 million in Uruguay (CEPAL [2002], Table 283).

91 The Unification Church, popularly known as the 'Moonies', is a religious movement founded in 1954 by Rev. Sun Myung Moon. Long controversial, the sect owns a vast business conglomerate in several countries, including a bank, a luxury hotel, two newspapers and vast tracts of land in Uruguay. There, the sect has been suspected of money-laundering activities and of courting right-wing politicians. See 'The Moonies have landed', *The Economist*, 7/11/1998; Blixen (1998); *Semanario Brecha* [BRE], 5/5/2000.

92 Gillespie (1995), p. 240.

93 Martin [6/6/2000].

94 Businessperson No. 2 [2/6/2000].

95 Ramírez [28/6/2000].

96 Businessperson No. 1 [15/5/2000].

97 Businessperson No. 2 [2/6/2000].

98 Aguirre [9/6/2000].

99 Heber [26/5/2000].

100 *EO*, 22/10/1994; www.bhu.com.uy/documentos/historia.htm.

101 *BRE*, 28/5/1999.

102 The following account is based on *POS*, 8–15–22/1/1999; *CRU*, Carpeta No. 3231/1998, pp. 126–145, pp. 223–242. Risi refused to be interviewed by the author. In a short telephone conversation [19/6/2000] he denied ever having had a significant participation in the fundraising activities of his sector, FB. All other evidence points to the contrary.

103 Lacalle [4/7/2000].

104 Businessperson No. 1 [15/5/2000].

105 *LRU*, 9–10/7/1996; *LM*, 10/7/1996; *LM*, 16/7/1996; *UN*, 10/7/1996; *OPI*, 19/7/1996.

106 Partido del Nuevo Espacio [NE] (1997).

107 *EO*, 22/10/1994.

# chapter five | state funding and party system dynamics: a look at costa rica and uruguay

## INTRODUCTION

The notion that Direct State Funding (DSF) exerts an 'ossifying' influence on the party system is one of the most common objections levelled against it. Drafted by incumbents, subsidy laws – it is said    tend to raise serious barriers for political newcomers. Thus protected, established parties have come to resemble a 'cartel', largely sheltered from electoral competition.

This book has already cast doubts on the validity of this argument. In Chapter one, the survey of the evidence from developed democracies suggested that neither electoral volatility nor party system fragmentation seem to suffer dramatic alterations in the wake of the introduction of DSF. Moreover, it showed that to the extent that any changes were visible they pointed towards *greater* volatility and fragmentation than before. This chapter will now look in more detail at the evidence yielded by the long-term evolution of the Costa Rican and Uruguayan party systems. In both, DSF is relatively generous and allocated in strict accordance to electoral results, thereby creating, in principle, the kind of inertial force that troubles the subsidies' critics. Moreover, in both countries, subsidy schemes have incorporated (in 1971–91 in Costa Rica, and since 1984 in Uruguay) a mechanism of pre-election disbursements allocated according to *previous* electoral results, thus reinforcing the protection of established parties. If any kind of 'freezing' effect exists, then these two countries appear as very promising places to find it.

While, in typical fashion, the effects of state funding on the dynamics of the party system have been hardly discussed at all in Uruguay, the topic has featured prominently in political discussions in Costa Rica for more than forty years. More than anything, the introduction in 1971 of pre-election disbursements – limited to parties that achieved 5 per cent of the vote in the previous election – spawned a long and bitter debate, during which subsidies came to be seen by most journalists, academics and politicians as *the* defining force behind the behaviour of the Costa Rican party system. 'What I see' – wrote in a typical statement the leader of a minor party in 1990 – 'is the evident fact that it is the unfair distribution of the pre-electoral state funds that has led us to the nefarious two-party system'.[1] In the same vein, the mechanism was called an 'artificial generator of a two-party system... that made impossible the free participation and fair competition in all the elections celebrated in (Costa Rica) over 20 years'.[2] These criticisms appeared vindicated in 1991, when the country's Constitutional Court struck down the 1971 reform, embracing wholeheartedly the 'ossification' argument. According to the Court,

> ...financing the parties according to their electoral past...is tantamount to *fossilising the political options of the Costa Rican people*, granting the traditional parties an odious monopoly and excluding the rest from an equitable participation, if not from all practical feasibility, insofar as the growth of the state subvention has truncated, in practice, any other financing option.[3]

The following pages will challenge these views. In line with the observations made in Chapter one, it will be argued that electoral subsidies have *not* frozen, in any visible way, the party systems of Costa Rica and Uruguay. The chapter will suggest that, contrary to what is commonly assumed, the Costa Rican subsidy, and in particular its much-criticised scheme of pre-election advances, was not a significant factor in the conformation of a two-party system or in the electoral performance of recipient parties. Moreover, it will be shown that the elimination of pre-election advances, considered an important milestone in Costa Rica's recent electoral history, had minimal effects – probably negative ones – on the electoral opportunities enjoyed by new and minor parties. We will also see that Uruguay's subsidy scheme has actually stimulated secular increases in the fragmentation, fractionalisation and volatility of the party system. Ultimately, electoral subsidies appear as a marginal factor in the complex dynamics that define the persistence and change of party systems.

## COSTA RICA

Gauging the influence of DSF on the evolution of the Costa Rican party system entails significant methodological problems. The most obvious one is the concomitance of both variables. Costa Rica's modern party system, defined by the dominant presence of the PLN and by the cleavage bequeathed by the 1948 civil war, precedes only by a few years the formalisation of the country's electoral subvention system in 1956. A comparison between the performance of the party system before and after the introduction of DSF is thus precluded. Attempting to sideline the concomitance issue, the following analysis will focus on the effects of the scheme of pre-electoral public loans used in 1971–91. This allows for a clearer inter-temporal evaluation of the effects of the instrument as well as a certain fidelity to the thrust of the critique against electoral subsidies in the country. Usually, the harshest criticisms have been directed, by and large, against pre-electoral advances of state funds rather than the subsidy system as such.[4]

The ingrained notion that Costa Rica's state funding system is an unfair instru-

Graph 5.1: *Disproportionality of DSF distribution, Costa Rica 1958–2002 (1)*

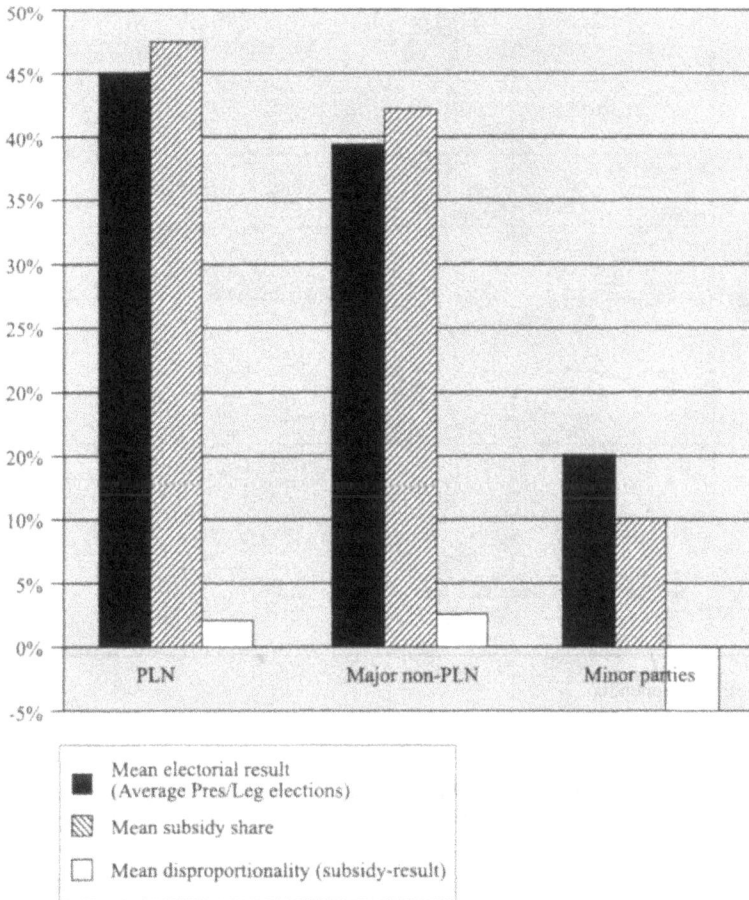

Note: (1) 2002 subsidy allocation figures are projections according to the parties' electoral share rather than actual disbursements by the National Comptroller (CGR)
Sources: See Appendix

ment, bent on preserving the status quo, derives part of its force from the limited access to public funds that minor parties have generally enjoyed over the last twelve elections (Graph 5.1). Even after the electoral 'earthquake' of 2002, the average share of the subsidy received by parties other than the PLN and its major opponents over the whole period stands at 10.1 per cent of the total. This proportion, moreover, is significantly lower than the mean percentage of their vote (15.1 per cent). The *under*-subsidisation of minor parties, largely due to the fragmentation of their votes into myriad groups that fall short of the subsidy's threshold, mirrors an equivalent *over*-subsidisation of major parties.

Graph 5.2: *Party system fragmentation in Costa Rica, 1953–2002*

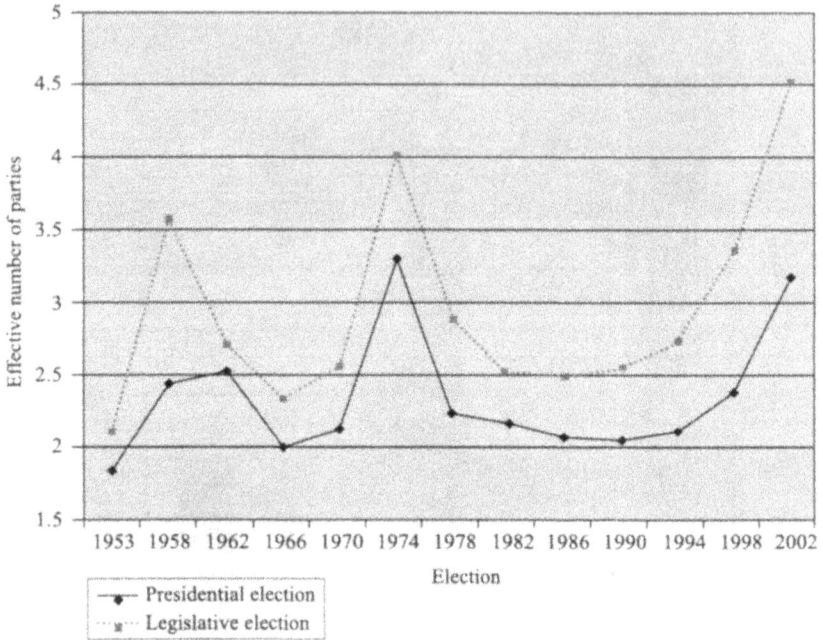

Sources: See Appendix

Is such a lopsided distribution inherently unfair? It seems difficult to argue against the fairness of a system of proportional post-electoral reimbursement, such as the one used in Costa Rica in 1956–1971 and since 1991. In this case the subvention is neutral from an electoral standpoint and its allocation reflects the popular will. The system may of course harm newcomers and minor parties in subtler ways, but its timing and allocation rules are hardly objectionable from a normative standpoint. Much more dubious is, however, the neutrality of a subsidy system that incorporates substantial pre-election funds distributed according to previous electoral results, as was the case in Costa Rica during 1971–91. Such a system may well generate a built-in advantage for major parties. Rather than a mere *consequence* of the electoral outcome, the allocation of public funding becomes, presumably, one of the *causes* behind it. Did pre-election advances 'freeze' electoral results and contribute decisively, as claimed, to the emergence of a two-party system in Costa Rica?

Graph 5.2, which portrays the evolution of the fragmentation of the Costa Rican party system over half a century, evinces that certain qualifications are essential when labelling the country's party format. As is plain to see, there is a far from negligible difference in the party system's format at presidential and legislative elections. While, in general, a two-party system[5] (i.e., an Effective Number of

Parties [ENP] around 2) has prevailed in presidential contests, it has clearly been absent in legislative elections. There, the ENP has been nearly always above 2.5, and was approaching 3.5 even before the electoral upheaval of 2002. Such figures are hardly suggestive of a two-party system.

The reasons for this heterogeneity are scarcely mystifying. The use of a plurality formula in the Costa Rican presidential election, reinforced with a 40 per cent threshold, exerts a powerful centripetal force that tends to concentrate the vote in two large parties or coalitions. This force does not exist in legislative elections, where proportional representation (PR) rules apply. In the Costa Rican system, the fragmenting influence of PR is, however, counterbalanced by the presence of several small electoral districts, the use of a moderate electoral threshold and, above all, by electoral concurrence. As Shuggart and Carey have argued, in presidential regimes concurrence transfers the centripetal effects of presidential competition on to legislative elections.[6] The combination of both competitive dynamics – centripetal in presidential contests and moderately centrifugal in legislative ones – should yield precisely the usual format of the Costa Rican party system: two large parties or blocs in presidential contests, and a few more competitors in legislative elections.

The crucial thing to note here is that the key pieces of the country's current electoral system are much older than its subsidy scheme, not to speak of the mechanism of pre-election advances. The plurality formula with a 40 per cent threshold was introduced in 1936, the electoral threshold for legislative elections in 1946, electoral concurrence in 1949, and the use of the current province-wide electoral districts in the early nineteenth century.[7] This explains why bipolarity in presidential elections was already a common occurrence before the adoption of pre-election subsidies, as shown by results in 1953, 1966 and 1970. The recurrence of such bipolarity can in fact be traced as far back as 1889, and most certainly to the immediate pre-civil-war period (1936–44), when Costa Rica already had a stable two-party system (ENP below 2.1).[8]

While this suggests that pre-election subsidies were not a *necessary* condition for the emergence of a two-party system in presidential elections, it is even clearer that they were not a *sufficient* condition to generate it after 1971. If the backers of the 1971 reform had set their minds on 'freezing' the two-party system of 1970 – an intention that enactors of the amendment reject to this day[9] – then the results of the 1974 election must have come as a disappointment. The disbursement of pre-election funds proved unable to prevent a proliferation of successful presidential candidates and an acute fragmentation of the party system.

The bipolar competition certainly came back in 1978. Yet, its return took place *despite* pre-electoral subsidies and their allocation rules. As we will soon see, those rules favoured some of the parties that were heavily defeated, i.e. the National Unification Party (PU) and National Independent Party (PNI), while severely discriminating against the new Unity Coalition (CU), which won the election and became, henceforth, the PLN's main competitor. Rather than to the presence of subsidies, the return of electoral bipolarity was largely due to the success of the historical anti-PLN forces – alongside other groupings – in forming a unified bloc. This achievement was not unprecedented: it had already happened in 1958 – around Mario Echandi, the National Union Party's (PUN) presidential candidate – and, more clearly, in 1966 and 1970 with the formation of National Unification, first as a coalition and later as a party. In all these cases, the electoral coalescence of anti-PLN forces took place in the absence of pre-election loans.

Pre-election subsidies not only failed to help the creation of an anti-PLN electoral bloc. In fact, they actively *hindered* its transformation into a unified political party. In 1981, responding to a query from the CU authorities, the TSE resolved that election subsidies accrued to the coalition *as a whole* and not to its member parties. Hence, not only would the coalition lose its pre-election entitlement in case one of the parties left it, but the defecting party would also walk away empty-handed.[10] This decision became a legal deterrent that bound coalition members together.

This centripetal force faded, however, in 1982, when a reform of the Electoral Code (EC) introduced explicit rules to distribute public funds between coalition partners. Member parties could now dismember an electoral alliance without forfeiting their own right to claim pre-election advances. Defecting parties would receive a proportion of the entitlement of the whole coalition, according to the rules laid out by the coalition covenant or, in lieu of this, to the number of legislative seats that the party had won as part of the alliance's candidate lists.[11] With the new rules, member parties could have left the CU without bearing any financial consequence for their decision. The fact that none of the four member parties defected throughout the long fusion process that led to the creation of the PUSC in late 1983 suggests that pre-election loans were hardly the main tie that bound them together. As in 1977, when they had forged the coalition, the four parties were well aware that their failure to stay together would doom them to relive their 1974 disappointment, when the PLN won the presidency with a paltry 43.4 per cent of the vote thanks to the fragmentation of its opponents. Rather than pre-election loans, the key force that bound CU members together until they merged into the PUSC was the bipolar logic imposed by the plurality formula. And also, presumably, the name recognition attached to an alliance whose formation had required a complex negotiation and which had already achieved a significant electoral presence. At this point, the fate of the small left-wing coalition United People (CPU) is revealing. In its case, given the practical impossibility of challenging for the presidency, the centrifugal impulse became irresistible. In 1985, the Popular Vanguard Party (PVP) left the alliance, carrying along three-quarters of the CPU's entitlement to subsidy advances for the 1986 election.[12]

Even if pre-election subsidies were considered, implausibly, the crucial centripetal force within the CU, their allocation rules were a major obstacle for the transformation of the coalition into a new political party. The new entity would of course lack an electoral past and, therefore, any right to claim pre-electoral funding. The idea of the merger had been first floated in 1980 when the CU was in power. The project foundered, however, when the PLN and even some sectors

Table 5.1: *Pre-election subsidies vs. subsidy recipients' electoral results in Costa Rica, 1970–1990*

| Election | 1970 | | 1974 | | 1978 | | 1982 | | 1986 | | 1990 | |
|---|---|---|---|---|---|---|---|---|---|---|---|---|
| Party | Pre-election subsidy (%) | Vote leg. election (%) | Pre-election subsidy (%) | Vote leg. election (%) | Pre-election subsidy (%) | Vote leg. election (%) | Pre-election subsidy (%) | Vote leg. election (%) | Pre-election subsidy (%) | Vote leg. election (%) | Pre-election subsidy (%) | Vote leg. election (%) |
| PLN | 0 | 50.7 | 57.1 | 40.9 | 48.3 | 38.9 | 42.9 | 55.2 | 58.7 | 47.8 | 52.6 | 41.9 |
| CU/PUSC | – | – | – | 8.0 | 43.4 | 49.4 | 29.1 | 33.6 | 41.5 | 46.0 | 46.2 | – |
| National Unification Party (PU) | 0 | 35.9 | 42.9 | 24.7 | 33.8 | 3.2 | – | – | – | – | – | – |
| National Independent Party (PNI) | – | – | 0 | 10.0 | 9.5 | 0.8 | – | – | – | – | 0 | 0.8 |
| United People Coalition (CPU) | – | – | – | – | 0 | 7.7 | 7.4 | 6.4 | 1.6 | 2.7 | 0 | 3.3 |
| People's Vanguard Party (PVP) | – | – | – | – | – | – | – | – | 4.8 | 2.4 | – | – |
| Alajuelense Democratic Action Party (PADA) | – | – | – | – | – | – | 0 | 1.3 | 0.5 | 0.4 | – | – |
| Cartaginesa Agrarian Unity Party (PUAC) | 0 | 0.5 | 0 | 1.2 | 0.4 | 1.0 | 0 | 0.8 | 0.5 | 1.2 | 1.2 | 1.2 |
| Limonense Authentic Party (PAL) | – | – | – | – | 0 | 0.4 | 0.4 | 0.4 | 0.4 | 0.3 | 0.3 | 0.3 |

Sources: See Appendix.

within the CU refused to agree to *ad-hoc* legislation in order to authorise the transfer of pre-electoral entitlements from CU members on to the new party that would emerge from their fusion.[13] In 1982, a controversial negotiation between the CU and the PLN, back in control of the presidency, enabled the transmission of subsidy rights in return for the CU's support of the PLN's legislative agenda. Once cleared of financial obstacles, the CU merged into the PUSC.[14] The consolidation of the anti-PLN forces, and thus of Costa Rica's contemporary two-party system, had more to do with the deliberate *bending* of subsidy allocation rules than with their rigorous application.

Once bipolarity returned to presidential elections in 1978, it stayed virtually unchanged until 1998. Whether the electoral hegemony of the two large parties and the failure of challengers to emerge owed little or much to the presence of pre-election loans is difficult to assert conclusively. At any rate, some evidence suggests that pre-election loans played a marginal role in securing the stability of the two-party system. Indeed, the notion that pre-election subsidies were the key element that 'fossilised the political options of the Costa Rican people', as the Constitutional Court memorably stated, assumes that subsidy advances were decisive for the electoral fate of recipient parties. Table 5.1 compares the allocation of pre-election public funding with the beneficiaries' electoral performance over the system's twenty-year existence.

Four clusters of cases can be identified from the table, and in none of them do pre-election subsidies seem to have played a significant role:

1) The first group comprises the cases of the PLN throughout the period and of the CU/PUSC from 1982 onwards. These cases fail to evince any direct correlation between access to pre-election subsidies and electoral outcomes. While expecting a perfect adjustment between both variables would be an absurd example of reductionism, the fact that the party that collected the largest share of pre-election subsidies lost the election in three out of five cases in the period (1978, 1982 and 1990) is noteworthy. Yet, it may be argued that the crucial fact is not whether access to the largest quota of pre-electoral funding led to the recipient's electoral victory, but whether access to generous funding protected *both* major parties against potential challengers and thus preserved their electoral hegemony. At this point the obvious should be pointed out: the PLN, in particular, consistently reaped strong electoral results well before the introduction of pre-election subsidies. Moreover, the next group of examples shows that the protection of the recipients' electoral position was not, by any means, a necessary consequence of the system.

2) The second group includes parties that received significant shares of pre-election funds and yet could not prevent an electoral meltdown and even their eventual demise. The PU offers a striking example of this. In 1978 the party was virtually wiped out from the political landscape, despite claiming one-third of the available advances (almost US$2.7 million). A simultaneous collapse, albeit from a lower electoral position, affected the PNI. More gradual, although equally clear, is the case of the Left. After an unexpectedly good electoral showing in 1978, the

CPU received a useful share of public loans in 1982, only to see its support dwindle into insignificance in successive elections. Finally, at a much lower level, the small regional PADA ebbed away precisely in the wake of its first publicly subsidised campaign.

3) The sample's other two regional parties, the PUAC and the PAL, form the third cluster. At 1.21 per cent, the PUAC achieved its best electoral performance in 1974 *without* pre-election funding. It would return to a similar level towards the end of the period after a few hiccups in the middle. Meanwhile, electoral variations are truly minimal for the PAL. It achieved in 1978, *without* pre-election funds, the electoral share that, by and large, it would continue to obtain until 1990. In both cases, pre-election advances preceded neither a significant electoral advance, nor an electoral breakdown. At most, the loans enabled the cultivation of an electoral allotment that had already been acquired.

4) The last case is that of the CU in 1978, the one example in which access to pre-election funds coexists with explosive electoral growth. In this case, the disproportion between the share of pre-election loans received (8 per cent) and the electoral outcome (43.4 per cent in the legislative election and 50.5 per cent in the presidential one) is of a magnitude that cannot be solely or even mainly explained by access to public funds. In fact, the evidence suggests that the CU may have run its campaign entirely without recourse to state funds, since the PRD, the only coalition member to be entitled to public loans after its showing in 1974, had all but spent them during the coalition's expensive 1977 presidential primary. Along with the electoral collapses undergone by the PU and the PNI, the CU's maiden victory in 1978 is, if anything, a remarkable demonstration of the inability of pre-election subsidies to explain electoral results and petrify the party system.

That the Costa Rican subsidy scheme has not petrified results may be best appreciated through an analysis of the evolution of electoral volatility since 1958 (Graph 5.3).

As Graph 5.3 shows shows, post-civil-war electoral results in Costa Rica have been anything but stable. Mean electoral volatility in Costa Rica (20.6 per cent for the presidential election and 21.9 per cent for the legislative election) stands well above the highest averages detected in the survey of electoral results in seven developed democracies included in Chapter one.[15] And this is particularly true after the introduction of pre-election public funding in 1971. It is precisely in the wake of the latter that electoral instability reached its most significant peak, with three consecutive high-volatility elections (1974, 1978 and 1982).

The graph suggests that post-civil war electoral volatility is probably more related to the level of fractionalisation of the political blocs that emerged from the war (PLN/anti-PLN) than to the availability of public funding. Out of all the elections in which *both* blocs have converged solidly behind single presidential candidacies (1966, 1970, 1978, 1982, 1986, 1990, 1994 and 1998), only those of 1978 and 1982 show volatility figures higher than 20 per cent. Moreover, the 1978 datum merely registers the system's return to the bipolar (PLN/anti-PLN) situation of 1970 after the atypical result of 1974. A high volatility election was necessary

Graph 5.3: *Electoral volatility in Costa Rica, 1958–2002*

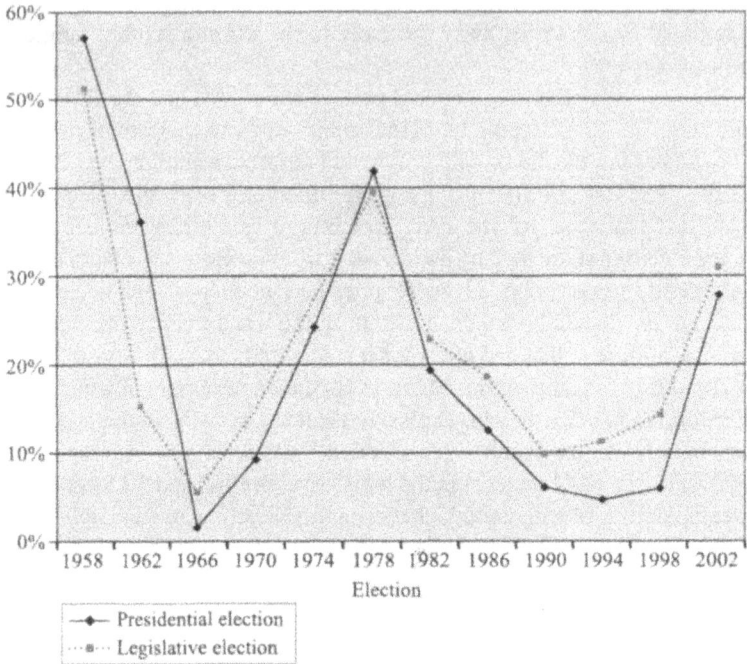

Election

—◆— Presidential election
····■···· Legislative election

Sources: See Appendix

to restore *normality* in the system.

So far, the findings of this story may be summarised as follows: the system of pre-electoral public funding was neither a necessary nor a sufficient condition for the emergence of a two-party format in Costa Rica's presidential elections and, if anything, probably hindered its emergence; the mechanism failed to generate a two-party system in legislative elections which, in fact, has hardly ever existed; the scheme had, most likely, a marginal effect on the performance of all the recipient parties; and, finally, public subsidies have not fossilised results in any electoral arena. On close scrutiny, the effects of pre-election subsidies on the dynamics of the Costa Rican party system appear simply insignificant.

Such conclusions vividly contrast with the public joy triggered by the Court's decision to eliminate public funding advances in 1991. In the words of the revellers, the Costa Rican political system was leaving behind a dark night of electoral injustice in order to move, finally, towards a fair competition. Rodrigo Gutiérrez-Sáenz, a left-wing deputy at the time, summed up the prevailing sense of elation:

This constitutional ruling achieved something that was virtually impossible to attain through any other way: that, legally, all parties will participate in the next electoral process under equal conditions and starting from the same line; what happens later will only hinge on their own efforts (...) From 1994...it will be possible to write a new and fair page of political democracy in this country.[16]

As usual, reality proved more stubborn than envisaged. Minor parties, which greeted the ruling as a vindication of their long-standing grievances, soon realised that the absence of pre-election funding had not improved their situation and, in fact, had probably made it worse.[17] Following a period of intense legislative activity aimed at restoring the mechanism according to the principles laid out by the Court's ruling,[18] major parties failed to reach an agreement before the 1994 election and, again, before the 1998 and 2002 campaigns. This was hardly fortuitous. Major parties also realised that pre-election subsidies were less relevant than previously thought, and were not worth the political inconvenience of drafting new unpopular legislation. More importantly, they were well aware that a similar system of electoral funding could be re-created *de facto* without bearing any political price for it. Alas, the new scheme would prove beyond the reach of minor parties.

As explained in Chapter three, after 1991 the PLN and PUSC financial managers resorted to a traditional financial method to cash the public subvention in advance: the issuing and selling of party bonds, backed by the expectation of the state's post-electoral reimbursement of expenses. If prior to 1991 parties ceded to investors the bonds that they received directly from the state during the campaign, after 1991 they simply transferred, using their own documents, their eventual right to collect the subsidies to be disbursed after the election. The financial costs attached to this system were, of course, much higher. An immediately tradable public bond is, naturally, more attractive to investors than a party-issued document that may only be cashed after the election, and then only if certain conditions are met (i.e. achieving the subsidy threshold and documenting the expenses to the electoral authorities' satisfaction). Discounts demanded by bond-takers shot up significantly, forcing the parties to relinquish part of their public funds. However heavy it became, the new financial burden was far from enough to deprive major parties of abundant resources collected against their future subsidies.

The crucial word in the whole scheme is *expectation*. The value of the entitlement transferred by the parties is determined by the expectation of a given electoral result. The realisation of each successive bond issued by the parties requires a higher electoral result than the previous one. Naturally, the higher the bond's realisation potential, the easier to find willing takers for the document and the lower the financial cost borne by the party. This is the key point. While the PLN and the PUSC have been able to sell, so far, a reasonably certain electoral probability, which allows them to transfer an equally certain subsidy entitlement, minor parties are not endowed with a comparable expectation.[19] Even when emerging parties have real chances of claiming the subsidy, the uncertainty about their electoral result – typically close to the subsidy threshold – and their administrative ability to document expenses, turn their bonds into a risky investment.

The bias once attributed to pre-electoral subsidies lingers, only it is more intense. If under the old rules a few minor parties regularly gained access to pre-election public funding, the new system, while impeccably neutral *de jure*, nearly precludes *de facto* the realisation of subsidies by new and minor parties. We have already seen how during the 1997–8 campaign, even a successful minor grouping, the Democratic Force Party (PFD), was unable to sell a single party bond amongst the same Costa Rican banks that were busy trading in the documents issued by both major parties. Moreover, the highly successful campaign of the emerging Citizen Action Party (PAC) in 2002 only managed to retail its bonds amongst financial operators once opinion polls showed, midway through the campaign, that it was seriously challenging both traditional parties. The PAC only began reaping benefits from the public funding system once it became clear that it was *not* a minor party.[20] The obstacles faced by emerging parties in cashing the subsidies during the campaign set in motion a perverse sequence that deprives them, in practice, of state funding. If funds cannot be borrowed during the campaign, they will not be spent and, therefore, no expenses will be documented before the electoral authorities. Even if the party surpasses the subsidy threshold, in the absence of receipts its subsidy entitlement will be lost. This is not hypothetical. In 1998, the Agrarian Labour Action Party (PALA), a regional group that elected one deputy after a very thrifty campaign, gave up its entitlement to public funds (nearly US$100,000) when it became evident that it would not be able to legitimately document its outlays.[21] Four years later, the same happened, on a much larger scale, to the PAC. It had to forego more than US$1.6 million in subsidies, which it simply could not back with receipts.[22]

It is tempting to argue, nonetheless, that the growth in the electoral share of non-traditional parties over the last three elections is the ultimate proof that the elimination of pre-election subsidies has had a clear 'defrosting' effect on the Costa Rican party system. Plausible as it seems, this proposition is not supported by the evidence. In fact, the increase in the vote for non-traditional parties, whose causes are yet to be fully grasped, has taken place in the absence of any significant change in the financial gap that separates their electoral efforts from those of the PLN and the PUSC. Graph 5.4 shows the 1990–8 inter-party distribution of electoral advertising investment, a variable obviously sensitive to the parties' availability of campaign funds.[23]

The data show that the derogation of pre-election public funding – which operated during the 1989–90 campaign, but not in the next two election cycles – made no difference to the media presence enjoyed by non-traditional parties. After 1991, the latter have increased dramatically their share of the vote despite paltry economic resources, limited access to the media, and even very poor electoral recognition amongst the voters. In 2000, two years after the minor parties' 1998 electoral breakthrough, opinion polls continued to show that while the PLN and the PUSC were known by nearly every voter in the country, a large proportion of the electorate had never heard of their challengers. Nearly 25 per cent of the voters

Graph 5.4: *Distribution of electoral advertising disbursements per party in Costa Rica, 1990–98*

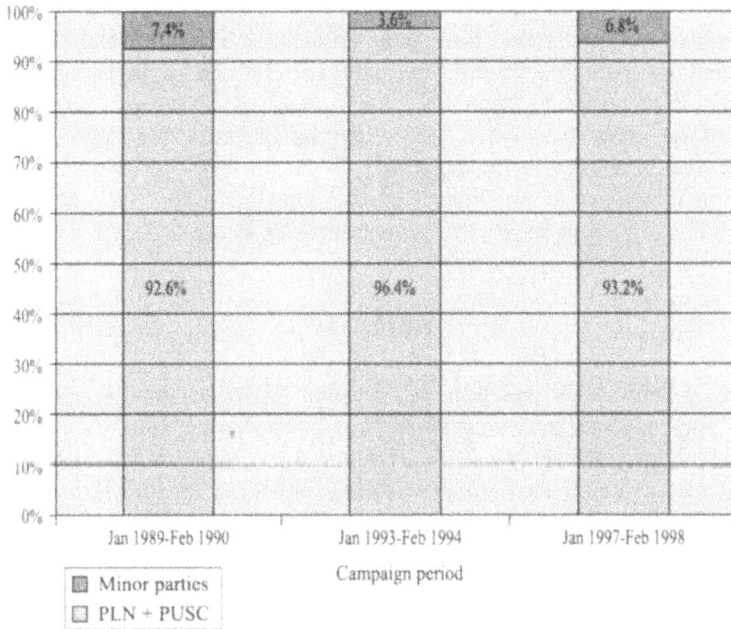

Sources and methods: See Appendix

were not aware of the existence of the PFD, a figure that climbed to 60 per cent for the Libertarian Movement (ML), and nearly 80 per cent for the Costa Rican Renovation Party (PRCO) and the National Integration Party (PIN). And those were the ones *with* seats in the Legislative Assembly.[24] Quite simply, campaign conditions faced by emerging parties in Costa Rica remain as tough as ever.

For two decades, Costa Rica's pre-electoral subsidies, controversial from the outset, became a simple and popular explanation for all sorts of political pathologies and misfortunes. The evidence shows, however, that their effects were severely over-estimated and that joy at their elimination was premature at best and, at worst, mistaken. If the scheme introduced in 1971 certainly failed to benefit emerging parties, it seems clear that it harmed them far less than they thought and could only marginally explain their electoral failure. In all likelihood the current subsidy rules make things even more difficult for emerging parties, despite their apparent electoral neutrality. The previous paragraphs suggest that with or without pre-electoral state funding, major parties enjoy a huge economic advantage that owes less to the text of the law than to their own electoral past and prospects, their name recognition and, in general, all the benefits attached to the prolonged exercise of power. Rather than a direct *cause* of their electoral hegemony, the crushing economic advantage enjoyed by major parties looks more like the *conse-quence* of their electoral predominance.

Yet, as shown by the 2002 election, in spite of massive economic handicaps emerging parties continue to flourish in Costa Rica. Their electoral success is a vivid demonstration that whatever the economic chasm between parties, no party system is impregnable to the arrival of new competitors. The proclaimed fossili-sation of the Costa Rican party system, and the decisive role ascribed to DSF in it, have been no more than pious myths.

Let us now move to the Uruguayan case, where DSF may indeed have had a visible effect on the party system, but not in the expected direction.

## URUGUAY

Uruguay's DSF system has been in operation far longer than any other in the world. Since its enactment predates by only five years the country's 1933 demo-cratic breakdown, the scheme's effects on the party system may only be appreci-ated after the resumption of normal electoral competition in 1942. Henceforth, and up until the 1973 coup, DSF would largely operate as a proportional post-electoral reimbursement of expenses, roughly similar to the current Costa Rican scheme. Since the transitional election of 1984, the system has also included early dis-bursements of public funds, allocated, in principle, according to the results of the previous election. This reform, enacted, unlike in Costa Rica, without so much as a hint of controversy, has given Uruguay's current subsidy rules more than a pass-ing resemblance to those applied in Costa Rica between 1971 and 1991. The Uruguayan scheme displays, however, two crucial differences from the Costa Rican one. First, recipients have never been required to meet an electoral thresh-old to access the funds. Second, since 1958, subsidies have been disbursed direct-ly to internal party actors, rather than central party authorities. These two features make the Uruguayan subvention not merely unlikely to freeze the party system, but indeed quite likely to achieve the opposite effect.

Has the Uruguayan party system remained stable since 1942? As previous chapters should have already suggested, the obvious answer is no. Let us quanti-fy just how profound its transformation has been (Graph 5.5).

Uruguay's ENP grew continuously and significantly between 1962 and 1989, only to decline partially in the last two elections. Even so, since 1989 fragmenta-tion has stayed at a higher level than at any other period during the previous sixty years. The past four decades have seen, as we know, the replacement of the secu-lar two-party system with a multi-party format, in which the FA has come to chal-lenge the hegemony of the PC and the PN. While the FA's arrival in 1971 is the most visible landmark in the process, the changes in the country's electoral dynamic had indeed started in the 1950s with the PN's reunification and momen-tous electoral victory in 1958. The latter marked the end of nearly one century of *Colorado* rule. If anything, the consolidation of the public funding system in the

Graph 5.5: *Party system fragmentation in Uruguay, 1942–99*

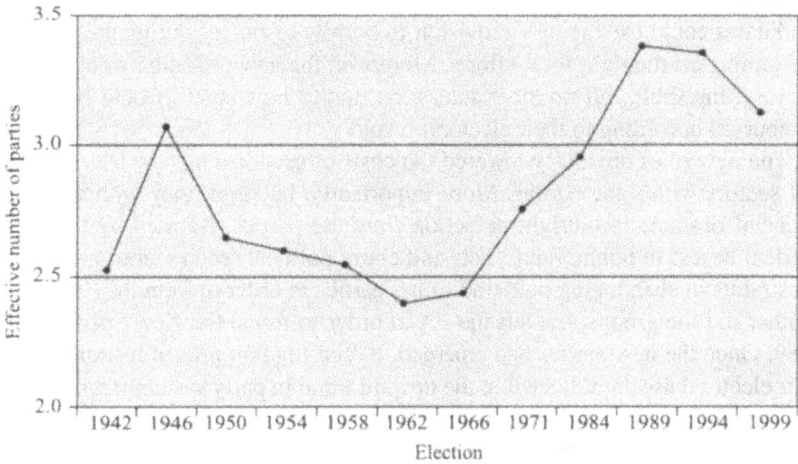

1950s seems to have anticipated the *melting* of an electoral competition that had remained essentially frozen for most of the country's early democratic life.

The entrenchment of Uruguay's traditional two-party system was already evident, of course, well before the introduction of DSF, and probably owed little to any factor connected to political finance. Even the patronage structures that both traditional parties came to control at most reinforced a set of pre-existing institutional incentives strongly geared towards the electoral predominance of two large parties. As in Costa Rica, those institutional levers included the plurality formula employed in presidential elections, the rigid concurrence of electoral timetables, and the ban on ticket-splitting. Crucially, it also included the use of DSV, which facilitated the channelling of political conflicts within both traditional parties, and offered a formidable protection against their dismemberment. Last but not least, the stability of the party system owed much to the sheer fixity of traditional political identities, in many ways older than the Uruguayan nation. It is remarkable that such a powerful combination of historical and institutional factors proved unable to forestall the rise of electoral challengers and the long-term transformation of the party system. The thaw of the latter arrived in the 1950s and is yet to end.

While electoral subsidies were not related to the early ossification of Uruguay's two-party system, they were connected in more than one way to its demise. Rather than merely co-existing with dramatic transformations in the party system, state subsidies in fact *nurtured* them. The 1958 decision to eliminate central party control over subsidy disbursements removed one of the few institutional levers still in place to control internal dissent in both traditional parties. Willing political entrepreneurs would henceforth enjoy autonomous access to public funds. Even in the absence of pre-election advances, presidential and legislative candidates could use the new provision to borrow resources during the campaign and jump-start their electoral efforts. Moreover, the new provision would have no electoral threshold: *all* political actors, no matter how small, would be directly reimbursed according to their electoral result.

The new rules obviously lowered the costs of establishing new lists and political sectors *within* the parties. More importantly, however, they withdrew a key financial obstacle to outright defection *from* the parties. Boosted by their independent access to public funds, lists and entire political sectors faced no financial constraints in abandoning both traditional parties in order to form the FA in 1971. Neither did the groups that left the FA in order to found the New Space (NE) in 1989. Once the new parties had emerged, public funding proved instrumental for their electoral ascent, reflected in the upward trend in party system fragmentation. In Chapter four, we have already seen how, more than any other funding source, electoral subsidies endow the FA and the NE with a fighting chance against traditional opponents largely reliant on private donors. DSF has provided the Uruguayan Left with an essential material base from which to exploit fertile political ground. Insufficient as they may be to explain the Left's electoral success, subsidies, in all likelihood, have been vital for it.

The trend towards greater political fragmentation has been mirrored, with more intensity, within the parties themselves. Since the 1950s the latter's internal fractionalisation has been not only intense, but also increasing. The decentralisation of subsidy disbursements in 1958 facilitated a proliferation of internal party actors, already aided by the very low entry barriers posed by DSV and extreme PR. As already seen in Chapter two, the number of candidate lists fielded in elections to the Chamber of Representatives (ChR) has increased dramatically since the 1950s (Graph 5.6).

The importance of subsidy decentralisation as an incentive to create new lists is not easy to establish. Most contemporary politicians dismiss it as an irrelevance, noting that the creation of new lists is underpinned by a purely political calculation. However, congressional proceedings suggest that in the 1950s Uruguayan politicians were well aware of the importance of public funds for the parties' internal cohesion. In 1953, an attempt to disburse public funding directly to the legislators, rather than to the parties' central authorities, was defeated in a congressional committee amidst fears that it would fuel party division.[25] When a similar amendment was finally approved in 1958, one legislator noted approvingly:

> This bill solves a fundamental problem in the electoral struggle, which concerns, above all, the resources of the parties. There are political groups that, because of a small divergence, split from the authorities or have a dispute with them. All the resources that have been gathered for four years, through costly contributions, then get to be used by only one part of the group, to the harm of the other part. Not one cent is given to the dissident part... (...) The solution

Graph 5.6: *Party fractionalisation in Uruguay, 1942–99*

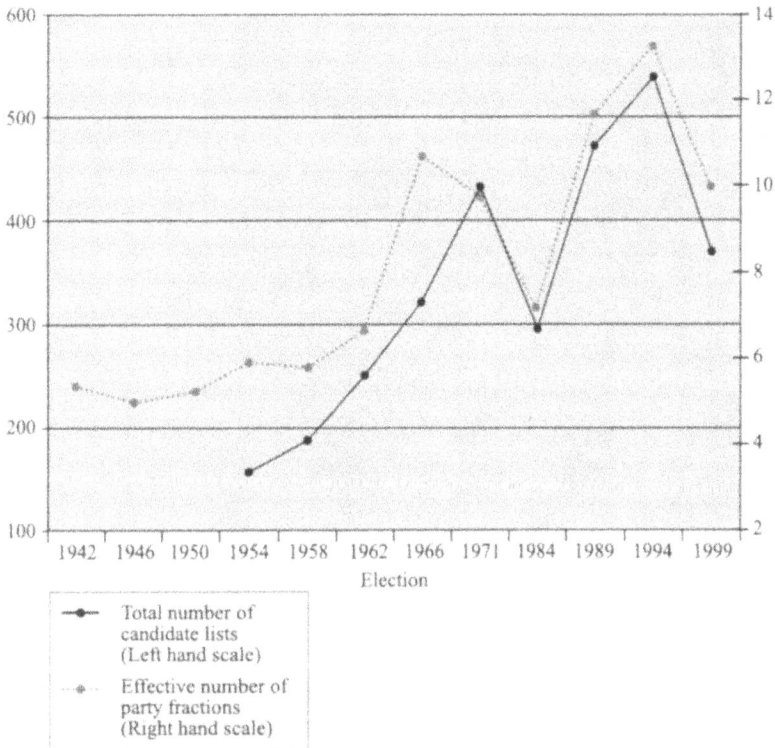

Legend:
- Total number of candidate lists (Left hand scale)
- Effective number of party fractions (Right hand scale)

Sources: See Appendix

provided by this project is beneficial, for it allows the equality of all the groups or political parties in the forthcoming elections.[26]

At any rate, the rules approved in 1958 were an addition to a process of internal disarticulation in the parties that had already been nurtured by the country's electoral system, the disappearance of historic leaderships, and a mounting economic crisis. In the following thirteen years, the number of ChR lists would rise 230 per cent, nearly doubling in both traditional parties alone. After a sharp drop in 1984, related to the parties' organisational reconstitution after a long authoritarian hiatus, it resumed its vigorous growth until 1994.

Far from being contained by the reintroduction of pre-electoral loans in 1984, the post-transition bout of list proliferation was aided by it. While allocated, in principle, according to past electoral results, the advances have repeatedly benefited new political sectors, as we saw in Chapter four. Financially limited as they may be, subsidy advances have been eagerly sought by new actors: more than one-third of the ChR lists that received advances in the run-up to the 1994 election had

Graph 5.7: *Fractionalisation in Uruguayan parties, 1942–99 (moving average of three elections)*

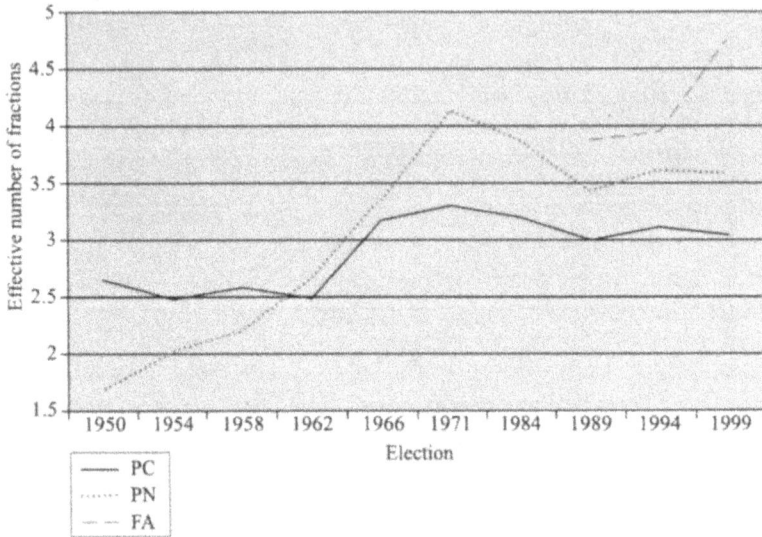

Sources: See Appendix

no previous political participation.

Perhaps more importantly, the growing atomisation in the parties' electoral *offer* has been reflected in increasingly fractionalised electoral *outputs*. Even after a sizeable drop in the last election cycle, the current effective number of party fractions nearly doubles the level of sixty years ago (see Graph 5.6 above). The chart suggests that the correlation between the number of ChR lists and fractionalisation is remarkable, and that any factor – including financial – that influences the former probably influences the latter as well.[27] The growth in the number of party fractions is, no doubt, related to the increase in the number of effective parties, i.e., the emergence of the FA with its own vast array of internal groupings. Indeed, when the evolution of fractionalisation in *each* party is taken in isolation, the data fail to show clear statistical trends.[28] Even so, to the extent that any kind of long-term tendency can be identified within each party, it is in all cases towards greater internal atomisation (Graph 5.7).

The dramatic expansion in the electoral offer – partially fuelled by the subsidy rules – probably contributed to high and growing levels of electoral volatility in Uruguay. This phenomenon is particularly visible *inside* the parties, where the proliferation of viable electoral options has been, of course, more acute. Graph 5.8 displays the evolution of electoral volatility in Uruguay since 1946.

While over the last six decades, levels of inter-party volatility have been moderate and largely stable in Uruguay (9.4 per cent on average), the parties' internal volatility has been extraordinarily high. Measured by the results of lists of Senate

Graph 5.8: *Electoral volatility in Uruguay, 1946–99 (1)*

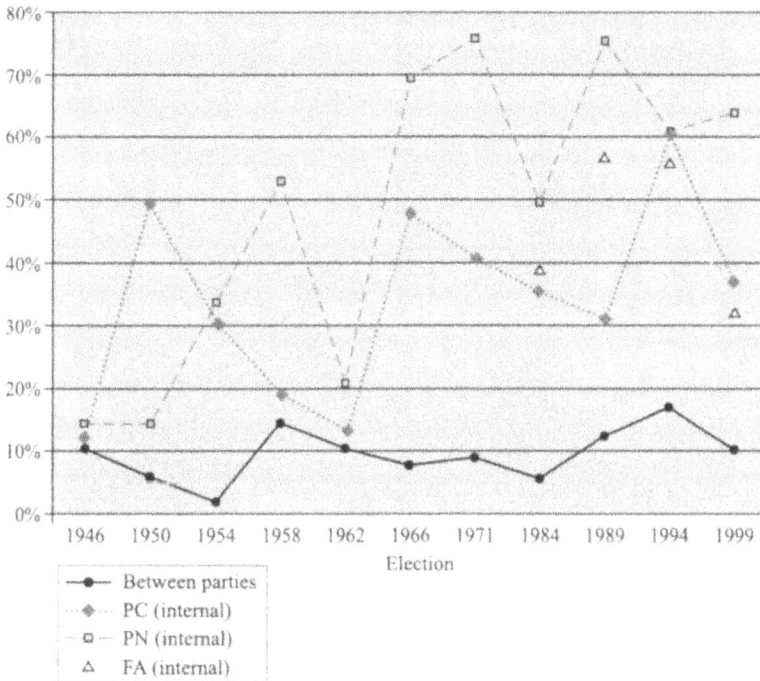

Note: (1) PN figures for 1942–54 include results of the National Independent Party (PNIU).
Sources: See Appendix

candidates, the PC's average internal volatility for the whole period stands at 34.3 per cent. The figure climbs to 45.6 per cent in the FA (since 1984 only) and 48.2 per cent in the PN.[29] Internal volatility has not fallen below 30 per cent for *any* party since 1962. The combination of general fidelity to parties and notorious fickleness with respect to fractions is not casual. Faced with an ever-growing set of electoral and even ideological options in each party, Uruguayan voters can afford to experiment with their votes without threatening the success of their preferred party at the polls. The FA offers a clear example of this. The party's uninterrupted electoral ascent has been marked, nonetheless, by dramatic electoral oscillations between its moderate and recalcitrant left-wing sectors. In fact, every posttransition election has yielded a large internal majority for a different fraction within the alliance.

While remarkably high most of the time, intra-party volatility has evolved in a jagged fashion. However, as with party fractionalisation, insofar as a secular tendency may be identified it is towards higher levels of instability (Graph 5.9).[30]

Thus, evidence that the Uruguayan subsidy scheme exerts any ossifying influence on the party system or that, indeed, the latter has been ossified at all during

Graph 5.9: *Intra-party electoral volatility in Uruguay, 1946–99 (moving average of three elections) (1)*

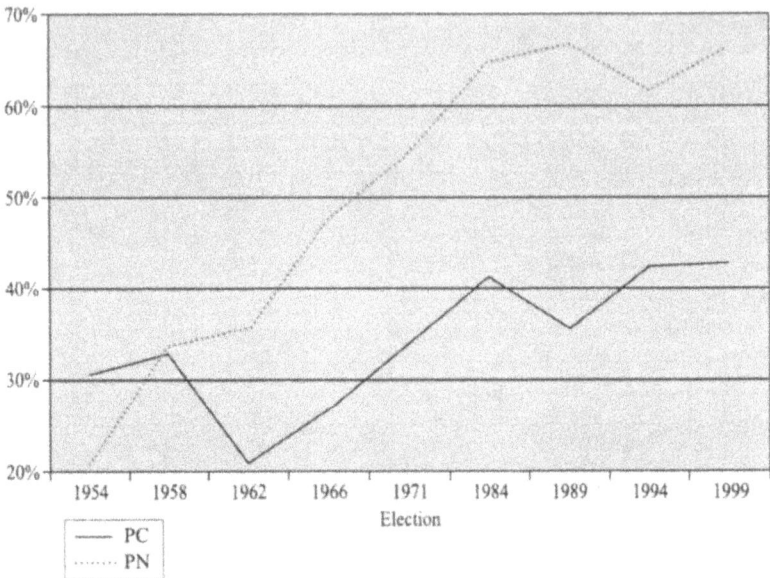

Note: (1) PN figures for 1942–54 include results of the National Independent Party (PNIU).
Sources: See Appendix

the past sixty years, is conspicuous by its absence. It is indeed very likely that electoral subsidies have at least made a modest contribution to the profound trans-formations undergone by the Uruguayan party system in the past decades. As noted above, the subsidy's role in the financial viability of the Left's electoral efforts is in itself a relevant factor in the demise of the country's historical two-party system. But this section also shows that, by allowing virtually unrestricted and independent access to public funding to any political actor, the Uruguayan subvention facilitates in obvious ways the fragmentation of the party system, the fractionalisation of parties, and the volatility of electoral preferences. Emerging parties and fractions have faced very few obstacles to obtaining at least some state funds to support their campaigns. Far from offering a protection to the electoral status quo, the Uruguayan subsidy system tends, in many ways, to undermine it.

## CONCLUSION

The Costa Rican and Uruguayan systems of electoral funding are financially gen-erous schemes, designed and modified by incumbents. They have rewarded par-ties in strict accordance to their votes and, on occasion, electoral past. According to a widespread interpretation, both systems *should* have created a strong inertial effect on the party system. Yet, there is no sign of this. DSF has neither ossified electoral results nor prevented the emergence of significant challengers to the status quo in either country. If there is any kind of freezing effect in either country let us agree that it is a fairly hidden one.

Quite to the contrary, the Uruguayan case suggests that, by fiat or by fluke, DSF may indeed play a role in stimulating the emergence and success of new political actors. Whether it does so or not seems to depend more on the subsidy's eligibility barriers than on its allocation rules or the timing of its disbursements. As the comparison of Costa Rica and Uruguay shows, even in the absence of strongly egalitarian allocation norms (such as flat subventions for all competitors), the mere elimination of electoral thresholds and cumbersome claiming procedures greatly facilitates the efforts of emerging political actors. At a minimum, the knowledge that all political actors will eventually claim *some* state funds markedly improves their access to credit during the campaign.

Whether access to the subsidy by emerging political actors should be encouraged or not is, of course, a complex normative discussion that can only be touched upon in this chapter. Indeed, while it is plausible to argue that DSF could and should be an instrument to provide *all* electoral competitors with a minimal material base to run an effective campaign, it is also true that a strongly redistributive allocation of the subsidy – even if politically feasible – elicits serious normative objections. As the German Constitutional Court noted in its 1992 landmark ruling, such a system would essentially separate the parties' financial situation from their level of popular support. Objectionable or not, a proportional distribution of public funds forces the parties to attract voters in order to secure the inflow of state resources.

If not sufficient to argue for strong redistribution, the Costa Rican experience shows, nevertheless, the deleterious effect that active discrimination against minor and new parties can have on the subsidy's own legitimacy. Whatever the ultimate effects of DSF on the party system, the idea that new and minor parties have been unfairly treated by Costa Rica's subsidy rules is no pious myth. While useful to their own electoral purposes, the public bitterness of minor parties at the subvention scheme is nonetheless justified and stands in stark contrast to the utter lack of controversy that has accompanied the long life of Uruguay's threshold-free subsidy system. Furthermore, the alarmingly low name recognition enjoyed by minor parties in Costa Rica points towards a flaw in the democratic process that could be partially redressed by easing their access to public funds during the campaign. Reforming the eligibility rules of the Costa Rican subsidy is advisable not out of any duty to stimulate the electoral success of emerging parties –obviously, no such obligation exists – but out of respect for voters' right to be informed of their electoral options.

More than anything, this chapter, as the rest of this book, should convey a sober idea of the political effects of electoral subsidies. Even the fragmenting influence ascribed to the Uruguayan subsidy system, while real, is probably very limited and has at most intensified pre-existing trends. The fact is that parties and party systems persist and change for reasons far more substantive and elusive than the allocation of state funds. After all, a powerful array of institutional and historical factors were not able to protect indefinitely the electoral hegemony of traditional parties in Uruguay, nor were dire economic disadvantages enough to thwart the recent emergence, with full force, of new parties in Costa Rica. Electoral subsidies, as electoral rules in general, can hardly row against the tide: they will not single-handedly subvert a stable party system, nor will they preserve one that is ripe for change. Crucial as it may be sometimes, money is not the only currency in the town of politics.

## NOTES

1  I. F. Azofeifa in *La Nación* [*LN*], 18/1/1990.
2  E. Quesada in *LN*, 30/6/1991.
3  Sala Constitucional de la Corte Suprema de Justicia, Costa Rica [SCCR], Vote No. 980–91 of 24/5/1991 (author's emphasis).
4  In 1988, 73 per cent of those polled were against pre-electoral state financing (*La Prensa Libre* [*LPL*], 12/2/1988). The popular rejection of the state funding system as such has remained at lower levels: 64 per cent and 57 per cent were against it in 1993 and 2000, respectively (UNIMER [1993], CID-Gallup [2000]).
5  It should be noted that the term *two-party system* has been used here to depict some situations in which, in fact, there were not two large competitive parties, but, rather, one party – the PLN – and one opposition coalition.
6  Shuggart and Carey (1992), pp. 226–58.
7  Chacón-Pacheco (1975); Casas-Zamora and Briceño-Fallas (1991).
8  Bendel (1993), p. 335; Jiménez-Zeledón (1996), pp. 998–1009; Peeler (1996), p. 82; R. Tovar in *LN*, 1/2/1987.
9  Laclé [7/9/1999].
10  Tribunal Supremo de Elecciones, Costa Rica [TSE], Vote No. 2335 of 27/8/1981.
11  Electoral Code [EC], article 193, as modified by Law No. 6833 of 21/12/1982.
12  See TSE, Vote No. 661 of 8/3/1985.
13  See *LN*, 4/9/1980; *LN*, 10–11/9/1980; Pérez-Brignoli (1999), p. 59.
14  On the creation of the PUSC see Pérez-Brignoli (1999), pp. 57–65; Tovar (1986), pp. 93–7; Araya-Alfaro et al. (1986), pp. 184–237. See also R. A. Calderón in *Semanario Universidad* [*SU*], 5/8/1983.
15  In that sample, which includes 1945–96 parliamentary elections only, Israel (14.5 per cent) and France (14.3 per cent) appear at the top, while Switzerland (5.4 per cent) and Austria (5.5 per cent) are at the bottom.
16  *LN*, 28/1/1992.
17  See *LPL*, 7/3/1992; *LPL*, 21/7/1993; *LN*, 9/7/1993; *La República* [*LR*], 16/6/1993; *Al Día* [*AD*], 17/6/1993.
18  The Court deemed unlawful any system of pre-election funding solely based on previous electoral results and without proper rules to guarantee the repayment of state loans by recip-

ient parties. It also ruled out the disbursement of public funds at any period other than the official campaign (SCCR, Vote 980–91 of 24/5/1991).

19  Note that the electoral floor of both traditional parties and the degree of certainty about it may well change after the electoral 'earthquake' of 2002.

20  *LN*, 15/12/2001.

21  Vargas-Artavia [4/10/1999]; TSE, Oficio No. 2022 of 24/4/1998.

22  *LN*, 5/2/2002; *LN*, 3/7/2002.

23  The chart shows investment according to official rates, rather than actual disbursements.

24  CID-Gallup, January 2000.

25  CRU, Carp. 1711/1953, pp. 28–35.

26  Deputy Oribe-Coronel, in Cámara de Representantes del Uruguay [CRU], DS 528, p. 130.

27  See Vernazza (1991), pp. 51–2.

28  Buquet et al. (1998), p. 43

29  My intra-party estimates differ from those given by Altman and Chasquetti (2000), for the period 1989–99. Mine are generally higher. Even theirs put average internal volatility at 27.8 per cent for the PC, 53.4 per cent for the PN, and 40.7 per cent for the FA.

30  Graph 5.9 excludes the FA. Since the FA has participated in five elections, the use of the moving average method to measure volatility yields only two observations (50.2 per cent for 1984–94, and 47.9 per cent for 1989–99) and thus no observable trend.

# | conclusion

Public financing of elections means no more Watergates

Senator Edward Kennedy[1]

...the lack of transparency of private funding enables the great corporate interests that control the economy of our countries to impose their own agendas on governments, congresses and docile parliaments through the unlimited financing of parties and candidates, which will then represent their particular interests and not those of the people who elect them. This is a breeding ground for corruption in the public administration, since the representative is not accountable to his electors, but loyal to those who paid his campaign expenditures.

Félix Ulloa[2]

...the mass media, particularly television, are the main reason – in this age of 'videocracy' – why parties need great sums of money for their election campaigns. Indeed, the parties have had to increase substantially their budgets insofar as their campaigns have become, more and more, television-based. This leads parties, under pressure to raise large sums of money, to engage in illegal acts.

Daniel Zovatto[3]

When it comes to campaign finance it is necessary to operate within radical and utterly transparent limits and restrictions.

Ottón Solís[4]

There are no simple truths about political finance. Each of the emphatic statements quoted above, typical of public debates on political finance, is more controversial than its author had intended. More than most fields in political science, the study of the funding of elections and parties is pervaded by preconceptions and opinions disguised as facts. The scientific enterprise of comparative political finance thus faces a double hurdle: it must overcome not just our current ignorance, but also entrenched prejudices. Since most of the findings of this research have already been laid out in the conclusions to each of the preceding chapters, this final reflection will mostly recapitulate some of the main themes that have emerged throughout the work.

## HETEROGENEITY, CONTINGENCY AND METHOD

The first theme is the heterogeneity of political finance regulations and state funding systems, and the contingency of their effects. This research has demonstrated that there is hardly *an* institution of state funding that can be readily advocated or criticised in the abstract, but a myriad of schemes with vastly different levels of generosity, recipients, allocation procedures, and disbursement modes. This heterogeneity impinges on the consequences of subsidy systems and on the possibility of making sweeping generalisations about them. Just in the last chapter we saw how relatively minor variations in design – such as the presence or absence of an eligibility threshold or the decentralisation of recipients within the parties – can visibly alter the effects of similar subsidy schemes on electoral competition. But this is only one source of contingency. Even more crucial, perhaps, are the multiple ways in which the wider institutional and political framework affects the consequences of subsidies, and of political finance rules in general. This book has provided numerous examples of this mediating impact. It should be enough to recall that the higher cost of Uruguayan elections with respect to Costa Rican ones; the lower overall financial relevance of the Uruguayan subsidy scheme despite its greater generosity; the almost complete decentralisation of fundraising practices in Uruguay as opposed to their centralisation in Costa Rica; the pervasiveness of the practice of multiple-giving in Uruguay; the stronger ideological motives that underpin business donations in Uruguay; and the Uruguayan subsidy's crucial role in protecting political pluralism, are largely the result of the South American country's peculiar voting rules and of the format and ideological make-up of its party system. The point is a simple one: when it comes to predicting the effects of political finance rules, the politico-institutional framework *matters*. In more than one way, we must understand before we can predict.

Ultimately, the issue concerns the method and approach of comparative political finance as a discipline. If the field is to be practically relevant, the unlikely quest for law-like generalisations should be dropped and replaced by more modest and realistic scientific goals: perhaps the production of systematic, richly textured and empirically grounded accounts of political finance practices in many different contexts. Although more descriptive than explanatory in nature, such accounts would help to debunk many of the suspect conventional truths that pervade the field today and thus provide a sound basis for political finance regulation. Moreover, by inductively linking these narratives to the categories of a refined typology of political finance systems, and to particular regime structures, electoral systems and party systems, carefully bounded empirical regularities may well appear over time. This monograph has merely hinted at this long-term research programme. For the time being, let us only claim as one of the modest merits of this work having emphasised the importance of context for political finance rules. But the real job remains to be done.

## STATE FUNDING, FUNDRAISING AND INTEGRITY

A second major theme concerns the role of state funding in moderating fundraising practices and questionable exchanges between donors and politicians. On this issue the findings of the research are neither encouraging nor entirely dispiriting. The cases of Costa Rica and Uruguay certainly demonstrate that the presence of a generous dose of state funds does not prevent most parties from aggressively courting business interests as part of their fundraising activities. Indeed, contrary to Senator Kennedy's dictum, political finance scandals continue to surface with regularity, especially in Costa Rica. However, the book also suggests that the disappointment with the failure of public funding to eradicate unsavoury fundraising practices should be tempered with a less sombre view of fundraising procedures. In the cases of Costa Rica and Uruguay the popular demonology that sees a private donation behind every policy decision and campaign finance as the root of all political evils is simply misguided. In both countries, exchanges between private donors and politicians have emerged as remarkably subtle and contingent and, ultimately, less risky for the integrity of the political system than normally assumed.

The reasons for this rather sanguine perception are numerous and worth recalling. First, there is the sheer complexity of the motives that animate most political donors. While it would be foolhardy to deny the centrality of instrumental motives in their behaviour, the preceding chapters suggest that instrumental calculations are frequently blurred by a broader set of reasons, ranging from long-standing personal loyalties to candidates to strong ideological allegiances to, or fears of, particular parties. Second, with very few exceptions, private political donations are simply too small to purchase public policies on a grand scale in either country. This is as much a result of the generosity of state funding as of many other factors, including the incentives created by the Uruguayan electoral system for the fragmentation of contributions and the subtle codes that govern the communication between fundraisers and donors, which keep explicit q*uid pro quos* at a minimum. The vagueness of such exchanges and the perception that the politicians' bargaining position improves dramatically after the electoral moment – notably in Costa Rica, where consecutive re-election is absent at all levels – turns large political donations into a gamble that few donors are willing to take. Third, the pre-eminence of personal ties between fundraisers and donors, and the conspicuous lack of co-ordination between political contributors, have emerged as two central features of fundraising dynamics in Costa Rica and Uruguay. Together, these traits contribute to atomise political donations, focus the donors' instrumental motives on the procurement of individual rather than collective benefits, and, ultimately, hinder the 'hijacking' of state policies by generous lobbies. Fourth, despite exciting great fears and mistrust (often justified in the past), the use of foreign sources of electoral funding is generally limited and probably diminishing in both countries. Fifth, there is the critical importance of reputation and trust in fundraising procedures conducted within a numerically small business elite. The reputation for trustworthiness that is a pre-requisite for the appointment and success of political fundraisers in both countries is a significant, if fallible, barrier against gross legal and ethical abuses, particularly if coupled, as in Costa Rica, with an increasingly aggressive probing of political finance issues by the press.

Whether some of these traits are peculiar to small countries with relatively transparent political and business practices (at least in the Latin American context) remains an open question that only broader comparisons can answer. At any rate, these features suggest the usefulness of probing the social networks and codes that underpin fundraising activities, only rarely examined in the literature. Peculiar or not, these traits amount to a dynamic that falls well short of the indiscriminate purchasing of state policies and decisions that populates most media reports and many academic analyses. In reality, the vast majority of private political donations in Costa Rica and Uruguay are construed as no more than instruments to ease access to policy-makers and their goodwill in case of necessity. In most cases, they are understood as insurance policies of sorts, able to secure the attention of policy-makers but not the positive outcome of the donor's request. They buy a resource, not a result.

This is not to say that private contributions are harmless for democracy or that their regulation is irrelevant. Large political donations may indeed jeopardise crucial democratic values. This book has argued that by bestowing privileges of access on a very limited circle of business donors they tax in an obvious way the value of political equality in Costa Rica and Uruguay. Even if political donations are mostly an insurance policy – generic, contingent and unreliable – it is clear that access to such a policy is unequally distributed and unaffordable for most citizens. Moreover, donations may indeed distort the public interest, and have been shown to do so in the past. The point here is one of emphasis. This volume strongly suggests that neither in Costa Rica nor in Uruguay private political contributions compromise regularly, visibly and pervasively the integrity of the political system. Whatever their flaws and risks, political finance practices are *not* a major threat to democracy in either country. In all likelihood, they are not even a crucial source of political corruption. Evidence from both countries hints at a more complex reality in which large political contributions may on occasion distort the public interest *with the help of other concomitant factors*, ranging from pre-existing personal commitments between donors and policy-makers to outright bribing. Corrupting political contributions do exist, but hardly ever travel alone.

The connection between political contributions and bribing, in particular, deserves close attention in future research. In this regard an intriguing hypothesis is worth exploring: the importance of political contributions as a corrupting device may be inversely proportional to the frequency of bribing as a mechanism to purchase public decisions. Popular and academic perceptions of the consequences of political finance have been strongly shaped by the experience of Western developed democracies where administrative corruption is, on the whole, rare and strongly frowned upon. In such an environment, large political contributions appear as a second-best option for instrumentally motivated interests aiming to secure specific political outcomes. In developed democracies political donations may be the currency that buys political decisions and political finance the venue where most corruption scandals take place. Elsewhere things may be very different. Indeed, the same interests would probably find large political donations an irrational and ineffective investment in a corruption-laden environment where public decisions can be routinely purchased through simple bribing. In that case, donations will at most operate as a mechanism to ease political access rather than as the down payment for a political decision; they will often serve, that is, as a mere prelude to bribes. Simply put, in this analysis political contributions could be a considerably greater threat to the public interest in the US than in Costa Rica, and in Costa Rica than in Nigeria. If this is true, then we face a paradox: the more widespread corrupt practices are, the less relevant political finance becomes as a corrupting device.

## STATE FUNDING AND POLITICAL EQUALITY

The limited impact of state funding on questionable fundraising practices in Costa Rica and Uruguay contrasts, however, with its visible effects on political and electoral equality. On this matter, the experiences of Costa Rica and Uruguay tend to confirm the claims of defenders of state funding and offer very little, if any, support for the fears of its critics. The evidence has conspicuously failed to back the latter's contention that subsidies bias the electoral arena in favour of established parties and prevent the entry of newcomers; that, in other words, they 'freeze' the party system. If anything, the opposite appears to be true: direct subsidies tend to co-exist with increasing electoral volatility and a higher number of parties.

But the preceding chapters do not merely suggest that state funding does not harm political equality, rather they show that subsidies help to protect it in several ways. As seen above, subsidies have been instrumental in providing the Uruguayan Left with the material means to challenge the electoral dominance of traditional parties, overwhelmingly favoured by business donors. In doing so, public funds have become not just a protection of electoral equality but also an important safeguard for pluralism in Uruguay. Such a role has been less obvious in Costa Rica, where major parties share an ideological outlook as much as a constituency. However, even in Costa Rica state funding has advanced political equality in a more restricted but similar way: by opening pathways to power for individual politicians who lack particularly close links to the country's business elite. The experience of open presidential primaries in Costa Rica offers a powerful reminder of the importance of this point. Devoid of state support, open party primaries have become an increasingly intractable obstacle for aspiring politicians in

Costa Rica. A subsidy-free national election – a much larger obstacle than primaries – would almost surely put the presidency beyond the reach of all but the wealthiest or best business-connected politicians. And in this lies, perhaps, the crux of the matter. Whatever imperfections state subsidies may have, the reconstruction of fundraising procedures in Costa Rica and Uruguay suggests that they are the sole check to the overwhelming dominance of business interests in the funding of campaigns and, ultimately, to the political influence than comes with it. Even in the two most egalitarian countries of Latin America, subsidies prevent political finance from being totally controlled by an extraordinarily narrow set of interests. And in doing so, they help to even out the political arena. If, as some believe, subsidies are an evil, then let us agree than in Latin America they are a necessary evil.

## ELECTORAL COSTS AND THE MEDIA

In exploring the political effects of state funding, the book has yielded findings that challenge other aspects of the conventional knowledge in political finance. In particular, this work suggests that widespread beliefs about the evolution and nature of electoral expenditure – neatly encapsulated by Daniel Zovatto's quote – may need extensive qualification. The book shows that neither in Costa Rica nor in Uruguay have the costs of elections skyrocketed in the recent past. Evidence from the Costa Rican case shows that the cost of national elections is now lower than twenty-five years ago, and that it has actually plummeted in per capita terms. The Costa Rican case suggests that if any increase in the *total* cost of politics (i.e. beyond national elections) has happened at all it is not due to any inexorable dynamic in electoral expenses but to the opening up of new electoral arenas, such as open presidential primaries. More democracy certainly costs more money. But there is nothing inevitable about the enlargement of democratic arenas.

Moreover, both case studies demonstrate that the notion that television advertising expenses are the bulk of electoral disbursements is not nearly as self-evident as most analysts and even politicians would have us believe. Indeed, in Costa Rica, television outlays trail organisational disbursements – salaries, rental of party branches, etc. – by a long margin. Even in Uruguay, where advertising budgets are proportionally larger than in Costa Rica, given the sheer magnitude of the rate rebates enjoyed by the parties television probably comprises no more than a third of overall electoral outlays. If anything, this volume suggests that the problem in Costa Rican and Uruguayan campaigns is not too much expenditure on television but exactly the opposite: that parties pay *too little* for their publicity and, to different degrees, have become addicted to enormous rate discounts. The latter, in effect, turn network owners into singularly large and powerful political donors.

In any case, the book, once more, cautions against grand generalisations. The comparison of Costa Rica and Uruguay suggests that the composition of electoral outlays is closely linked to the incentives and burdens created by electoral laws, and to organisational traditions that vary from party to party. It is, largely, a local phenomenon. Quite simply, there are no universal 'electoral spending triggers'.


## THE LIMITS OF POLITICAL FINANCE REFORM

Last but not least, the evidence presented throughout the work should encourage more sober thinking about political finance regulation. We have seen, after all, how subsidies have a minor impact on the evolution of the party system, how their effectiveness in preventing problematic funding practices is rather limited, and how many basic fundraising dynamics are remarkably similar in our two cases, despite the presence of extensive legal controls in Costa Rica and their complete absence in Uruguay. The Costa Rican case indeed provides a textbook example of how the introduction of political finance controls does not guarantee their implementation and of the questionable benefits derived from weakly applied rules. The income reports currently submitted by the Costa Rican parties, poorly monitored by the electoral authorities, have at most facilitated the overseeing role of the press, ultimately a much more powerful restraint on objectionable funding practices.

No reform, even a well conceived one, will smoothly recast deeply ingrained political finance practices or the popular perceptions about them. Would-be political finance reformers should be under no illusions about the unrewarding nature of their endeavours. There is, after all, very little evidence that the enactment and even the proper implementation of political finance rules help to increase the legitimacy of political systems or the popular standing of reforming actors. The struggle to legitimise political finance activities is, at best, an uphill battle, and at worst an unwinnable one. When deregulated, these activities breed suspicion and damning mythologies; when poorly regulated, they nurture disappointment with reform and scepticism about the politicians' motives; when rigorously regulated, they beget scandals about illegal funding and increased cynicism about politics. Political finance reformers may fail even when they succeed.

This is not a call for inaction. The dangers of deregulation of political finance for democracy may be far greater than those derived from the alternatives. Rather, this is a reminder of the inevitable price of any reform and an appeal to would-be reformers to moderate their expectations and those of the public. The results of political finance rules in securing central democratic tenets will inevitably fall short of the intentions of even the best-willed and most careful reformer. New funding sources and practices will replace old ones, and unexpected ways of taking advantage of the existing legislation will be developed in due course by political participants. As with the construction of democracy itself, the configuration of an effective political finance system is a dynamic process, a never-ending journey in which preciously few stations are likely to be an unqualified success. Moreover, even the most successful reformer must acknowledge that the use of money to fund parties and candidates is merely one of the channels through which economic resources influence politics. As Alexander Heard noted, '(t)he inherent power of wealth exists without regard to how political campaigns are paid for'.[5] Whatever lofty ambitions we may harbour, political finance reform is no more than an exercise in damage limitation.

## NOTES

1  Quoted by Pulzer (2001), p.1
2  Ulloa (2001). Ulloa is a former magistrate of El Salvador's Supreme Electoral Tribunal.
3  Zovatto (1998), p. XLIX
4  *La Nación* [*LN*], 21/10/2002. Solís is a former presidential candidate (PAC) in the 2002 Costa Rican election.
5  Heard (1960), p. 90.

# bibliography

Abdala, Washington (1993), *Corrupción en Uruguay: Opiniones sin Censura*; Montevideo, Editorial Sudamericana.

----- [25/4/2000] (Deputy [FB and PC]), interview, Montevideo.

'Abitab: Información institucional'. Downloaded from the Internet: http://www.abitab.com.uy/ab_fr1_ins.htm.

Achard, Diego [17/5/2000] (former personal secretary of PN leader Wilson Ferreira), interview, Montevideo.

Adamany, David and Agree, George (1975), *Political Money*; Baltimore, Johns Hopkins University Press.

Advertising executive [10/5/2000] (media advisor to L15 and PC), interview, Montevideo.

Agree, George (1980), 'Commentary', in Malbin, Michael, ed., *Parties, Interest Groups and Campaign Finance Laws*, Washington DC, American Enterprise Institute for Public Policy Research.

Aguiar, César (1984), *Partidos y Elecciones*; Montevideo, CIEDUR.

Aguiar, Roberto (1994), 'The cost of election campaigns in Brazil' in Alexander, Herbert and Shiratori, Rei, eds, *Comparative Political Finance among the Democracies*; Boulder, Westview Press.

Aguilar, Luis and Esquivel, Max (1991), *Problemática de la Tendencia del Derecho Electoral Costarricense hacia la Conformación de un Sistema Bipartidista*, San José, Tesis de Grado, Universidad de Costa Rica.

Aguilar-Bulgarelli, Oscar (1969), *Costa Rica y sus Hechos Politicos de 1948. Problematica de una Decada*; San Jose, Editorial Costa Rica.

Aguirre, Gonzalo (1986), 'Es deseable una reforma electoral?' in Nohlen, Dieter and Rial, Juan, eds, *Reforma Electoral: Posible, Deseable?* Montevideo, FESUR-Ediciones de la Banda Oriental.

----- [9/6/2000] (former Vice-President of the Republic and presidential pre-candidate [PN]), interview, Montevideo.

Aguirre-Bayley, Miguel (2000), *Frente Amplio: La Admirable Alarma de 1971*, Montevideo, La República. Second edition.

Ahumada, Alexis [16/6/2000] (financial manager [MPP and FA]), interview, Montevideo.

*Al Día* [*AD*] (San José), various years.

Alcántara, Manuel and Crespo, Ismael (1992), *Partidos Políticos y Procesos Electorales en Uruguay (1971–1990)*, Madrid, CEDEAL.

----- Cordero, Luis Alberto and González, María Lourdes (1997), 'El finan ciamiento partidario en Alemania, Argentina, Canada, Chile y Costa Rica'. Paper presented at the Council for Freely Elected Heads of Government, Carter Centre, Atlanta, Georgia, April 28–29.

Alemán-Velasco, Miguel (1995), *Las Finanzas de la Politica*, Mexico, D. F., Editorial Diana.

Alexander, Herbert (1979), ed., *Political Finance*; London, Sage.

----- (1980), 'Political finance regulation in international perspective', in Malbin, Michael, ed., *Parties, Interest Groups and Campaign Finance Laws*; Washington DC, American Institute for Public Policy Research.

----- (1989), 'American Presidential elections since public funding, 1976–84', in Alexander, Herbert, ed., *Comparative Political Finance in the 1980s*, Cambridge, Cambridge University Press.

----- (1992), *Financing Politics*; Washington DC, Congressional Quarterly Press.

----- et al. (1997), *New Realities, New Thinking: Report of the Task Force on Campaign Finance Reform*; Citizens' Research Foundation/University of Southern California. Downloaded from the Internet: http://www.usc.edu/dept/CRF/DATA/newrnewt.htm

----- and Corrado, Anthony (1995), *Financing the 1992 Election*; New York, M. E. Sharpe.

----- Goss, Eugene R. and Schwartz, Jeffrey A. (1992), *Public Financing of State Elections: A Data Book on Tax-Assisted Funding of Political Parties and Candidates in Twenty-Four States*; Los Angeles, Citizens' Research Foundation.

----- and Shiratori, Rei (1994), eds, *Comparative Political Finance among the Democracies*; Boulder, Westview Press.

Allen, Michael Patrick and Broyles, Philip (1991), 'Campaign finance reforms and the presidential campaign contributions of wealthy capitalist fami lies', *Social Science Quarterly*, Vol. 72, No. 4 (December).

Almond, Gabriel and Genco, Stephen J. (1977), 'Clouds, clocks, and the study of politics', *World Politics*, Vol. 29, No. 4 (July).

Alonzo, Tomás [9/5/2000] (BROU manager), interview, Montevideo.

Altman, David and Chasquetti, Daniel (2000), 'Patterns of incumbent's turnover at the Uruguayan Congress (1985–1999): An institutional account'. Paper presented at the conference of the Midwest Political Science Association; Chicago, Illinois, April 2000.

Altmann, Fernando [28/9/1999] (former Deputy and party treasurer [PU]), inter view, San José.

Alvarez, Antonio [7/12/1999] (former Deputy and presidential pre-candidate [PLN]), interview, San José.

Alvarez-Conde, Enrique (1994), 'Algunas propuestas sobre la financiación de los partidos políticos', in Alvarez-Conde, Enrique et al., *La Financiación de los Partidos Políticos; Madrid*, Centro de Estudios Constitucionales.

Amr, Dina and Lisowski, Rainer (2001), 'Political finance in Old Dominions: Australia and Canada', in Nassmacher, Karl-Heinz, *Foundations for Democracy: Approaches to Comparative Political Finance*; Baden-Baden, Nomos.

Andren, Nils (1970), 'Partisan motivations and concern for system legitimacy in the Scandinavian deliberations on public subsidies', in Heidenheimer,

Arnold, ed., *Comparative Political Finance: The Financing of Party Organizations and Election Campaigns*; Levington, DC, Heath and Company.

Andreoli, Selva [13/6/2000] (advertising advisor to the FA), interview, Montevideo.

Anglade, Christian (1970), 'Party finance models and the classification of Latin American parties', in Heidenheimer, Arnold, ed., *Comparative Political Finance: The Financing of Party Organizations and Election Campaigns*, Levington, DC, Heath and Company.

Araya, Rolando [14/12/1999] (former Deputy, Secretary-General and presidential candidate [PLN]), interview, San José.

Araya-Alfaro, Ana Julia et al. (1986), *Enfoque Jurídico-Político del PUSC en Costa Rica*; San José, Tesis de Grado, Universidad de Costa Rica.

Araya-Fernández, Sergio [27/1/1999] (Director of Political Training at the Costa Rican Institute of Political Studies [ICEP]), interview, San José.

Araya-Herrera, Mayela (1996), *Las Partidas Específicas en el Sistema Político Costarricense, un Estudio de Caso: La Administración Calderón Fournier, 1990–94*; San José, Tesis de Grado, Universidad de Costa Rica.

Araya-Pochet, Carlos (1982), *Liberación Nacional en la Historia Política de Costa Rica, 1940–80*; San José, Editorial Nacional de Textos.

Arbilla, Danilo [3/7/2000] (director *Semanario Búsqueda*), interview, Montevideo.

Ardaya, Gloria and Verdesoto, Luis (1998), 'Financiación de los partidos políticos y las campañas electorales en Ecuador', in Del Castillo, Pilar and Zovatto, Daniel, eds, *La Financiación de la Política en Iberoamérica*; San José, IIDH-CAPEL.

Ares-Pons, Roberto (1990), 'Blancos y Colorados', in Caetano, Gerardo and Rilla, José, eds, *Los Partidos Uruguayos y su Historia (I): El Siglo XIX*; Montevideo, ICP-FCU.

Arias, Oscar (1976), *Quién Gobierna en Costa Rica? Un Estudio del Liderazgo Formal en Costa Rica*; San José, EDUCA.

----- [30/8/1999] (former President of the Republic [PLN]), interview, San José.

Asamblea Constituyente de Costa Rica [ACCR] (1949), *Actas de la Constituyente de 1949*; San José, Imprenta Nacional.

Asamblea General del Uruguay [AGU] (various years), Diario de Sesiones (DS).

Asamblea Legislativa de Costa Rica [ALCR], Expediente Ley No. 2036.

----- Expediente Ley No. 2667.

----- Expediente Ley No. 4765.

----- Expediente Ley No. 7094.

----- Expediente Legislativo A45-E8008.

----- Expediente Legislativo 7675.

----- Expediente Legislativo 7898.

----- Expediente Legislativo 10200.

-----   Expediente Legislativo 10386.
-----   Expediente Legislativo 10684.
-----   Expediente Legislativo 10934.

Asociación Uruguaya de Agencias de Publicidad [AUDAP] (various years), offi cial television advertising fares.

Astori, Danilo [1/6/2000] (Senator [AU and FA]), interview, Montevideo.

Austin, Reginald and Tjernström, Maja (2003), eds, *Funding of Political Parties and Election Campaigns*; Stockholm, International IDEA.

Avril, Pierre (1994), 'Regulation of political finance in France', in Alexander, Herbert and Shiratori, Rei, eds, *Comparative Political Finance among the Democracies*; Boulder, Westview Press.

'Banca de Cubierta Colectiva de Quinielas de Montevideo'. Downloaded from the Internet: http://www.lotteryinsider.com/lottery/bccq.htm.

Banco Central de Costa Rica [BCCR], various documents from Departament of Economic Research.

Banco Central del Uruguay [BCU], various documents from Department of Economic Research.

'Banco Hipotecario del Uruguay: Historia y galería de presidentes'. Downloaded from the Internet: www.bhu.com.uy/documentos/historia.htm.

Banco Nacional de Costa Rica [BNCR] (1997), *Reglamento para la Financiación de los Gastos Justificables en que incurran los Partidos Políticos con ocasión de la Campaña Electoral, 1994–98*; San José.

Baráibar, Carlos [17/4/2000] (Deputy [AU and FA]), interview, Montevideo.

Barandiarán, Gabriel [25/4/2000] (former Deputy and Secretary of Finance [NE]), interview, Montevideo.

Barbé, Carlos [20/3/2000] (member of Board of Directors of Banco de la República Oriental del Uruguay), interview, Montevideo.

Bardi, Luciano and Morlino, Leonardo (1994), 'Italy: tracing the roots of the Great Transformation', in Katz, Richard and Mair, Peter, eds, *How Parties Organize: Change and Adaptation in Party Organizations in Western Democracies*; London, Sage.

Barreiro, Lina (1998), 'El financiamiento de los partidos políticos paraguayos', in Del Castillo, Pilar and Zovatto, Daniel, eds, *La Financiación de la Política en Iberoamérica*; San José, IIDH-CAPEL.

Bartolini, Stefano (1983), 'The membership of mass parties: the Social Democratic experience, 1889–1978', in Daalder, Hans and Mair, Peter, eds, *Western European Party Systems: Continuity and Change*; London, Sage.

Batlle, José Luis [2/6/2000] (Senator and Secretary General [L15 and PC]), inter view, Montevideo.

Bayardi, José [4/5/2000] (Deputy [VA and FA), interview, Montevideo.

Bell, John Patrick (1971), *Crisis in Costa Rica: The 1948 Revolution*; Austin, University of Texas Press.

Bendel, Petra (1993), 'Partidos políticos y sistemas de partidos en

Centroamérica', in Nohlen, Dieter, ed., *Elecciones y Sistemas de Partidos en América Latina*; San José, IIDH-CAPEL.

Benecke, Dieter [4/7/2000] (Representative, Konrad Adenauer Foundation), inter view, Montevideo.

Berhorst, Anja [21/10/1999] (assistant to the regional director for Latin America of the Friedrich Naumann Foundation), interview, San José.

Bille, Lars (1994), 'Denmark: the decline of the membership party', in Katz, Richard S. and Mair, Peter, eds, *How Parties Organize: Change and Adaptation in Party Organizations in Western Democracies*; London, Sage.

Blackburn, Robert (1995), *The Electoral System in Britain*; London, Macmillan.

Blanco-Valdés, Roberto (1994), 'Consideraciones sobre la necesaria reforma del sistema español de financiación de los partidos políticos', in Alvarez-Conde, Enrique et al., eds, *La Financiación de los Partidos Políticos*; Madrid, Centro de Estudios Constitucionales.

Blechinger, Verena and Nassmacher, Karl-Heinz (2001), 'Political finance in non-Western democracies: Japan and Israel', in Nassmacher, Karl-Heinz, *Foundations for Democracy: Approaches to Comparative Political Finance*; Baden-Baden, Nomos.

Blixen, Samuel (1998), 'Rev. Moon's Uruguayan money-laundry', *The Consortium for Independent Journalism*. Downloaded from the Internet: http://www.consortiumnews.com/1990s/consor16.html.

Bogdanor, Vernon (1982), 'Reflections on British Political Finance', *Parliamentary Affairs*, Vol. XXV, No.4, (Autumn).

----- (1997), 'Would you pay to clean up politics?', *The Times* (London), 2/11/1997.

Booth, John (1999), 'Costa Rica: the roots of democratic stability', in Diamond, Larry; Hartlyn, Jonathan; Linz, Juan and Lipset, Seymour, eds, *Democracy in Developing Countries*, Latin America; Boulder, Lynne Reiner.

Borge and Asociados (various years), *Encuesta Nacional de Opinión Pública*; San José.

Bottinelli, Oscar (1993), 'Estructura y funcionamiento de los partidos políticos en el Uruguay', in Bodemer, Klaus and Laurnaga, María Elena, eds, *Estructura y Funcionamiento de los Partidos Políticos: Una Reforma Posible*; Montevideo, FESUR-Ediciones Trilce.

----- (1999), 'El nuevo sistema apunta a producir un cambio en la cultura política', in Cribari, Pedro et al., eds, *Uruguay después del Balotaje: El Impacto de la Reforma y el Nuevo Escenario Político*; Montevideo, Cauce Editorial.

Brewer-Carías, Alan (1991), 'Consideraciones sobre el financiamiento de los par tidos políticos en Venezuela', in *Memoria del IV Curso Annual Interamericano de Elecciones-Volumen II*; San José, IIDH-CAPEL.

Briffault, Richard (1999), 'Public funding and democratic elections', *University of Pennsylvania Law Review*, Vol. 148, No. 2 (December).

Brito-González, José (1988), 'El financiamiento estatal de los partidos', in Rey, Juan Carlos et al., *Visión General de las Reformas: Financiamiento de los Partidos, Clientelismo e Ideología*; Caracas, Consejo Supremo Electoral.

Brown Jr., Clifford W.; Powell, Lynda W. and Wilcox, Clyde (1995), *Serious Money: Fundraising and Contributing in Presidential Nomination Campaigns*; Cambridge, Cambridge University Press.

Brüner, F. H. (1998), 'Investigating illegal financing of political parties'. Report prepared for the Third European Conference of Specialised Services in the Fight Against Corruption, Madrid, 28–30 October 1998; Council of Europe.

Bruschera, Oscar (1966), *Los Partidos Tradicionales en el Uruguay*; Montevideo, Ediciones del Río de la Plata.

Buquet, Daniel (1997), 'Reforma política y gobernabilidad democrática en Uruguay: la reforma constitucional de 1996', *Revista Uruguaya de Ciencia Política*, No. 10.

----- Chasquetti, Daniel and Moraes, Juan Andrés (1998), *Un Enfermo Imaginario? Fragmentación Política y Gobierno en Uruguay*; Montevideo, Instituto de Ciencia Política.

Burgués, Antonio [11/11/1999] (former party treasurer [PLN]), interview, San José.

Burnell, Peter and Ware, Alan (1998), eds, *Funding Democratization*; Manchester, Manchester University Press.

Businessperson No. 1 [15/5/2000], interview, Montevideo.

Businessperson No. 2 [2/6/2000] (former President of Uruguay's National Chamber of Commerce), interview, Montevideo.

Businessperson No. 3 [24/5/2000], interview, Montevideo.

Businessperson No. 4 [5/7/2000], interview, Montevideo.

Caetano, Gerardo et al. (1985), *De la Tradición a la Crisis: Pasado y Presente de Nuestro Sistema de Partidos*; Montevideo, CLAEH-Ediciones de la Banda Oriental.

----- et al. (2002), *Dinero y Política: El Financiamiento de los Partidos en la Democracia*; Montevideo, Ediciones de la Banda Oriental – Goethe Institut – Unidad para la Promoción de la Democracia – Instituto de Ciencia Política.

----- and Rilla, José (1985), 'El sistema de partidos: raíces y permanencias', in Caetano, Gerardo et al., *De la Tradición a la Crisis: Pasado y Presente de Nuestro Sistema de Partidos*; Montevideo, CLAEH-Ediciones de la Banda Oriental.

----- and Rilla, José, eds (1990), *Los Partidos Uruguayos y su Historia (I): El Siglo XIX*; Montevideo, ICP-FCU.

----- and Rilla, José (1999), *Historia Contemporánea del Uruguay: De la Colonia al Mercosur*; Montevideo, CLAEH-Editorial Fin de Siglo.

----- Rilla, José; and Pérez, Romeo (1988), 'La partidocracia uruguaya: Historia y teoría de la centralidad de los partidos políticos,' *Cuadernos del CLAEH*, No. 44 (April).

----- Rilla, José; and Pérez, Romeo (1989), 'Cambios recientes en el sistema político uruguayo concebido como una partidocracia', in Instituto de Ciencia Política de la Universidad de la República Oriental del Uruguay, *Los Partidos Políticos de Cara al 90*; Montevideo, ICP-FCU-FESUR.

Caja Costarricense del Seguro Social [CCSS] (various years), payroll archives.

Calderón-Fournier, Rafael Angel [16/9/1999] (former President of the Republic [PUSC]), interview, San José.

Cámara de Representantes del Uruguay [CRU] (1989), *Elecciones del 25 de Noviembre de 1984*; Montevideo, Cámara de Representantes.

----- (1994), *Elecciones del 26 de Noviembre de 1989*; Montevideo, Cámara de Representantes.

----- (1999), *Elecciones del 27 de Noviembre de 1994*; Montevideo, Cámara de Representantes.

----- (various years), Diario de Sesiones (DS).

----- Carpeta 1711/1953.

----- Carpeta 2464/1954.

----- Carpeta 2222/1958.

----- Carpeta 3085/1966.

----- Carpeta 1369/1991.

----- Carpeta 3231/1998.

Cámara de Senadores del Uruguay [CSU] (various years), Diario de Sesiones (DS).

----- Carpeta 1292/1993.

----- Carpeta 943/1997.

----- Repartido No.2299/1998

Camby, Jean-Pierre (1995), *Le Financement de la Vie Politique en France*; Paris, Montchrestien.

Carazo, Rodrigo [29/9/1999] (former President of the Republic [CU]), interview, Escazú.

Carey, John (1996), *Term Limits and Legislative Representation*; Cambridge, Cambridge University Press.

----- (1997), 'Strong candidates for a limited office: Presidentialism and political parties in Costa Rica', in Mainwaring, Scott and Shuggart, Mathew Sobert, eds, *Presidentialism and Democracy in Latin America*; Cambridge, Cambridge University Press.

Carlevaro, Marcela [14–16/6/2000] (administrative assistant for South America, Friedrich Naumann Foundation), interview, Montevideo.

Casas-Zamora, Kevin (2001), 'Contribución estatal a los partidos políticos en Costa Rica: apuntes sobre sus efectos en la dinámica del sistema de partidos', in Rovira, Jorge, ed., *La Democracia de Costa Rica ante el Siglo XXI*; San José, Editorial Universidad de Costa Rica – Fundación

Friedrich Ebert.

----- (2002), *Paying for Democracy in Latin America: Political Finance and State Funding for Parties in Costa Rica and Uruguay*; Oxford, D.Phil Thesis, University of Oxford.

----- (2003), 'Subsidios electorales y financiemiento de campañas en el Uruguay', *Cuadernos del CLAEH*, No. 86/87 (August).

----- and Briceño-Fallas, Olman (1991), *Democracia Representativa en Costa Rica? Análisis del Sistema de Elección de Diputados y sus Perspectivas de Cambio*; San José, Tesis de Grado, Universidad de Costa Rica.

Castrillo, Francisco (1977), *Régimen Jurídico de la Deuda Política*; San José, Tesis de Grado, Universidad de Costa Rica.

Castro, Oscar [18/5/2000](President of the Financial Commission [FA]), inter view, Montevideo.

Castro-Méndez, Mauricio (2001), 'Comentarios sobre la situación de la libertad sindical en Costa Rica'. Downloaded from the Internet: http://www.democraciadigital.org/derechos/arts/0109sindical.html.

Cataldi, Alfonso [5/6/2000] (Secretary of the EC on Legal Matters), interview, Montevideo.

Centro de Estudios para la Justicia Social con Libertad [CEJUL] (1989), *El Estado y la Financiación de los Partidos Políticos en Costa Rica*; San José, Varitec.

Centro de Información, Documentación y Educación Electoral de Paraguay. Loose document mailed to the author.

Cepeda-Ulloa, Fernando (1997), *Financiacion de Campañas Políticas*; Bogotá, Editorial Ariel.

Cerdas, Rodolfo (1998), 'Financiación de partidos y campañas electorales', in Del Castillo, Pilar and Zovatto, Daniel, eds, *La Financiación de la Política en Iberoamérica*; San José, IIDH-CAPEL.

----- [20/9/1999] (former Deputy [Frente Popular]), interview, San José.

Chacón, Maruja [7/9/1999] (former TSE magistrate), interview, San José.

Chacón-González, Francisco [21/12/1999] (pre-campaign official [PLN]), tele phone conversation with the author.

Chacón-Pacheco, Nelson (1975), *Reseña de Nuestras Leyes Electorales*; San José, n.p.

Chaples, Ernest (1981), 'Public campaign finance: New South Wales bites the bul let', *The Australian Quarterly*, Vol. 53, No.1 (Autumn).

----- (1989), 'Public funding of elections in Australia', in Alexander, Herbert, ed., *Comparative Political Finance in the 1980s*; Cambridge, Cambridge University Press.

Chávez, Román [22/10/1999] (former President of the Costa Rican Chamber of Construction), interview, San José.

Chief Electoral Officer of Canada (1993), *Thirty-fifth General Election 1993: Contributions and Expenses of Registered Political Parties and Candidates*; Ottawa, Chief Electoral Officer of Canada.

Chinchilla, Rafael Angel [9/9/1999] (former General Comptroller of the Republic), interview, San José.

Ciaurro, Gian Franco (1989), 'Public financing of parties in Italy', in Alexander, Herbert, ed., *Comparative Political Finance in the 1980s*; Cambridge, Cambridge University Press.

CID-Gallup (various years), *Encuesta de Opinión Pública*; San José.

CIFRA (various years), Opinion poll database; Montevideo.

Cocchi, Angel (1986), 'El sistema electoral uruguayo: historia y estructura actu al', in Nohlen, Dieter and Rial, Juan, eds, *Reforma Electoral: Posible, Deseable?*; Montevideo, FESUR-Ediciones de la Banda Oriental.

----- (n.d.), *Un Sistema Político Centenario*; Montevideo, Peitho-CAPEL.

*Código Electoral – Ley Orgánica del Tribunal Supremo de Elecciones y del Registro Civil* (1997); San José, Tribunal Supremo de Elecciones.

Comisión Económica para América Latina y el Caribe [CEPAL] (1999), 'Indicators of economic and social development in Latin America and the Caribbean'. Downloaded from Internet: http://www.cepal.org/publica ciones/estadísticas/6/icg2006/parte1anu99.pdf.

----- (2001), *Anuario Estadístico de América Latina y el Caribe*; Santiago, CEPAL.

----- (2002), *Anuario Estadístico de América Latina y el Caribe*; Santiago, CEPAL.

Commission of the European Communities, Proposal for a Council Regulation on the Statute and Financing of European Political Parties, 13/2/2001. Downloaded from the Internet: http://europa.eu.int/smartapi/cgi.

Committee on Financial Aid to Political Parties (1976), *Report* (Houghton Report); London, Her Majesty's Stationery Office.

Committee on Standards in Public Life (1998), *The Funding of Political Parties in the United Kingdom*, Volume 1 (Neill Report); London, The Stationery Office.

Congressional Quarterly (1992), *Congressional Campaign Finances: History, Facts and Controversy*; Washington DC, Congressional Quarterly.

Consejo de Estado del Uruguay [CEst] (various years), Diario de Sesiones (DS).

----- Carpeta 201/1981.

Consejo Nacional Electoral de Venezuela, *El Financiamiento de las Campañas Electorales, Memoria*; Caracas, IFES.

Constenla, Guillermo [20/9/1999] (former Deputy, former campaign manager and campaign treasurer [PLN]), interview, San José.

*Constitución de la República Oriental del Uruguay* (1997); Montevideo, Cámara de Senadores.

*Constitución Política de la República de Costa Rica* (1999); San José, La Nación.

Contraloría General de la República, Costa Rica [CGR] (1997), Reglamento sobre el pago de los gastos de los partidos políticos.

----- (various years), Departamento de Estudios Especiales, various loose documents.

----- Departamento de Estudios Especiales, Informe No. 95–98.
----- Departamento de Estudios Especiales, Informe No. 158–90.
----- Departamento de Estudios Especiales, Informe No. 161–90.
----- Departamento de Estudios Especiales, Informe No. 167–90.
----- Departamento de Estudios Especiales, Informe No. 70–94.
----- Departamento de Estudios Especiales, Informe No. 85–94.
----- Departamento de Estudios Especiales, Informe No. 92–94.
----- Departamento de Estudios Especiales, Informe No. 95–98
----- Departamento de Estudios Especiales, Informe No. 96–98
----- Departamento de Estudios Especiales, Informe No. 97–98.
----- Departamento de Estudios Especiales, Informe No. 99–94.
Coppedge, Michael (1998), 'The dynamic diversity of Latin American party systems', *Party Politics*, Vol. 4, No.4.
Cordes, Doris and Nassmacher, Karl-Heinz (2001), 'Mission impossible: can any one control the unlimited increase of political spending?', in Nassmacher, Karl-Heinz, ed. *Foundations for Democracy: Approaches to Comparative Political Finance*; Baden-Baden, Nomos.
Corrado, Anthony (1993), *Paying for Presidents: Public Financing in National Elections*; New York, Twentieth Century Fund Press.
----- et al. (1997), *Campaign Finance Reform: A Sourcebook*; Washington DC, The Brookings Institution.
Corte Electoral del Uruguay [CE] (1989), *Leyes de Elecciones*; Montevideo.
----- (1999), *Leyes de Elecciones*; Montevideo.
----- (2000), Electoral results, Elections 31/10/1999, 28/11/1999 y 14/5/2000. Loose documents from the Electoral Archive.
----- Circular No. 4765 of 27/12/1971.
Cortés-Ramos, Alberto (2001), 'Cultura política y sistema de partidos en Costa Rica: Nuevas tendencias en el 2002?', in Rovira, Jorge, ed., *La Democracia de Costa Rica ante el Siglo XXI*; San José, Editorial UCR – Fundación Friedrich Ebert.
Costa-Bonino, Luis (1995), *La Crisis del Sistema Político Uruguayo: Partidos Políticos y Democracia hasta 1973*; Montevideo, FCU.
Coto, Walter [6/9/1999] (former Deputy and Secretary General [PLN]), interview, San José.
Council of Europe (COU) (2000), 'Summary of member and observer states' replies to political party and candidate funding questionanaire'. Downloaded from the Internet: http://www.coe.int.
----- Parliamentary Assembly, Recommendation 1516, 22/5/2001. Downloaded from the Internet: http://assembly.coe.int/Documents/Adopted Text/ta01/EREC1516.htm.
Cox, Gary (1997), *Making Votes Count: Strategic Coordination in the World's Electoral System*; Cambridge, Cambridge University Press.
----- and Thies, Michael (2000), 'How much does money matter? 'Buying' votes in Japan, 1967–1990', *Comparative Political Studies*, Vol. 33, No.

1 (February).

Crain, W. M.; Tollison, R. and Leavens M. (1988), 'Laissez-faire in campaign finance', *Public Choice*, Vol. 56, No. 3 (March).

Cribari, Pedro et al., eds (1999), *Uruguay después del Balotaje: El Impacto de la Reforma y el Nuevo Escenario Político*; Montevideo, Cauce Editorial.

Cruickshank, Eduardo (1984), *El Derecho a la Deuda Política Adelantada*; San José, Tesis de Grado, Universidad de Costa Rica.

Da Silva, Sebastián [29/6/2000] (Deputy and campaign manager of *Lista 903* [DN and PN]), interview, Montevideo.

Dahl, Robert (1956), *A Preface to Democratic Theory*; Chicago, University of Chicago Press.

----- (1989), *Democracy and its Critics*; New Haven, Yale University Press.

De Cuadro, Artigas [13/6/2000] (former President of the Rural Federation), inter view, Montevideo.

De la Calle, Humberto (1998), 'Financiación de los partidos políticos y las cam pañas electorales en Colombia', in Del Castillo, Pilar and Zovatto, Daniel, eds, *La Financiación de la Política en Iberoamérica*; San José, IIDH-CAPEL.

De la Cruz, Vladimir [13/9/1999] (former presidential candidate [PFD]); inter view, San José.

Del Castillo, Pilar (1985); *La Financiación de Partidos y Candidatos en las Democracias Occidentales*; Madrid, Siglo XXI Editores.

----- (1989), 'Financing of Spanish political parties', in Alexander, Herbert, ed., *Comparative Political Finance in the 1980s*; Cambridge, Cambridge University Press.

----- (1992), 'Financiación de los partidos políticos: la reforma necesaria', in González-Encinar, José Juan, ed., *Derecho de Partidos*; Madrid, Espasa-Calpe.

----- (1993), 'La financiación de los partidos políticos: propuestas para una reforma', in Instituto de Investigaciones Jurídicas, *Aspectos Jurídicos del Financiamiento de los Partidos Políticos*; México D.F., UNAM.

----- (1994), 'Objetivos para una reforma de la legislación sobre financiación de los partidos políticos', in Alvarez-Conde, Enrique et al., *La Financiación de los Partidos Políticos*; Madrid, Centro de Estudios Constitucionales.

----- (1998), 'La financiación de los partidos políticos en España', in Del Castillo, Pilar and Zovatto, Daniel , eds, *La Financiación de la Política en Iberoamérica*; San José, IIDH-CAPEL.

----- and Zovatto, Daniel (1998), eds, *La Financiación de la Política en Iberoamérica*; San José, IIDH-CAPEL.

Della Porta, Donatella (1996), 'Actors in corruption: business politicians in Italy', *International Social Science Journal*, Vol. XLVIII, No.3 (September).

Dent, Alberto [22/12/1999] (former campaign treasurer [PUSC]), interview, San José.

'Derecho a la información'. Downloaded from the Internet: www.serpaj.org.uy /INF99/derecho_infor.htm.

*Diario de Costa Rica* [*DCR*] (San José), various years.

Díaz-Santana, Héctor (1998), 'CEP: proyecto reforma del estado y financiamien to de partidos políticos', Santiago de Chile, Centro de Estudios Públicos, mimeo.

Dix, Robert (1989), 'Cleavage structures and party systems in Latin America', *Comparative Politics*, Vol. 22, No. 1 (October).

Donnay, Patrick and Ramsden, Graham (1996), 'Public financing: lessons from Minnesota', Citizens Research Foundation. Downloaded from the Internet: http://www.usc.edu/dept/CRF/NET/PAPERS/paper4.htm.

Downs, Anthony (1957), *An Economic Theory of Democracy*; New York, Harper Collins.

Drysch, Thomas (1993), 'The new French system of political finance', in Gunlicks (Arthur), ed., *Campaign and Party Finance in North America and Western Europe*; Boulder, Westview Press.

Dutrénit, Silvia (1996), 'El Frente Amplio y la reproducción de la identidad política,' *Nueva Sociedad*, No.144 (July-August).

Duverger, Maurice (1988 [1951]), *Los Partidos Políticos*; Mexico D.F., Fondo de Cultura Economica.

Dworkin, Ronald (1997), 'The Curse of American Politics', in Corrado, Anthony *et al.*, eds, *Campaign Finance Reform: A Sourcebook*; Washington D. C., Brookings Institution Press.

*The Economist* (London), 25/5/1996, 'Drugs are back'.

----- 29/6/1996, 'Well I never, says the president'.

----- 8 –12/2/1997, 'How to cut the cost of politics'.

----- 8–12/2/1997, 'Politicians for rent'.

----- 7/11/1998 'The Moonies have landed'.

*El Día* [*ED*] (Montevideo), various years

*El Eco* [*ECO*] (Montevideo), various years.

*El Financiero* [*EF*] (San José), various years.

*El Nuevo Diario* (Managua), 15/10/2000.

*El Observador* [*EO*] (Montevideo), various years.

*El Observador Económico* (Managua), No. 112.

*El País* [*EP*] (Montevideo), various years.

*El Panamá América* (Panama City), 14/8/2001.

*El Popular* [*ELP*] (Montevideo), various years.

'Elecciones libres internas – Domingo 25 de Abril'. Downloaded from the Internet: http://www.uruguaytotal.com/internas.htm.

Errandonea, Alfredo (1989), 'Notas sobre la caracterización del sistema de partidos en Uruguay', in Instituto de Ciencia Política de la Universidad de la República Oriental del Uruguay, *Los Partidos Políticos de Cara al 90*; Montevideo, ICP-FCU-FESUR.

Ersson, Svante and Lane, Jan-Erik (1998), 'Electoral instability and party system change', in Pennings, Paul and Lane, Jan-Erik, eds, *Comparing Party System Change*; London, Routledge.

Espinal, Rosario and Jiménez, Jacqueline (1998), 'El financiamiento de los partidos políticos en la República Dominicana', in Del Castillo, Pilar and Zovatto, Daniel, eds, *La Financiación de la Política en Iberoamérica*; San José, IIDH-CAPEL.

Este Diario [ESTD] (Montevideo), various years.

Euchner, Ch. and Maltese, J.A. (1992) *Selecting the President: From Washington to Bush*; Washington DC, Congressional Quarterly Inc.

*European Journal of Political Research [EJPR]*, various years.

European Parliament (1991), *The Funding of Political Parties in European Community Member States*; Directorate General for Research, European Parliament.

European Union (EU), Treaty of Nice (Declaration 11), 26/2/2001. Downloaded from the Internet: http://europa.eu.int/comm/nice_treaty.

Ewing, Keith D. (1992), *Money, Politics and Law: A Study of Electoral Campaign Finance Reform in Canada*; Oxford, Clarendon Press.

*Excelsior [EXC]* (San José), various years.

*Extra [EXT]* (San José), various years.

FA media advisor [27/4/2000], interview, Montevideo.

Fabregat, Julio (1950), *Elecciones Uruguayas*, 1925–1946; Montevideo, Poder Legislativo.

----- (1957), *Elecciones Uruguayas*, 1950–1954; Montevideo, Poder Legislativo.

----- (1959), *Elecciones Uruguayas*, 1958; Montevideo, Poder Legislativo.

----- (1963), *Elecciones Uruguayas*, 1962; Montevideo, Poder Legislativo.

----- (1967), *Elecciones Uruguayas*, 1966; Montevideo, Poder Legislativo.

----- (1972), *Elecciones Uruguayas*, 1971; Montevideo, Poder Legislativo.

Fachler, Moisés (27/4/1998), Letter to the PLN's Superior Executive Committee.

----- [22/9/1999] (former party treasurer and pre-campaign manager [PLN]), interview, San José.

----- [20/12/1999], telephone conversation with the author.

Federal Election Commission (1993), *The Presidential Public Funding Program*; Washington DC, Federal Election Commission.

----- (1998), *Annual Report 1997*; Washington DC, Federal Election Commission.

----- (1999), 'States with special tax or public financing provisions'. Downloaded from the Internet: http://fecweb1.fec.gov/pages/Chart4.htm.

Feoli, Juan Carlos [20/9/1999] (former pre-campaign treasurer and manager [PLN]), interview, San José.

Ferdinand, Peter (1998), 'Building democracy on the basis of capitalism: towards an East Asian model of party funding', in Burnell, Peter and Ware, Alan, eds, *Funding Democratization*; Manchester, Manchester University Press.

Ferguson, Thomas (1995), *Golden Rule: The Investment Theory of Party Competition and the Logic of Money-Driven Political Systems*; Chicago, University of Chicago Press.

Fernández, Oscar (1991), 'Costa Rica: una bipolaridad partidaria hoy apenas cuestionada', *Anuario de Estudios Centroamericanos*, Vol. 17, No. 2.

----- (1993), 'La financiación política en Costa Rica: los altibajos de una larga e interminable negociación', in Pedone, Luis, *Sistemas Eleitorais e Processos Políticos Comparados: A promessa de democracia na América Latina e Caribe*; Brasilia, Organisacao dos Estados Americanos-Conselho de Desenvolvimiento Científico e Tecnológico-Universidade de Brasilia.

----- (1994), 'Costa Rica: la reafirmación del bipartidismo', *Nueva Sociedad*, Vol. 131 (May–June).

----- (1996), 'Los partidos políticos: Su interrelación y sus rasgos centrales en la sociedad costarricense,' *Anuario de Estudios Centroamericanos*, Vol. 22, No. 2.

Ferreira-Rubio, Delia M. (1997a), ed., *Financiamiento de los Partidos Políticos*; Buenos Aires, Fundación Konrad Adenauer-CIEDLA.

----- (1997b), 'Dinero y partidos políticos en Argentina', in Ferreira-Rubio, Delia M., ed., *Financiamiento de los Partidos Políticos*; Buenos Aires, Fundación Konrad Adenauer-CIEDLA.

Fiallos, Mariano (1998), 'Financiación de los partidos políticos y las campañas electorales en Nicaragua', in Del Castillo, Pilar and Zovatto, Daniel, eds, *La Financiación de la Política en Iberoamérica*; San José, IIDH-CAPEL.

Figueres, José María [3/11/1999] (former President of the Republic [PLN]), interview, Ochomogo.

*The Financial Times* (London), 12–13/11/1997.

Finch, M. H. J. (1981), *A Political Economy of Uruguay since 1870*; London, Macmillan Press.

Fishman, Luis [1/12/1999] (former Deputy, campaign manager and presidential pre-candidate [PUSC]), interview, San José.

Flores-Silva, Manuel [14/4/2000] (former Senator [PC]), interview, Montevideo.

Flórez-Estrada, Antonio [28/1/2000] (General Manager *La Nación*), interview, San José.

Fonseca, Oscar [24/11/1999] (President TSE), interview, San José.

Franco, Rolando (1985), *Democracia 'a la Uruguaya': Análisis electoral*, 1925–1985; Montevideo, Editorial El Libro Libre. Second Edition.

----- (1986), 'El sistema electoral uruguayo en una perspectiva comparada', in Franco, Rolando, ed., *El Sistema Electoral Uruguayo: Peculiaridades y Perspectivas*; Montevideo, Fundación Hans Seidel. Volume I.

Frente Amplio (1999), *Estatutos del Frente Amplio*; Montevideo, Comisión Nacional de Propaganda.

Galiarcho, Juan Luis and Berbell, Carlos (1995), *FILESA: Las Tramas del Dinero*

*Negro en la Política*; Madrid, Ediciones Temas de Hoy.

Gandini, Jorge [12/4/2000] (former Deputy and Senator [PN]), interview, Montevideo.

García-Rubio, Carlos (1994), *Lo que el Cable nos Dejó: Televisión para Abonados, Comunicación y Democracia en el Uruguay*; Montevideo, Ediciones de la Pluma.

Geddes, Barbara and Ribeiro-Neto, Artur (1992), 'Institutional sources of corruption in Brazil', *Third World Quarterly*, Vol. 13, No. 4.

Gidlund, Gullan (1991a), 'Public investments in Swedish democracy', in Wiberg, Matti, ed., *The Public Purse and Political Parties: Public Financing of Political Parties in Nordic Countries*; Helsinki, The Finnish Political Science Association.

----- (1991b), 'Conclusions: the nature of public financing in the Nordic states', in Wiberg, Matti, ed., *The Public Purse and Political Parties: Public Financing of Political Parties in Nordic Countries*; Helsinki, The Finnish Political Science Association.

----- and Koole (2001), 'Political finance in North of Europe: The Netherlands and Sweden', in Nassmacher, Karl-Heinz, *Foundations for Democracy: Approaches to Comparative Political Finance*; Baden-Baden, Nomos.

Gillespie, Charles G. (1995), *Negociando la Democracia: Políticos y Generales en Uruguay*; Montevideo, ICP-FCU.

Gillespie, Richard (1998), 'Party funding in a new democracy: Spain', in Burnell, Peter and Ware, Alan, eds, *Funding Democratization*; Manchester, Manchester University Press.

Giuria, Raúl [25/4/2000] (former Deputy, member of the Executive Committee of the *Lista 71* [MH and PN]), interview, Montevideo.

González, Luis Eduardo (1986a), 'Doble voto simultáneo y Ley de Lemas', in Franco, Rolando, ed., *El Sistema Electoral Uruguayo: Peculiaridades y Perspectivas – Volume I*; Montevideo, Fundación Hans Seidel.

----- (1986b), 'Legislación electoral, partidos y gobernabilidad', in Nohlen, Dieter and Rial, Juan, eds, *Reforma Electoral: Posible, Deseable?*; Montevideo, FESUR-Ediciones de la Banda Oriental.

----- (1991a), 'Legislación electoral y sistemas de partidos: el caso uruguayo,' *Revista Uruguaya de Ciencia Política*, No. 4.

----- (1991b), *Political Structures and Democracy in Uruguay*; Notre Dame, University of Notre Dame Press.

----- (1993), *Estructuras Políticas y Democracia en Uruguay*; Montevideo, ICP-FCU.

----- (1999), 'Introducción: los partidos establecidos y sus desafiantes', in González, Luis Eduardo et al., *Los Partidos Políticos Uruguayos en Tiempos de Cambio*; Montevideo, FCU.

----- and Gillespie, Charles (1994), 'Presidentialism and democratic stability in Uruguay', in Linz, Juan and Valenzuela, Arturo, eds, *The Failure of Presidential Democracy: The Case of Latin America, Volume 2*;

Baltimore, The Johns Hopkins University Press.

González, Rolando [17/9/1999] (former Deputy and Secretary General [PLN]), interview, San José.

González-Varas, Santiago (1995); *La Financiación de los Partidos Políticos*; Madrid, Dykinson.

Goodwin-Gill, Guy S. (1998), *Codes of Conduct for Elections*; Geneva, Inter-Parliamentary Union.

Grentzke, Janet M. (1989), 'PACs and the Congressional supermarket: the currency is complex', *American Journal of Political Science*, Vol. 33, No. 1 (February).

Gross, Kenneth A. (1997), 'The enforcement of campaign finance rules: a system in search of reform', in Corrado, Anthony et al., eds, *Campaign Finance Reform: A Sourcebook*; Washington DC, Bookings Institution Press.

Guardia, Fernán [20/10/1999] (party treasurer [PUSC]), interview, San José.

*The Guardian* (London), 12–13/11/1997.

*The Guardian* (London), 4/12/1999, 'European politics plagued by funding scandals'.

Guevara, Otto [24/9/1999] (former Deputy and presidential candidate [ML]), interview, San José.

Guidobono, Alberto (1986), 'La clase política uruguaya y el sistema electoral', in Franco, Rolando, ed., *El Sistema Electoral Uruguayo: Peculiaridades y Perspectivas – Volume II*; Montevideo, Fundación Hans Seidel.

Gunlicks, Arthur (1993), ed., *Campaign and Party Finance in North America and Western Europe*; Boulder, Westview Press.

----- (1995), 'The new German Party Finance Law', *German Politics*, Vol. 4, No. 1 (April).

Gutiérrez-Sáenz, Rodrigo [1/11/1999] (former Deputy and presidential candidate [CPU]), interview, San José.

Hall, Richard and Wayman, Frank W. (1990), 'Buying time: the moneyed interests and the mobilization of bias in congressional committees', *American Political Science Review*, Vol. 84, No. 3 (September).

Hansard Society Commission (1991), *Agenda for Change: The Report of the Hansard Society Commission on Election Campaigns*; London, The Hansard Society for Parliamentary Government.

Heard, Alexander (1960), *The Costs of Democracy*; Chapel Hill, University of North Carolina Press.

Heber, Luis Alberto [26/5/2000] (Senator [MH and PN]), interview, Montevideo.

Heidenheimer, A.J. (1963), 'Comparative party finance: notes on practices and toward a theory', *Journal of Politics*, Vol. 25, No.4 (November).

----- (1970), 'Major modes of raising, spending and controlling political funds during and between elections campaigns', in Heidenheimer, Arnold, ed., *Comparative Political Finance: The Financing of Party Organizations and Election Campaigns*; Levington, DC, Heath and Company.

----- et al. (1989), eds, *Political Corruption: A Handbook*; New Brunswick, Transaction Publishers.

----- and Langdon, Frank C. (1968), *Business Associations and the Financing of Political Parties: A Comparative Study of the evolution of Practices in Germany, Norway and Japan*; The Hague, Martinus Nighoft.

Hernández-Naranjo, Gerardo (1998), *El Sistema de Partidos en Costa Rica, 1982 –1994*; San José, Tesis de Maestría, Universidad de Costa Rica.

Hernández-Rodríguez, Oscar (2001), 'El quiebre del voto en las elecciones de Presidente y diputados: Costa Rica, 1962–1998', in Rovira, Jorge, ed., *La Democracia de Costa Rica ante el Siglo XXI*; San José, Editorial UCR – Fundación Friedrich Ebert.

Heywood, Paul (1995), 'Sleaze in Spain', *Parliamentary Affairs*, Vol. 48, No. 4.

----- (1996), 'Continuity and change: analysis of political corruption in Spain', in Little, Walter and Posada-Carbó, Eduardo, eds, *Political Corruption in Europe and Latin America*; Macmillan-Institute of Latin American Studies, University of London.

Hine, David (1996), 'Political corruption in Italy', in Little, Walter and Posada-Carbó, Eduardo, eds, *Political Corruption in Europe and Latin America*; Macmillan-Institute of Latin American Studies, University of London.

Hofnung, Menachem (1996a), 'Public financing, party membership and internal party competition', *European Journal of Political Research*, Vol. 29 (January).

----- (1996b), 'The public purse and the private campaign: political finance in Israel', *Journal of Law and Society*, Vol. 23, No. 1 (March).

Huneeus, Carlos (1998a), 'Chile's new democracy: political funding and economic transformation', in Burnell, Peter and Ware, Alan, eds, *Funding Democratization*; Manchester, Manchester University Press.

----- (1998b), 'El financiamiento de los partidos políticos y las campañas electorales en Chile', in Del Castillo, Pilar and Zovatto, Daniel, eds, *La Financiación de la Política en Iberoamérica*; San José, IIDH-CAPEL.

Hutchinson, Robert (1975), *Vesco*; New York, Praeger.

IBOPE (1999), media advertising reports, Montevideo.

Ifrán, Geraldine and Gallegos, Miguel (1999), 'Legitimidad y tratamiento fiscal de las donaciones a los partidos políticos,' *Revista Guía Financiera*, No. 1102, April 18.

*The Independent* (London), 12–13/11/1997.

Instituto de Ciencia Política de la Universidad de Heilderberg (1988), *El Sistema Electoral del Uruguay: Característica, Evolución y Efectos*; Santo Domingo, Fundación Friedrich Ebert.

Instituto de Ciencias Políticas de la Universidad de la República [ICP] (various years), election database.

Instituto Nacional de Estadística del Uruguay [INE] (2000), 'Principales Indicadores'. Downloaded from the Internet: http://www.ine.gub.uy/principal.htm.

International IDEA (1997), *Voter Turnout from 1945 to 1997: A Global Report on Political Participation*; Stockholm, International IDEA.

International Labour Organisation [ILO] (1997), *World Labour Report 1997–98*;

Geneva, ILO.

International Monetary Fund [IMF] (2000), *International Financial Statistics –*
*September 2000*; Washington DC, IMF.

International Organisation of the Francophonie [OIF], Declaration of Bamako
(paragraph 5.b.11), 3/11/2000. Downloaded from the Internet:
http://www.francophonie.org/oif/actions/rtf/Declaration_de_bamako.rtf.

International Parliamentary Union [IPU], Resolution adopted without a vote by
the 94th Inter-Parliamentary Conference (paragraph 5.c), 13/10/1995.
Downloaded from the Internet: http://www.ipu.org/conf-e/94-1.htm.

Issacharoff, Samuel and Karlan, Pamela S. (1999), 'The hydraulics of campaign
finance reform', *Texas Law Review*, Vol. 77, No. 7 (June).

Jacobson, Gary (1978), 'The effects of campaign spending in congressional elections', American Political Science Review, Vol. 72, June.

----- (1979), 'Public funds for congressional campaigns: who would benefit?',
in Alexander, Herbert, ed., *Political Finance*; London, Sage.

----- (1985), 'Money and votes reconsidered: congressional elections,
1972–1982', *Public Choice*, Vol. 47, No. 1.

Jain, Randir (2001), 'Electoral financing in India', in Nassmacher, Karl-Heinz,
*Foundations for Democracy: Approaches to Comparative Political*
*Finance*; Baden-Baden, Nomos.

Janda, Kenneth (1980), *Political Parties: A Cross-National Survey*; New York,
The Free Press.

Jenson, Jane (1991), 'Innovation and equity: the impact of public funding', in
Seidle, F. Leslie, ed., *Comparative Issues in Party and Election Finance*;
Toronto, Dundurn Press.

Jiménez-Zeledón, Mariano (1996), *Sistemas de Partidos Políticos, Sistemas*
*Electorales y Regímenes Políticos de Costa Rica, 1821–1995*; San José,
Tesis de Grado, Universidad de Costa Rica.

Johnston, Michael (1996), 'The search for definitions: the vitality of politics and
the issue of corruption', *International Social Science Journal*, Vol.
XLVIII, No. 3 (September).

Johnston, R. J. (1986), 'A further look at British political finance', *Political*
*Studies*, Vol. 34 (September).

----- (1987), *Money and Votes: Constituency Campaign Spending and*
*Election Results*; London, Croom Helm.

----- and Pattie, Charles (1993), 'Great Britain: twentieth century parties oper-
ating under nineteenth century regulations', in Gunlicks, Arthur, ed.,
*Campaign and Party Finance in North America and Western Europe*;
Boulder, Westview Press.

Jones, Mark (1995), 'A guide to the electoral systems of the Americas', *Electoral*
*Studies*, Vol. 14, No. 1.

Kaltefleiter, Werner and Nassmacher, Karl-Heinz (1995), 'El actual sistema de
financiamient de los partidos políticos en Alemania', in Thesing, Josef
and Hofmeister, Wilhelm, eds, *Partidos Políticos en la Democracia;*

*Buenos Aires*, Fundación Konrad Adenaer-CIEDLA.

Katz, Richard S. (1996), 'Party organizations and finance', in Le Duc, Lawrence; Niemi, Richard G. and Norris, Pippa, eds, *Comparing Democracies: Elections and Voting in Global Perspective*; London, Sage Publications.

----- *et al.* (1992), 'The membership of political parties in European democracies, 1960–1990', *European Journal of Political Research*, Vol. 22, No. 3.

----- and Kolodny, Robin (1994), 'Party organization as an empty vessel: parties in American politics', in Katz, Richard S. and Mair, Peter, eds, *How Parties Organize: Change and Adaptation in Party Organizations in Western Democracies*, London, Sage.

----- and Mair, Peter (1992), eds, *Party Organizations: A Data Handbook of Party Organizations in Western Democracies, 1960–90*; London, Sage Publications.

----- and Mair, Peter (1994), eds, *How Parties Organize: Change and Adaptation in Party Organizations in Western Democracies*; London, Sage.

----- and Mair, Peter (1995), 'Changing models of party organization and party democracy', *Party Politics*, Vol. 1, No. 1 (January).

----- and Mair, Peter (1996), 'Cadre, catch-all or cartel: a rejoinder', *Party Politics*, Vol. 2, No. 4.

King, Anthony (1969), 'Political parties in Western Democracies', *Polity*, Vol. 2, No. 2.

King, Gary; Keohane, Robert and Verba, Sidney (1994), *Designing Social Inquiry*; Princeton, Princeton University Press.

Kinzo, Maria D'Alva (1998), 'Funding parties and elections in Brazil', in Burnell, Peter and Ware, Alan, eds, *Funding Democratization*; Manchester, Manchester University Press.

Kirchheimer, Otto (1966), 'The transformation of the Western European party systems', in La Palombara, Joseph and Weiner, Myron, eds, *Political Parties and Political Development*; Princeton, Princeton University Press.

Klee, Gudrun (1993), 'Financing parties and elections in small European democracies: Austria and Sweden', in Gunlicks, Arthur, ed., *Campaign and Party Finance in North America and Western Europe*; Boulder, Westview Press.

Koole, Ruud (1989), 'The "modesty" of Dutch party finance', in Alexander, Herbert, ed., *Comparative Political Finance in the 1980s*; Cambridge, Cambridge University Press.

----- (1996), 'Cadre, catch-all or cartel? a comment on the notion of the cartel party', *Party Politics*, Vol. 2, No. 4.

----- (2001), 'Political finance in Western Europe: Britain and France', in Nassmacher, Karl-Heinz, *Foundations for Democracy: Approaches to Comparative Political Finance*; Baden-Baden, Nomos.

Kopecky, Petr (1995), 'Developing party organizations in East-Central Europe: what type of party is likely to emerge?', *Party Politics*, Vol. 1, No. 4.

Kumado, Kofi (1996), ed., *Funding Political Parties in West Africa*; Accra, Friedrich Ebert Foundation.

*La Gaceta [LG]* (San José), May 1998–December 1999.

*La Mañana [LM]* (Montevideo), various years.

*La Mañana [LM]* (Montevideo), various years.

*La Nación [LN]* (San José), various years.

*La Prensa Libre [LPL]* (San José), various years.

*La Prensa Panamá*, (Panama City), 22/7/1995.

*La República [LRU]* (Montevideo), various years.

*La República [LR]* (San José), various years.

Laakso, Marku and Taagepera, Rein (1979), 'Effective number of parties: A measure with application to Western Europe', *Comparative Political Studies*, Vol. 12, No. 1 (April)

Lacalle, Luis Alberto [4/7/2000] (former President of the Republic [MH and PN]), interview, Montevideo.

Laclé, Rolando [7/9/1999] (Deputy [PU and PUSC]), interview, San José.

Lamorte, Aldo [31/5/2000] (former mayoral candidate and member of National Junta [UC]), interview, Montevideo.

Lassús, César [14/6/2000] (commercial manager, Channel 12), interview, Montevideo.

Latinobarómetro (2000), 'Informe de Prensa-Encuesta Latinobarómetro 1999 –2000'. Downloaded from the Internet: http://www.latinobarometro.cl.

----- (2002), 'Informe de Prensa-Encuesta Latinobarómetro 2001-2002'. Downloaded from the Internet: http://www.latinobarometro.cl.

Le Duc, Lawrence; Niemi, Richard and Norris, Pippa. (1996), 'Introduction: the present and future of democratic elections', in Le Duc, Lawrence; Niemi, Richard G. and Norris, Pippa, eds, *Comparing Democracies: Elections and Voting in Global Perspective*; London, Sage.

Lehoucq, Fabrice (1997), *Lucha Electoral y Sistema Político en Costa Rica 1948–1998*; San José, Editorial Porvenir.

----- (1998), *Instituciones Democraticas y Conflictos Politicos en Costa Rica*; San Jose, EUNA.

Leonard, Dick (1975), *Paying for Party Politics: The Case for Public Subsidies*; London, PEP.

León-Páez, Eduardo [1/12/1999] (former campaign treasurer [PUSC]), interview, San José.

Levush, Ruth et al. (1991) *Campaign Financing of National Elections in Foreign Countries*; Washington DC, Law Library of Congress.

Lewis, Paul G. and Gortat, Radzislawa (1995), 'Models of party development and questions of state dependence in Poland', *Party Politics*, Vol. 1, No. 4.

----- (1998), 'Party funding in post-communist East-Central Europe', in Burnell, Peter and Ware, Alan, eds, *Funding Democratization*; Manchester, Manchester University Press.

Lijphart, Arend (1994), *Electoral Systems and Party Systems*; Oxford, Oxford

University Press.

Linton, Martin (1994), *Money and Votes*; London, Institute for Public Policy esearch.

Linz, Juan and Stepan, Alfred (1996), *Problems of Democratic Transition and Consolidation: Southern Europe, South America and post-Communist Europe*; Baltimore, The Johns Hopkins University Press.

Liphart, Arend (1975), 'The comparable-cases strategy in comparative research', *Comparative Political Studies*, Vol. 8, No. 2 (July).

Little, Walter and Posada-Carbó, Eduardo (1996), eds, *Political Corruption in Europe and Latin America*; London, Macmillan.

Lorenzo, Fernando [3/4/2000] (former campaign manager [NE]), interview, Montevideo.

'Lotería Uruguaya: leyes y decretos'. Downloaded from the Internet: http://www.loteria.gub.uy.

Lowenstein, Daniel Hays (1989), 'On campaign finance reform: the root of all evil is deeply rooted', *Hofstra Law Review*, Vol. 18, No. 2 (Fall).

Macedo, Nelson [9/6/2000] (former campaign manager and member of Political Board [FA]), interview, Montevideo.

MacIntyre, Alasdair C. (1978), 'Is a science of comparative politics possible?', in Lewis, Paul G. et al., eds, *The Practice of Comparative Politics*; London, Longman.

Mackie, Thomas and Rose, Richard (1991), *The International Almanac of Electoral History*, 3rd Edition; London, Macmillan.

Mainwaring, Scott and Scully, Timothy (1995), 'Introduction: party systems in Latin America', in Maiwaring, Scott and Scully, Timothy, eds, *Building Democratic Institutions: Party Systems in Latin America*; Stanford, Stanford University Press.

Mair, Peter (1994), 'Party organizations: from civil society to the state', in Katz, Richard S. and Mair, Peter, eds, *How Parties Organize: Change and Adaptation in Party Organizations in Western Democracies*, London, Sage.

----- (1996), 'Comparative politics: an overview', in Goodin, Robert and Klingemann, Hans-Dieter, eds, *A New Handbook of Political Science*; Oxford, Oxford University Press.

----- (1997), *Party System Change: Approaches and Interpretations*; Oxford, Oxford University Press.

Marchesano, Antonio (1986), 'Introducción', in Franco, Rolando, ed., *El Sistema Electoral Uruguayo: Peculiaridades y Perspectivas*; Montevideo, Fundación Hans Seidel. Volume I.

Marius, Jorge Leonel and Bacigalupe, Juan Francisco (1998), *Sistema Electoral y Elecciones Uruguayas, 1992–1998*; Montevideo, Fundación Konrad Adenauer.

Martin, Beate [6/6/2000] (Representative, Friedrich Ebert Foundation), interview, Montevideo.

Martins, José de Souza (1996), 'Clientelism and corruption in contemporary Brazil', in Little, Walter and Posada-Carbó, Eduardo, eds, *Political Corruption in Europe and Latin America*; Macmillan-Institute of Latin American Studies, University of London.

Mayer, Kenneth (1998), 'Public financing and electoral competition in Minnesota and Wisconsin', Citizens' Research Foundation. Downloaded from the Internet: http://www.usc.edu/dept/CRF/DATA/ mayer.htm.

Mayorga, René (1998), 'El financiamiento de los partidos políticos en Bolivia', in Del Castillo, Pilar and Zovatto, Daniel, eds, *La Financiación de la Política en Iberoamérica*; San José, IIDH-CAPEL.

Meckstroth, Theodore (1975), ' "Most Different Systems" and "Most Similar Systems": a study in the logic of comparative inquiry', *Comparative Political Studies*, Vol. 8, No. 2 (July).

Mediciones & Mercado (various years), media advertising reports. Montevideo.

Mejía, Thelma et al (2001), 'El verdadero "negocio" de la política', Tegucigalpa, unpublished manuscript.

Melchionda, Enrico (1997), *Il finanziamento della politica*; Roma, Riuniti.

Méndez, Rodolfo [15/11/1999] (former presidential pre-candidate and campaign manager [CU and PUSC]), interview, San José.

Mendilow, Jonathan (1992), 'Public party funding and party transformation in multiparty systems', *Comparative Political Studies*, Vol. 25, No. 1 (April)

----- (1996), 'Public party funding and the schemes of mice and men: the 1992 elections in Israel', *Party Politics*, Vol. 2, No. 3.

----- and Rusciano, Frank (2001), 'The effects of public funding on party participation', in Nassmacher, Karl-Heinz, ed. *Foundations for Democracy: Approaches to Comparative Political Finance*; Baden-Baden, Nomos.

Mény, Ives (1996), 'Corruption French style', in Little, Walter and Posada-Carbó, Eduardo, eds, *Political Corruption in Europe and Latin America*; Macmillan-Institute of Latin American Studies, University of London.

----- (1996), 'Politics, corruption and democracy: the 1995 Stein Rokkan Lecture', *European Journal of Political Research*, Vol. 30 (September).

Michelini, Felipe [11/5/2000] (Deputy [NE]), interview, Montevideo.

Michelini, Rafael [10/5/2000] (Senator and former presidential candidate [NE]), interview, Montevideo.

Mieres, Pablo (1992), 'Acerca de los cambios del sistema de partidos uruguayo', *Cuadernos del CLAEH*, No.62.

----- (1994), *Desobediencia y Lealtad: El Voto en el Uruguay de Fin de Siglo*; Montevideo, CLAEH-Editorial Fin de Siglo.

----- (1997), 'La reforma constitucional de 1996 en Uruguay y sus posibles efectos sobre los partidos y el sistema de partidos,' *Cuadernos del CLAEH*, No. 80.

----- [20/3/2000] (Deputy [NE]), interview, Montevideo.

Millán, Hermes [26/5/2000] (former National Secretary of Finance, 1990–92

[COM]), interview, Montevideo.

Miller, Warren and Merrill Shanks, J. (1996), *The New American Voter*; Cambridge, Harvard University Press.

Miró-Quesada, Francisco (1998), 'Financiación de los partidos políticos y las campañas electorales en el Perú', in Del Castillo, Pilar and Zovatto, Daniel, eds, *La Financiación de la Política en Iberoamérica*; San José, IIDH-CAPEL.

Molina, Guillermo and Suyapa, Maritza, (1998), 'Financiación de los partidos políticos y las campañas electorales en Honduras', in Del Castillo, Pilar and Zovatto, Daniel, eds, *La Financiación de la Política en Iberoamérica*; San José, IIDH-CAPEL.

Monestier, Felipe (1999), 'Partidos por dentro: la fraccionalización de los partidos políticos en el Uruguay (1954–1994)', in González, Luis Eduardo et al., *Los Partidos Políticos Uruguayos en Tiempos de Cambio*; Montevideo, FCU.

Montenegro, Maximiliano (2002), 'Fuga de capitales en Argentina'. Downloaded from the Internet: http://www.globalizacion.org/argentina/ArgentinaFuga Capitales.htm.

Montero, Rodolfo [21/12/1999] (party treasurer [PFD]), interview, San José.

Moreira, Constanza (2000), 'Elecciones en Uruguay 1999: Comportamiento electoral y cultura política'. Paper presented at the XXIIth International Congress of the Latin American Studies Association; Miami, Florida, March 16–18.

Morlino, Leonardo (1996), 'Crisis of parties and change of party system in Italy', *Party Politics*, Vol. 2, No. 1.

Müller, Wolfgang (1994), 'The development of Austrian party organizations in the post-war period', in Katz, Richard S. and Mair, Peter, eds, *How Parties Organize: Change and Adaptation in Party Organizations in Western Democracies*; London, Sage.

Muñoz, Walter [21/10/1999] (former Deputy and presidential candidate [PIN]), interview, San José.

Nassmacher, Hiltrud and Nassmacher, Karl-Heinz (2001), 'Major impacts of political finance regimes (Introduction)', in Nassmacher, Karl-Heinz, ed. *Foundations for Democracy: Approaches to Comparative Political Finance*; Baden-Baden, Nomos.

Nassmacher, Karl-Heinz (1989), 'Structure and impact of public subsidies to political parties in Europe: the examples of Austria, Italy, Sweden and West Germany', in Alexander, Herbert, ed., *Comparative Political Finance in the 1980s*; Cambridge, Cambridge University Press.

----- (1993), 'Comparing party and campaign finance in Western Democracies', in Gunlicks, Arthur, ed., *Campaign and Party Finance in North America and Western Europe*; Boulder, Westview Press.

----- (1994), 'Citizens' cash in Canada and the United States', in Alexander, Herbert and Shiratori, Rei, eds, *Comparative Political Finance among* the Democracies; Boulder, Westview Press.

----- (2001a), ed., *Foundations for Democracy: Approaches to Comparative Political Finance*; Baden-Baden, Nomos.

----- (2001b), 'Comparative political finance in established democracies (Introduction)', in Nassmacher, Karl-Heinz, ed. *Foundations for Democracy: Approaches to Comparative Political Finance*; Baden-Baden, Nomos.

----- (2001c), 'Political finance in West Central Europe: Austria, Germany, Switzerland', in Nassmacher, Karl-Heinz, Foundations for Democracy: *Approaches to Comparative Political Finance*; Baden-Baden, Nomos.

----- and Nassmacher, Hiltrud (2001), 'Major impacts of political finance regimes', in Nassmacher, Karl-Heinz, *Foundations for Democracy: Approaches to Comparative Political Finance*; Baden-Baden, Nomos.

Navas-Carbo, Xiomara (1993), 'La regulacion del financiamiento de los partidos políticos y de la campaña electoral en America Latina', in Nohlen, Dieter, ed., *Elecciones y Sistemas de Partidos en America Latina*; San Jose, CAPEL/IIDH.

Nelson, Candice J. (1990), 'Loose cannons: independent expenditures', in Nugent, Margaret Latus and Johannes, John R., eds, Money, *Elections and Democracy: Reforming Congressional Campaign Finance*; Boulder, Westview Press.

*The New Republic* (Washington D.C.), 16–23/4/1977.

*The New York Times*, 2/11/1997, 'After 1996, campaign finance laws in shreds'.

----- 3/4/1997, 'Campaign finance: development so far'.

----- 25/11/1997, 'Cost of '96 campaign sets record at $2.2 billion'.

----- 13/5/1998, 'Democrats and Republicans step up pursuit of 'soft money''.

----- 26/12/1996, 'In political money game, the year of big loopholes'.

----- 5/9/1996, 'Loopholes allow presidential race to set a record'.

----- (n.d.) 'The 50 largest political contributors'. Downloaded from the Internet: http://www.nytimes.com/library/politics/1226campaign-funds.1.GIF.htm.

Nicholson, Marlene Arnold (1977), 'Buckley vs. Valeo: the constitutionality of the Federal Election Campaign Act Amendments of 1974', *Wisconsin Law Review*, 323.

Njaim, Humberto (1998), 'Una parte de la historia: El financiamiento de la política (partidos políticos, campañas electorales y otros aspectos) en Venezuela', in Del Castillo, Pilar and Zovatto, Daniel, eds, *La Financiación de la Política en Iberoamérica*; San José, IIDH-CAPEL.

Nohlen, Dieter (1986), 'Un balance', in Nohlen, Dieter and Rial, Juan, eds, *Reforma Electoral: Posible, Deseable?*; Montevideo, FESUR-Ediciones de la Banda Oriental.

----- (1995), *Sistemas Electorales y Partidos Políticos*; México D.F., UNAM-Fondo de Cultura Economica.

----- and Rial, Juan eds, (1986), *Reforma Electoral: Posible, Deseable?*;

Montevideo, FESUR-Ediciones de la Banda Oriental.

Nunes, José [4/10/2000] (Secretary of Propaganda and former National Secretary of Finance [PS and FA]), interview, Montevideo.

Oduber, Daniel (1996), *Raíces del Partido Liberación Nacional: Notas para una Evaluación Histórica*; San José, EUNED. Second Edition.

Olivero, Roberto H. (1994), *El Financiamiento de los Partidos Politicos en Argentina: Un Problema de Cultura Politica y Valores Sociales*; Buenos Aires, Instituto Internacional de Investigaciones Interdisciplinarias.

Open Secrets (2002a), '2000 Presidential race: total raised and spent'. Dowloaded from the Internet: www.opensecrets.org/2000elect/index/AllCands.htm.

----- (2002b), 'Soft money's impact at a glance'. Downloaded from the Internet: http://www.opensecrets.org/softmoney/softglance.asp.

Organisation of American States [OAS], Inter-American Democratic Charter (Article 5), 11/9/2001. Downloaded from the Internet: http://www.oas.org.

Otero, Jorge (1993), 'Los partidos políticos uruguayos: Reflexiones históricas y diagnóstico de la situación actual', in Bodemer, Klaus and Laurnaga, María Elena, eds, *Estructura y Funcionamiento de los Partidos Políticos: Una Reforma Posible*; Montevideo, FESUR-Ediciones Trilce.

Pacheco, Miguel [20/1/2000] (former pre-campaign financial director [PLN]), interview, San José.

Pacheco-Salazar, Ovidio [23/11/1999] (former Deputy and Secretary General [PUSC]), interview, San José.

Pajares-Montolío, Emilio (1998), *La Financiación de las Elecciones*; Madrid, Congreso de los Diputados.

Palda, Filip and Palda, Kristian (1998), 'The impact of campaign expenditures on political competition in the French legislative elections of 1993', *Public Choice*, Vol. 94.

Pallares, Laura and Stolovich. Luis (1991), *Medios Masivos de Comunicación en el Uruguay: Tecnología*, Poder y Crisis; Montevideo, Centro Uruguay qIndependiente.

Palma, Carlos [15/10/1999] (former Secretary General [PUSC]), interview, San José.

Paltiel, Khayyam Zev (1970), 'Contrasts among the several Canadian political finance cultures', in Heidenheimer, Arnold J., ed., *Comparative Political Finance: The Financing of Party Organizations and Election Campaigns*; Lexington, DC Heath and Company.

----- (1979), 'The impact of election expenses legislation in Canada, Western Europe, and Israel', in Alexander, Herbert, ed., *Political Finance*; London, Sage.

----- (1980), 'Public financing abroad: contrasts and effects', in Malbin (Michael), ed., *Parties, Interest Groups and Campaign Finance Laws*, Washington DC, American Enterprise Institute for Public Policy Research.

----- (1981), 'Campaign finance: contrasting practices and reforms', in Butler,

David; Penniman, Howard and Ranney, Austin, eds, *Democracy at the Polls: A Comparative Study of Competitive National Elections*; Washington D.C., American Enterprise Institute for Public Policy Research.

----- (1989), 'Canadian election expense legislation, 1963–85: a critical appraisal or was the effort worth it?', in Alexander, Herbert, ed., *Comparative Political Finance in the 1980s*; Cambridge, Cambridge University Press.

Panebianco, Angelo (1988), *Political Parties: Organization and Power*; Cambridge, Cambridge University Press.

Panizza, Francisco (1990), *Uruguay: Batllismo y Después: Pacheco, Militares y Tupamaros en la Crisis del Uruguay Batllista*; Montevideo, Ediciones de la Banda Oriental.

Park, Chan Wook (1994), 'Financing political parties in South Korea: 1988–1991', in Alexander, Herbert and Shiratori, Rei, eds, *Comparative Political Finance among the Democracies*; Boulder, Westview Press.

Partido Colorado [PC] (1984), *Por un Uruguay para Todos: Programa de Principios y Carta Orgánica del Partido Colorado*; Montevideo, Diario El Día-Fundación José Batlle y Ordóñez.

Partido del Nuevo Espacio [NE] (1994), Informe de Egresos Campaña 1994.

----- (1995), Resumen Campaña Financiera 1995.

----- (1997), *Código de Conducta y Normas de Transparencia*; Montevideo.

----- (1999a), Estado de Resultados del Partido (Campaña Elecciones 1999).

----- (1999b), Presupuesto de Campaña (Junio-Octubre de 1999).

----- (1999c), Rendición de Cuentas, Lista 99000 de Montevideo.

Partido Fuerza Democrática [PFD], Contribution reports submitted to the TSE, from March 1997 to November 1999.

Partido Liberación Nacional [PLN] (1971), *Nuestra Posición sobre el Pago de la Deuda Política*; San José, PLN.

----- (1999), *Estatuto*; San José.

----- (29/3/1990), Official letter submitted to the TSE.

----- (7/4/1994), Official letter submitted to the TSE.

----- (1994–98), Accounting statements.

----- (1997–99), Contribution reports submitted to the TSE, from March 1997 to November 1999.

Partido Nacional [PN] (1999), *Carta Orgánica*; Montevideo.

----- (various years), Archivo del Honorable Directorio (AHD)

Partido Unidad Social Cristiana [PUSC] (23/4/1990), Official letter submitted to the TSE;

----- (25/4/1994), Official letter submitted to the TSE;

----- (1997–99), Contribution reports submitted to the TSE, from March 1997 to November 1999.

----- (1999), *Estatutos*; San José.

Pasquino, Gianfranco (1982), *Degenerazione dei partiti e reforme istituzionale*;

Roma, Laterza Editori.

Pattie, Charles J.; Johnston R. J. and Fieldhouse, Edward A. (1995), 'Winning the local vote: The effectiveness of constituency campaign spending in Great Britain, 1983–1992', *American Political Science Review*, Vol. 89, No. 4 (December).

Pedersen, Mogens N. (1990), 'Electoral volatility in Europe, 1948–1977', in Mair, Peter, ed., *The West European Party System*; Oxford, Oxford University Press.

----- and Bille, Lars (1991), 'Public financing and public control of political parties in Denmark', in Wiberg, Matti, ed., *The Public Purse and Political Parties: Public Financing of Political Parties in Nordic Countries*; Helsinki, The Finnish Political Science Association.

Peeler, John (1996), 'Democratización inicial en América Latina: Costa Rica en el contexto de Chile y Uruguay', *Anuario de Estudios Centroamericanos*, Vol. 22, No.2.

----- (2001), 'La política de élites y la política económica: la democracia en Costa Rica y Venezuela', in Rovira, Jorge, ed., *La Democracia de Costa Rica ante el Siglo XXI*; San José, Editorial UCR – Fundación Friedrich Ebert.

Penino, Nelson [20/6/2000] (Vice-President of Uruguay's Chamber of Industry), telephone conversation with the author.

Pérez, Romeo (1984), 'Los partidos en el Uruguay moderno,' *Cuadernos del CLAEH*, No. 31.

----- (1990), 'La dimensión popular de las divisas', in Caetano, Gerardo and Rilla, José, eds, *Los Partidos Uruguayos y su Historia (I): El Siglo XIX*; Montevideo, ICP-FCU.

Pérez-Brignoli, Héctor (1999), *Historia del Partido Unidad Social Cristiana*; San José, ICEP-Fundación Konrad Adenauer.

Pérez-Pérez, Alberto (1970), *La Ley de Lemas*; Montevideo, FCU.

Pesonen, Pertti (1974), 'Impact of public financing of political parties: the Finnish experience', Helsinki, Institute of Political Science, University of Helsinki.

The Pew Research Centre (1999), 'Too much money, too much media say voters'. Downloaded from the Internet: www.people-press.org/reports/display .php3?ReportID=54.

Pierre, Jon and Widfeldt, Anders (1994), 'Party organizations in Sweden: colossuses with feet of clay or flexible pillars of government', in Katz, Richard S. and Mair, Peter, eds, *How Parties Organize: Change and Adaptation in Party Organizations in Western Democracies*; London, Sage.

----- Svasand, Lars and Widfeldt, Anders (2000), 'State subsidies to political parties: confronting rhetoric with reality', *West European Politics*, Vol. 23, No. 3 (July).

Pinilla, Erasmo (1998), 'La experiencia panameña en materia de financiamiento público'. Paper delivered at the IV Conference of the Interamerican Union of Electoral Authorities; Ottawa, Canada, July 26–28.

Pinto-Duschinsky, Michael (1981), *British Political Finance*, 1830–1980; Washington DC, American Enterprise Institute.

----- (1985), 'Trends in British political funding, 1979–1983', *Parliamentary Affairs*, Vol. 38, No. 3 (Summer).

----- (1989), 'Trends in British party funding, 1983–1987', *Parliamentary Affairs*, Vol. 42, No. 2 (April).

----- (1991a), 'The party foundations and political finance in Germany', in Seidle, F. Leslie, ed., *Comparative Issues in Party and Election Finance*; Toronto, Dundurn Press.

----- (1991b), 'Foreign political aid: the German political foundations and their US counterparts', *International Affairs*, Vol. 67, No. 1 (January).

----- (1996), 'International political finance: the Konrad Adenauer Foundation and Latin America', in Whitehead, Laurence, ed., *The International Dimensions of Democratization: Europe and the Americas*; Oxford, Oxford University Press.

----- (2002), 'Financing politics: a global view', *Journal of Democracy*, Vol. 13, No. 4 (October).

Pivel-Devoto, Juan (1994), *Historia de los Partidos Políticos en el Uruguay*; Montevideo, Cámara de Representantes.

Pizarro-Leongómez, Eduardo (1997), 'El financiamiento de las campañas electorales en Colombia', in Ferreira-Rubio, Delia M., ed., *Financiamiento de los Partidos Políticos*; Buenos Aires, Fundación Konrad Adenauer-CIEDLA.

Pizzorno, Alessandro (1990), 'Parties in Pluralism', in Mair, Peter, ed., *The West European Party System*; Oxford, Oxford University Press.

Poguntke, Thomas (1994), 'Parties in a legalistic culture: the case of Germany', in Katz, Richard S. and Mair, Peter, eds, *How Parties Organize: Change and Adaptation in Party Organizations in Western Democracies*; London, Sage.

Pollock, James Kerr (1932), *Money and Politics Abroad*; New York, Alfred A. Knopf.

Poole, K. T. and Romer, T. (1985), 'Patterns of political action committee contributions to the 1980 campaigns for the United States House of Representatives', *Public Choice*, Vol. 47, No. 1.

Posada-Carbó, Eduardo (n.d.), 'Colombia', background paper for IDEA *Handbook on Funding of Parties and Election Campaigns*; Stockholm, IDEA.

Posadas, Juan Martín (1992), 'El papel del estado con respecto a la televisión en Uruguay', in Rama, Claudio, ed., *Las Industrias Culturales en Uruguay*; Montevideo, Arca Editorial.

Programa de Naciones Unidas para el Desarrollo [PNUD] – Uruguay (1999), *Desarrollo Humano en Uruguay, 1999*; Montevideo, PNUD-Uruguay.

Proyecto Estado de la Nación (1999), *Estado de la Nación en Desarrollo Humano Sostenible – Informe No. 5*; San José, Proyecto Estado de la Nación.

----- (2000), *Estado de la Nación en Desarrollo Humano Sostenible – Informe No. 6*; San José, Proyecto Estado de la Nación.

----- (2001), *Auditoría Ciudadana sobre la Calidad de la Democracia*; San José, Proyecto Estado de la Nación.

Prud'homme, Jean Francois; Barquin-Alvarez, Manuel; Alcocer, Jorge (1993), eds, *Dinero y Partidos: Propuestas para regular los ingresos y los gastos de los partidos politicos*; Mexico D.F., CEPNA/Nuevo Horizonte Editores/Fundacion Friedriech Ebert.

Przeworski, Adam (1991), *Democracy and the Market: Political and Economic Reforms in Eastern Europe and Latin America*; Cambridge, Cambridge University Press.

----- and Teune, Henri (1970), *The Logic of Comparative Social Enquiry*; Wiley, New York.

Pujas, Veronique and Rhodes, Martin (1998), 'Party finance and political scandal in Latin Europe', Florence, European University Institute, Robert Schuman Centre.

Pulzer, Peter (2001), 'Votes and resources: political finance in Germany', *German Politics and Society*, Vol. 19, No. 1 (Spring).

Queirolo, Rosario (1999), 'La tradicionalización del Frente Amplio: la confictividad del proceso de cambio', in González, Luis Eduardo *et al.*, *Los Partidos Políticos Uruguayos en Tiempos de Cambio*; Montevideo, FCU.

Qvortrup, Mads (1997), 'Uruguay's constitutional referendum, 8 December 1996', *Electoral Studies*, Vol. 16.

Radiccioni, José [23/5/2000] (member of finance commissions 1971, 1989, 1994 and 1999 campaigns [PN]), interview, Montevideo.

Radunski, Peter (1999), 'Management de la comunicación política: la americanización de las campañas electorales', in Thesing, Josef and Priess, Frank, eds, *Globalización, Democracia y Medios de Comunicación*; Buenos Aires, Fundación Konrad Adenauer – CIEDLA.

Rae, Douglas (1967), *The Political Consequences of Electoral Laws*; New Haven, Yale University Press.

Rama, Germán (1971), *El Club Político*; Montevideo, Arca Editorial.

----- (1987), *La Democracia en Uruguay: Una Perspectiva de Interpretación*; Montevideo, Arca Editorial.

Ramírez, Juan Andrés [28/6/2000] (former presidential pre-candidate and candidate [DN and PN]), interview, Montevideo.

Real de Azúa, Carlos (1981), *El Patriciado Uruguayo*; Montevideo, Ediciones de la Banda Oriental.

----- (1984), *Uruguay: Una Sociedad Amortiguadora?*; Montevideo, CIESU-Ediciones de la Banda Oriental.

República Oriental del Uruguay [ROU], Ministerio de Economía y Finanzas,

Oficio No. 11529 of 4/7/1996.

Restrepo, Diego and Rendón, Sandra (1995), 'Efectos políticos y económicos de la financiación estatal de los partidos políticos y las campañas electorales', Bogotá, Departamento Nacional de Planeación, mimeo.

*Revista Posdata [POS]* (Montevideo), various years.

*Revista Tres [TRES]* (Montevideo), various years.

Rey, Juan Carlos et al. (1988), *Visión General de las Reformas: Financiamiento de los Partidos, Clientelismo e Ideología*; Caracas, Consejo Supremo Electoral.

Rhodes, Martin (1997), 'Financing party politics in Italy: a case of systemic corruption', *West European Politics*, Vol. 20, No. 1 (January).

Rial, Juan (1984), *Partidos Políticos, Democracia y Autoritarismo*; Montevideo, CIESU-Ediciones de la Banda Oriental.

----- (1986), 'Sistema electoral y gobernabilidad', in Franco, Rolando, ed., *El Sistema Electoral Uruguayo: Peculiaridades y Perspectivas – Volume II*; Montevideo, Fundación Hans Seidel.

----- (1998), 'Financiación de partidos políticos en Uruguay', in Del Castillo, Pilar and Zovatto, Daniel, eds, *La Financiación de la Política en Iberoamérica*; San José, IIDH-CAPEL.

Risi, Osvaldo [19/6/2000] (former member of financial committee [FB and PC]), telephone conversation with the author.

Rodríguez-Camusso, Francisco [28/4/2000] (former Senator and Deputy [PN and FA]), interview, Montevideo.

Rojas-Bolaños, Manuel (1994), 'Democratizar los partidos o la sociedad,' *Revista Parlamentaria*, Vol. 2, No. 2.

Romero, Cira (1998), 'El financiamiento público y la sociedad civil en Venezuela', in Consejo Nacional Electoral de Venezuela, *El Financiamiento de las Campañas Electorales*, Memoria; Caracas, IFES.

Rosas, Mario [21/6/2000] (Treasurer of the National Executive Committee [PC]), interview, Montevideo.

Rose, Richard (1974), *The Problem of Party Government*; London, Macmillan.

Rovira, Jorge (1988), *Estado y Política Económica en Costa Rica, 1948–1970*; San José, Editorial Porvenir.

----- (1994), 'Costa Rica 1994: Hacia la consolidación del bipartidismo?', *Espacios*, No. 1 (July–September).

----- (1998), 'Costa Rica. Elecciones generales, 1 de febrero de 1998', *Boletín Electoral Latinoamericano*, No. XIX, January–June.

----- (2001), ed., *La Democracia de Costa Rica ante el Siglo XXI*; San José, Editorial Universidad de Costa Rica – Fundación Friedrich Ebert.

Royal Commission on Electoral Reform and Party Financing (1991), *Reforming Electoral Democracy: Volume 1*; Canada, Royal Commission on Electoral Reform and Party Financing.

Ruiz, Marco Vinicio [10/12/1999]) (President of the Chamber of Industry), interview, San José.

Ruostetsaari, Ilkka and Mattila, Mikko (2002), 'Candidate-centred campaigns and their effects in an open list system: the case of Finland', in Farrell, David M. and Schmitt-Beck, Rüdiger, eds, *Do Political Campaigns Matter? Campaign Effects in Elections and Referendums*; London, Routledge.

Sala Constitucional de la Corte Suprema de Justicia, Costa Rica [SCCR], Vote No. 980–91of 24/5/1991.

----- Vote No. 1750-97 of 21/3/1997.

Sánchez, Carlos Ariel (1998), 'Financiamiento estatal a los partidos y movimientos políticos', Bogotá, mimeo.

Sánchez-Campos, Fernando F. (forthcoming), 'Cambios políticos en Centroamérica: el desalineamiento electoral en Costa Rica', *Revista Bicentenario*, Vol. 2, No. 1.

Sánchez-Gutiérrez, Arturo (1998), 'El financiamiento público en el sistema electoral mexicano', in Consejo Nacional Electoral de Venezuela, *El Financiamiento de las Campañas Electorales*, Memoria; Caracas, IFES.

Sanguinetti, Julio María [12/4/2000] (former President of the Republic [FB and PC]), interview, Montevideo.

Sartori, Giovanni (1986), 'The influence of electoral laws: faulty laws or faulty method?', in Lijphart, Arend and Grofman, Bernard, eds, *Electoral Laws and their Political Consequences*; New York, Agathon Press.

----- (1992), *Partidos y Sistemas de Partidos: Marco para un Análisis*, 2nd Edition; Madrid, Alianza Editorial.

----- (1994), 'Comparacion y metodo comparativo', in Sartori, Giovanni and Morlino, Leonardo, eds, *La Comparacion en las Ciencias Sociales*, Madrid, Alianza Editorial.

----- (1997), *Comparative Constitutional Engineering: An Inquiry into Structures, Incentives and Outcomes*; Basingstoke, Macmillan Press.

Sassoon, Donald (1975), 'The funding of political parties in Italy', *Political Quarterly*, Vol. 46.

Scarrow, Susan (1994), 'The "paradox of enrolment": assessing the costs and benefits of party membership', *European Journal of Political Research*, Vol. 25, No. 1.

Schattschneider, E. E. (1975 [1960]), *The Semi-Sovereign People*; Fort Worth, Harcourt Brace Jovanovich College Publishers.

Schefold, Dian (1995), 'Financiamiento de los partidos políticos: análisis comparado de los sistemas europeos', in Thesing, Josef and Hofmeister, Wilhelm, eds, *Partidos Políticos en la Democracia*; Buenos Aires, Fundación Konrad Adenaer-CIEDLA.

Schleth, Uwe and Pinto-Duschinsky, Michael (1970), 'Why public subsidies have become the major source of party funds in Germany, but not in Great Britain', in Heidenheimer, Arnold, ed., *Comparative Political Finance: The Financing of Party Organizations and Election Campaigns*, Levington, DC, Heath and Company

Schyfter, Miguel [9/12/1999] [former President of the Chamber of Industry), interview, San José.

Selle, Per and Svasand, Lars (1991), 'Membership in party organizations and the problem of the decline of parties', *Comparative Political Studies*, Vol. 23, No. 4 (January).

*Semanario Brecha [BRE]* (Montevideo), various years.

*Semanario Búsqueda [BUS]* (Montevideo), various years.

*Semanario Búsqueda [BUS]* (Montevideo), various years.

*Semanario Crónicas [CRO]* (Montevideo), various years.

*Semanario Demos [DEMOS]* (Montevideo), various years.

*Semanario Marcha [Marcha]* (Montevideo), various years.

*Semanario Opinión [OPI]* (Montevideo), various years.

*Semanario Prensa de los Viernes [PV]* (Montevideo), various years.

*Semanario Universidad [SU]* (San José), various years.

*Servicios Publicitarios Computarizados [SPC]* (various years), media advertising reports, San José.

Shiratori, Rei (1994), 'Political finance and scandal in Japan', in Alexander, Herbert and Shiratori, Rei, eds, *Comparative Political Finance among the Democracies*; Boulder, Westview Press.

Shockley, John S. (1983), 'Money in politics: judicial roadblocks to campaign finance reform', *Hastings Constitutional Law Quarterly*, Vol. 10, Spring.

Shugart, Matthew Soberg and Carey, John (1992), *Presidents and Assemblies: Constitutional Design and Electoral Dynamics*; Cambridge, Cambridge University Press.

Skocpol, Theda and Somers, M. (1980), 'The use of comparative history in macro-social inquiry', *Comparative Studies in Society and History*, Vol. XXII.

Smith, Bradley A. (2001), *Unfree Speech: The Folly of Campaign Finance Reform*; Princeton, Princeton University Press.

Sobrado, Antonio [8/9/1999] (TSE magistrate), interview, San José.

Solari, Aldo (1986), 'El sistema de partidos y el régimen electoral en el Uruguay', in Franco, Rolando, ed., *El Sistema Electoral Uruguayo: Peculiaridades y Perspectivas – Volume I*; Montevideo, Fundación Hans Seidel.

----- (1988), *Uruguay: Partidos Políticos y Sistema Electoral*; Montevideo, El Libro Libre-FUCCYT.

Solís, Alex (1994), 'El financiamiento de los partidos políticos,' *Revista Parlamentaria*, Vol. 2, No. 2 (December).

Sontheimer, Kurt (1974), 'The funding of political parties in West Germany', *Political Quarterly*, Vol. 45.

Sorauf, Frank J. (1992), *Inside Campaign Finance: Myths and Realities*; New Haven, Yale University Press.

----- (1994), 'Politics, experience, and the First Amendment: the case of American campaign finance', *Columbia Law Review*, Vol. 94, No. 4 (May).

Sotelo-Rico, Mariana (1999), 'La longevidad de los partidos tradicionales uruguayos desde una perspectiva comparada', in González, Luis Eduardo et al., *Los Partidos Políticos Uruguayos en Tiempos de Cambio*, Montevideo, FCU.

Spaett, Gunther [22/10/1999] (Representative, Konrad Adenauer Foundation), interview, San José.

Stanbury, William T. (1993a), 'Financing federal politics in Canada in an era of reform', in Gunlicks, Arthur, ed., *Campaign and Party Finance in North America and Western Europe*; Boulder, Westview Press.

----- (1993b), *Money in Politics: Financing Federal Parties and Candidates in Canada*, Toronto, Dundurn Press.

Stone, Samuel (1975), *La Dinastía de los Conquistadores*; San José, EDUCA.

*The Sunday Times* (London), 16/11/1997.

Sundberg, Jan (1987), 'Exploring the basis of declining party membership in Denmark: a Scandinavian comparison', *Scandinavian Political Studies*, Vol. 10, No. 1.

----- (1994), 'Finland: nationalized parties, professionalized organizations', in Katz, Richard S. and Mair, Peter, eds, *How Parties Organize: Change and Adaptation in Party Organizations in Western Democracies*, London, Sage.

Suñol, Julio (1978), *Robert Vesco compra una república*; San José, Editorial La República.

Sunstein, Cass R. (1994), 'Political equality and unintended consequences', *Columbia Law Review*, Vol. 94, No. 4 (May).

Svasand, Lars (1991), 'State subventions for political parties in Norway', in Wiberg, Matti, ed., *The Public Purse and Political Parties: Public Financing of Political Parties in Nordic Countries*; Helsinki, The Finnish Political Science Association.

----- (1994), 'Change and adaptation in Norwegian party organizations', in Katz, Richard S. and Mair, Peter, eds, *How Parties Organize: Change and Adaptation in Party Organizations in Western Democracies*; London, Sage.

Thelen, Kathleen and Steinmo, Sven (1992), 'Historical institutionalism in comparative politics', in Steinmo, Sven; Thelen, Kathleen and Longstreth, Frank, eds, *Structuring Politics: Historical Institutionalism in Comparative Analysis*; Cambridge, Cambridge University Press.

Thompson, Dennis (1993), 'Mediated corruption: the case of the Keating Five', *American Political Science Review*, Vol. 87, No. 2 (June).

*The Times* (London), November 12–17/11/1997.

Torres-Rivas, Edelberto and Aguilar, Carla (1998), 'Financiación de partidos y campañas electorales: el caso guatemalteco', in Del Castillo, Pilar and Zovatto, Daniel, eds, *La Financiación de la Política en Iberoamérica*; San José, IIDH-CAPEL.

Tovar, Roberto (1986), *PUSC: Bosquejo Histórico*; San José, LIL.

----- [1/11/1999] (former Deputy, party treasurer and campaign manager

[PUSC]), interview, San José.

Transparency International (2000), 'Press release: bribes to political parties an increasing threat to democracy'. Downloaded from the Internet: http://www.transparency.org/pressreleases archive/2000.

----- (2002), 'Corruption perception index 2002'. Downloaded from the Internet: http://www.transparency.org/pressreleases archive/2002.

Trejos, Juan José [25/10/1999] (former Deputy and presidential pre-candidate [PUSC]), interview, San José.

Trías, Vivián (1990a), 'Entre los caudillos y el Imperio', in Caetano, Gerardo and Rilla, José, eds, *Los Partidos Uruguayos y su Historia (I): El Siglo XIX*; Montevideo, ICP-FCU.

----- (1990b), 'La significación de las divisas en la historia nacional', in Caetano, Gerardo and Rilla, José, eds, *Los Partidos Uruguayos y su Historia (I): El Siglo XIX*; Montevideo, ICP-FCU.

Tribunal Supremo de Elecciones, Costa Rica [TSE] (1954), *Cómputo de Votos y Declaratorias de Elección 1953*; San José, TSE.

----- (1959), *Cómputo de Votos y Declaratorias de Elección 1958*; San José, TSE.

----- (1963), *Cómputo de Votos y Declaratorias de Elección 1962*; San José, TSE.

----- (1967), *Cómputo de Votos y Declaratorias de Elección 1966*; San José, TSE.

----- (1971), *Cómputo de Votos y Declaratorias de Elección 1970*; San José, TSE.

----- (1975), *Cómputo de Votos y Declaratorias de Elección 1974*; San José, TSE.

----- (1979), *Cómputo de Votos y Declaratorias de Elección 1978*; San José, TSE.

----- (1983), *Cómputo de Votos y Declaratorias de Elección 1982*; San José, TSE.

----- (1987), *Cómputo de Votos y Declaratorias de Elección 1986*; San José, TSE.

----- (1991), *Cómputo de Votos y Declaratorias de Elección 1990*; San José, TSE.

----- (1995), *Cómputo de Votos y Declaratorias de Elección 1994*; San José, TSE.

----- (1996), *Elecciones en Cifras*; San José, TSE.

----- (1997), Reglamento sobre el pago de los gastos de los partidos políticos.

----- (1999), *Cómputo de Votos y Declaratorias de Elección 1998*; San José, TSE.

----- (2002), 'Elecciones 2002 – escrutinio definitivo'. Downloaded from the Internet: www.tse.go.cr.

----- (various years), Electoral Archive.

----- Oficio No. 2022 of 24/4/1998.

----- Vote No. 2235 of 27/8/1981.

----- Vote No. 661of 8/3/1985.

----- Vote No. 1750-97 of 21/3/1997.

----- Vote No. 1548 of 31/8/1999.

Tsatsos, Dimitris Th. (1992), ed., *Parteienfinanzierung im europaischen Vergleich. Die Finanzierung der politischen Parteien in den Staaten der Europaischen Gemeinschaft*; Baden-Baden, Nomos.

Ulloa, Félix (2001), 'El financiamiento de la política', *Boletín Probidad*, No. 26 (December 20). Downloaded from Internet: http://probidad.org/local/boletines/2001.

*Ultimas Noticias* [*UN*] (Montevideo), various years.

'Un año de Jorge Batlle – Mapa Político', *El Observador* (Montevideo). Downloaded from the Internet: http://www.observa.com.uy/elobser vador/ED010314/home.html.

UNIMER (various years), *Encuesta Nacional de Opinión*; San José.

United Nations [UN](1998), 'Demographic yearbook 1995: population of capital cities and cities of 100,000 and more inhabitants.' Downloaded from the Internet: http://www.un.org/depts/unsd/demog.

United Nations Development Program [UNDP] (2001), 'Human Development Report 2001, Statistical Annex'. Downloaded from the Internet: http://www.undp.org/hdr2001/back.pdf.

Urcuyo, Constantino (1992), *Más Democracia*; San José, Ediciones Sanabria.

----- [23/11/1999] (former Deputy and presidential advisor [PUSC]), inter view, San José.

Urruty, Carlos [23/2/2000] (President of the Electoral Court), interview, Montevideo.

Vaillant, Víctor [28/4/2000] (former Deputy and presidential pre-candidate [PC]), interview, Montevideo.

Valdés, Eduardo (1998), 'Finaciación de los partidos políticos y las campañas electorales en la República de Panamá', in Del Castillo, Pilar and Zovatto, Daniel, eds, *La Financiación de la Política en Iberoamérica*; San José, IIDH-CAPEL.

Valdés-Prieto, Salvador et al. (2000), 'Proposiciones sobre el financiamiento de la actividad política', *Estudios Políticos*, No. 78 (Otoño).

Valdez, Martín [10/4/2000] (former President of the Directorate's Central Commission of Finance [PN]), interview, Montevideo.

Van Biezen, Ingrid (2000), 'Party financing in new democracies: Spain and Portugal', *Party Politics*, Vol. 6, No. 3 (July).

----- and Nassmacher, Karl-Heinz (2001), 'Political finance in Southern Europe: Italy, Portugal, Spain', in Nassmacher, Karl-Heinz, *Foundations for Democracy: Approaches to Comparative Political Finance*; Baden-Baden, Nomos.

Vanger, Milton (1968), *José Batlle y Ordóñez: El Creador de su Epoca*, 1902 –1907; Buenos Aires, EUDEBA.

----- (1983), *El País Modelo: José Batlle y Ordóñez 1907–1915*; Montevideo, Arca Editorial-Ediciones de la Banda Oriental.

Vargas, Marcos [28/10/1999] (former campaign treasurer [PLN]), interview, San José.

Vargas-Aguilar, Carlos (1995), 'Algunos aspectos de deuda política y su relación con la Contraloría General de la República', *Fiscalización y Gestión Pública*, Vol. 1, No. 3.

----- [6/12/1999] (chief auditor of electoral expenses at the CGR), interview, San José.

Vargas-Artavia, Guido [4/10/1999] (former Deputy [Partido Acción Laborista Agrícola], interview, San José.

Vargas-Benavides, Luis Fernando [23/9/1999] (General Comptroller of the

Republic), interview, San José.

Vega-Carballo, José Luis (1982) *Poder Político y Democracia en Costa Rica*; San José, Editorial Porvenir.

----- (1983), *Hacia una Interpretación del Desarrollo Costarricense: Ensayo Sociológico*; San José, Editorial Porvenir.

----- (1992), 'Political parties, party systems and democracy in Costa Rica', in Goodman, Louis; Leogrande, William M. and Mendelson, Johanna, eds, *Political Parties and Democracy in Central America*; Boulder, Westview Press.

Venturini, Angel (1989), *Estadíticas Electorales 1917–1989 y Temas Electorales*; Montevideo, Ediciones de la Banda Oriental.

Vernazza, Francisco (1991), 'Minoristas, mayoristas y generalistas en el sistema electoral uruguayo', *Revista Uruguaya de Ciencias Políticas*, No. 3.

Vertiente Artiguista [VA] (2000), Presupuesto tentativo elecciones de Mayo 2000.

Villalobos, Guillermo [25/11/1999] (Director of the Centre for Democratic Studies of Latin America [CEDAL] and coordinator of the socio-political cal programme of the Friedrich Ebert Foundation in Costa Rica), interview, San José.

Villasuso, Juan Manuel (2001), 'Procesos electorales y política económica en Costa Rica', in Rovira, Jorge, ed., *La Democracia de Costa Rica ante el Siglo XXI*; San José, Editorial UCR – Fundación Friedrich Ebert.

Villegas, Rafael A. (1997), 'Financiamiento de partidos políticos y procesos electorales: El papel de los organismos electorales,' *Documentos de Trabajo de CIAPA*, Vol. 1, No. 4 (February).

----- [17/9/1999] (former President of the TSE), interview, San José.

Visillac, Michel [23/5/2000] (advertising advisor to the VA and the FA), interview, Montevideo.

Von Armin, Hans Herbert (1993), 'Campaign and party finance in Germany', in Gunlicks (Arthur), ed., *Campaign and Party Finance in North America and Western Europe*; Boulder, Westview Press.

Von Beyme, Klaus (1985), *Political Parties in Western Democracies*, Aldershot, Gower Publishers.

----- (1995), *La Clase Política en el Estado de Partidos*; Madrid, Alianza Editorial.

Walecki, Marcin (2001), 'Political finance in Central Eastern Europe', in Nassmacher, Karl-Heinz, *Foundations for Democracy: Approaches to Comparative Political Finance*; Baden-Baden, Nomos.

*The Washington Post*, 19/3/2002, 'Campaign finance bill nears final Senate vote'.

----- 5/4/2002, 'Secret Taiwan fund sought friends, influence abroad'.

Webb, Paul D. (1994), 'Party organizational change in Britain: the iron law of centralization?', in Katz, Richard S. and Mair, Peter, eds, *How Parties Organize: Change and Adaptation in Party Organizations in Western Democracies*; London, Sage.

Weinstein, Martin (1975), *Uruguay: The Politics of Failure*; London, Greenwood Press.

Weisleder, Saúl (1997), 'El financiamiento político: una cuestión de escogencias', in Urcuyo, Constantino, ed., *Partidos Políticos y Gobernabilidad: La Dimensión Política del Desarrollo Humano*; San José, PNUD.

----- [23/9/1999] (former Deputy and party treasurer [PLN]), interview, San José.

Welch, W. P. (1976), 'The effectiveness of expenditures in state legislative races', *American Political Quarterly*, Vol. 4 (July).

Wells, Henry (1962), *Government Financing of Political Parties in Puerto Rico*; Princeton, Citizens' Research Foundation.

White, Elaine (1997), 'El financiamiento de los partidos políticos en Costa Rica', in Ferreira-Rubio, Delia M., ed., *Financiamiento de los Partidos Políticos*; Buenos Aires, Fundación Konrad Adenauer-CIEDLA.

Whitehead, Laurence (1996), 'Comparative politics: democratization studies', in Goodin, Robert and Klingemann, Hans-Dieter, eds, *A New Handbook of Political Science*, Oxford, Oxford University Press.

----- (2002), *Democratization: Theory and Experience*; Oxford, Oxford University Press.

Wiberg, Matti (1991a), ed., *The Public Purse and Political Parties: Public Financing of Political Parties in Nordic Countries*; Helsinki, The Finnish Political Science Association.

----- (1991b), 'Public financing of parties as Arcana Imperii in Finland', in Wiberg, Matti, ed., *The Public Purse and Political Parties: Public Financing of Political Parties in Nordic Countries*; Helsinki, The Finnish Political Science Association.

Williams, Robert (2000), ed., *Party Finance and Political Corruption*; Basingstoke, Macmillan.

Woldenberg, José; Becerra, Ricardo and Salazar, Pedro (1998), 'El modelo de financiación de los partidos políticos en México', in Del Castillo, Pilar and Zovatto, Daniel, eds, *La Financiación de la Política en Iberoamérica*; San José, IIDH-CAPEL.

World Bank (2000), 'Selected World Development Indicators'. Downloaded from the Internet: http://www.worldbank.org/poverty/wdrpoverty/report/c12a.pdf.

----- (2001), *World Development Indicators*. Downloaded from the Internet: http://www.worldbank.org/data/wd2001/pdfs/tab5_10.pdf.

----- (2002), *World Development Indicators*. Downloaded from the Internet: http://www.worldbank.org/data/wdi2002/tables/table1-1.pdf.

Wright, John R. (1985), 'PACs, contributions, and roll calls: an organizational perspective', *American Political Science Review*, Vol. 79, No. 2 (June).

Xavier, Mónica [1/6/2000] (Senator, member of the campaign management team [PS and FA]), interview, Montevideo.

Yankelewitz, Samuel [20/10/1999] (President of the Union of Chambers of the Private Sector), interview, San José.

Yashar, Deborah (1995), 'Civil war and social welfare: the origins of Costa Rica's competitive party system', in Mainwaring, Scott and Scully, Timothy R., eds, *Building Democratic Institutions: Party Systems in Latin America*; Stanford, Stanford University Press.

Zovatto, Daniel (1998), 'La financiación política en Iberoamérica: una visión preliminar comparada', in Del Castillo, Pilar, and Zovatto, Daniel, eds, *La Financiación de la Política en Iberoamérica*; San José, IIDH-CAPEL.

# | appendix

## SOURCES AND METHOD OF TABLES AND GRAPHS

The following is a summary of the sources of the information included in tables and graphs throughout the book. More detailed information on sources, as well as comprehensive methodological notes on tables 1.4, 1.8, 3.2, 3.7, 3.8, 4.1 and 4.5, and graphs 3.3, 3.5, 4.1 and 5.4 can be found in Casas-Zamora (2002) or obtained from the author at <u>kevin_casas@yahoo.com</u>.

## INTRODUCTION

**Table A.1**
A: Costa Rica, *Estado de la Nación* (2000); Uruguay, INE (2000). B: United Nations (1998). C: World Bank (2002). D: UNDP (2001). E: UNDP (2001). F: CEPAL (1999). G: Costa Rica, *Estado de la Nación* (2000); Uruguay, PNUD-Uruguay (1999).

## CHAPTER ONE

**Tables 1.1–1.4, 1.6–1.9**
Argentina: Ley 23.298 Orgánica de los Partidos Políticos (30/9/1985); Decreto 396/89 of 31/7/1989; Decreto 2089/92 of 16/11/1992; Decreto 485/97 of 29/5/1997; Navas-Carbó (1993); Ferreira-Rubio (1997); Del Castillo and Zovatto (1998).
Australia: Paltiel (1981); Levush et al. (1991); Le Duc, Niemi and Norris (1996); Committee on Standards in Public Life (1998); Amr and Lisowski (2001).
Austria: Le Duc, Niemi and Norris (1996); Katz and Mair (1992); Nassmacher (1993); Committee on Standards in Public Life (1998); Nassmacher (2001c).
Belgium: European Parliament (1991); Katz and Mair (1992); Goodwin-Gill (1998); Committee on Standards in Public Life (1998).
Bolivia: Ley Electoral 1997; Navas-Carbó (1993); Del Castillo and Zovatto (1998).
Brazil: Navas-Carbó (1993); Del Castillo and Zovatto (1998).
Canada: Canada Elections Act; Chief Electoral Officer of Canada (1993); Stanbury (1993b); Committee on Standards in Public Life (1998); Amr and Lisowski (2001).
Chile: Ley Orgánica Constitucional de los Partidos Políticos, No. 18.603 (11/3/1987); Navas-Carbó (1993); Del Castillo and Zovatto (1998).

Colombia: Ley 130 of 23/3/1994; Navas-Carbó (1993); Pizarro-Leongómez (1997); Del Castillo and Zovatto (1998).

Costa Rica: *Constitución Política de la República de Costa Rica* (1999); Código Electoral (1997); White (1997); LN, 4/6/2001; LN, 23/4/2002.

Denmark: Pedersen and Bille (1991); European Parliament (1991); Katz and Mair (1992); Committee on Standards in Public Life (1998).

Dominican Republic: Del Castillo and Zovatto (1998).

Ecuador: Ley de Partidos Políticos (10/2/1979); Navas-Carbó (1993); Del Castillo and Zovatto (1998).

El Salvador: Navas-Carbó (1993); Del Castillo and Zovatto (1998); *La Prensa Gráfica*, 10/3/2002.

Finland: Wiberg (1991); Council of Europe (2000); Katz and Mair (1992); Ruostetsaari and Mattila (2002).

France: European Parliament (1991); Doublet (1997); Drysch (1993); Avril (1994); Camby (1995); Goodwin-Gill (1998); Committee on Standards in Public Life (1998); Koole (2001).

Germany: Gunlicks (1995); Kaltefleiter and Nassmacher (1995); González-Varas (1995); Committee on Standards in Public Life (1998); Nassmacher (2001c); Pulzer (2001).

Greece: European Parliament (1991); Levush et al. (1991); Le Duc, Niemi and Norris (1996).

Guatemala: Navas-Carbó (1993); Del Castillo and Zovatto (1998); Ley Electoral y de Partidos de 1985.

Honduras: Navas-Carbó (1993); Del Castillo and Zovatto (1998); Mejía et al. (2001).

India: Levush et al. (1991); Committee on Standards in Public Life (1998); Jain (2001).

Ireland: Paltiel (1981); European Parliament (1991); Katz and Mair (1992); Committee on Standards in Public Life (1998).

Israel: Levush et al. (1991); Mendilow (1992); Hofnung (1996 a–b); Blechinger and Nassmacher (2001).

Italy: European Parliament (1991); Levush et al. (1991); Bardi and Morlino (1994); Le Duc, Niemi and Norris (1996); Rhodes (1997); Committee on Standards in Public Life (1998); Van Biezen and Nassmacher (2001).

Japan: Levush et al. (1991); Shiratori (1994); Le Duc, Niemi and Norris (1996); Ferdinand (1998); Blechinger and Nassmacher (2001).

Luxembourg: European Parliament (1991); Committee on Standards in Public Life (1998).

Mexico: Alemán-Velasco (1995); Del Castillo and Zovatto (1998); Sánchez-Gutiérrez (1998).

Netherlands: European Parliament (1991); Levush et al. (1991); Katz and Mair (1992); Le Duc, Niemi and Norris (1996); Committee on Standards in Public Life (1998); Gidlund and Koole (2001).

New Zealand: Paltiel (1981); Committee on Standards in Public Life (1998).

Nicaragua: Nicaragua: Ley Electoral de 2000; Navas-Carbó (1993); Del Castillo and Zovatto (1998); *El Nuevo Diario*, 15/10/2000; *El Observador Económico* (2001), No. 112; *El Observador Económico* (2001), No. 112.
Norway: Svasand (1991); Katz and Mair (1992); Le Duc, Niemi and Norris (1996), Council of Europe (2000).
Panama: Navas-Carbó (1993); Pinilla (1998); Del Castillo and Zovatto (1998); Tribunal Electoral de Panamá (www.tribunal-electoral.gob.pa/elec/elec04.html).
Paraguay: Código Electoral (1997); Navas-Carbó (1993); Del Castillo and Zovatto (1998).
Peru: Ley No. 26.859, Ley Orgánica de Elecciones (29/9/1997); Navas-Carbó (1993); Del Castillo and Zovatto (1998).
Portugal: European Parliament (1991); Van Biezen (2000); Van Biezen and Nassmacher (2001).
South Korea: Park (1994); Ferdinand (1998).
Spain: European Parliament (1991); Del Castillo (1992); González-Varas (1995); Pajares-Montolío (1998); Committee on Standards in Public Life (1998); Van Biezen and Nassmacher (2001).
Sweden: Gidlund (1991a); Katz and Mair (1992); Nassmacher (1993); Le Duc, Niemi and Norris (1996); Committee on Standards in Public Life (1998); Gidlund and Koole (2001).
Switzerland: Le Duc, Niemi and Norris (1996); Goodwin-Will (1998); Nassmacher (2001c).
Taiwan: Levush et al. (1991); Le Duc, Niemi and Norris (1996); Ferdinand (1998).
Turkey: Levush et al. (1991).
UK: Pinto-Duschinsky (1981); European Parliament (1991); Katz and Mair (1992); Blackburn (1995); Le Duc, Niemi and Norris (1996); Committee on Standards in Public Life (1998); Koole (2001).
USA: Alexander, Goss and Schwartz (1992); Federal Election Campaign Laws (1997); Federal Election Commission (1993); Corrado et al. (1997).
Uruguay: Ley No. 8312 of 13/10/1928; Ley No. 17157 of 4/8/1999; Ley No. 17237 of 5/4/2000; Bottinelli (1993); TRES, 9/4/1999.
For all countries: Pinto-Duschinsky (2002), Austin and Tjernström (2003).
**Table 1.9**
Registered voters and election dates except for Costa Rica: International IDEA (www.idea.int/vt/index.cfm); Costa Rica: Tribunal Supremo de Elecciones (www.tse.go.cr). Exchange rates: International Monetary Fund (2000).
**Tables 1.10, 1.11**
Political finance data: Germany, Austria, Sweden, Norway, Finland and Italy: calculated from Katz and Mair (1992). Spain: Pajares-Montolío (1998). Mexico: calculated fom Woldenberg et al. (1998) and Sánchez-Gutiérrez (1998); Canada: calculated from Chief Electoral Officer of Canada (1993)
Electoral results: For all countries except Mexico: Mackie and Rose (1991) and *European Journal of Political Research* (*EJPR*) updates. Mexico: http://www.georgetown.edu/pdba/Elecdata/Mexico/mexico.html.

**Tables 1.12, 1.13**

For all countries except Spain, data calculated from Katz and Mair (1992). For Spain, data calculated from Pajares-Montolío (1998), pp. 420–421, 426–427, 441–442; Del Castillo (1992), p.159.

**Table 1.14**

For all countries, data on party membership, DSF per voter and DSF dependence calculated from Katz and Mair (1992). Converted into constant US$ of 1990, using exchange rates and deflator from IMF International Financial Statistics.

Data on voting age population for all countries from International IDEA (1997).

**Table 1.15**

Data calculated from Katz and Mair (1992).

**Graph 1.2**

Financial data calculated from Katz and Mair (1992); electoral results from Mackie and Rose (1991) and EJPR updates.

**Graph 1.3**

Data calculated from Mackie and Rose (1991) and EJPR updates.

Dates of enactment of DSF: Table 1.6 and its sources.


CHAPTER TWO

**Table 2.2**

TSE (1996); TSE (2002); TSE, *Cómputo de Votos y Declaratorias de Elección* (various years)

**Table 2.3**

A, B, C: Data calculated from CID-Gallup, July 1997. D: Data calculated from Borge and Asociados, October 1997.

**Table 2.4**

Nominal figures: 1953–98: TSE, Archivo Electoral; CGR, Departamento de Estudios Especiales; 2002: LN, 23/4/2002.

Constant and per voter figures: Author's own calculation using deflator and exchange rates from BCCR, Departamento de Investigaciones Económicas; and number of registered voters from TSE, *Cómputo de Votos y Declaratorias de Elección* (various years) and TSE (2002).

**Table 2.7**

Fabregat (various years); Cámara de Representantes del Uruguay (various years); Corte Electoral del Uruguay (2000); Franco (1984), p. 57.

**Table 2.8**

1954–94: Monestier (1999), p. 52; 1999: Moreira (2000), p. 15.

**Table 2.9**

CIFRA, Opinion poll database.

**Table 2.10**

Nominal figures: CRU, Carp. 1711/1953, p. 23; Law No. 11603 of 9/10/1950;

Law No. 12145 of 13/10/1954; Law No. 12561 of 15/10/1958; Law No. 13107 of 15/10/1962; Law No. 13574 of 15/10/1966; Law No. 14012 of 1/9/1971; Law No. 15320 of 31/8/1982; Law No. 15673 of 6/11/1984; Law No. 16103 of 1/11/1989; Law No. 16567 of 16/8/1994; Law No. 17157 of 4/8/1999; Law No. 17237 of 5/4/2000; and rates of UR from INE (2000).

Constant and per voter figures: author's own calculation using deflator from INE (2000); exchange rates from BCU, Department of Economic Research; and number of registered voters from Marius and Bacigalupe (1998), tables 04.04.01.01–05 and CE (2000).

**Graph 2.1**

Author's own elaboration based on Pérez-Brignoli (1999), p. 56. Other data taken from Aguilar-Bulgarelli (1969), TSE (1996); TSE, *Cómputo de Votos y Declaratorias de Elección* (various years); TSE (2002).

**Graph 2.2**

Author's own elaboration based on Fabregat (various years); Cámara de Representantes del Uruguay (1989), (1994) and (1999); CE (2000); Cocchi (n.d.); Aguirre-Bayley (2000).

**Graph 2.3**

Author's own elaboration based on Batlle [2/6/2000]; Lacalle [4/7/2000]; Macedo [9/6/2000]; Aguirre-Bayley (2000); CE (2000); 'Un año de Jorge Batlle,' *EO*.

**Graph 2.4**

1985: González (1993), p.159; 1999: EO, 7/3/1999.


CHAPTER THREE


**Tables 3.1, 3.3, 3.4, 3.6**

CGR, Departamento de Estudios Especiales.

**Table 3.2**

Author's own calculation based on: SPC (various years); ALCR, Exp. Leg. 10934, p. 4103; *LR*, 2/6/1993; *LR*, 31/1/2001; *LN*, 29/1/2001; *LN*, 8/6/2001; Alvarez [7/12/1999]; Chacón-González [20/12/2999]; Fachler [20/12/1999]; Trejos [25/10/1999]; Vargas [23/9/1999].

**Table 3.5**

A-B: CGR, Departamento de Estudios Especiales; C: Table 3.2; D: See text p. 138; E-F: Author's own calculation.

**Table 3.7, 3.8**

A, E: Author's own calculation based on reports from SPC (various years).

B, F: CGR, Departamento de Estudios Especiales.

C, D, G, H: Author's own calculation.

**Graph 3.1**

Expenditure figures from Table 3.1.

State funding figures from CGR, Departamento de Estudios Especiales.

Number of registered voters from TSE, *Cómputo de Votos y Declaratorias de Elección* (various years).

**Graph 3.2**

PLN: Official letters submitted to the TSE, dated 29/3/1990 and 7/4/1994.
PUSC: Official letters submitted to the TSE, dated 23/4/1990 and 25/4/1994.
For all parties: CGR, Departamento de Estudios Especiales.

**Graphs 3.3, 3.5**

Author's own calculation based on reports from SPC (various years).

**Graph 3.4**

Author's own calculation based on expenditure figures taken from Table 3.1 and state funding figures from CGR, Departamento de Estudios Especiales.


CHAPTER FOUR

**Table 4.1**

Author's own calculation based on: NE (1994), (1995) and (1999 a,b,c); Mediciones & Mercado (1994) and 1999); AUDAP (1994) and (1999); Law No. 16567 of 26/8/1994; Law No. 17237 of 14/4/2000; INE (2000); CRU (1999); CE (2000); Advertising executive [10/5/2000]; Andreoli [13/6/2000]; Astori [1/6/2000]; Barandiarán [25/4/2000]; Batlle [2/6/2000]; Castro [18/5/2000]; FA media advisor [27/4/2000]; Gandini [12/4/2000]; Lamorte [31/5/2000]; Lassús [14/6/2000]; F. Michelini [11/5/2000]; Ramírez [28/6/2000]; Visillac [23/5/2000].

**Table 4.2**

Uruguay: Expenditure per party: Table 4.1 and Graph 4.1; Registered voters: 1994: CRU (1999); 1999–2000: CE (2000).
Costa Rica: Expenditure per party: Table 3.1 and Table 3.5. Registered voters: TSE (various years).

**Tables 4.3, 4.4**

Subsidy value calculated from Law No. 16567 of 26/8/1994, No. 17157 of 20/8/1999 and No. 17237 of 14/4/2000; UR values from INE (2000); electoral results from CRU (1999) and CE (2000).
Expenditure per party: Table 4.1 and Graph 4.1.

**Table 4.5**

A, D, E: ROU, Ministerio de Economía y Finanzas, Oficio No. 11529 of 4/7/1996. Information on lists from ICP (various years).
B: Total subsidisation per party calculated from Law No. 16567 of 26/8/1994; UR values from INE (2000); electoral results from CRU (1999).
C: Total expenditure per party calculated from Table 4.1 and Graph 4.1.

**Graph 4.1**

Author's own calculation based on: Heber [26/5/2000], De Cuadro [16/6/2000], CRU (1999), CE (2000) and Table 4.1.

**Graph 4.2**

Author's own calculation based on NE (1994), (1995), (1999 a,b,c).

**Graph 4.3**

ANCAP-ANCEL-ANP-ANTEL-BHU-OSE-UTE: IBOPE (1999).

IMM: Mediciones & Mercado (various years).

**Graph 4.4**

Author's own elaboration based on Mediciones & Mercado (various years).

CHAPTER FIVE

**Table 5.1, Graphs 5.1–5.3**

Author's own elaboration based on electoral results from TSE, *Cómputos y Declaratorias de Elección* (various years), and TSE (2002). Subsidy figures from CGR (various years), except for 2002. Figures for 2002 from *LN*, 23/4/2002.

**Graph 5.4**

Author's own elaboration based on SPC (various years).

**Graphs 5.5–5.9**

Author's own elaboration based on Fabregat (various years); CRU (1989), (1994) and (1999); and CE (2000). Number of party lists: Chapter two, Table 2.8.

# index

## G

www.ingramcontent.com/pod-product-compliance
Lightning Source LLC
Chambersburg PA
CBHW072054020426
42334CB00017B/1499